Pre-removal Choctaw History

The Civilization of the American Indian Series

Pre-removal Choctaw History

EXPLORING NEW PATHS

Edited by

GREG O'BRIEN

UNIVERSITY OF OKLAHOMA PRESS : NORMAN

ALSO BY GREG O'BRIEN

Choctaws in a Revolutionary Age, 1750–1830 (Lincoln, Neb., 2002)
(ed. with Tamara Harvey) *George Washington's South* (Gainesville, Fla., 2004)

Library of Congress Cataloging-in-Publication Data

Pre-removal Choctaw history : exploring new paths / edited by Greg O'Brien.
  p. cm. — (Civilization of the American Indian ; vol. 255)
  Includes bibliographical references and index.
  ISBN 978-0-8061-3916-6 (cloth)
  ISBN 978-0-8061-4848-9 (paper)
  1. Choctaw Indians—History. 2. Choctaw Indians—First contact with Europeans. 3. Choctaw Indians—Government relations. I. O'Brien, Greg, 1966–
E99.C8.P77 2008
976.004'97387—dc22
                                                                   2007034422

Pre-removal Choctaw History: Exploring New Paths is Volume 255 in The Civilization of the American Indian Series.

The paper in this book meets the guidelines for permanence and durability of the Committee on Production Guidelines for Book Longevity of the Council on Library Resources, Inc. ∞

Copyright © 2008 by the University of Oklahoma Press, Norman, Publishing Division of the University. Paperback published 2015. Manufactured in the U.S.A.

All rights reserved. No part of this publication may be reproduced, stored in a retrieval system, or transmitted, in any form or by any means, electronic, mechanical, photocopying, recording, or otherwise—except as permitted under Section 107 or 108 of the United States Copyright Act—without the prior written permission of the University of Oklahoma Press. To request permission to reproduce selections from this book, write to Permissions, University of Oklahoma Press, 2800 Venture Drive, Norman OK 73069, or email rights.oupress@ou.edu.

Contents

	Acknowledgments	vii
	Editor's Introduction	ix
CHAPTER 1	The Coming of Age of Choctaw History *Greg O'Brien*	3
CHAPTER 2	Ohoyo Chishba Osh: Woman Who Stretches Way Back *LeAnne Howe*	26
CHAPTER 3	Countering "A Powerful Indefiniteness": Doing Choctaw Ethnohistory in the Liminal Space between History and Archaeology *Patricia Galloway*	48
CHAPTER 4	Choctaw Factionalism and Civil War, 1746–1750 *Patricia Galloway*	70
CHAPTER 5	Protecting Trade through War: Choctaw Elites and British Occupation of the Floridas *Greg O'Brien*	103
CHAPTER 6	The Choctaw Defense of Pensacola in the American Revolution *Greg O'Brien*	123
CHAPTER 7	The Conqueror Meets the Unconquered: Negotiating Cultural Boundaries on the Post-Revolutionary Southern Frontier *Greg O'Brien*	148
CHAPTER 8	Native Americans, the Market Revolution, and Culture Change: The Choctaw Cattle Economy, 1690–1830 *James Taylor Carson*	183

| CHAPTER 9 | Choctaws and Missionaries in Mississippi before 1830 *Clara Sue Kidwell* | 200 |
| CHAPTER 10 | Greenwood LeFlore: Southern Creole, Choctaw Chief *James Taylor Carson* | 221 |

Appendix A. Choctaw Negotiations with the United States at Hopewell, South Carolina, 1785–1786   237

Appendix B. The Hopewell Treaty Signed by the Choctaws and the United States   248

Contributors   253

Index   255

Acknowledgments

I wish to thank several people for making this book possible. Alessandra Jacobi Tamulevich and Charles Rankin of the University of Oklahoma Press suggested the need for such a work when I met with them at the 2004 annual meeting of the American Society for Ethnohistory in Chicago. I am especially thankful to Alessandra for her patience and support in seeing this book brought to publication. Shelia Smith, the office manager for the Department of History at the University of Southern Mississippi and all-around good person, retyped all of the previously published essays. Graduate student Misty Grantham helped proofread the previously published articles. My colleague Kyle Zelner offered suggestions on some of the new essays, though he should not be held responsible for any mistakes or the interpretations therein. Thanks are also due to Colin Calloway for providing me a stint as the Gordon Russell Visiting Professor in Native American Studies at Dartmouth College in fall 2004, which enabled me to have time to organize the collection. All of the contributors to this volume—LeAnne Howe, Patricia Galloway, Clara Sue Kidwell, and James Carson—responded positively and enthusiastically to the opportunity to publish new essays or to reprint older pieces. I hope they are pleased with the final product. My wife, Jodi Pettazzoni, endured with patience and support, as always, my discussion of the project. I dedicate the book to our children—Conor and Kayla—who remind me daily why history must be told and written, for the empowerment of future generations.

Editor's Introduction

A decade before the Treaty of Dancing Rabbit Creek in 1830, which called for the removal of Choctaws to Indian Territory, west of the Mississippi River, Choctaw elders lamented that their children and grandchildren no longer bothered to learn history. One unnamed Choctaw man explained to British missionary Adam Hodgson in 1820 that "great changes had taken place among the Indians, even in his time." Previously, children were "collected on the bank of the river" after ritual morning bathing "to learn the manners and customs of their ancestors, and hear the old men recite the traditions of their forefathers." The children "were assembled again, at sunset for the same purpose and were taught to regard as a sacred duty, the transmission to their posterity of the lessons thus acquired." But now "this custom is . . . abandoned . . . except . . . where there is, here and there, an old ancient fellow, who upholds the old way."[1] Two years later an elderly Choctaw man named Chahta Immataha offered another description of how Choctaw traditional education had changed. He explained that a "long time ago, before the white man came, it was a custom with the old men, after they had become too feeble from age and decrepitude to pursue the chase, for them to remain at home with the women and children; assist them in the cultivation of their little farm patches, and carefully teach the traditional [Choctaw] history to the children." All Choctaws once knew the traditional history of their people, he continued, but "when the white people came and brought with them [alcohol] old men as well as the young [got] drunk, & the traditional teaching ceased."[2] In 1823 another unnamed Choctaw chief told missionary Cyrus Byington, "When he was a boy it was customary for the oldest men in the nation to give long talks to the boys, concerning the former wars of Choctaws, Chickasaws, &c.," but that form of education was now neglected.[3] In 1828 another missionary, Reverend Alfred Wright, discovered that Choctaw elders had once "assemble[d] the youth and children of their respective towns and rehearse[d] to them those . . . stories which embodied all their traditional knowledge." "In this way," he continued, "was their traditional knowledge, depending alone on the

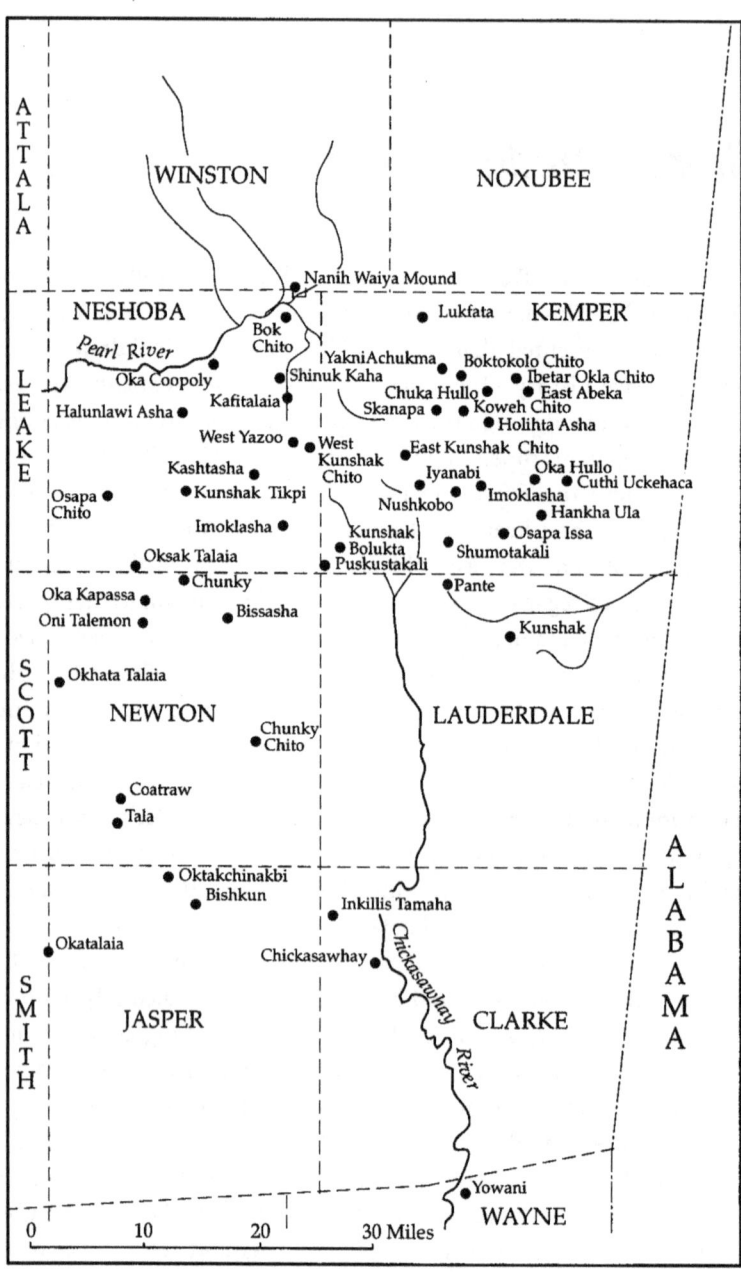

Choctaw villages in Mississippi during the nineteenth century. Reproduced, with permission, from Clara Sue Kidwell, *Choctaws and Missionaries, 1818–1918* (Norman: University of Oklahoma Press, 1995).

INTRODUCTION   XI

memory for its preservation, transmitted from generation to generation." But "since their intercourse with the whites, [the Choctaws] have in a great measure lost the knowledge of their ancient traditions," and "the little that is now known, is retained only in the memories of a few old men who have survived their own generation."[4]

One hundred and eighty years later, Wright's pessimism about the state of Choctaw history seems overstated. Though Choctaw people have suffered, persevered, and sometimes welcomed extraordinary changes in their culture, their history before the removal era of the 1830s has not disappeared. Multilayered histories of the Choctaws before removal have been written using a wide array of sources including Choctaw oral traditions, language, artifacts, and rituals; French, British, Spanish, and U.S. government records; missionary accounts; archeological studies; and other data. Choctaw people have also used these records and their own recollections and understandings to tell their history. Though appearing nearly two hundred years after Choctaw elders first complained about the need to teach more Choctaw history—they might reasonably ask what took so long—this book brings together much of the innovative work recently completed on pre-removal Choctaw history. This collection could not have been compiled just a few years ago. Choctaw history has undergone a dramatic transformation in the past couple of decades as scholars from a variety of disciplines have trained their analytical eyes on many aspects of Choctaw history and culture. This shift in Choctaw history is connected to larger trends in American Indian history and ethnohistory but also stems from the unique interests and backgrounds of the people writing about Choctaw history today. Reverend Wright might be shocked about how much we do know about pre-removal Choctaw history, but his lament reminds us that there is still much to learn.

To keep the length of this volume manageable, its scope has been limited to research on pre-removal Choctaw history. Readers should not take from this organizational paradigm that little or no Choctaw history after the 1830s has been written; in fact, there is just as significant an outpouring of work on nineteenth- and twentieth-century Choctaw history, which I will discuss briefly in the opening chapter. Indian removal is arguably the most important history-changing event for Choctaws and other eastern Indian groups after contact with Euro-Americans. Forced removal killed thousands of Native people, tore apart families, and forced most eastern Indians off of a land base that was (and is) full of sacred sites, burials, family-owned agricultural fields, and hunting grounds. Banished west of the Mississippi River, most Choctaws and other eastern Indians had to recreate their lives, villages, farms, and governments while continuing to deal with an imperious U.S. government and its various levels of officials, traders, soldiers, and missionaries. For the few thousand Choctaws who remained in Mississippi, life became equally hard as they tried to maintain claims to land and preserve family ties and culture in a society devoted to racial segregation and oppression. Unsurprisingly, few histories have attempted to breach the pre-removal/post-removal barrier.

Readers are also cautioned that the new and reprinted essays included in this volume are a representative sample of the new work on pre-removal Choctaw history and not a comprehensive collection. Decisions about what to include were based on several factors, including whether or not permission could be obtained to reprint a previously published article at a reasonable cost. Presented chronologically and covering more than a century of Choctaw history, the essays in this collection serve as a useful primer on pre-removal Choctaw history. The previously published chapters originally appeared in a variety of journals and essay collections, making it difficult to read them together. All of these essays were written as stand-alone articles or chapters; this collection does not include excerpts from the numerous books written on pre-removal Choctaw history, though many of the essays do naturally reflect the arguments and evidence used by these authors in their respective books. A fuller picture of all the work of recent years will be found in the first and third chapters, which seek in different ways to organize the historiography of pre-removal Choctaw history.

This collection will enable the reader to experience the varieties of recent research on the Choctaw Indians in one place and arranged chronologically from precontact Choctaw history to the immediate pre-removal period up to 1830. *Pre-removal Choctaw History* is intended for high school and college students, researchers, and the general public interested in Choctaw and southeastern Indian history. By highlighting the latest work being done on Choctaw history, this collection emphasizes how ethnohistory and the "new Indian history" have impacted study on the Choctaws and southeastern Indians more generally. This collection will also be useful as a textbook in ethnohistorical techniques of research and writing and in the new ways that scholars are studying American Indians. Two of the five contributors—LeAnne Howe and Clara Sue Kidwell—are themselves Choctaw, and they embody the shift in topical focus and depth of research being completed on Choctaw history. Once a rare occurrence, scholars of American Indian descent are now

INTRODUCTION   XIII

making major impacts on the way that Native history is told and investigated, and Choctaw scholars are no exception. Other Choctaw scholars and their works are discussed in the first chapter. The other three contributors, Patricia Galloway, James Taylor Carson, and myself, are scholars with backgrounds in anthropology and history who have written extensively on Choctaw history. No other volume of essays incorporating recent scholarly research focuses exclusively on the Choctaws or on any other southeastern Indian group. Southeastern Indian ethnohistory has progressed rapidly in the last decade or so to the point that such collections are not only convenient but are necessary as we all try to keep up with the fast-developing scholarship.

Though the structure of the collection is chronological, each essay examines a different topic, utilizes a different set of sources, and employs a unique approach to Choctaw history. In a new essay, writer and documentary filmmaker LeAnne Howe utilizes documentary data, oral traditions, and literary creativity to delve into the origins of corn and the role of women among the Choctaws. Anthropologist, archivist, and literary specialist Patricia Galloway shares in a new piece how she became interested in Choctaw history while working for the Mississippi Department of Archives and History in the 1970s and 1980s. Her ground-breaking essay explaining the Choctaw civil war as an interethnic conflict is also reprinted here. Historian James Taylor Carson is represented by his previously published essays that reassess the place of chief Greenwood LeFlore and that expose the gender implications of Choctaw immersion in the American market economy in the early nineteenth century. Native American studies professor Clara Sue Kidwell's important article on the interaction of Christian missionaries and Choctaws in pre-removal Mississippi is included to shed light on an important and often misunderstood phase of cross-cultural interaction in Choctaw and Mississippi history. My previously published articles on the Choctaw-Creek war of the 1760s and 1770s and on the first diplomatic meeting between the Choctaws and the United States at Hopewell, South Carolina, in 1785–1786 are included, as are two new essays describing the historiography of Choctaw studies and Choctaw military actions at Pensacola, Florida, during the American Revolution.

Appendix A consists of the previously unpublished record of "talks" from the Hopewell Treaty negotiations between the United States and the Choctaws. The document is an excellent tool that educators can use to explore issues of U.S.-Indian relations, methods of diplomacy, trade, Choctaw politics, gender roles, and more. The proceedings of the Hopewell treaty negotiation expose a very different picture of what the treaty meant to the Choctaws than does examination of the signed treaty itself, and it provides a note of caution to aspiring students of Indian history to be sure to seek out Indian perspectives on key events arising from intercultural contact. The signed treaty is reprinted in appendix B for comparison. Similarly, as reading this collection will make clear, trying to understand early American history from the perspectives of American Indians gives us a deeper understanding of the realities of life in the colonial and early national Southeast. In many ways we are just now reaching the point where we can say that we understand what contact between Indians, Europeans, and Africans meant to all parties concerned. Students of Choctaw and southeastern Indian history have reshaped in recent years our understanding of the South, its culture, and its history. Though much more is known now about Choctaw history than in Reverend Wright's day, there is much yet to learn. But I think those Choctaw elders of the early nineteenth century would be proud to see the work represented by this volume and would look to the future with anticipation that a renewed interest in Choctaw and southeastern Indian history is upon us.

NOTES

1. Adam Hodgson, *Letters from North America Written During a Tour in the United States and Canada*, 2 vols. (London: Hurst, Robinson, 1824), 2:243.
2. Gideon Lincecum, "Traditional History of the Chahta Nation: Translated from the Chahta" (typescript version, Gideon Lincecum Papers, Center for American History, University of Texas at Austin, 1861), 7.
3. "Mission among the Choctaws: Elliot," *Missionary Herald* 19 (1823): 115.
4. Alfred Wright, "Choctaws: Religious Opinions, Traditions, &c.," *Missionary Herald* 24 (1828): 178–79.

Pre-removal Choctaw History

CHAPTER 1

The Coming of Age of Choctaw History

Greg O'Brien

It is an understatement to write that pre-removal Choctaw history has undergone a dramatic transformation since the 1980s. In the last quarter century our knowledge of Choctaw history, and southeastern Indian history generally, has grown by leaps and bounds to the point that new studies about the Choctaws and other southeastern Indians are frequently on the cutting edge of new Indian history.[1] This historiographical essay will examine this development while also drawing attention to topics that need further investigation, highlighting published documentary sources vital to understanding pre-removal Choctaw history, and showing how the contributions in this collection of essays have contributed to the maturation of Choctaw studies.

Until the past couple of decades, one scholar and one book from the early twentieth century dominated our understanding of Choctaw history and culture. Anthropologist John Swanton's *Source Material for the Social and Ceremonial Life of the Choctaw Indians*, originally published in 1931, is the starting point for all subsequent scholarship on Choctaw history and the most important work on Choctaw history published in the first three-quarters of the twentieth century.[2] Swanton described Choctaw oral traditions, material culture, social organization, government structure, notions of property, rules about crime, women, childbirth, naming, education, marriage, gender roles, recreation, warfare, burial customs, religion, and healing. Written in ethnological fashion without much sense of change over time, Swanton's work on the Choctaws reflected the concerns and organizing principles of anthropologists of the early twentieth century. Swanton explained the apparent lack of traditional knowledge among early-twentieth-century Choctaws, for example, by writing that they lacked "pronounced native institutions," which "made it easy for them to take up with foreign customs and usages." The Choctaws "became with great rapidity poor subjects for ethnological study," and were a "meek" people besides.[3] Swanton's search for pristine cultural traits among twentieth-century Choctaws forced him to pursue other sources of information on Choctaw history when his informants failed to live up to his expectations.

Swanton completed his Ph.D. in anthropology at Harvard in 1900, conducted research among Northwest Coast peoples, and then joined the Bureau of American Ethnography (BAE), where he remained until his death in 1958. After joining the BAE he turned his scholarly gaze to the Native South, seeking out Indian informants in Oklahoma, Texas, and Louisiana and mining archives for material on the histories and cultures of the South's first peoples. His major works include analyses of various lower Mississippi Valley Indian tribes (the Creeks, the Choctaws, the Chickasaws, and the Caddos), southeastern Indian folklore and oral history, and various southeastern Indian languages, and a monumental text, *Indians of the Southeastern United States*, published in 1946.[4] He was the first scholar to focus intensely on the entire Native Southeast, and he filled that void for half a century. Nearly every book published on the Choctaws and southeastern Indians since the mid-twentieth century includes Swanton as a source.

Recent works on southeastern Indian history, however, use the data and reprinted (and translated) primary source material in Swanton's studies much more than his interpretations. Swanton's reliance on the notion of a southeastern "culture area," borrowed from his mentor, the anthropologist Franz Boas, led him to assume too much general cultural similarity among southeastern Indian groups while underemphasizing the diversity of the Choctaws and other southeastern Indian peoples.[5] Many recent authors, including this one, have been critical of Swanton's overreliance on structural and dualistic paradigms to explain southeastern Indian belief systems, social structure, and political organization. For example, Swanton's attempt to portray Choctaw society as divided into "red" and "white" moieties (an anthropological concept describing the division of society into two basic units based on common lineal descent with particular political and cultural duties), whereby the "red" moiety supplied war chiefs and the "white" moiety provided "peace" chiefs, does not fit the evidence about Choctaw culture and history.[6]

Swanton did make prolific and, for his time, innovative use of documentary sources to gain insight into southeastern Indian cultures. He mined published and archival sources and quoted heavily from primary documents created by Euro-Americans to craft a snapshot of traditional beliefs and practices that he felt were no longer in existence or remembered by twentieth-century southeastern Indians. At times he was willing to question the reliability of written sources, particularly when the document creator seemed to be inserting too much of his or her own perspective or agenda.[7] The reprinted documentary excerpts and Swanton's bibliographies still encourage students of Choctaw and southeastern Indian history to start with his works and branch out from there, even if paying slight attention to his interpretations. But there are problems even here. Swanton did not always read his documents critically enough, and he sometimes fit vague references into his preconceived structural frameworks.[8] He also did not make extensive use of documents not written in or translated into English. He made no travels to archives in Seville or Paris, and he did not have access to the wealth of printed, photographic, and digitized sources now available. Moreover, "his research methods were 'less than meticulous.'"[9] Though extremely valuable as starting points for investigating southeastern Indian culture and Choctaw history, Swanton's documentary sources should never be viewed as a complete data set.

For at least the first half of the twentieth century, Swanton dominated the study of the Choctaws and other southeastern Indians not only because he was the most prolific writer about their cultures and societies but also because he was conducting innovative research that combined fieldwork with extensive use of documentary sources. He combined historical and anthropological methodologies to create a fuller picture of the Native Southeast than had ever existed before.[10] Swanton should be viewed as a major transitional figure in the development of ethnohistory as a scholarly field. His basic approach to studying American Indians came to characterize what ethnohistory and the new Indian history, at their most basic level, are: the combination of historical and anthropological research methods to thoroughly interpret particular peoples and their cultures.

Swanton was the most important scholar of Choctaw history and culture for the first three-quarters of the twentieth century, but he was not the only one. The famed Oklahoma historian Angie Debo, a contemporary of Swanton, published her doctoral dissertation in history from the University of Oklahoma as *The Rise and Fall of the Choctaw Republic* in 1934.[11] Debo's work is based on deep research in primary sources and focuses primarily on the post-removal period, especially after the Civil War, as Choctaws grappled with rebuilding their lives and government in Indian Territory (Oklahoma). In no-holds-barred fashion, Debo exposed the U.S. government's successful efforts to dissolve the Choctaw polity as Oklahoma moved toward statehood in 1907. In 1959 Choctaw scholar Anna Lewis, who like Debo earned a Ph.D. in history from the University of Oklahoma, wrote a well-researched biography of the prominent chief and warrior Pushmataha.[12] Though dated in many of its interpretations, Lewis's book is the only significant treatment of Pushmataha's life and career to date. Among other sources, Lewis utilized excerpts from Gideon Lincecum's "Life of Apushimataha," published by the Mississippi Historical Society in 1906.[13] Historian Mary Elizabeth Young analyzes the aftermath of Indian removal in Mississippi and Alabama in *Redskins, Ruffle-shirts, and Rednecks* (1961).[14] She exposes the long and intricate story of corruption by American officials and settlers in acquiring Choctaw and other Indian lands. In 1970, historian Arthur DeRosier published what is still the only book-length treatment of the Choctaw experience with Indian removal.[15] DeRosier's *The Removal of the Choctaw Indians* is exclusively a political study of Choctaw-U.S. relations but remains indispensable by providing a chronological narrative of this crucial moment in Choctaw and American history. Two years later, historian W. David Baird published a biography of the prominent nineteenth-century Choctaw man Peter Pitchlynn that includes some information and discussion of the pre-removal period.[16] Baird's work, much like Lewis's biography of Pushmataha, relies on original research in primary sources but fails to assess Choctaw actions from a culturally informed perspective. In 1980 geographer Jesse McKee and sociologist Jon Schlenker published a useful survey of Choctaw history from precontact times to the late twentieth century that broke little new ground but provides a useful baseline for understanding major events in Choctaw history.[17] Another survey of Indian history in Mississippi from the era of European contact to the end of the eighteenth century, written by independent scholar Mary Ann Wells in 1994, includes much material on the Choctaws and relies heavily on published primary sources.[18] Like most survey-level books, the books by McKee and Schlenker and Wells, though valuable as reference works, are more descriptive than thesis driven and when published did not reflect scholarly trends in American Indian history and ethnohistory.

Not until the 1980s did scholars begin to fully take up the challenge established by Swanton to conduct ethnohistorical research that combined anthropological, historical, and Indian approaches to explaining Choctaw history. These newer works were born out of the intellectual ferment stimulated by Indian activism in the 1960s and 1970s and the rise of ethnohistorical approaches to history. The principal organization responsible for developing these new approaches to American Indian history is the American Society for Ethnohistory (ASE). Formed in the mid-1950s, the ASE has brought anthropologists, historians, American Indians, and other scholars together to share methods and research. The focus on ethnological data, participant observation, archaeology, and theory from anthropology was joined with the documentary and archival research and emphasis on change over time from history. A new methodology arose from this collaboration that focuses on culture as a basic component of human societies. Ethnohistorians argue that only by understanding the cultures of Indian people and others in the Americas can we begin to comprehend how they viewed the world around them and why they acted the way that they did (and do). In order to gain an understanding of American Indian culture, ethnohistorians utilize information about linguistics, oral traditions, material objects, rituals, music, religion, politics, economics, as well as theoretical approaches derived from the study of other indigenous peoples. Such insight comes from archaeology, written documents, languages, songs, literature, interviews with Native people, and even astronomy, biology, geology, and geography. Ethnohistorians will make use of any source that offers insight into culture and, thus, into Native ways of thinking. Topics studied by ethnohistorians include Indian-European relations, warfare, gender, diplomacy, biography, trade, religion, and ideology. The rise of social history among American historians since the 1960s, especially among early Americanists, has further fueled the acceptance and growth of culturally informed ethnohistorical studies of the diverse peoples living in North America in the colonial and early national periods. Historians now understand that Indian people were crucial participants in nearly every aspect of early American history. In recognition of the new ethnohistorical focus of most works on American Indians, many early Americanists refer to the explosion of works on American Indian history and Indian-European relations in the past few decades as the "new Indian history." They distinguish this new scholarship from the "old Indian history" that preceded it and that operated under Euro-American paradigms such as "savagery" versus "civilization" and that tended to deny Indians agency in their own history.[19]

The first major reexamination of Choctaw history that sought to move beyond the older descriptive works was prominent western historian Richard White's *The Roots of Dependency* (1983).[20] Utilizing "dependency theory" and a world-systems approach, White examines the histories of the Choctaws, Pawnees, and Navajos as they transitioned from a time of relative independence to a state of dependence on the American economy and the U.S. government. White describes how the Choctaws became enmeshed in the Euro-American market economy in the eighteenth century, starting with the trade in whitetail deerskins, and argued that this development transformed their society for the worse by the early nineteenth century. White's thesis about the pre-removal era of Choctaw history is summarized near the end of his discussion of the Choctaws:

> If any single factor is to be isolated as critical for understanding the fate of the Choctaws, it is market. The market and liquor emptied the forests of game; they brought into the nation the white traders who intermarried, pushed cattle herds into the borderlands, and started cotton plantations. The market forced land sales; it created distinctions of wealth unknown in the older order which it crippled.[21]

White's analysis is thesis driven, and he perceptively uses geographical and environmental data to show how change within Choctaw society occurred. For the first time, a scholar looking at pre-removal Choctaw history had suggested reasons for cultural change other than the power of "civilization" over "savagery" or the supposed natural appeal of Christianity and other American values (White clearly did not view the "market" as an inherently positive change agent). Yet, White only describes part of the story of pre-removal Choctaw history. The Choctaws in his book are still less historical actors with diverse motivations than victims of impersonal forces over which they had little control. For example, White does not adequately take into account the role of some Choctaws in encouraging economic and cultural change for reasons other than acculturation to American values, such as enhancing their own status and power, and he does not explain how cultural continuity could exist within such a devastating onslaught of market forces. White's story ends with the start of Indian removal and leaves readers wondering if the "crippled" Choctaws could possibly have survived after that time as a unique people with the ability to adapt and endure.

Another major book by a historian dealing with some aspect of Choctaw history is Daniel Usner's *Indians, Settlers, and Slaves in a Frontier Exchange Economy* (1992).[22] As its title suggests, Usner's book is a social history of the lower Mississippi Valley from the arrival of the French in 1699 to the end of the American Revolution. As the group with the largest population in the area, the Choctaws loom large in Usner's book as political players, whom the French viewed as the "key to the country," and as major trading partners of France and Britain in the deerskin exchange system. Usner exposes how Indians, Europeans, and Africans shaped the local-level economic and social systems in the region and how the culture in this pre-American South resulted from the interactions of all three groups. Usner advances our knowledge of Choctaw history by shedding light on the various ways that Choctaws and other Indians participated in trade with Europeans without weakening their political and cultural positions as White had argued. After the publication of *Indians, Settlers, and Slaves* it is no longer possible to ignore the fundamental contributions by Indians and Africans to the Gulf South's colonial history. Usner followed in 1998 with the publication of a collection of essays that again deal with the social and socioeconomic histories of Indians in the lower Mississippi Valley.[23] In this collection Usner examines, among other topics, the Choctaw role in transitioning Mississippi to a cotton economy in the early nineteenth century, the American Indian (especially Choctaw), presence in nineteenth-century New Orleans, and the portrayal of Indians (again especially Choctaws) in nineteenth-century images in the lower South. Usner's books reflect the movement to social history typical of recent early American history, but he calls for "greater attention to culture" in studying the Choctaws and other southeastern Indians "in order to advance our understanding of what this all meant to the participants themselves."[24]

Though her works concerning the Choctaws began to be published long before Usner made his suggestion to focus on culture, anthropologist and literary specialist Patricia Galloway has focused on culture and much more in Choctaw history. It is not an exaggeration to say that Patricia Galloway has radically and completely transformed our understanding of the Choctaw past. Since the early 1980s nearly all works that discuss Choctaw history exhibit Galloway's influence and acknowledge her findings. Not only has Galloway nearly single-handedly moved pre-removal Choctaw history into the modern age, she has remained a prolific scholar with a seemingly insatiable curiosity about Choctaw history and culture. Her entry into Choctaw studies and her continuing interest in "doing Choctaw ethnohistory" is explained nicely in her original essay in this volume. Luckily, for those of us who have tried to keep abreast of her frequent writings, she has recently published a collection of many of her more important and hard-to-find articles.[25]

Several of Galloway's essays made significant impacts on our understanding of Choctaw and southeastern Indian history and deserve mention here.

One of the earliest essays by Galloway that had an immediate effect on Choctaw studies is her article on the Choctaw Civil War of 1746–50, which is reprinted in this volume.[26] Appearing originally in the *Journal of Mississippi History* in 1982, Galloway's article demonstrates that the Choctaws were not "revolting" against a European power, though some Frenchmen were killed, but instead were fighting a civil war. Galloway exposes the diverse ethnic composition of the people who called themselves "Chahtas" and argues persuasively that the conflict could only be understood through an awareness of the contingent nature of Choctaw political loyalties. Suddenly that conflict made more sense as she argues that the Western Division Choctaws dominated by the *Imoklasha* ethnic group waged war against Eastern Division Choctaws dominated by the *Inholahta* ethnic group. The causes of the conflict stemmed from disputes between the two divisions over whether France or Britain should be the Choctaws' primary trading partner, but the fierceness and longevity of the war can only be explained by the ethnic divisions among the Choctaws rather than any supposed loyalty to European powers. Thus, by understanding more deeply than previous scholars how Choctaw society and politics worked, Galloway opens the door to better comprehension of eighteenth-century Choctaw culture and history as a whole.

Galloway made another major contribution to Choctaw history in 1989 with her essay "'The Chief Who Is Your Father': Choctaw and French Views of the Diplomatic Relation," published in the important collection *Powhatan's Mantle: Indians in the Colonial Southeast*.[27] For the first time, a scholar attempted to understand diplomacy between the Choctaws and Europeans from a Choctaw perspective. Recognizing that the matrilineal structure of Choctaw society permeated every aspect of their lives, Galloway demonstrates that the Choctaws accepted the French use of the term "father" in diplomacy because to the Choctaws a "father" was a "kind, indulgent" nonrelative "who had no authority over them."[28] For the French and other European diplomats, however, "father" meant someone who told his "children" how to behave. Thus, a basic cultural misunderstanding occurred repeatedly in the eighteenth century with neither side completely living up to the obligations that they expected from the other. Diplomacy for the Choctaws was necessary to establish trade relations, and the use of familial terminology by the French made sense to the Choctaws even as they disagreed about the obligations of "fathers." Choctaw trade could only occur after strangers had been converted into fictive kin. The Choctaws consistently tried to establish responsibilities and titles among French officials in order to have them protect Choctaw interests among the French, but the French never entirely understood their role, and misunderstanding frequently resulted.

In 1994 two essays by Galloway appeared that address distinct and crucial eras in pre-removal Choctaw history. One essay, published in the journal *Ethnohistory*, focuses on the major meeting between the Choctaws and Britain that occurred at Mobile in 1765.[29] Britain had just acquired claims to the Gulf Coast region from France after the Treaty of Paris ended the Seven Years' War in 1763. Though British fur traders had traveled to Choctaw villages and Choctaws had journeyed to British settlements at Charles Town and other locations throughout the eighteenth century, this was the first meeting that formally acknowledged the new ties between the two powers. Galloway exposes the intricate political maneuvering employed by the Choctaws as well as the diverse ethnic and divisional makeup of the "Choctaw Confederacy." The evidence, as presented by Galloway, clearly shows the divergent yet complementary motivations of chiefs from different villages and lineages as they competed for access to British trade and recognition from British officials of their high status.

Galloway's other major essay published in 1994 explains why by the seventeenth century the Choctaw polity should be viewed as a confederacy. Published in an important collection of essays on southeastern Indians edited by Charles Hudson and Carmen Chaves Tesser, Galloway's "Confederacy as a Solution to Chiefdom Dissolution: Historical Evidence in the Choctaw Case" opens an entirely new understanding of the Choctaw past and Choctaw origins.[30] Her chapter brings together archeological, cartographic, documentary evidence, and Choctaw oral traditions, to show how the diverse ethnic groups she writes about in other essays came together to form the Chahta people. In the aftermath of Hernando de Soto's expedition through the Southeast in the early 1540s, the multitown, chiefdom-level societies that the Spanish encountered, and which archaeologists call the "Mississippians," either disappeared, moved, joined other peoples, or decentralized into smaller, less hierarchical societies. It is thought that deadly European diseases such as smallpox caused this dramatic transformation and dislocation in the Southeast. Galloway looks for evidence to explain the diverse origins of the Choctaws in this period between the 1540s and 1700 and their location in central-eastern Mississippi. After marshalling the data, Galloway concludes that

> the "native" core of the emerging Choctaw tribe was made up of people who had never been part of a multilevel chiefdom, possibly the people

who had built the Nanih Waiya mound on the headwaters of the Pearl River but never settled thickly around it—the people who shared the "prairies culture of groups that would emerge as Chakchiumas and Chickasaws. If these people were reached at all by disease at an early date, it probably did affect them substantially. They were then joined by people from the east who had not been badly affected either—the remnants of the devolved Moundville chiefdom, who had moved down to the mouth of the Black Warrior [River] before the coming of Europeans, then on down the Tombigbee [River], and then in the seventeenth century were pushed westward into what were probably their former hunting grounds by the pressure of European-allied Indians. From the southwest came people related to the Natchez, perhaps the remnant of a great chiefdom on the lower Pearl [River]. The two incoming groups settled respectively the eastern and southern part of the "homeland" area that had not been settled before because it was poorly suited to the floodplain agriculture of the Mississippian adaptation.[31]

In essence, this explanation of Choctaw origins is also the central thesis of Galloway's important book, *Choctaw Genesis, 1500–1700*, published in 1995. The book lays out all of the minute detail and evidence that went into Galloway's momentous conclusion about the origins of the Choctaws. Her thesis helps to explain, among other things, why there are different Choctaw oral traditions about their origins that emphasize either their migration to present-day central Mississippi or their emergence from the Nanih Waiya mound. If distinct ethnic groups joined together after the 1540s, it makes sense that they retained different oral traditions about their respective origins. With Galloway's understanding of Choctaw origins, evidence from the eighteenth and later centuries that shows the divisional and ethnic distinctiveness among the Choctaws makes more sense, and interpreting Choctaw politics as a confederacy enables us to see more clearly the contingent nature of Choctaw foreign relations and domestic affairs. All future research on the Choctaws will be impacted and strengthened by these findings.

Another major book on pre-removal Choctaw history also appeared in 1995 by Choctaw scholar Clara Sue Kidwell.[32] Her work on the interaction between the Mississippi Choctaws and Christian missionaries was the first sustained investigation of a crucial era and series of events in early-nineteenth-century Choctaw history. An article published in 1987 by Kidwell and reprinted in this collection, "Choctaws and Missionaries in Mississippi before 1830," outlines many of the major conclusions of her later book.[33] Protestant missionaries from the American Board of Commissioners for Foreign Missions traveled to Choctaw villages at the invitation of several Choctaw chiefs. Kidwell exposes how the missionaries introduced new ideas and cultural changes to the Choctaws, yet ironically also worked to preserve the Choctaw language and empower Choctaw elites with new knowledge and new skills to participate in the American economy. By 1830 the missionaries had only converted about 250 Choctaws to Christianity, out of a population of some 15,000, but by establishing schools that taught Choctaw children reading, writing, and math, they had given Choctaw leaders the power to "deal with the white men on their own terms." "It is ironic," Kidwell writes, "that the most tangible and possibly the most lasting result of missionary activity among the Choctaw in Mississippi was the preservation of the Choctaw language." By producing English-Choctaw dictionaries and Bibles printed in the Choctaw language, the missionaries "helped to make possible the continuation of language in Choctaw communities and to preserve the identity that has sustained those communities to the present."[34] In her book-length treatment of the topic, Kidwell exposes in more detail the political machinations and disputes among Choctaw leaders, American Board opposition to Indian removal, and Mississippi Choctaw life after removal. Kidwell also makes notable use in her book of Choctaw oral traditions and interpretations of spirituality, as well as the Choctaw language, to provide an ethnohistorical interpretation of this period of Choctaw history that explained Choctaw actions from Choctaw perspectives.

Ethnohistorical examination of pre-removal Choctaw history grew quickly after the seminal publications by Galloway and Kidwell in 1995. James Taylor Carson contributed to our understanding of pre-removal Choctaw history that same year with an article in *Ethnohistory* that analyzes Choctaw adoption of the horse.[35] Using linguistic and other evidence, he shows that Choctaws considered the horse in much the same way they did deer—as animals that could be eaten when necessary and as items crucial to the fur trade economy of the eighteenth and early nineteenth century. Choctaws raised horses but used them most often as pack animals to transport deerskins to market and to carry European merchandise back to their villages rather than as implements of war, as was more common with Plains Indians. Carson continued this focus on the impact of European animals on Choctaw culture with his 1997 article, reprinted in this volume, about the Choctaw adaptation of cattle into their economy and lifeways.[36] Carson places this aspect of the Choctaw economy squarely within the recent literature on the market revolution of the early-nineteenth-century United States and urges readers to consider American Indian contributions to and encounters with the market revolution. Carson employs an explicitly ethnohistorical approach to his analysis and discovers a crucial element of Choctaw gender roles; men and women each adapted cows into their lives but in starkly different ways. Men tended to view cattle as sources of meat or as items to be sold at market, whereas women emphasized the renewable characteristic of cow's milk and the products to be made from it. Both men and women had adopted this European animal using their particular gender-specific Choctaw cultural meanings and terminology.

In 1999 Carson built upon this initial focus on Choctaw culture change with his book *Searching for the Bright Path: The Mississippi Choctaws from Prehistory to Removal*.[37] Like Richard White a decade and a half before, he examines the impact of European contact and the market on Choctaw society, but he comes away with a very different interpretation. Carson sees cultural continuities where White sees degradation. Carson argues that until at least 1830 the Choctaws maintained four key aspects of their culture: a gendered division of labor, a matrilineal kinship system, a political structure based on chiefly power, and a cosmology or belief system with roots in the Mississippian past. Carson acknowledges and shows that aspects of Choctaw culture changed after European arrival, but he insists that there was much more to the story than just change and that, therefore, students of Choctaw history need to look deeper within Choctaw understandings of their world in order to more accurately assess what was happening. In the second essay by Carson reprinted in this volume, published originally in 2003, he applies this basic notion to the seemingly paradoxical career of Choctaw leader Greenwood LeFlore.[38] LeFlore, Carson argues, exhibited behavior and cultural beliefs that combined his biological heritage of Choctaw and French while living in a time of U.S. ascendancy in the early to mid-nineteenth century. LeFlore arranged elements of his diverse heritage in ways that made sense to him and lived as both a Choctaw chief and a "southern Creole." Unlike many of his contemporaries—Choctaw and American—LeFlore saw no contradiction in the dual nature of his being.

In 1999 my first published essay on Choctaw history appeared, and, though I emphasize a different era of pre-removal Choctaw history than Carson, I too seek to understand Choctaw actions by a more thorough examination of Choctaw culture. In "Protecting Trade through War: Choctaw Elites and British Occupation of the Floridas," reprinted in this volume, I seek to understand why the Choctaws and Creeks fought a war from 1766 to 1776.[39] It became clear to me that both Choctaw and Creek chiefs let the war erupt after a series of small-scale killings in order to direct the energies of their young men away from the British and toward a Native enemy. French abandonment and British occupation of the Gulf Coast after the Seven Years' War ended in 1763 precipitated a crisis in Choctaw and Creek societies as British traders ignored Indian customs about how to conduct trade, and Indian men responded with attacks on the traders. War against another Indian group became a solution for elites as they tried to assert some social control in a society that increasingly ignored chiefly authority and had alienated the source of needed trade goods.

I continued my ethnohistorical examination of late-eighteenth-century century Choctaw history in my 2002 book, *Choctaws in a Revolutionary Age, 1750–1830*. When I started researching this project, I soon realized that there is an immense amount of archival and published documents pertaining to Choctaw history from the eighteenth century onward. I decided to follow the careers of individual Choctaws during the late eighteenth century as they appeared in French, British, Spanish, and American documents. Two men, Franchimastabé and Taboca, figured prominently in Choctaw political affairs in the last half of the eighteenth century. Though they hailed from the same village cluster of West Yazoo in the Western Division, their paths diverged: Taboca remained wedded to an ancient understanding of power and spirituality as the basis of his immense authority, while Franchimastabé became reliant on Euro-Americans and their merchandise as the basis of his authority. They represent in microcosm what happened to Choctaw society as a whole by the start of the nineteenth century. My emphasis on individual decision making was added to an understanding of Choctaw culture to explain how Choctaw culture changed and demonstrated continuities. Some Choctaw elites chose to participate in the market economy because it made cultural sense for them to do so and enhanced or preserved their high status. Other Choctaws, the majority through the era of Indian removal, continued to define their place in the world via notions of spiritual power, gender-specific obligations, and minimal contact with Euro-Americans.

My other essays in this volume include a previously published analysis of the first treaty negotiation between the Choctaws and the United States in 1786 and a new essay on the Choctaw role in defending British Pensacola from Spanish attack during the American Revolution.[40] The transcription of the talks between the Choctaws and the United States, published for the first time in this volume in Appendix A, revealed that the Choctaws had very different goals in mind for this negotiation than did the Americans. The Choctaws wanted trade, and they constructed the sacred space and rituals necessary to convert the Americans to fictive kin and trading partners. The Americans, however, sought to exert their new post–Revolutionary War power over all Indians who had aided Britain. Neither side successfully enforced its will on the other. My new essay examines the reasons that the Choctaws defended Pensacola during the American Revolution, and it corrects the mistaken impression propounded by many scholars that the Choctaws supported the United States in that conflict.

Choctaw scholar LeAnne Howe contributed to our understanding of pre-removal Choctaw history with her novel *Shell Shaker* in 2001.[41] She draws parallels between Red Shoes, whose killing of Frenchmen in 1746 precipitated the Choctaw civil war, and a partially fictionalized chief of the Choctaw Nation of Oklahoma in the late twentieth century. Both men relied on violence or the threat of violence to get their way, and both men introduced outsiders to the Choctaw community with detrimental impacts. Uniting the seemingly disparate stories is a family whose female descendants deal with the modern chief through a combination of smarts, perseverance, and appeal to spiritual influence. Though a work of fiction, *Shell Shaker* is based on deep research in historical sources and on first-hand experience with Choctaw culture and values. Howe's new essay on Ohoyo Chishba Osh, the Unknown Woman, for this collection is similarly based on documentary evidence and her informed interpretation of the Choctaw past. The traditional story of Ohoyo Chishba Osh credits her with introducing corn to the Choctaws, and Howe explores whether or not she was an actual person. Howe offers important insight into the roles of corn agriculture and women within Choctaw society and culture, while simultaneously offering a reinterpretation of an ancient oral tradition. In Howe's essay, it becomes clear that oral traditions first written down in the nineteenth century still have meaning and are being understood in new ways today.

A recent book-length work on pre-removal Choctaw history is Choctaw scholar Michelene Pesantubbee's book on Choctaw women published in 2005.[42] Pesantubbee sheds light on the changing role of Choctaw women within early-eighteenth-century Choctaw history; however the thesis and paradigms employed in the book are problematic. Pesantubbee argues for a declensionist interpretation of the status of Choctaw women, as their roles became devalued during the era of French contact from 1699 to 1763. According to Pesantubbee, so-called beloved, or high-status, women seem to disappear from the French documentary record early in the eighteenth century, while the importance of female-dominated agriculture seems to subside as well. Pesantubbee credits the oppressive French patriarchy and the Catholic Church for causing this dramatic culture change among the Choctaws. If she had carried her story past 1763, she may have arrived at a different conclusion. Starting in the early nineteenth century, gender roles did begin to change for some Choctaw families who participated in the American market economy, as elite women became spinners of cotton rather than farmers. But the subsistence, corn-based economy persisted for at least another century after 1763; women played a role in tribal political matters throughout the pre-removal era (for the role of women in foreign relations at the time, see my essay in this volume, "The Conqueror Meets the Unconquered"), and notions of matrilineality endured well after removal. The circumstance of so many Choctaw women—including, among others, Anna Lewis, Clara Sue Kidwell, LeAnne Howe, Devon Mihesuah, Valerie Lambert, Donna Akers, and Michelene Pesantubbee—becoming academic historians and writers in the twentieth and twenty-first centuries attests to the perseverance and continued importance of women in Choctaw society.

Also in 2005, independent scholar Charles Weeks analyzed the intense treaty negotiations between the Choctaws, and other southeastern Indians, and the Spanish during the late eighteenth century. Spain sought firmer alliances with the southeastern Indian groups to counter American interference in the area, and it wanted additional settlements and trading posts along the Mississippi and Tombigbee rivers.[43] Despite only covering a five-year period from 1791 to 1795, Weeks's work exposes the motivations of Choctaws and other southeastern Indians as they confronted the need for trade, protected their sovereignty, and attempted to counter increasing American demands for their land by allying with the other major non-Indian power in the region. Weeks's analysis of these diplomatic maneuverings is solid and builds upon the ethnohistorical literature of the preceding decades. Of particular value to students of late eighteenth-century Choctaw history is the last third of the book which reprints several important and lengthy Spanish documents that are full of information about the Indian groups and individuals with whom the Spanish dealt. Translated talks by numerous Choctaw and other Indian leaders are found in the documents, thus offering unique insight into southeastern Indian perspectives and goals. Primary sources like the ones that

Weeks reproduced are the lifeblood of historians and ethnohistorians, and Weeks went far in exposing how valuable the Spanish sources from the late eighteenth century are in exposing key facts from that era in Choctaw history.

As research on pre-removal Choctaw history continues to grow, writers will follow Weeks's example to discover new documents and other sources to shed light on Choctaw history, and they will ask new questions of established sources. Since Swanton's time in the first half of the twentieth century, a number of important primary sources have been published that any student of the pre-removal period will want to examine. The first stop on the journey to researching Choctaw history are the numerous books and articles mentioned in this chapter and reprinted in this volume, as well as the dozens of other articles that these authors have written that are not discussed here. The notes and bibliographies of these books and articles on Choctaw history expose the sources those authors used and discovered. Next, researchers should read through the annotated bibliography on Choctaw studies put together by Clara Sue Kidwell and Charles Roberts in 1980.[44] Though somewhat out-of-date, it still remains a convenient place to find crucial sources. Another hard-to-find volume that reprints several key documents and sources on pre-removal Choctaw history is the late John Peterson's *Choctaw Source Book* that came out in 1985.[45] The Choctaw-English dictionary originally compiled by missionary Cyrus Byington remains in print, and updated studies of the Choctaw language have recently appeared.[46]

Beyond these publications, several important document collections are available in libraries and, in some cases, for sale. The following discussion highlights key compilations but is not a comprehensive list of all printed sources that discuss the Choctaws; for further document assemblages researchers must comb through the writings of other scholars, dig around in libraries, consult bibliographic databases, and ask librarians and archivists for help. Researchers looking for French documents will want to examine the five volumes titled *Mississippi Provincial Archives: French Dominion*.[47] Records from the various English colonies, especially in the South, are helpful, as are the volumes of British Indian Superintendent Sir William Johnson's papers.[48] In the mid-twentieth century, the American Historical Association and the East Tennessee Historical Society published the largest translated collections of late-eighteenth-century Spanish documents relevant to the American South and to Choctaw history, but Spanish documents have also appeared in other publications.[49] American documents that discuss the Choctaws in the period from 1776 through Indian removal in the 1830s have been reprinted in several collections.⁵⁰ Personal and official papers of the U.S. presidents from George Washington through Andrew Jackson, and assorted government officials from Mississippi Territorial governors to federal cabinet officers, Indian agents, and fur traders will also yield information on the pre-removal Choctaws. Newspapers from southern colonies and states are very useful. Missionary records, from the French Jesuits of the eighteenth century to the American Board of the early nineteenth century, shed light on historic events and cultural beliefs.⁵¹ Last, but not least, travel accounts by various Europeans and Americans who encountered the Choctaws expose key aspects of Choctaw life.⁵²

Researchers should keep in mind that, though numerous, these are only the published primary sources on pre-removal Choctaw history. Countless more documents exist in archives, some awaiting discovery. Nearly all of the authors discussed in this chapter utilized archival sources, so their bibliographies and endnotes are useful starting places to figure out which archives possess relevant materials. Key archives with known sizable collections on pre-removal southeastern Indian and Choctaw history include the National Archives, the Library of Congress, and the Smithsonian Institution in Washington, D.C.; the Mississippi Department of Archives and History in Jackson; the Alabama Department of Archives of History in Montgomery; the Georgia Department of Archives and History in Atlanta; the Tennessee Department of Archives and History in Nashville; the William L. Clements Library at the University of Michigan in Ann Arbor; the American Philosophical Society Library in Philadelphia; the Southern Historical Collection at the University of North Carolina in Chapel Hill; the Thomas Gilcrease Institute of American History and Art in Tulsa, Oklahoma, the Oklahoma Historical Society in Oklahoma City, and the Western History Collection at the University of Oklahoma in Norman; the Williams Research Center at the Historic New Orleans Collection; and the Huntington Library and Art Gallery in San Marino, California. Other archives in the United States will also hold useful information; while underused archives in Spain, France, and Britain await further exploration as well.

Although the authors highlighted in this chapter have explored numerous topics in pre-removal Choctaw history, many more subjects await analysis or reinterpretation. Neglected topics include the interaction between Choctaws and peoples of African descent and the Choctaw adoption of racial slavery. Several recent works have begun exploring this long-neglected aspect of intercultural relations in the South but none have yet focused on the Choctaws.⁵³ The Choctaw role, apparently only as victims, in the Indian slave trade in the late seventeenth and early eighteenth centuries needs further examination.[54] More work is warranted on women and changing gender dynamics after the end date of Pesantubbee's work in 1763.[55] Community studies of particular Choctaw villages may help expose further the diversity of Choctaw experiences.[56] Relations between the Choctaws and their Native neighbors, such as the Creeks, Alabamas, Chakchiumas, Chickasaws, Caddos, and Osages, need further explication. Diplomatic meetings with Euro-Americans, such as those studied by Charles Weeks and others, should provide further insight into both the political maneuverings at work within Choctaw society at a given moment and the methods that Choctaws employed to craft successful diplomacy. The precise Choctaw role in Euro-American wars, such as the Seven Years' War, the U.S. war against the Ohio Valley Indian Confederacy in the 1790s, and the War of 1812 (especially Choctaw participation in that war against the Red Stick Creek Indians and in the Battle of New Orleans) demands more analysis. Why did Choctaws fail to accept Tecumseh's offer to join in the pan-Indian fight against the United States, for example?[57] There is always room for biographical studies that employ ethnohistorical methods; we need to know more about well-known Choctaw men such as Pushmataha and Mushulatubbee, as well as less-well-known men and women who impacted the direction of Choctaw history or exemplified key aspects of that history. The historiographical gap between pre-removal and post-removal studies needs to be bridged by scholars willing to do original research in both eras.[58] An ethnohistorical study of Choctaw removal, along the lines that Michael Green accomplished for Creek removal, would shed new light on that dark chapter in Choctaw history.[59] The ongoing relationship between Mississippi Choctaws and those who left for Indian Territory in the 1830s and after deserves greater attention. Book-length studies of the impact of Choctaw and general southeastern Indian culture on the customs of the South and on the trajectory of southern history will reshape our understanding of who and what made the South "southern." Other topics will surely arise and are quite likely being studied right now. Choctaw history has come of age, and the future of Choctaw studies looks bright.

NOTES

1. Dan Usner made this point a decade ago in *American Indians in the Lower Mississippi Valley: Social and Economic Histories* (Lincoln: University of Nebraska Press, 1998), 1.

2. John R. Swanton, *Source Material for the Social and Ceremonial Life of the Choctaw Indians* (1931; repr. Tuscaloosa: University of Alabama Press, 2001).

3. Swanton, *Source Material*, 2.

4. In their original form and by order of publication Swanton's major publications include *Indian Tribes of the Lower Mississippi Valley and Adjacent Coast of the Gulf of Mexico*, Bureau of American Ethnology Bulletin 43 (Washington, D.C.: U.S. Government Printing Office, 1911); Cyrus Byington, *A Dictionary of the Choctaw Language*, ed. Swanton and Henry S. Halbert, Bureau of American Ethnology Bulletin 46 (Washington, D.C.: U.S. Government Printing Office, 1915); *Early History of the Creek Indians and Their Neighbors*, Bureau of American Ethnology Bulletin 73 (Washington, D.C.: U.S. Government Printing Office, 1922); "Social Organization and Social Usages of the Indians of the Creek Confederacy," in *Forty-Second Annual Report of the Bureau of American Ethnology, 1924–1925, 1927* (Washington, D.C.: U.S. Government Printing Office, 1928), 279–325; "Social and Religious Beliefs and Usages of the Chickasaw Indians," in *Forty-Fourth Annual Report of the Bureau of American Ethnology, 1926–1927* (Washington, D.C.: U.S. Government Printing Office, 1928), 169–273; *Myths and Tales of the Southeastern Indians*, Bureau of American Ethnology Bulletin 88 (Washington, D.C.: U.S. Government Printing Office, 1929); *Source Material for the Social and Ceremonial Life of the Choctaw Indians*, Bureau of American Ethnology Bulletin 103 (Washington, D.C.: U.S. Government Printing Office, 1931); *Source Material on the History and Ethnology of the Caddo Indians*, Bureau of American Ethnology Bulletin 132; (Washington, D.C.: U.S. Government Printing Office, 1942); and *The Indians of the Southeastern United States*, Bureau of American Ethnology Bulletin 137 (Washington, D.C.: U.S. Government Printing Office, 1946).

5. Jason Baird Jackson, *Yuchi Ceremonial Life: Performance, Meaning, and Tradition in a Contemporary Indian Community* (Lincoln: University of Nebraska Press, 2003), 16–17.

6. Swanton, *Source Material for the Social and Ceremonial Life of the Choctaw Indians*, 76–79; Greg O'Brien, *Choctaws in a Revolutionary Age, 1750–1830* (Lincoln: University of Nebraska Press, 2002), 15, 19; and Greg Urban, "The Social Organizations of the Southeast," in *North American Indian Anthropology: Essays on Society and Culture*, ed. Raymond J. DeMallie and Alfonso Ortiz (Norman: University of Oklahoma Press, 1994), 173.

7. For an example, see Patricia Galloway, *Choctaw Genesis, 1500–1700* (Lincoln: University of Nebraska Press, 1995), 333.

8. O'Brien, *Choctaws in a Revolutionary Age*, 19.

9. Thomas J. Pluckhahn and Robbie Ethridge, eds., *Light on the Path: The Anthropology and History of the Southeastern Indians* (Tuscaloosa: University of Alabama Press, 2006), 5.

10. Usner, *American Indians in the Lower Mississippi Valley*, 3.

11. Angie Debo, *The Rise and Fall of the Choctaw Republic* (1934; repr. Norman: University of Oklahoma Press, 1961).

12. Anna Lewis, *Chief Pushmataha, American Patriot: The Story of the Choctaws' Struggle for Survival* (New York: Exposition Press, 1959).

13. Gideon Lincecum, "Life of Apushimataha," *Publications of the Mississippi Historical Society* 9 (1906): 415–85; repr. as Lincecum, *Pushmataha: A Choctaw Leader and His People* (Tuscaloosa: University of Alabama Press, 2004).

14. Mary Elizabeth Young, *Redskins, Ruffleshirts, and Rednecks: Indian Allotments in Alabama and Mississippi, 1830–1860* (Norman: University of Oklahoma Press, 1961).

15. Arthur H. DeRosier Jr., *The Removal of the Choctaw Indians* (Knoxville: University of Tennessee Press, 1970).

16. W. David Baird, *Peter Pitchlynn: Chief of the Choctaws* (Norman: University of Oklahoma Press, 1972).

17. Jesse O. McKee and Jon A. Schlenker, *The Choctaws: Cultural Evolution of a Native American Tribe* (Jackson: University Press of Mississippi, 1980).

18. Mary Ann Wells, *Native Land: Mississippi, 1540–1798* (Jackson: University Press of Mississippi, 1994).

19. For historiographical overviews of the development and impact of ethnohistory, see James Axtell, "Ethnohistory: An Historian's Viewpoint," *Ethnohistory* 26, no. 1 (1979): 1–13; Axtell, "Colonial American without the Indians: Counterfactual Reflections," *Journal of American History* 73 (1987): 981–86; James H. Merrell, "Some Thoughts on Colonial Historians and American Indians," *William and Mary Quarterly* 46 (1989): 94–119; Neal Salisbury, "The Indians' Old World: Native Americans and the Coming of Europeans," *William and Mary Quarterly* 53, no. 3 (1996): 435–58; Philip J. Deloria, "Historiography," in *A Companion to American Indian History*, ed. Deloria and Neal Salisbury (Malden, Mass.: Blackwell, 2002), 6–24; and Nicolas G. Rosenthal, "Beyond the New Indian History: Recent Trends in the Historiography on the Native Peoples of North America," *History Compass* 4 (2006): 962–74.

20. Richard White, *The Roots of Dependency: Subsistence, Environment, and Social Change among the Choctaws, Pawnees, and Navajos* (Lincoln: University of Nebraska Press, 1983).

21. White, *The Roots of Dependency*, 146.

22. Daniel H. Usner Jr., *Indians, Settlers, and Slaves in a Frontier Exchange Economy: The Lower Mississippi Valley before 1783* (Chapel Hill: University of North Carolina Press, 1992).

23. Usner, *American Indians in the Lower Mississippi Valley*.

24. Ibid., 12.

25. Patricia Galloway, *Practicing Ethnohistory: Mining Archives, Hearing Testimony, Constructing Narrative* (Lincoln: University of Nebraska Press, 2006).

26. Patricia Galloway, "Choctaw Factionalism and Civil War, 1746–1750," *Journal of Mississippi History* 44 (1982): 289–327.

27. Patricia Galloway, "'The Chief Who Is Your Father': Choctaw and French Views of the Diplomatic Relation," in *Powhatan's Mantle: Indians in the Colonial Southeast*, ed. Peter H. Wood, Gregory A. Waselkov, and M. Thomas Hatley (Lincoln: University of Nebraska Press, 1989), 254–78.

28. Ibid., 255.

29. Patricia Galloway, "'So Many Little Republics': British Negotiations with the Choctaw Confederacy, 1765," *Ethnohistory* 41 (1994): 513–37.

30. Patricia Galloway, "Confederacy as a Solution to Chiefdom Dissolution: Historical Evidence in the Choctaw Case," in *The Forgotten Centuries: Indians and European in the American South, 1521–1704*, ed. Charles Hudson and Carmen Chaves Tesser (Athens: University of Georgia Press, 1994), 393–420.

31. Ibid., 399.

32. Clara Sue Kidwell, *Choctaws and Missionaries in Mississippi, 1818–1918* (Norman: University of Oklahoma Press, 1995).

33. Clara Sue Kidwell, "Choctaws and Missionaries in Mississippi before 1830," *American Indian Culture and Research Journal* 11, no. 2 (1987): 51–72.

34. Ibid., 69–70.

35. James Taylor Carson, "Horses and the Economy and Culture of the Choctaw Indians, 1690–1840," *Ethnohistory* 42 (1995): 495–513.

36. James Taylor Carson, "Native Americans, the Market Revolution, and Culture Change: The Choctaw Cattle Economy, 1690–1830," *Agricultural History* 71, no. 1 (1997): 1–18.

37. James Taylor Carson, *Searching for the Bright Path: The Mississippi Choctaws from Prehistory to Removal* (Lincoln: University of Nebraska Press, 1999).

38. James Taylor Carson, "Greenwood LeFlore: Southern Creole, Choctaw Chief," *Journal of Mississippi History* 65, no. 4 (2003): 355–73.

39. Greg O'Brien, "Protecting Trade through War: Choctaw Elites and British Occupation of the Floridas," in *Empire and Others: British Encounters with Indigenous Peoples, 1600–1850*, ed. Martin Daunton and Rick Halpern (Philadelphia: University of Pennsylvania Press, 1999), 149–66.

40. Greg O'Brien, "The Conqueror Meets the Unconquered: Negotiating Cultural Boundaries on the Post-Revolutionary Southern Frontier," *Journal of Southern History* 68 (2001): 39–72.

41. LeAnne Howe, *Shell Shaker* (San Francisco: Aunt Lute Books, 2001).

42. Michelene E. Pesantubbee, *Choctaw Women in a Chaotic World: The Clash of Cultures in the Colonial Southeast* (Albuquerque: University of New Mexico Press, 2005).

43. Charles A. Weeks, *Paths to a Middle Ground: The Diplomacy of Natchez, Boukfouka, Nogales, and San Fernando de las Barrancas, 1791–1795* (Tuscaloosa: University of Alabama Press, 2005).

44. Clara Sue Kidwell and Charles Roberts, *The Choctaws: A Critical Bibliography* (Bloomington: Indiana University Press, 1980).

45. John H. Peterson, *A Choctaw Source Book* (New York: Garland, 1985).

46. Byington, *A Dictionary of the Choctaw Language*. See also, Marcia Haag and Henry Willis, eds., *Choctaw Language and Culture: Chahta Anumpa* (Norman: University of Oklahoma Press, 2001); and George A. Broadwell, *A Choctaw Reference Grammar* (Lincoln: University of Nebraska Press, 2006).

47. Dunbar Rowland, Albert G. Sanders, and Patricia Galloway, eds., *Mississippi Provincial Archives: French Dominion*, 5 vols. (vols. 1–3: Jackson: Mississippi Department of Archives and History, 1927–32; vols. 4–5: Baton Rouge: Louisiana State University Press, 1984).

48. For South Carolina, see William McDowell, ed., *Colonial Records of South Carolina: Documents Relating to Indian Affairs*, 3 vols. (Columbia: South Carolina Department of Archives and History, 1955–70). For West Florida see Dunbar Rowland, ed., *Mississippi Provincial Archives: English Dominion* (Nashville, Tenn.: Brandon Printing, 1911); and John J. Juricek, ed., *Georgia and Florida Treaties*, vol. 12 of *Early American Indian Documents: Treaties and Laws, 1607–1789*, ed. Alden T. Vaughan (Washington, D.C.: University Publications of America, 2001). For British-Indian relations during the American Revolution see K. G. Davies, ed., *Documents of the American Revolution, 1770–1783*, 21 vols. (Shannon: Irish University Press, 1972). For William Johnson, see Alexander C. Flick, ed., *The Papers of Sir William Johnson*, 14 vols. (Albany: University of the State of New York, 1921–65).

49. Lawrence Kinnaird, trans. and ed., *Spain in the Mississippi Valley, 1765–1794*, 3 vols. (Washington, D.C.: U.S. Government Printing Office, 1949); D. C. Corbitt and Roberta Corbitt, eds., "Papers from the Spanish Archives Relating to Tennessee and the Old Southwest, 1783–1800," *East Tennessee Historical Society Publications*, vols. 9–49 (1937–77); and Manuel Serrano y Sanz, ed., *España y los Indios Cherokis y Chactas en la segunda mitad del siglo XVIII* (Seville: Tip. de la Guia Oficial, 1916), also published in English as Samuel Dorris Dickinson, trans. and ed., *Spain and the Cherokee and Choctaw Indians in the Second Half of the Eighteenth Century* (Idabel, Okla.: Museum of the Red River, 1995).

50. For example, see Dunbar Rowland, ed., *The Mississippi Territorial Archives, 1798-1803* (Nashville, Tenn.: Brandon Printing, 1905); Clarence E. Carter, ed., *The Territory of Mississippi, 1798–1817*, vol. 5 of *The Territorial Papers of the United States* (Washington, D.C.: U.S. Government Printing Office, 1937); and *American State Papers: Indian Affairs* (Washington, D.C.: Gales and Seaton, 1832).

51. Reuben Gold Thwaites, ed., *The Jesuit Relations and Allied Documents: Travels and Explorations of the Jesuit Missionaries in New France, 1610–1791*, 73 vols. (New York: Pageant Book Co., 1959); and *Papers of the American Board of Commissioners for Foreign Missions* (Woodbridge, Conn.: Research Publications, 1985), microfilm.

52. Two of the more important such travel accounts for Choctaw history are Jean Bernard Bossu, *Travels through That Part of North America Formerly Called Louisiana* (London, 1771); and Bernard Romans, *A Concise Natural History of East and West Florida*, ed. Kathryn E. Holland Braund (Tuscaloosa: University of Alabama Press, 1999).

53. James F. Brooks, ed., *Confounding the Color Line: The Indian-Black Experience in North America* (Lincoln: University of Nebraska Press, 2002); Lisa Bier, *American Indian and African American People, Communities, and Interactions: An Annotated Bibliography* (Westport, Conn.: Praeger, 2004); Tiya Miles, *Ties That Bind: The Story of an Afro-Cherokee Family in Slavery and Freedom* (Berkeley: University of California Press, 2005); Claudio Saunt, *Black, White, and Indian: Race and the Unmaking of an American Family* (New York: Oxford University Press, 2005); Tiya Miles and Sharon P. Holland, eds., *Crossing Waters, Crossing Worlds: The African Diaspora in Indian Country* (Durham, N.C.: Duke University Press, 2006); and Gary Zellar, *African Creeks: Estelvste and the Creek Nation* (Norman: University of Oklahoma Press, 2007).

54. Alan Gallay, *The Indian Slave Trade: The Rise of the English Empire in the American South* (New Haven, Conn.: Yale University Press, 2002).

55. Greg O'Brien, "'Trying to Look Like Men': Changing Notions of Masculinity among Choctaw Elites in the Early Republic," in *Southern Manhood: Perspectives on Masculinity in the Old South*, ed. Craig Friend and Lorri Glover (Athens: University of Georgia Press, 2004), 49–70.

56. For a community study on the Creeks, see Joshua A. Piker, *Okfuskee: A Creek Indian Town in Colonial America* (Cambridge, Mass.: Harvard University Press, 2004).

57. John Sugden, "Early Pan-Indianism: Tecumseh's Tour of the Indian Country, 1811–1812," *American Indian Quarterly* 10, no. 4 (1986): 280–82.

58. For the beginnings of such work, see Donna Akers, *Living in the Land of Death: The Choctaw Nation, 1830–1860* (East Lansing: Michigan State University Press, 2004).

59. Michael D. Green, *The Politics of Indian Removal: Creek Government and Society in Crisis* (Lincoln: University of Nebraska Press, 1982).

CHAPTER 2

Ohoyo Chishba Osh

WOMAN WHO STRETCHES WAY BACK

LeAnne Howe

In this essay I will examine the nature of Choctaw stories. Whether written down or "as told to," the impact of our stories is still reverberating throughout our lands. An important element in my essay is the mix of an oral story, history, and my own narrative about the woman who brought the Choctaw people corn.

Our core beliefs, sacred knowledge, cultural heroes and heroines, and our nation's histories come to us through the telling of stories. For example, how many of us can remember learning the story of George Washington and the cherry tree? He could not tell a lie and confessed to his father that he'd chopped down the cherry tree. For Americans, George Washington and the cherry tree incident has become a core narrative. Whether true or not, the story exemplifies the qualities every American wishes for in a U.S. president, namely truthfulness.

In *On Literature*, novelist and literary critic Umberto Eco writes, "Certain characters have become somehow true for the collective imagination because over the course of centuries we have made emotional investments in them. We all make emotional investments in any number of fantasies which we dwell on either with open eyes or half-awake."[1] Eco goes on to talk about the kinds of fictional attributes that Europeans apply to living persons. "We have to find a space in the universe where these characters live and shape our behavior to such an extent that we choose them as role models for our life, and for the lives of others, so that we are clear about what we mean when we say that someone has an Oedipus complex, or a Gargantuan appetite, that someone behaves quixotically, is as jealous as Othello, doubts like Hamlet, is an incurable Don Juan, or is a Scrooge."[2]

For American Indians, stories have a different responsibility. Traditional or core stories rarely point out personal characteristics; rather, they tell of certain epitomizing events.[3] Creation stories are told to establish a tribe's place of origin. Peopling stories are told to explain how they came together on a specific land site. Migration stories are told to explain where and why the people relocated. So it is indeed unfortunate that over the last century American Indian stories have been relegated to the status of myth and legends—first by the early ethnographers, and currently by children's authors. A quick Internet search using the phrase "American Indian stories" will yield twenty web pages containing book titles that attach the words "myth," "legend," "lore," and "tale" to the titles of indigenous stories. This may explain why Louis Owens once took umbrage and wrote, "The dilemma begins with the word *Indian*." Perhaps no other utterance in American language is so "enveloped in an obscuring mist," so "entangled, shot through with shared thoughts, points of view, alien value judgments and accents."[4] I agree with Owens's assessment that "Indian" stories were not necessarily intended to become captive to the whims of non-Native uses, specifically non-Native children's book authors. We need to review American Indian core narratives through a more focused historical lens in order to better understand our past, our present, and our future.[5] So it is with this view in mind that I began to question the story of Ohoyo Chishba Osh, the Unknown Woman (or the Woman Who Stretches Way Back, as my subtitle suggests), who brought corn seeds to the Choctaws.

The story of Ohoyo Chishba Osh was first published by Horatio Bardwell Cushman in 1899.[6] Because of Cushman's love for the Choctaws (he was born in 1822 in the Choctaw homelands and grew up speaking Choctaw with his boyhood tribal friends), his unwavering support for the Choctaw Nation during the time of allotment (the so-called progressive era of the late nineteenth century [1896–1905]), and his penchant for flowery language, the story has been largely dismissed as a mythic tale.

Was Ohoyo Chishba Osh a real person or a fictional character? Was she an agricultural broker from a far away place who came into the Choctawan homelands trading meat for corn kernels? If so, how did the Choctaws relate to her community? How does the story reveal core values and beliefs of the Choctaw people? Finally, how are we, Choctaw people today, informed by this epitomizing event? These questions and others will undoubtedly lead to more historical debate, but one thing is certain: Choctaw stories are the literary and intellectual traditions of the Choctaw people, whether or not the narratives are "as told to." As the Choctaw-Chickasaw scholar Philip Carroll Morgan argues in an essay on the letters of Choctaw James McDonald, "Some scholars from each band, tribe and nation need to realize both the responsibility and the opportunity to discover the roots of their own intellectual traditions. An excellent place to begin this voyage of discovery is with primary research in the library, museum, tribal government, and private archives, which in the past have been the academic terrain of historians and folklorists but have been largely ignored by literary critics."[7] In other words, if Choctaw stories function as national narratives, if we have Choctaw literary nationalism, and I believe we do, then it's time Choctaw scholars interrogate these ancestral stories. We have a great deal to learn from them—even if they have been written down by an invited tribal guest such as Cushman.

OVERTURE

In 1964 Robert Kingsbery photographed Marie Gibson standing in front of three large cast-iron pots of *pashofa* cooking over an open fire. The picture was taken outdoors, and, judging by the size of the pots, each must have held at least five gallons of the creamy white corn soup. Marie Gibson stirs the pashofa with a large wooden paddle. The photograph is an eloquent witness to the role women play in southeastern Indian culture. First, it captures the reality of the moment—she, the woman, mother, grandmother is preparing a great deal of corn soup, enough for a tribe. Second, because the photograph was shot outdoors there is a sense of place coded in it: she, the woman, is connected to the land and the crops harvested from it. Third, the image hints at the roots of this event, the timelessness of Indian women preparing corn. Today the Kingsbery image appears on the back of a Chickasaw Historical Society postcard with the words, "Promoting and Preserving Our Heritage." The "moccasin telegraph" (in this case) is a postcard, and the image being communicated through the U.S. postal system underlies the theme of this essay: corn is the gift of woman.

Pashofa is also the first traditional dish my Choctaw mother, Christine Billy Poynor, taught me how to prepare. It's a corn soup made from pearl hominy or cracked corn sold at roadside vegetable stands or at the small independent grocery stores in both the Choctaw and Chickasaw nations. The corn must be soaked overnight in water. The next day, add it to a large pot of boiling water. Cook for two hours, then add fresh meat (nowadays the Choctaws prefer pork) and unsalted butter. Once the corn is soft, add several pinches of oak ash to the pot for flavoring (think Liquid Smoke) and salt and pepper to taste. The pashofa will be very creamy and delicious. This recipe has been passed on for generations—from my grandmother Lucinda Billy to my mother and me. Now I have passed it to you.

My great-grandmother was Catherine Thompson (Chickasaw-Choctaw). She made pashofa as well as another corn soup called hominy. She would begin with a quart of oak ash, four quarts of water, and two quarts of dried kernels. The process for making hominy takes a little longer because you must boil the ash and water for about a half hour until the mixture is bubbling. Once the mixture is bubbling, take it off the stove and let it cool. Strain the mixture through a cheesecloth and return it to a crock-pot along with the kernels. Cook until the hulls loosen from the kernels and drain the liquid. Wash and rewash the corn until the hulls float atop the water and can be discarded. Then you can follow the recipe above, although it will not be creamy.

By this time you may be asking yourself what these two recipes have to do with the story of Ohoyo Chishba Osh. Perhaps it would be simplest to admit that corn and the preparation of foods derived from corn have been lifelong passions of mine. Certainly receiving these recipes marked the beginning of my interest in southeastern traditional foods. However, in early 1990 while I was researching Choctaw history for my novel *Shell Shaker* I came across the story of Ohoyo Chishba Osh.[8] It was unusual because the story is about a Native woman traveler. In so many instances, whether primary or secondary sources, the transcribers *and* the storytellers are males. However, the Cushman story is different. I asked my mother if she knew the story of Ohoyo Chishba Osh, and she said she didn't. I explained that I'd found a couple of stories about how our tribe first received corn: In one version a black bird brought corn (*tanchi*) to a Choctaw boy. In another story it is an unknown woman who left seeds atop the mound. My mother and I talked at length about the stories and finally decided that either could be correct. Events were not always the same for everyone in our old homelands because the towns and communities were spread across a vast territory.

A few weeks later my mother telephoned me to say that she had been talking with her oldest sister to get a better opinion of the meaning of Ohoyo Chishba Osh. She said the name could mean that the woman "stretched way back and was from a far away place, somewhere not known to us." Again we talked about where the woman could have come from, and my mother said she and her sister did not know. That was over fifteen years ago. While my research interests have changed somewhat since then, I still continue to ruminate about the woman who brought the Choctaws corn. Was Ohoyo Chishba Osh from somewhere in Mexico, or from a place much farther south? My aunt and mother would not speculate, but I don't believe they thought she was an invented character either. So what about the coming of corn? Who brought the Choctaws the seeds? Was it the rain, the birds, a woman, or someone or something else?

Modern scientists tell us that the wild grass teosinte, which became corn, developed in central Mexico some seven thousand years ago. "From Mexico maize spread north into the Southwestern United States and south down the coast to Peru. About 1,000 years ago, as Indian people migrated north to the eastern woodlands of present day North America, they brought corn with them."[9] With all the interest in transnationalism among academics in American Indian studies and American studies, stories like the one about Ohoyo Chishba Osh should yield a great deal of interest in the development of the Choctaws' transnational trading networks. We have the stories, so what can we learn from them? Following is the story of Ohoyo Chishba Osh, as translated by Cushman. For emphasis, I have italicized some of the words and will come back to them later in the essay.

> In the days of many moons ago, two Choctaw hunters were encamped for the night in the swamps of the Alabama river. The two hunters having been unsuccessful in the chase of that and the preceding day, found themselves on that night with nothing to satisfy the cravings of their hunger except a black hawk which they had shot with an arrow. *Sad reflections* filled their hearts as they thought of their rather sad disappointments and of their suffering families at home, while the gloomy future spread over them its dark pall of despondency, all serving to render them unhappy indeed. They cooked the hawk, and sat down to partake of their poor and scanty supper, when their attention was drawn from their gloomy foreboding by the low but distinct tones strange yet soft and plaintive as the melancholy notes of the dove, but produced by what, they were unable to even conjecture. At different intervals it broke the deep silence of the early night with its seemingly muffled notes of woe; and as the nearly full orbed moon slowly ascended the eastern sky the strange sounds became more frequent and distinct. With eyes dilated and fluttering hearts they looked up and down the river to learn

whence the sounds proceeded, but no object except the sandy shores glittering in the moonlight greeted their eyes, while the dark waters of the river seemed alone to give response in murmuring tones to the strange tones that continued to float upon the night air from a direction they could not definitely locate; but happening to look behind them in the direction opposite the moon they saw a woman of wonderful beauty standing upon a mound a few rods distant. Like an *illuminating shadow*, she had suddenly appeared out of the *moon-lighted* forest. She was loosely clad in a *snow-white raiment*, and bore in the folds of her drapery a wreath of fragrant flowers. She beckoned them to approach, while she seemed surrounded by a *halo of light* that gave to her a supernatural appearance. Their imagination now influenced them to believe her to be the Great Spirit of their nation, and that the flowers she bore were representatives of loved ones who had passed from earth to bloom in the spirit land.

The mystery was solved. At once they approached [the spot] to where she stood and offered their assistance in any way they could be of service to her. She replied she was very hungry, where upon one of them ran and brought the roasted hawk and handed it to her. She accepted it with grateful thanks; but after eating a small portion of it, she handed the remainder back to them replying that she would remember their kindness when she returned to her home in the happy hunting grounds of her father, who was *Shilup Chitoh Osh*—the Great Spirit of the Choctaws. She then told them that when the next mid-summer moon should come they must meet her at the mound upon which she was standing. She then bade them an affectionate *adieu* and was at once borne away upon a gentle breeze and mysteriously as she came, so she disappeared. The two hunters returned to their camp for the night and early next morning sought their homes, but kept the strange incident a profound secret to themselves. When the designated time rolled around the midsummer full moon found the two hunters at the foot of the mound but *Ohoyo Chishba Osh* was nowhere to be seen. They remember she told them they must come to the very spot where she was then standing they at once ascended to the mound and found it covered with a strange plant, which yielded an excellent food, which was ever afterwards cultivated by the Choctaws, and named by them *Tanchi* (corn).[10]

Many who read Cushman's translation may think he missed his calling as a romance novelist. However, the story has a great deal of value when we pull the text apart and study it. The unknown woman's story then becomes a kind of syncretism, a history collapsing many events together that profoundly influences Choctaw culture: an eclipse; the rituals and accords around the summer solstice in southeastern Indian societies; the role of women in land tenure; and the role of women as both daughter of and creator of early Choctaw lifeways, including the production of corn. In this way the story of Ohoyo Chishba Osh literally becomes a story of survival. Her seeds made it possible for the Choctaws to grow into one of the largest Indian confederacies in the Southeast.

OHOYO CHISHBA OSH: THE WOMAN'S GOT CORN!

When I examine a story, anyone's story, I look first at where the story is set. The unknown Choctaw who narrated the story of Ohoyo Chishba Osh to Cushman locates the two Choctaw hunters along the Alabama River. Naming the particular water route as the Alabama River would seem to be one of the keys to authenticating the story. At this place along the Alabama River corn is unknown to the two Choctaw hunters. What the name of the river was previous to contact with Europeans is another question. But at the time the story was told to Cushman, let's assume that both storyteller and translator understood the location to be the Alabama River. Second, Choctaw hunters were traveling widely throughout the central southeastern homelands to hunt before the coming of corn. (Choctaws still hunt in the Southeast despite the federal government's removal of the Choctaw people in 1831—an irony that must not go unwritten here.) Of further importance, the Alabama River is formed in central Alabama by the confluence of the Tallapoosa and Coosa rivers north of where the city of Montgomery is located. The river flows southwest to Mobile where it joins the Tombigbee to form the Mobile River that eventually empties into Mobile Bay. This is another key of the story. Traders from as far away as Mexico and beyond could use the coastlines of North and South America to eventually enter the Southeast at the Bay of Mobile. We know from scholars such as Patricia Galloway that indigenous people had traveled widely throughout the Southeast for centuries by using the river systems.[11] We also know that in the nineteenth century, as well as today, the Alabama River was vital to the transportation of goods and to the region's economy. Though more research is needed, there is little reason not to presume that the Choctaws (and other tribes) in prehistory were using the rivers to effect trade between North and South America—which brings us back to the story of Ohoyo Chishba Osh.

After a very unsuccessful day of hunting, the two weary hunters sit down to a meal of roasted hawk. We are told that they worry about their loved ones who are probably hungry too. The sadness of the two men is interrupted by the call of a low, soft voice: "distinct tones strange yet soft and plaintive as the melancholy notes of the dove, but produced by what, they were unable to even conjecture. At different intervals it broke the deep silence of the early night with its seemingly muffled notes of woe[,] . . . while the dark waters of the river seemed alone to give response in murmuring tones to the strange tones that continued to float upon the night air from a direction they could not definitely locate." The river responds to the soft call and issues a response.

The call and response technique is the hallmark of Choctaw song and dance. A man issues the call, and dancers line up and sing the response. During the response, women sometimes double men at the octave.[12] The call and response technique narrated in the story of Ohoyo Chshba Osh is emblematic of Choctaw song and dance and reaffirms for me that a Choctaw must have told the story to Cushman.

First, the two men by the Alabama River before the age of corn. Next, they hear a call and response coming from the natural world.

The two men in the story respond to the call, "but happening to look behind them in the direction opposite the moon they saw a woman of wonderful beauty standing upon a mound a few rods distant. Like an *illuminating shadow*, she had suddenly appeared out of the *moon-lighted* forest."

Could this "illuminating shadow" be the description of a lunar eclipse? Historical documents reveal that Choctaws consider eclipses, equinoxes, and solstices powerful events, and I have used the autumnal equinox in my stories to delineate important events.[13] Given that the unknown woman is standing in a shadow during a lunar eclipse, and the men see her as the daughter of the sun, a powerful metaphor for creation, can we also read this narrative as the birth of Choctaw matrilineal culture? If mother grows the children that become her tribe and if a woman has brought the seeds that will grow a crop that increases the population across all directions and all boundaries, the narrative has broad implications. Certainly Choctaw culture becomes matrilineal and culturally focused around women as the literal and fictive heads of the families. But how did Choctaw culture become matrilineal? Could this lifeway be tied to the coming of corn? If this story is indeed as old as it appears can we also begin to read it with other narrative possibilities? In the story of Ohoyo Chishba Osh, the men feed her meat, and she rewards them with seeds, actions symbolic of men and women's roles in Choctaw culture. Men hunt. Women grow the crops. Again much more research by scholars considering a wide range of disciplines, documents, and fieldwork will be necessary. But this is work for scholars who will consider what Choctaw literary nationalism is and how our stories function.

The story builds on. First, the two men by the Alabama River before the age of corn. Next, they hear a call and response coming from the natural world. She appears reflected in the light to the two Choctaw hunters.

The unknown woman tells the hunters to return to the mound the following mid-summer and that "she would remember their kindness when she returned to her home in the happy hunting grounds of her father, . . . *Shilup Chitoh Osh*." It can be noted that *Shilup Chitoh Osh*, also means "Big Shadow" or "Big Shade." The storyteller twice invokes the notion of the "Great Spirit." In the first reference, "Their imagination now influenced them to believe her to be the Great Spirit of their nation." And later on, "*Shilup Chitoh Osh*—the Great Spirit of the Choctaws." Before Christianity the Great Spirit was called "Hashtali," the eye of the Sun. After Christianity, other terms can be found in the Choctaw translation of the Old Testament by Cyrus Byington that mean "Great Spirit" or "God the Father." But I said earlier in the essay that I would return to discuss the italicized words, *Shilup Chitoh Osh, sad reflection, illuminating shadow, moon-lighted, snow-white raiment,* and *halo of light*. Perhaps it's the use of these particular words that finally convinced me that Cushman was translating from a Choctaw speaker. In the Choctaw language it is the intensity and grayness, the dullness or brightness of a thing that determines how it is spoken of. While Cushman grew up speaking Choctaw he may not have known the formal nuances of the language, but he intuitively understood the meaning and translated the descriptions as he was told.[14] How a big shade came is described through that Choctaw worldview. The unknown woman brought a powerful gift and is described as "surrounded by a *halo of light*."

The story continues to build. First, the two men by the Alabama River before the age of corn. Next, they hear a call and response coming from the natural world. She appears reflected in the light to the two Choctaw hunters. She brings a gift. She leaves instructions.

When I first read the story of Ohoyo Chishba Osh, I was puzzled at the mention of the mound in the story. It couldn't have been Nanih Waiya because the story is set along the Alabama River. The Nanih Waiya mound is located along the Pearl River in Winston County, Mississippi. While Choctawan mounds once populated the landscape in the Southeast, it wasn't until I came across the writings of Jane Mt. Pleasant, a Tuscarora associate professor at Cornell University, that I resolved the meaning of the mound in the story of Ohoyo Chishba Osh.

> Certainly when the Europeans arrived in the northeast, the agriculture they encountered was very different from what they knew. It was different in two primary ways. First, the primary crop that the Iroquois were growing was corn.... They had no draft animals and no plows....
> Agronomists also now know that there are a lot of good reasons for planting on mounds. First, it is a handy way to control plant populations. Corn is very sensitive to population, and a very easy way to control the number of plants per field is to simply limit the number that you plant per mound. Also, because planting in mounds does not involve tillage, it is excellent for preventing soil erosions. It also is an excellent way to improve the soil's physical composition; all of the plant residues from the corn and any weeds when they die become concentrated in the mound, and the organic matter improves the soil. Mound planting also concentrates and recycles nutrients. Corn has to have nutrients to grow, and Iroquois people did not have access to inorganic fertilizers at a feed and fertilizer store.... Finally mound planting facilitates weed control. Weed spread is reduced by gaps between mounds, and it is much easier to deal with weeds in one hill at a time rather than weeds that spread across an entire field. Though developed by people with no science training the Three Sisters system of the Iroquois was mimicked by mainstream farmers and studied by mainstream scientists. It made an enormous contribution to modern agriculture but has been almost completely forgotten.[15]

Although Mt. Pleasant is talking about Iroquois agriculture, her discussion of corn, beans, and squash—the Three Sisters—nicely explains the importance of the mound.

In the story of Ohoyo Chishba Osh, not only does the Unknown Woman bring a powerful gift to the Choctaws, but she also shows the men that the seeds should be planted on a mound.

Mt. Pleasant also goes on to explain in "The Three Sisters" that the Iroquois women have been planting corn for eight hundred years. Yet she worries about American Indians losing touch with the natural world. "I believe that losing the ability and the desire to grow corn sustainedly threatens our cultural identity and political and economic survival."[16]

The Chickasaw Nation headquartered in Ada, Oklahoma, may have had similar concerns as Jane Mt. Pleasant when they created a program to teach their high school students how to grow corn, beans, squash, and a variety of other indigenous plants. I was told by one of the participants in the program that lack of good nutrition is another concern. The Chickasaw Gardens program is a part of Chickasaw Enterprises. Corn, beans, and squash are but a few of the crops that have been planted by the Chickasaws and harvested and sold at the annual Chickasaw Fair held in the fall at Tishomingo, Oklahoma.

The story continues. First, the two men by the Alabama River before the age of corn. Next, they hear a call and response coming from the natural world. She appears reflected in the light to the two Choctaw hunters. She brings a gift. She leaves instructions. The Choctaw men discover corn. The story continues.

"UNKNOWN WOMEN"

The following story is titled "Unknown Women," because it signifies all American Indian women in the historical documents. It is in the form of a Native drama influenced by the story of Ohoyo Chishba Osh.

First Character—The Spirit

Minimal staging and props. All action takes place on an empty darken stage. Use spot lighting to highlight actors during narration.

From the landscape of imagination,
I noiselessly dream beneath clouds
illuminated like bleach on blue silk
And in a vision
I am told to create a poem
to live inside of.

There is breath
inhaling past and present forms everything—
tender shoots of cosmic energy
aim their sperm into the sun
and she spasms
launching a pulpy sweet body.

I become irresistible in a dress
made of *Fichik isi nala sil h hi*
brilliant white stars.
Serene, yet steamy,

I use the light coming from inside me to attract attention.
Something thrives and mounts the mist

silhouetted insinuations
we form people,
things with underpinnings.
Purpose.
All properties that are necessary,
but not sufficient to define.

What they will say is
my poem is *Anuk la mampa*.
Anuk la mampa
the power of thought
represented as food.

Are you surprised?
Look beyond me. Us. It. This moment. Can you see what just
　happened?
Copper masks made by my children appear in the Field Museum's case.
They rest in the future—from the past—folded together
pinioned to a web of metallic shadows. *Huh*, the power of poetry!
I feel just like William Shakespeare will feel in a distant moment,
from my words, generations of artists are born.

A refrain that is the signature melody for First Character—The Spirit.

First Character—The Spirit

I begin to think of myself as a cosmic dress.
Here are my underpinnings:

Ho tan tona: "She who seeks—goes along and gets there."
Be-ia—ya e-e-hona (Baiyillihona): "She who follows another and gets
　there."
Ho tima: "She who seeks and gives advice."
Mantema: "To go and carry or deliver something sacred or particular."
Wak a ya tema (Wakayatima): "Get up and deliver it."

I deliver myself unto you now. My intent is breath and mind, the power
　of thought
represented as food. *Anuk la mampa*. I AM the one you long for.

Use a sound to evoke Ohoyo Chishba Osh—The Unknown Woman.

Ohoyo Chishba Osh—The Unknown Woman

It has been my experience that the most intimate thing we do, we accomplish with haste.

This is true for me, as well.
I came in haste.
I am *Ohoyo Chishba Osh*—The Unknown Woman. I begin my story in the middle . . .

It was a time of white moons:

Two of my people are camped for the night in the swamps along the river *Ali Bamu*. They hunger and eat the carcasses of birds. Pitiful, they need me for strength. As the two warriors listen to the gloomy sounds of water lapping against the black muddy shore, they cry out for longing, the noun, I mean, *Na Bano*, and like an illuminating shadow I appear to the Choctaw hunters.

Loosely clad in the cool white mist, I wear a wreath of fragrant flowers in my hair and beckon for them to approach. It is then I fall to my knees and produce a sound I will never again utter as *Ohoyo Chishba Osh*.
With my own hands
I slay all reason
tear out my hair
and tassel the four directions with my seed.
The warriors inhale me. I am mercy in their mouths.
I become Corn Woman.
And I am mercy in their mouths.

Fade out music.

Ohoyo Chishba Osh—The Unknown Woman

People have speculated about my life, but the truth is, I was a romantic, bred for giving.
"In the beginning" I will say, "I desired to be a Host." A provider. Savior of the World. Being a host is an imprecise calling, I know, and a dangerous one. I will not tell it all, just the parts I want to giveaway.

The sound of shaking shells beneath narration.

Corn is grown in more countries in the world than any other food crop,

And *Yakni Achukma* exports more corn than any other land in the world.

I suppose I am fully realized now. Did you know that in Romania I am boiled with potatoes to make a mush—and that the Romanians say I am their traditional food? In Cairo, Egypt I am the same breakfast cereal as in Battle Creek, Michigan. However the Turks, always the bossy ones, claim I originated in their homelands. But it's their custom to allege that all things come from Turkia and the Ottoman Empire.

After my first dream, I went into the protective Earth. Out of boredom I sometimes created a world for myself that was full of desire. I had no way of knowing that it was wrong to covet a precarious existence. For instance, when a rainbow landed on my belly I tried to propel myself toward the arch—and it singed the silk of my vulva. As a result, I will turn all the shades of the rainbow during growing season. For a while I was a little embarrassed by this and sank deeper into the soil until the rains came and I had trouble breathing. Naked, I twisted upward and a friendly worm gave me the final push. Afterwards, I began to grow easily in sunlight.

Then one day there came a small boy, lean, not by choice but by circumstance. "I am looking for a host," he says to no one in particular. He wears the same dirty clothes he wore when he arrived. He represents the Old World well, and like the Old World, he refuses to wash or braid his colorless, lifeless, hair. In fact, the only thing that does change about him is his expression. In time, his young body with its pallid flat cheeks will harden to stone.

"I will find the host," he says persistently.

"But I am here for everyone," I answer. "See my praying rows."

He doesn't see anything, but metal and machinery. Eventually, a Hummer races toward him squealing its tires past generations of my people. The Legendary H1. The Old World freezes, blinded by high beams and technology, and in an instant, the boy leaps off the road. The Hummer stops to gas up on ethanol, a mixture made of corn and oil, then accelerates along a dark road made by the God of Tourists.

In the twinkling of an eye another earnest white man appears, this one being a kind of evolved-God-himself. He says, "Being God isn't a job so much as second nature. No fixed rules except this: both hands get used in the taking of everything." "Imagine," he says, "as far as the eye can see miles and miles of empty, but gleaming red earth. By day, it's Egypt and the Arabian Desert, by night, Monument Valley where the Navajos dress like Apaches. Like you, he says, whatever I visualize comes true."

After a time we begin to breathe like one person, the same heartbeat, the same hunger. *Na Bano*. We sleep side-by-side, but never touch. His God has told him that our union will never yield anything, not even relief. So when we do it, we do it apart. I am easily aroused and easily satisfied and each kernel I produce represents an orgasm. He is repulsed by my sex, but likes to fondle my ears—finally he rips them off one-by-one, my drying ears with their cooking smells. He weaves them into a wreath he will wear around his neck to fertility parades.[17]

See the suspended animation behind his eyes as he sends in the cows to gorge on my flesh and blood. It seems everything comes down to my eradication. No, not eradication, my use as a shape changer. What an erotic disaster I have become.

I am dragged against my will through a million fields of those who purposely deform my body. Blind. Deaf. Friendless. Sometimes I am tortured with acids that swell my body beyond grace. Eventually, the son of God sends agronomists disguised as angels to study me. They take field trips and write exhaustive notes about their experiences with corn. I am no longer beautiful, nor represented as food for thought.

I am corn whiskey
Mother's milk to the addicted.
Because of me,
my first children
are wizened at my breasts.
Suckled to death.

See the nitrate plow tilling the rivers and waterways.
My poem swerves and takes a mean curve
forming a pattern of struggle.
Watchful geese
shrouded in my mist
wait for blessings
to surface as dead fish.
Baby alligators patiently stand guard
in the narrow bayous where I came down as food.
I warn you—someday they will grow into warriors on a killing spree.
What has happened to my poetic vision?

I am completely blue now.
For Greeks,
change meant their Gods became
intellectual concepts.
Psyche, Venus, Ego, Mercury.
I wonder if this has already happened to me?
Is Corn Woman a concept? *Huh*!
Never real. A myth. A commodity?
Blue Corn Chips.
White Corn Chips?
Red again.
I am a buck-twenty a bag in some markets.

And you claim you never devour anything with a face
Shame on you Mary Tyler Moore!
Everything is alive
Everything is past
Present
Future
Something endures.
And I tell you now
I dreamed the vision that is you.
And I issue the call.

Red Woman Responds

She enters the stage in a huff carrying a set of books marked "Indian" in large letters. Plops them on a small square table.

Go ahead ask me. Subjects are on the table, but I don't think you'll find any answers.

Use sarcastic voice.

She said, everything is related
Everything is past and present
Everything is future
Something survives and endures, huh?

God damn, I hate that New Age shit!
Who does she think she is?
Ohoyo Chishba Osh—The Unknown Woman—steps into the second spotlight. She appears soulful and sad as she stares at her ancestor, Red Woman Responds.

Red Woman Responds

I'll grant you, she has a habit of being an enigmatic as hell. She loves to answer questions with questions, and she dismisses her enormous influence with "*huh*," as if she didn't know it. I'll tell you right now, if she is THE CORN WOMAN, I'm Little Red Riding Hood.

Ohoyo Chishba Osh—The Unknown Woman holds up a sign that says, LITTLE RED RIDING HOOD WAS AN INDIAN.

Red Woman Responds

Red Woman Responds looks at the sign and continues her monologue.

If she's not a seething mass of contradictions I don't know what is. She's always doing shit like this.

Pause

She once said, "I'm distrustful of ethnographers like John Swanton or even John Neihardt so that makes me very guarded with my stories." Despite her voice, low and soft as satin, her words come in *rat-a-tat* stream of nervous energy. Is Corn Woman the nervous type? I don't think so.

Ohoyo Chishba Osh—The Unknown Woman holds up another sign that says, I AM TOO NERVOUS.

Red Woman Responds

Red Woman responds, ignores the sign.

She says, "Authors tend to get it all wrong. Really, you shouldn't believe everything you read." Well, listen honey, Indians no longer tell stories, not new ones anyway, so the books are all we have.

Personally I think she's just on a mission to let you know she isn't certifiable. That is weird, in and of itself, since she's just spent the last fifteen minutes letting you know weird she is. Explaining how she tore her own hair out of her scalp, turned her orgasms into kernels of corn, and then there was the time—not too long ago—when she said she liked to wear men's underwear. Talk about kinky. And now she wants you to know all that stuff isn't that strange if you think about it—or better yet, if you don't think about it.

Sure, she likes the attention an awful lot—and I'll grant you she has a kind of strange intensity you don't normally see after high school. But describing herself as Corn Woman, full of desire, and "being completely blue." Oh please. I know for a fact that she eats corn on the cob, and corn tortillas. So she can't be the reincarnation of Corn Woman. One does not eat one's self.

Ohoyo Chishba Osh—The Unknown Woman pulls out a bag of corn chips and eats one. Spotlight fades. Striking sticks.

Choctaw Woman Calls

I'll tell you what I know—one red woman to another:

Over the centuries, Choctaws and other Red People have seemed to produce only one idea: the freedom to create and grow. A long time ago a Choctaw would leave behind every extraneous comfort and go to live in the swamp—to dream.

Perhaps we deserved the reputation we gained for this kind of escapism. "Primitive." The idea of absolute zero is purely Choctaw. It made us entirely useless as builders of empires, but incalculable in spirit. The ethnographers, anthropologists, and historians, even New Agers, who've tried to discover the meaning of being Native, or Indigenous, or Choctaw have found nothing to document, but a longing to know more.

Now here is all you need to know!

The Southeastern Ceremonial symbol of the Hand should appear in spotlights lights, blue, red, yellow, green, all around the stage. Women hold out their hands.

Choctaw Woman Calls

Here is the power! The vision. And it grows under your fingernails, crawls up your sleeves and enters . . . You.

Spotlight on the four women as they change places and costumes onstage.

Red Woman Responds

How could I have been so foolish to stop believing in the power of story?

Women hold hands.

Ohoyo Chishba Osh—The Unknown Woman

This IS the season when constellations turn—and spring arrives.
We are the daughters of creation.
We are Food for thought.
We carry the old within us.
And in return for the gift of corn, we create new stories.

Women begin call and response song.

Red Woman Responds

What are you waiting for?

Choctaw Woman Calls

Get up and deliver the stories. Look way beyond us—what do you see?
A corn plant appears on a screen behind the women.

CONCLUSION

"It is the lucid vertigo of a language," says Eco, "that is trying to redefine the world while it redefines itself in the full knowledge that, in an age that is still uncertain, the key to the revelation of the world can be found not in the straight line, but only in the labyrinth."[18]

So what about the story of Ohoyo Chishba Osh, the Unknown Woman. I am no longer content to consider only the history surrounding a particular story and person. I also want to understand the intellectual traditions that kept the story alive in memory long enough so that Cushman would decide it was important (to the Choctaws) to publish it in 1899.

Of course we must bear in mind the age of the story. Of course we must bear in mind that it isn't the only story of how corn came to the Choctaws. New stories about how corn came to the Choctaws are being written (and told) all the time. In *Choctaw Language and Culture: Chahta Anumpa* by Marcia Haag and Henry Willis appears another story of corn called "Hvshtahlia-akosh Tanchi Atahli-tok" ("It Was the Great Spirit Who Provided Corn").

> Long ago, when the Choctaw people still lived in the West, a great famine fell upon the land, and so the women heard the children crying aloud and were sad; and so they brought this before the council and this is what they said to them: "The food is all gone. And because the deer and buffalo are getting scarce, there is no meat. The young ones and the old are dying. Tell us what we are to do."
>
> When the child had pondered this matter, he went and beseeched the Great Spirit, asking him, "Tell me what I must do."
>
> And so that night while he slept he dreamed that he heard an eagle cry, and then he looked up and saw a cornstalk fall to the earth, and then the seed scattered on the ground and it grew and the stalks produced corn. The corn was the staple food of our forefathers.
>
> On the next day he saw birds feeding near the moor where they roost. And a number of days later cornstalks began to appear, and when it grew it produced the corn that the Choctaws thrived on. The chief was happy and praised the Great Spirit.[19]

It is transliterated in Choctaw, then translated into English. The line at the end of the translation reads: "A modern tale adapted by Henry Willis." It doesn't take a literary critic to immediately see the vast differences in my play (above) and in Willis's story. They are two very different stories on the same event. Both stories involve a miracle. Both stories are written by Choctaws. Both stories add to the notion that Choctaw literary nationalism is not just an academic term, but also a living tradition.

Perhaps Umberto Eco is precisely correct when he says that the intangible power of stories—whether based on events or nonevents—creates our cultural truths. Certainly that is the case of the story of George Washington and the cherry tree. Yet, as said earlier, the story exemplifies a desire for honesty in our nation's leaders. As Eco says, "At one stage, they [stories] came to us through the voice of someone who was calling on an oral tradition."[20] This is true of the story of corn. But was Ohoyo Chishba Osh a real person? For me she is real. A living story. She is also a part of our tribal past. She came to us through a hundred generations of Choctaw storytellers until one day H. B. Cushman would write it down. And that is what I tell my own granddaughters when they say, "Grandma, *Pokni*, tell me a story."

I leave you with another true story. A metaphor for certain, but nevertheless true. When I was at my wits end trying to finish *Shell Shaker*, and yet knowing it was not quite right, I had a dream. An old woman came into my dreams carrying an empty pot in the crook of her arm. She pointed to the clay pot and said, "This is how we make the corn soup." Implied in her tone (in my dream) was that I had somehow made corn soup the wrong way. After she reappeared in my dream a second night I went back into the manuscript to find the mistake I'd made in "cooking the corn soup." I rewrote part of the text and the novel was published—after an unknown woman appeared in my dreams to help me make the soup.

Ah me.

NOTES

1. Umberto Eco, *On Literature*, trans. Martin McLaughlin (Orlando, Fla.: Harcourt, 2004), 10.

2. Ibid., 11.

3. For a fuller discussion see Ray Fogelson, "The Ethnohistory of Events and Non-Events," *Ethnohistory* 36, no. 2 (1989): 133–47.

4. Louis Owens, *Other Destinies* (Norman: University of Oklahoma Press, 1992), 7.

5. I will be using the words "story(ies)," "narrative(s)," and "history(ies)" interchangeably. For a fuller discussion on how I view these terms see LeAnne Howe, "The Story of America: A Tribalography," in *Clearing A Path: Theorizing The Past in Native American Studies*, ed. Nancy Shoemaker (New York: Routledge, 2002), 29–48.

6. Horatio B. Cushman, *The History of the Choctaw, Chickasaw, and Natchez Indians* (Greenville, Tex.: Headlight Printing House, 1899), 277–78.

7. Phillip Carroll Morgan, "Who Shall Gainsay Our Decision? Choctaw Literary Criticism in 1830," in *Reasoning Together: Native Critics in Dialogue*, ed. Craig S. Womack (Norman: University of Oklahoma Press, forthcoming).

8. I have written briefly about Ohoyo Chishba Osh in "The Story of America." Ohoyo Chishba Osh is also a character in a one-act play I wrote called "The Unknown Women," in *Evidence of Red* (Cambridge, Salt Publishing, 2005), 9–20.

9. "The History of Corn," Silos and Smokestacks National Heritage Area website, www.campsilos.org/mod3/students/c_history.shtml (accessed July 30, 2007).

10. Cushman, *History of the Choctaw, Chickasaw, and Natchez Indians*, 277–78.

11. See Patricia Galloway, *Choctaw Genesis* (Lincoln: University of Nebraska Press, 1995), for a fuller discussion of Choctaw territories in prehistory.

12. James Howard and Victoria Lindsay Levine, *Choctaw Music and Dance* (Norman: University of Oklahoma Press, 1990), 69.

13. Documents tell us that on September 17, 1540, the Spaniards reached Talisi and found it evacuated, but rich supplies had been left behind. One explanation is that the townspeople had left for their yearly celebrations. The Spaniards stayed in Talisi until after September 25, after the autumnal equinox, when Tuscalusa finally appeared with supplies, food, carriers, and women for de Soto. For extensive readings into what Fogelson calls events and nonevents, I recommend Dunbar Rowland and Albert G. Sanders, eds., *Mississippi Provincial Archives: French Dominion*, vols. 1–3 (Jackson: Mississippi Department of Archives and History, 1927–32).

14. See Marcia Haag and Henry Willis, *Choctaw Language and Culture: Chahta Anumpa* (Norman: University of Oklahoma Press. 2001), 13.

15. Jane Mt. Pleasant, "The Three Sisters: Care for the Land and the People," in *Science and Native American Communities: Legacies of Pain, Visions of Promise*, ed. Keith James (Lincoln: University of Nebraska Press, 2001), 129–30.

16. Ibid., 130.

17. Each September, during the first week of the month, the city of Urbana, Illinois, hosts a corn festival. Some men wear corn flowers around their necks.

18. Eco, *On Literature*, 101.

19. Haag and Willis, *Choctaw Language and Culture*, 154–55.

20. Eco, *On Literature*, 2.

CHAPTER 3

Countering "A Powerful Indefiniteness"

DOING CHOCTAW ETHNOHISTORY IN THE LIMINAL SPACE BETWEEN HISTORY AND ARCHAEOLOGY

Patricia Galloway

In 1931, on the first page of his *Source Material for the Social and Ceremonial Life of the Choctaw Indians,* John Reed Swanton famously said, after having made several brief observations of the attainments of other southeastern tribes, "The feeling of a student for the Choctaw . . . might be described as of a powerful indefiniteness." There is more that indicates Swanton's agreement with this view and the motivation for his writing the book he was introducing. He referred to the Choctaws as "poorly press agented," offering "little 'copy stuff,' in other words, as would interest officers of trading corporations or missionary societies or governmental functionaries back home, or such as could be used to circulate explorers' narratives." And he averred that the "absence of pronounced native institutions made it easy for them to take up with foreign customs and usages, so that they soon distanced all other of the Five Civilized Tribes except the Cherokee, who in many ways resembled them, and became with great rapidity poor subjects for ethnological study but successful members of the American Nation."[1] Indeed, Swanton observed, the only distinctly Choctaw cultural practice that had received much notice by non-Choctaws was their burial ritual. He intended, therefore, to set forth what could be gleaned from all the sources at his disposal, including ethnographic fieldwork, to establish a fuller ethnography and check another southeastern tribe off his list. Significantly for the purposes of this essay, Swanton himself found that to increase the data sources for Choctaw ethnography, he had to go into the field and discover data for himself. In many respects, as we now know, he succeeded beyond his wildest dreams, and the success of his work would effectively halt research on the broad history of the Choctaws for some fifty years.[2]

Although change had begun to nibble away at this situation by 1979, it was not yet very evident when I began to edit eighteenth-century French colonial documents pertaining to the colony of Louisiana for the series *Mississippi Provincial Archives: French Dominion* (hereafter *MPAFD*) for the Mississippi Department of Archives and History (MDAH).[3] These primary documents, in fact, provided my first encounter with the Choctaw Indians as portrayed by colonial observers, and my background reading made it pretty clear that very few other people who were interested in Choctaw history had spent much time with these untranslated French sources. The Choctaws were obviously the most important allies of the French, since not only were Choctaw affairs mentioned often in the colonial documents, but many explicitly identified Choctaws appeared in them. These were real, active people who emerged from these political and military reports, and they were obviously respected and sometimes feared by the French. As such, they could not be treated generically.

Responding to new trends in historical editing I aimed to clarify the identities of all people who appeared in the documents. Having set myself to read all the relevant documents, including the French ones in the existing archival series and a large quantity of the documents from the English Atlantic seaboard colonies, I began to realize that I had to disambiguate the identities of people, especially Indian people, who were identified by the same name. The two men who had preceded me in this editing task in the 1920s and 1930s had frequently taken the Indian names reported by the French to be individual names, but my reading suggested that in many cases more than one person bore the same name in the documents. I also suspected in my examination of existing material that Indian actions as portrayed by the French were more complex than my predecessors had understood. Their goal was to explain the European past of Mississippi; I wanted to help illuminate the past of all the people who had lived on that land. I realized that to prepare the manuscripts for publication, I would have to do a lot more than just clean up a few typos; the annotation of the two volumes would have to be recast conceptually, and I would have to know a lot more to do it. At a minimum, I would have to understand non-European naming systems and kinship. If I wanted to do the job right, I had to master the ethnography of the Choctaws and the other Native people who interacted with the French colony, because the primary French materials before me were so obviously significant to their history.[4]

Luckily, MDAH's collection of Mississippiana had fairly good holdings in colonial and Indian history, and the archives and its staff provided a rich and supportive research environment. Materials available to me on the spot included the already edited French documents and complete modern microfilm of the series from which they came;[5] copied colonial documents from British archives obtained by MDAH and edited documentary collections from most of the former English colonies of the Southeast; copied colonial documents from Spanish archives obtained by MDAH and an unpublished typescript translation of them; a few published personal accounts by observers like Jean-Bernard Bossu, Antoine Simon Le Page Du Pratz, André Penicaut, James Adair, William Bartram, and Bernard Romans; and nineteenth-century descriptions of the Choctaws by missionaries and other Euro-Americans who had had dealings with them. Many of the published materials were available to me in original editions purchased in the early days of MDAH at the turn of the twentieth century. For other French materials in Louisiana and Alabama archives and ancillary English materials at the William L. Clements Library in Ann Arbor, Michigan, MDAH sent me on brief trips to explore these archival holdings and to order copies of additional materials.

Printed secondary sources were also available to me, mostly at MDAH. These included the quasi-primary sources constituted by John Swanton's ethnographies with their encyclopedic data collected from historical sources and contemporary Indian people in the early twentieth century, Henry Halbert's voluminous writings about the Choctaws he knew through his work with Indian education in Mississippi, and Jean Delanglez's impressive critical analyses of sources in his work on the history of Jesuit missionaries.[6] Finally, the MDAH library assiduously collected current writings about the Choctaws, including De Rosier's account of Choctaw removal recently received, Clara Sue Kidwell and Charles Roberts's bibliography when it appeared in 1980 (which provided invaluable leads to materials that had escaped the notice of MDAH acquisitions librarians, particularly for periodical literature), and John Peterson's 1985 sourcebook of published ethnographic materials. Charles Hudson's *Southeastern Indians* (1976), less focused on the region but a great introduction to the literature on southeastern Indian cultures, was also on hand.[7] Finally, whenever I found out about something I needed but MDAH did not have, the staff of the library either purchased it or obtained it for me on interlibrary loan.[8]

Surprisingly, there had been almost no monographic writing by historians about the colonial history of the Choctaws by 1979, in spite of the wealth of data about them in the documentary sources: Kidwell and Roberts, in assembling their bibliography, found only the 1946 dissertation by Charles W. Paape about the Choctaws' civil war in the 1740s and Patricia Woods's more general 1978 dissertation about French-Indian relations.[9] There were no scholarly books about Choctaw history addressed specifically to the colonial period. American historians, avoiding the backwater of exploration history that tended to be occupied by amateurs, linguists, and anthropologists trolling for data, were focusing on Anglo colonial history, the American Revolution, and the early Republic and had simply ignored the Choctaw Indians of the colonial period.

A second and important line of investigation of Choctaw history in the colonial period was brought into play when I was unexpectedly called on to exercise my knowledge of eighteenth-century European manufactures of pottery and other objects, gained through four years of archaeological fieldwork in northern Europe. An incident of looting of Chickasaw burial sites near Tupelo came to my attention through my acquaintance with MDAH staff archaeologists. At the time, most archaeologists who lived and worked locally concentrated on the "prehistoric" period, while the very few "historic" archaeologists of the region concerned themselves with the archaeology of Europeans during the colonial period. Within the state only so-called relic collectors and avocational archaeologists even knew very much about the European trade goods to be found on Mississippi Indian eighteenth-century sites, and this was where I came in. Having excavated ceramics and other objects from the places where they were primarily manufactured and used in Europe, I was familiar with the European objects being found on Indian sites in Mississippi as well as with the classification systems and dating methods used by European archaeologists to analyze them.

There were a few exceptions to this lack of archaeological attention: the early work done by the Lower Mississippi Survey (LMS) exploiting La Salle and de Soto exploration accounts to connect Mississippian moundbuilders and "historic" Indians of the Mississippi Valley; Stuart Neitzel's extraordinary publications on excavations at the Grand Village of the Natchez Indians; Jeffrey Brain's work on the so-called Tunica Treasure looted from eighteenth-century Tunica burials at Angola Prison in Louisiana; and George Lankford's background work on European colonialism carried out as part of the Tennessee-Tombigbee Waterway archaeological projects.[10] But with Neitzel then employed in Louisiana and Brain at Harvard (and neither having directed their interest toward the Choctaws—that "powerful indefiniteness" at work again), it seemed that at that time I was the only person in Mississippi whose research program in archaeology did not exclude colonial-period Indians and who might take a serious interest in the archaeology of eighteenth-century Choctaws and how it fit with their history.

A third significant element that persuaded me to focus on writing about the Choctaws in addition to my work on the *MPAFD* volumes was interaction and acquaintance with scholars with similar interests as I began to develop essays on topics that overflowed from the *MPAFD* documentation task. By entering several intersecting networks of scholars I received the support of existing communities of practice willing to share unpublished materials and general research savvy. I attended my first meeting of the American Society for Ethnohistory (ASE) in 1981 in Colorado Springs, where I presented a paper about the Choctaw civil war, which would eventually be published in the *Journal of Mississippi History* and which is reprinted in this collection.[11] Because the meeting was held in the West, many Indian people attended, and I recall my nervousness on being introduced to Vine Deloria and his amusement when I immediately identified my research interest much as a Native person would identify tribal and clan affiliation.

At that conference and through the ASE, I learned who was doing what historical research on the southeastern tribes, and it became clear that there was plenty of room for a new researcher on Choctaw history: Clara Sue Kidwell, still at Berkeley, had established her interest and expertise in the nineteenth and early twentieth centuries; John Peterson at Mississippi State, whom I had already met and who had urged me to attend the ASE meeting, had done historical work on the Choctaws and was then doing sociological studies of twentieth-century Choctaws; and Richard White, then at Michigan State, was writing about Choctaws as part of a larger study (I became a manuscript reader of the Choctaw chapter of *Roots of Dependency* as a result of the ASE meeting).[12] No scholar seemed to be pursuing Choctaw ethnohistory primarily and in detail for the colonial period, however, and even less was any professional historian interested in pursuing Choctaw history before exploration and colonization. Although the archaeological literature seemed to take it for granted that the Choctaws were linked somehow with prehistoric

Mississippian culture (vaguely accepting into evidence the existence of the Nanih Waiya mound), there was no clear idea of the details of that historical development. Nevertheless, in at least the anthropological wing of ethnohistory I had found the interdisciplinary approach I was increasingly interested in taking.[13]

The following year I attended the French Colonial Historical Society (FCHS) conference for the first time, and found that there was significant interest within this group in the Indians of North America. As a result of presenting a paper on Jean-Baptiste Le Moyne de Bienville's application of the *lex talionis* to French murderers of Indians, I met David Miller, director of the Newberry Library's Center for the History of the American Indian, and Cornelius Jaenen, whose *Friend and Foe* I had already read and admired.[14] This connection reinforced the FCHS-ASE links (there was minor overlap in membership), and what was more important, it also introduced me to emerging discourses in French and European historiography, which took the work of the *Annales* school for granted in its more text-critical Le Roy Ladurie mode and was already incorporating postmodern questioning and postcolonial studies. Among practitioners of Louisiana colonial studies I could fill a gap by adding a focus on Native partners and allies to balance out a growing interest in enslaved Africans in Louisiana, and in general I had found a congenial group with good historical credentials who were nevertheless not considered to be "mainstream" American history practitioners.[15]

Because so little was known about what archaeologists were beginning to call the "protohistory" of the southeastern Indians, mostly because there was no documentary evidence and even ethnohistorians were still doubtful of or puzzled by the historical exactitude of Indian accounts of the deep past, it was natural that my archaeological background would be crucial here. Because of it and my already demonstrated editorial skills, I became de facto editor in 1981 of both the state journal *Mississippi Archaeology* and the MDAH *Archaeological Reports* series.[16] Working on these editing jobs, with two issues of the journal to fill and multiple archaeological reports to edit and see through the press every year, as well as actively participating in the Mississippi Archaeological Association, which I served as secretary-treasurer for some years, very quickly acquainted me with the current state of archaeology in Mississippi and the community of archaeologists who pursued work there.[17]

This situation and these contacts and colleagues provided me over a period of twenty years with opportunities to intervene in order to see that archaeology was done to support research on Choctaw history. Although I had worked as a field archaeologist for four years in Europe, I did not have the formal credentials required to carry out archaeological investigations in the United States. So if I wanted to get archaeology done, I would have to persuade credentialed archaeologists to do it. After the 1981 uproar over the looting of Chickasaw sites, I worked with a private cultural group in Tupelo and the Mississippi Humanities Council to put together a project to survey historic Chickasaw sites with a view to protecting them, extending work done in the region by MDAH in the 1930s.[18] Inspired by discussions about what Choctaw archaeology might look like with Chris Peebles, then directing archaeological work in Alabama as part of the Tennessee-Tombigbee Waterway project, I began investigating seriously what was already known, examining in detail the MDAH state archaeological site files for potential Choctaw sites in east-central Mississippi counties but expanding that search southward and westward based on what the colonial documents were suggesting about the possibility that the Choctaw tribe of the eighteenth century might have been a confederation of several groups.

Initially, Sam Brookes of MDAH assisted me in undertaking some road trips to follow up on specific areas and sites, especially along Sucarnoochee Creek and on the Pearl River, where there was a known eighteenth-century trail crossing. We did not find anything from the late prehistoric period on the Sucarnoochee (itself a relevant fact), but a reported mound site on the Pearl River first observed in 1977 turned out to be extremely impressive, rich, and not alone. Jerome Voss, who had just arrived at the University of Southern Mississippi, joined in 1982 our interest in the impressive Mill Creek site and the neighboring Lowe-Steen mound site. Under his aegis two students who had worked with Peebles, John Blitz and Baxter Mann, began work surveying the Choctaw homeland, studying Choctaw pottery in existing collections, and mapping the Mill Creek site.[19] Their work and its support for the possibility that the confederation thesis was correct sparked the interest of Vincas Steponaitis at the University of North Carolina, whose students Timothy Mooney and Patrick Livingood carried out projects at the Mill Creek site in the 1990s.[20]

Jim Parker, whom I had met through Chris Peebles in Alabama, was pursuing archaeological investigations in the early 1980s at the site of Fort Tombecbé, the French outpost nearest to the Choctaws, and I had the opportunity to excavate briefly at that site and to have early access to the finds from it.[21] Another piece of the puzzle was uncovered when archaeological investigation following the looting at the Pine Log Creek site in Alabama provided a profile of late-sixteenth-century pottery types, dated by the Spanish artifacts found there that were thought to have been left behind by the Tristán de Luna expedition.[22] Also in Alabama, work by Ian Brown at the Bottle Creek mound site in the Mobile-Tensaw delta, described by French explorers of the early eighteenth century, revealed further details.[23] Clearly there was an enormous amount of potential contribution that archaeology could make toward elucidating what was happening before and just as Europeans came onto the scene, and I used my position as editor of *Mississippi Archaeology* and the MDAH *Archaeological Reports* series to bring this work to light, thereby stirring additional interest.[24] The reputation I had thereby established as an archaeological editor meant that I was also called on to edit a book of essays on the late prehistoric "Southeastern Ceremonial Complex" of symbols and cultural features discussed at a gathering of archaeologists and objects sponsored by avocational archaeologist Lib Burke Jones and the Cottonlandia Museum in 1984; that work forced me to develop an improved understanding of the state of knowledge about the late Mississippian chiefdoms of the region.[25]

The "problem" of a lack of attention to Choctaw history by American historians and Americanist archaeologists was in fact due to two issues, not one. First, Choctaws were Indians, and ethnohistorians were still struggling for recognition in some quarters that Indians actually had histories at all. For historical archaeologists, whose very discipline was still making its colonialist justification, the archaeology of Indians without documentary backing was simply another discipline requiring mastery of techniques aimed at investigating "people without history." Second, at least during the period of interest to me, late prehistory to the end of the eighteenth century, the Choctaws had only tenuous relationships with people who spoke and wrote English. Ethnohistory, in other words, shared exclusion from the American historical and historical archaeology canon with the American colonial histories of Spain and France: what went on in the "original thirteen colonies" was all that mattered, and it was still all too common for American historical writing to occupy itself with English-speaking white males alone, at least partly because it was mostly practiced by English-speaking white males.

The lack of professional reward for this work was not a problem for me, since although I had no certificated training in American history or archaeology, my employer did not care: I was not trying to make tenure in the American professoriat. Instead, I was professionally occupied with tasks then emerging as those appropriate to public history. I was obliged during the course of my work for MDAH to make history work for the public, to present history to the public, and to make my research aspirations serve those goals.

As far as colonial history was concerned, I had the good fortune of being assigned to see that the observances of the La Salle bicentennial (in 1982) and the de Soto 450th (in 1991) were properly observed in scholarly fashion, and in both cases I rounded up experts and bribed them with honoraria to do and write up research they might not otherwise have done and whose results, which would impinge significantly on Choctaw history, I selfishly wanted to see. To make sure that others could see them too, in each case I made participation and honorarium contingent upon contribution of an essay to a volume of papers.[26]

In sum, I had experience in textual criticism and anthropological archaeology on the European model, as well as a good grounding in critical historical method. But the people I met practicing ethnohistory, colonial history, and archaeology, together with the entrepreneurial possibilities for practicing public history that I had at MDAH, made it possible for me to bring the efforts of more people to bear on the history of the Choctaws by creating several spaces in which such work could be rewarded and showcased. What also made a difference was the fact that I personally made a continuing investment in the three scholarly communities themselves, attending meetings, playing supporting roles, and steadily presenting the results of my own research.

I and other scholars alone did not determine the development of Choctaw ethnohistory during the 1980s and 1990s. Not nearly so much might have happened had the Mississippi Choctaws themselves not taken serious steps to pursue their own history at just this juncture, as a logical step toward greater autonomy. In 1963 the Mississippi Band of Choctaw Indians (MBCI) had established a K–12 school for their children in segregated Mississippi, though the band had been recognized by the federal government since 1945. In 1975 the tribal government completed the building of a hospital on the Pearl River reservation. That same year, the MBCI tribal council adopted a new constitution that provided for an executive office of tribal chief to replace the legislative office of council chairman. In 1980, under the leadership of Philip Martin, the first elected tribal chief, and tribal historian Bob Ferguson, the Mississippi Choctaws appointed a Choctaw Heritage Council to lead and assist in the creation of a museum of Choctaw history, inspired by the Museum of the Cherokee Indian in North Carolina. Members of the council included Choctaw members Philip Martin, Thallis Lewis, and Kenneth York; scholars like Charles Hudson, Arrel Gibson, John Peterson, and me; prominent Choctaw-heritage lawyer Tom Goldman; and the Cherokee-heritage singer Johnny

Cash.²⁷ Although the original intention to build a major new museum was not realized immediately, Heritage Council members assisted the Mississippi Choctaws with other projects, including the creation of a modest Choctaw Museum of the Southern Indian (1981) on the Pearl River reservation in an existing building and speaking on various public occasions like the annual Choctaw Fair.

The council also became a vehicle to sponsor efforts thenceforth centered on the museum and led by Thallis Lewis to assist older craftspeople to teach young people the traditional Choctaw crafts they practiced (basket weaving, drum and stickball-stick making, beadwork, and sewing traditional dress). I was personally involved with a project carried out by Choctaw curriculum specialist Bill Brescia, who developed a course for the Choctaw Central School called "Choctaw History, Culture, and Current Events" in the early 1980s. As part of that project I wrote a piece on what I knew at that time about Choctaw history during the colonial period to fit into a book of curriculum materials called *Choctaw Tribal Government: A New Era*.²⁸ As part of the Choctaw Central course, students wrote essays about Choctaw history, drawing on interviews they carried out with elders as part of the oral history program (part of a program to support bilingual education) developed by Lewis. These essays were published in three books, from 1983 to 1985.²⁹ Finally, the MBCI hired a tribal archaeologist, Kenneth Carleton, in 1990.

The successes of all these efforts together with that of the businesses developed under the aegis of Chahta Enterprises began to establish a firm foundation for the Choctaw economic self-determination advocated by Chief Martin, which would be capped by the prosperity ushered in through casino gambling, initiated with the opening of the Silver Star in 1994 and the Golden Moon in 2000. But prosperity and its changes have brought a progressive diminution of mastery of Choctaw tradition by the tribe's young people, an increasing concern to Chief Martin and other Mississippi Choctaw leaders. In a move to counter that trend the Mississippi Choctaws have undertaken several projects. In 1995, expanding on previous projects, they established a formal Cultural Affairs Program and formalized a set of cultural skills workshops. Oral history interviews of Choctaw elders have continued. For many years Choctaw cultural leaders like Roseanna Tubby and linguist Pat Kwachka have been developing language teaching materials, including a dictionary of Mississippi Choctaw, which is near completion.

These activities of the MBCI have in turn provided rich support for the representation of Choctaw history in the Mississippi State Historical Museum. I began development of a permanent exhibit covering the years 1500–1800 for the museum in 1994, after years of preparatory work. Our exhibit team decided to form a Community Advisory Committee consisting of representatives of the communities whose history would be represented in the exhibit. MBCI representatives were active in assisting with the project, providing critiques of exhibit text and materials, instructing exhibit designers on the construction of a funerary scaffold that represented the scourge of European diseases suffered by the Native people of the whole Southeast, hosting a public meeting in the Tribal Council Hall to discuss representation of the Choctaws in the exhibit, and ultimately sharing casino largesse by hosting the opening of the exhibit in Jackson in 1997. As the state historical museum moves toward the development of a new and much larger history center and museum in Jackson in the wake of Hurricane Katrina damage to the existing museum, Mississippi Choctaws continue to serve on its advisory committee. Meanwhile, they are working on developing a cultural education center at the Pearl River Community that will incorporate an archives, museum exhibits, production facilities for multimedia educational materials, and a home for collections of Choctaw objects, and I have been asked to assist that project by bringing my historical, archival, and museological work to bear on it.

In carrying out my own research and writing on Choctaw history, I was predisposed to using a multidisciplinary approach, but there was a significant recent model in the field that overshadowed everything else, even though it did not treat a southeastern tribe: Bruce Trigger's history of the Hurons, *The Children of Aataentsic*. This remarkable book influenced everyone working in ethnohistory who wanted to tackle "protohistoric" times and earlier, and I was no exception. I was also impressed with Trigger's continuing critical examination of the actual treatment of indigenous people in Canada and their virtual treatment in Canadian history, and his insistence on situating historical work on First Nations people.[30]

Trigger's skills as an archaeologist and his broad concern for using all the resources available for recovering evidence of the past charted for me a view of what ethnohistory could be if all resources were taken seriously, but like Swanton I had to work hard to find them and even to produce them, joining in the ongoing work of the many others already mentioned. One effect of the work I did in translating documents for *MPAFD* was that shortly after those volumes appeared in 1984, they became a significant resource for others to use, and they were used widely. The same held true for the beginning efforts at a Choctaw archaeology that I was beginning to publish in *Mississippi Archae-*

ology and in the MDAH *Archaeological Reports* series: these reports encouraged others and provided them with a basis for beginning new research. When I was finally able to finish *Choctaw Genesis 1500–1700* in 1995, it immediately began to encourage new work, especially by younger scholars. As a result of this synergy, there was a larger network of people working on Choctaw history than had been the case ten years earlier. The work even began to be mainstreamed as history Ph.D. students, particularly under the direction of Theda Perdue at Kentucky, began to take up work on Choctaw history.[31]

My own research has not come to a halt; in 2006 a book of essays was published, drawn from published and particularly unpublished work done over twenty-five years. Its title, *Practicing Ethnohistory: Mining Archives, Hearing Testimony, Constructing Narrative*, calls out the major elements of the work I have done in mining the archives of documents and artifacts; listening for the testimony of site plan, observer accounts, and oral traditions; and critically constructing a narrative that is more aimed at explaining the narratives I have found than at using the genre itself to formulate a single persuasive story.[32] As I completed that book new ideas for research have emerged, continuing some of the directions taken therein. Situated as I now am, teaching archivists in the School of Information at the University of Texas, I am especially focused on what I term the *archivization* of documents and archaeological objects and how that process shapes the stories that can be told.[33]

This whole scenario has been a local development within the larger story of the continuing contestation for historical meaning within Western, and now global, culture. Crucial to the development of a serious discourse on Choctaw history within the academy has been the larger epistemic shift from political to social history and the reflexive concern among historians to understand what degree of objectivity is even possible for their work. The scientific history paradigm that focused on formal proofs of documentary authenticity has been displaced by a model more open to concerns with historical sources themselves as intentional shapings of knowledge. Ethnohistorians, in their corner of the field, have begun to take more seriously than ever the need to share historical work with those whose history it is. On the archaeological side, Euro-American archaeology has been challenged by the emerging discourses of decolonization and the worldwide concern of indigenous people with excavation or repatriation of burials and other archaeological materials. In the United States this demand has finally been met through the passage of the Native American Graves Protection and Repatriation Act (NAGPRA) in 1990, which brought Native people to the table in substantive decision making in archaeology. Although older archaeologists have had their struggles with this new state of affairs, younger ones are learning to make the archaeology of living peoples a dialogic process, just as historians are now required to do. In all these cases, Native scholars have reinforced these trends, as they take leading roles in developing new approaches to the history of indigenous people in the Americas. An interesting emergent trend among indigenous librarians and archivists worldwide, which is promoting both the control of indigenous knowledge and records of that knowledge by indigenous people, is leading to the development of protocols for the management of and access to such materials; this trend will doubtless have a substantial impact on the writing of indigenous history and even on terms for the framing of indigenous history.[34]

I have tried to focus critical attention on these areas of struggle. I have ranted at archaeologists that they must not take documents at face value and that European documents were not the only valid source material to fill in their "historical" blanks; I have ranted at historians that archaeological research designs are themselves interested and likely to construct a biased view of any society to which they are applied. In both disciplines I nagged people to work on Choctaw historical issues, provided research assistance where I could, and worked hard to see that more work was made public. The time was right to undertake such an effort in this particular case: favorable academic trends and Choctaw concerns coincided in time; I was fortunate enough to be employed at MDAH, where my work could take advantage of an institutional lever; and I was able to influence a broader range of people by filling responsible positions in scholarly organizations in ethnohistory, history, and archaeology. One should never underestimate the power of service to facilitate progress.

But one should also question what constitutes progress. I am especially proud of the work that I have done and continue to do with the Mississippi Band of Choctaw Indians; I rejoice particularly in the collaborations that I have engaged in with Choctaw colleagues Clara Sue Kidwell and LeAnne Howe and have been happy to assist where I could in the research of Choctaw students like Michelene Pesantubbee.[35] There is an enormous amount of additional research to be done before Choctaw history is the subject of the amount of scholarship that has been written about the Iroquois or the Cherokees, but then "written" may prove to be less significant in the future as new media and communication modalities influence new stories and as the pervasiveness of the Internet lowers barriers to the dissemination of many stories—from Choctaw traditions to archaeological "gray literature." Further, scholarship itself is in the process of being redefined, such that it is not possible to make predictions that assume the continued persistence of a credentialing paradigm that requires a hierarchical structure of aspiration. Choctaw history is not likely to be neglected any more, and the participants in its pursuit are multiplying.

APPENDIX.
MISSISSIPPI DEPARTMENT OF ARCHIVES AND HISTORY AND MISSISSIPPI ARCHAEOLOGICAL ASSOCIATION, LIST OF PUBLICATIONS RELEVANT TO CHOCTAW HISTORY AND MISSISSIPPI INDIAN HISTORY, 1981–2000

Mississippi Department of Archives and History Archaeological Reports

No. 16, 1985. John Blitz. *An Archaeological Study of the Mississippi Choctaw Indians.*
No. 18, 1986. David Dye and Ronald Brister, eds. *The Protohistoric Period in the Mid-South, 1500–1700, Proceedings of the 1983 Mid-South Archaeological Conference.*
No. 20, 1987. John Sparks. *Prehistoric Settlement Patterns in Clay County, Mississippi.*
No. 26, 1997. David Morgan. *The Mississippi De Soto Trail Mapping Project.*
No. 27, 1997. Timothy Mooney. *Many Choctaw Standing: An Archaeological Study of Culture Change in the Early Historic Period.*
No. 30, 2000. John Blitz and Baxter Mann. *Fisherfolk, Farmers, and Frenchmen: Archaeological Explorations on the Mississippi Gulf Coast.*

Mississippi Archaeology *Articles (54)*

Vol. 16, no. 2 (December 1981)
Vincas P. Steponaitis. "Plaquemine Ceramic Chronology in the Natchez Region," 6–19.
Marvin T. Smith. "Sixteenth Century Spanish Beads," 19–22.

Vol. 17, no. 2 (December 1982)
John H. Blitz. "A Brief Outline and Bibliography of Southeastern Mississippi Prehistory, Part I," 16–26.
John D. Stubbs Jr. "A Preliminary Classification of Chickasaw Pottery," 50–57.

Vol. 18, no. 1 (June 1983)
Ian W. Brown. "Plaquemine Culture Houses in the Natchez Bluffs Region, Mississippi: Excavations at the Lookout Site," 14–26.

John H. Blitz. "A Brief Outline and Bibliography of Southeastern Mississippi Prehistory, Part II," 26–27.

Rufus A. Ward Jr. "English Earthenwares Associated with Early 19th Century Choctaw Sites," 37–45.

Vol. 18, no. 2 (December 1983)

Jerome A. Voss and John H. Blitz. "An Archaeological Survey in the Choctaw Homeland," 49–56.

Vol. 19., no. 1 (June 1984)

James F. Barnett Jr. "A New Building Location at the Fatherland Site (the Grand Village of the Natchez)," 2–11.

Vol. 19, no. 2 (December 1984)

Rufus Ward. "19th Century Choctaw Indian Reservation Sites in Lowndes County, Mississippi," 39–45.

Jeffrey P. Brain. "The De Soto Entrada into the Lower Mississippi Valley," 48–58.

Patricia Galloway. "Technical Origins for Chickachae Combed Ceramics: An Ethnohistorical Hypothesis," 58–66.

Vol. 20, no. 1 (June 1985)

Ann F. Ramenofsky. "The Introduction of European Disease and Aboriginal Population Collapse," 2–19.

James R. Atkinson. "The Ackia and Ougoula Tchetoka Chicasaw Village Locations in 1736 during the French-Chickasaw War," 53–72.

Vol. 20, no. 2 (December 1985)

Richard A. Weinstein. "Some New Thoughts on the De Soto Expedition through Western Mississippi," 2–24.

James R. Atkinson. "A Surface Collection from the Chickasaw Agency Site, 22-CS-521, on the Natchez Trace in Chickasaw County, Mississippi," 46–63.

Vol. 21, no. 1 (June 1986)

Jerome A. Voss and C. Baxter Mann. "Stylistic Variation in Historic Choctaw Ceramics," 43–58.

Sam McGahey. "A Compendium of Mississippi Dugout Canoes Recorded since 1974," 58–70.

James R. Atkinson. "The Location of the Nineteenth Century Choctaw Village of Wholkey in Chickasaw County, Mississippi," 70–72.

Vol. 21, no. 2 (December 1986)

James F. Barnett. "The Play Site (22-Ad-812): A Natchez Phase Burial in Natchez, Mississippi," 3–11.

Rufus Ward. "The Tombigbee Crossing of the De Soto Expedition," 62–68.

Vol. 22, no. 1 (June 1987)

Christopher S. Peebles. "The Rise and Fall of the Mississippian in Western Alabama: The Moundville and Summerville Phases, A.D. 1000 to 1600," 1–31.

James R. Atkinson. "The De Soto Expedition through North Mississippi in 1540–41," 61–74.

Vol. 22, no. 2 (December 1987)
James R. Atkinson. "Historic Chickasaw Cultural Material: A More Comprehensive Identification," 32–63.
Rufus A. Ward Jr. "Reconstructing the Topography of Protohistoric Aboriginal Sites: An Example from Clay County, Mississippi," 71–74.

Vol. 23, no. 1 (June 1988)
John H. Blitz. "Henry Collins and Southeastern Archaeology," 1–11.

Vol. 23, no. 2 (December 1988)
Tristram R. Kidder. "The Koroa Indians of the Lower Mississippi Valley," 1–42.

Vol. 24, no. 2 (December 1989)
Jay K. Johnson, Patricia K. Galloway, and Walter Belokon. "Historic Chickasaw Settlement Patterns in Lee County, Mississippi: A First Approximation," 45–52.
Gregory A. Waselkov. "A Summary of French Colonial Archaeology in Eastern 'Louisiane,'" 53–69.

Vol. 25, no. 2 (December 1990)
Evan Peacock and W. Frank Miller. "Protohistoric Settlement Patterns in Northeast Mississippi and the Cedar Glade Hypothesis," 45–57.
Jay K. Johnson. "Cedar Glades and Protohistoric Settlement: A Reply to Peacock and Miller," 58–62.
Jonathan Leader. "The Humber-McWilliams Site Brass Headdress: Preliminary Evidence for the Re-use of European Metal by Contact Period Native Americans in Mississippi," 63–69.

Vol. 26, no. 1 (June 1991)
Robert M. Heath. "Replication Experiments for the Manufacture of Sixteenth-Century Spanish Bells," 39–55.

Vol. 26, no. 2 (December 1991)
Jesse D. Jennings. "Adventures in Mississippi Archaeology: A Learning Experience," 7–18.

Vol. 27, no. 1 (June 1992)
Douglas C. Sims, Marie Elaine Danforth, Joseph A. Giliberti, Angele M. Montana, and Todd McMakin. "An Analysis of Diet in the Mississippian Population at Kellogg Village, Mississippi, Using Dental Indicators," 44–59.

Vol. 27, no. 2 (December 1992)
Tim Mooney. "Migration of the Chickasawhays into the Choctaw Homeland," 28–39.
Mary Evelyn Starr. "Preliminary Report on Ceramic Vessels from the 1991 Oliver Salvage," 40–55.

Vol. 29, no. 1 (June 1994)
John L. Cotter. "Archaeological Memoir of the Natchez Trace," 1–16.

Vol. 29, no. 2 (December 1994)
Kenneth Styer. "Testing the Weinstein Hypothesis: An Evaluation of Three Potential De Soto Contact Sites in Northwest Mississippi," 1–17.
Donald G. Hunter. "The Biloxi on Bayou Boeuf: An Ethnohistory and Analysis of Surface Collections from the Biloxi Village Site (16-Ra-60), Rapides Parish, Louisiana," 18–43.
Patricia Galloway. "Prehistoric Population of Mississippi: A First Approximation," 44–71.

Vol. 30, no. 1 (June 1995)
John H. Blitz, C. Baxter Mann, and Ray L. Bellande. "Fort Maurepas and Vieux Biloxi: Search and Research," 23–58.

Vol. 30, no. 2 (December 1995)
Jerome A. Voss. "The Persistence of Choctaw Pottery," 21–34.

Vol. 31, no. 1 (Summer 1996)
David W. Morgan. "Historic Period Chickasaw Indians: Chronology and Settlement Patterns," 1–39.

Vol. 31, no. 2 (Winter 1996)
S. Homes Hogue, Suzanne Bufkin, and Heather Rushing. "European Contact, Burial Behavior, Health, and Diet: A Case Study from Starkville, Mississippi," 1–22.

Vol. 32, no. 1 (Summer 1997)
Rufus Ward Jr. "Shell-Edge Decorated Ceramics," 27–39.

Vol. 32, no. 2 (Winter 1997)
Julie G. Markin. "Elite Stoneworking and the Function of Mounds at Moundville," 117–35.

Vol. 33, no. 2 (Winter 1998)
Jeffrey P. Brain. "A Note on the River of Anilco," 115–24.
Ian W. Brown. "Benjamin L. C. Wailes and the Archaeology of Mississippi," 157–91.

Vol. 34, no. 2 (Winter 1999)
Kenneth H. Carleton. "Nanih Waiya (22W1500): An Historical and Archaeological Overview," 125–55.
John H. House, Mary Evelyn Starr, and Leslie C. Stewart-Abernathy. "Rediscovering Menard," 156–77.

Vol. 35, no. 1 (Summer 2000)
Terry Lolley. "Archaeology at the Lyon's Bluff Site, A Mississippian and Protohistoric Settlement in Oktibbeha County, Mississippi," 1–14.
Samuel O. Brookes. "Archaeology from Memory: Lyon's Bluff, 1968," 15–22.
Patricia K. Galloway. "Archaeology from the Archives: The Chambers Excavations at Lyon's Bluff, 1934–35," 23–90.

NOTES

1. John R. Swanton, *Source Material for the Social and Ceremonial Life of the Choctaw Indians*, Bureau of American Ethnology Bulletin 103 (Washington, D.C.: U.S. Government Printing Office, 1931), 1–2.

2. John H. Peterson observed this fact in 1985 in his fine introduction to the edited anthology *A Choctaw Source Book* (New York: Garland, 1985), xi–xxiii; see p. xi. Peterson pointed to the shortcomings in both Swanton's fieldwork and his use of documents, both at least partly attributable to scholarly understandings and conventions of his time but both cloaked by the seeming authority of Swanton's work.

3. Three volumes of *MPAFD*, edited and translated by Dunbar Rowland and Albert Godfrey Sanders, had been published by 1932. I was tasked with working on volumes 4 and 5 (published by Louisiana State University Press in 1984 with subvention by the National Historical Publications and Records Commission) to complete the history of the Louisiana colony as it pertained to the lands of the state of Mississippi.

4. It was also necessary to apply the excellent scholarship that had developed about the Africans who were enslaved by the French and brought to the colony, but this was a lesser problem because so few Africans were brought to labor on the lands of Mississippi during the colonial period.

5. My primary focus was on the documents from colonial Louisiana (series C13A for letters received from Louisiana, plus some letters from the B series sent to Louisiana) in the Archives des Colonies, Centre des Archives d'outre-mer (now at Aix-en-Provence but then in Paris). See Henry Beers, *The French in North America: A Bibliographical Guide to French Archives, Reproductions, and Research Missions* (Baton Rouge: Louisiana State University Press, 1957). MDAH acquired microfilm of these materials in 1970 in partnership with the Library of Congress and several other archives and universities.

6. Swanton, *Source Material*; Swanton, *Indian Tribes of the Lower Mississippi Valley and Adjacent Coast of the Gulf of Mexico*, Bureau of American Ethnology Bulletin 43 (Washington, D.C.: U.S. Government Printing Office, 1911); and Swanton, *The Indians of the Southeastern United States*, Bureau of American Ethnology Bulletin 137 (Washington, D.C.: U.S. Government Printing Office, 1946), were mainstays, but MDAH had all the BAE bulletins. Most of the relevant writings of Henry S. Halbert are collected in John Peterson's *Choctaw Source Book*; similarly, the extraordinary writings of Jean Delanglez have now been collected by Mildred Mott Wedel in *A Jean Delanglez, S.J., Anthology* (New York: Garland, 1985). In the early 1980s I was able to obtain the original publications of Halbert and Delanglez in the MDAH library, from the *Publications of the Mississippi Historical Society* series for Halbert and from *Mid-America* for Delanglez.

7. Arthur H. De Rosier Jr., *The Removal of the Choctaw Indians* (Knoxville: University of Tennessee Press, 1970); Clara Sue Kidwell and Charles Roberts, *The Choctaws: A Critical Bibliography* (Bloomington: Indiana University Press, 1980); Peterson,

Choctaw Sourcebook; Charles Hudson, *The Southeastern Indians* (Knoxville: University of Tennessee Press, 1976).

8. For a comprehensive bibliography of the sources I used for the *MPAFD* volumes, see the bibliography that accompanies them.

9. Charles W. Paape, "The Choctaw Revolt: A Chapter in the Intercolonial Rivalry in the Old Southwest" (Ph.D. diss., University of Illinois, 1946); Patricia Dillon Woods, "French-Indian Relations on the Southern Frontier, 1699–1762" (Ph.D. diss., Louisiana State University, 1978).

10. Philip Phillips, James A. Ford, and James B. Griffin looked at the explorations of de Soto and La Salle in their *Archaeological Survey in the Lower Mississippi Alluvial Valley, 1940–1947*, Papers of the Peabody Museum of Archaeology and Ethnography 25 (Cambridge, Mass., 1951); Robert Stuart Neitzel, *Archaeology of the Fatherland Site: The Grand Village of the Natchez*, Anthropological Papers of the American Museum of Natural History 51, no. 1 (New York, 1965); Jeffrey P. Brain, *Tunica Treasure*, Papers of the Peabody Museum of Archaeology and Ethnology 71 (Cambridge, Mass., 1979); George Lankford, *Ethnohistory: A Documentary Study of Native American Life in the Lower Tombigbee Valley*, vol. 2 of *Cultural Resources Reconnaissance Survey of the Black Warrior-Tombigbee System Corridor, Alabama* (Mobile: University of South Alabama, Department of Geology and Geography, 1983). James A. Ford's *Analysis of Indian Village Site Collections from Louisiana and Mississippi*, Louisiana Department of Conservation Anthropological Study 2 (New Orleans, 1936), provided, however, a basis for an understanding of what was then considered "Choctaw" pottery.

11. Patricia Galloway, "Choctaw Factionalism and Civil War, 1746–1750," *Journal of Mississippi History* 44 (1982): 289–327.

12. Kidwell had completed her bibliography with Roberts, and had begun applying her interest in intellectual history through research work on the American missionaries to Choctaw country; John H. Peterson Jr., whose dissertation had been about the portrayal of the Choctaws in the work of Henry Halbert, had established a record of sociological work with the Mississippi Band of Choctaw Indians that was helping to underpin their establishment of tribally controlled infrastructure (e.g., "Three Efforts at Development among the Choctaws of Mississippi," in *Southeastern Indians Since the Removal Era*, ed. Walter L. Williams [Athens: University of Georgia Press, 1979]), had published on Choctaw history in two anthologies edited by Charles Hudson ("Indians in the Old South," in *Red, White, and Black: Symposium on Indians in the Old South* [Athens: University of Georgia Press, 1971] and "The Louisiana Choctaws at the End of the Nineteenth Century," in *Four Hundred Years of Southeastern Indian History* [Athens: University of Georgia Press, 1975]), and had drafted a chapter on Mississippi Choctaws for the *Southeast* volume of the *Handbook of North American Indians*; Richard White, *The Roots of Dependency: Subsistence, Environment, and Social Change among the Choctaws, Pawnees, and Navajos* (Lincoln: University of Nebraska Press, 1983).

13. In 1987 I was elected to the Executive Committee of the ASE for two years and served in that capacity again from 1998 to 2000.

14. My paper was published as "The Barthelemy Murders: Bienville's Establishment

of the *Lex Talionis* as a Principle of Indian Diplomacy," in *Proceedings of the Eighth Annual Meeting of the French Colonial Historical Society*, ed. E. P. Fitzgerald (Lanham, Md.: University Press of America, 1985), 91–103; Cornelius Jaenen, *Friend and Foe: Aspects of French-Amerindian Cultural Contact in the Sixteenth and Seventeenth Centuries* (New York: Columbia University Press, 1976).

15. In 1991, when the favored candidate for president of the FCHS fell ill, I was elected president; I edited and handled production of several volumes of the FCHS proceedings in the early 1990s and served as the second editor of *French Colonial History*, which replaced it.

16. Officially, Samuel O. McGahey, MDAH's chief archaeologist, was editor of *Mississippi Archaeology* until 1982 and I was listed as associate editor; he continued to support this work with final checking for accuracy until 1985. My name did not appear as editor of the *Archaeological Reports* series until 1983 (nobody had been listed as editor until that time).

17. A fact not well-understood by those who are not archaeologists is that the spatial specificity of archaeological knowledge ties archaeologists to specific stretches of country and many will work on one site or small region for their whole lives; hence the extreme importance of local and regional groups of archaeologists, who control knowledge of what are frequently unpublished or underpublished details of archaeological findings. My relationship with archaeologists in Mississippi and the southeastern region was mostly cordial, and I was accepted as a member of the Mississippi Association of Professional Archaeologists when it was formed in 1984.

18. I called on the Lower Mississippi Survey based at Harvard, which had long been involved with archaeology in Mississippi and had expertise on historic archaeology of Indians, for help in providing a graduate student with background in colonial trade goods to carry out the survey, and they proposed John Stubbs, who subsequently spent two years in Tupelo when the project was extended with purely local support. This project led to changes that in turn engaged the Chickasaw Nation of Oklahoma in the archaeology of their original homeland.

19. Among the publications coming from this work were: Jerome Voss and John Blitz, "An Archaeological Survey in the Choctaw Homeland," *Mississippi Archaeology* 18, no. 2 (1983): 49–56; Voss and Baxter Mann, "Stylistic Variation in Historic Choctaw Ceramics," *Mississippi Archaeology* 21, no. 1 (1986): 43–58; Blitz, *An Archaeological Study of the Mississippi Choctaw Indians*, Mississippi Department of Archives and History Archaeological Report 16 (Jackson, Miss., 1985). These publications fairly quickly multiplied the amount of relevant archaeology for the Mississippi Choctaws.

20. Timothy Mooney, *Many Choctaw Standing: An Archaeological Study of Culture Change in the Early Historic Period*, Mississippi Department of Archives and History Archaeological Report 27 (Jackson, Miss., 1997). This master's thesis was completed in 1994. Livingood presented a paper on his work at Mill Creek as "Investigation of Mississippian Mounds on the Middle Pearl River, Mississippi" at the 1999 Southeastern Archaeological Conference, Pensacola, Fla.

21. This was the Livingston University (now University of West Alabama) Fort Tombecbé Documentation and Research Project carried out from 1980–81. Jim Par-

ker, "Archaeological Test Excavations at 1SU7: The Fort Tombecbé Site," *Journal of Alabama Archaeology* 28, no. 1 (1982): whole issue; Joe Wilkins, "Outpost of Empire: The Founding of Fort Tombecbé and De Bienville's Chickasaw Expedition of 1736," in *Proceedings of the Twelfth Meeting of the French Colonial Historical Society*, ed. Philip P. Boucher and Serge Courville (Lanham, Md.: University Press of America, 1988), 133–53.

22. For Pine Log Creek archaeology, see Noel R. Stowe, Richard Fuller, Amy Snow, and Jennie Trimble, "A Preliminary Report on the Pine Log Cree Site: 1 Ba 462" (1982; report on file at the Center for Archaeological Studies, University of South Alabama, Mobile).

23. See the articles in the "Bottle Creek Research" issue of the *Journal of Alabama Archaeology* 39, nos. 1–2 (1993), edited by Ian Brown and Richard Fuller; and Brown, ed., *Bottle Creek: A Pensacola Culture Site in South Alabama* (Tuscaloosa: University of Alabama Press, 2003).

24. See the appendix for a list of relevant Choctaw-related archaeological publications I was able to get into print while at the MDAH.

25. Patricia Galloway, ed., *Southeastern Ceremonial Complex, Artifacts and Analysis* (Lincoln: University of Nebraska Press, 1989). My efforts to foster historic Indian archaeology and my editorial work on the archaeology of Mississippi were recognized in 1994 when I became president-elect of the Southeastern Archaeological Conference and then president in 1996. That visibility helped me to continue to promote the historical archaeology of Native people in the Southeast.

26. Patricia Galloway, ed., *La Salle and His Legacy: Frenchmen and Indians in the Lower Mississippi Valley* (Jackson: University Press of Mississippi, 1982); Galloway, ed., *The Hernando De Soto Expedition* (Lincoln: University of Nebraska Press, 1997); in addition, the Jackson teacher and scholar Dr. Charles Weeks, an expert in Mexican history, became interested in Spanish Mississippi and began to investigate the ethnohistory of Mississippi Indians under the Spanish colonial regime after having worked on a reader of Spanish documents for Mississippi schools under the Columbus Quincentenary initiatives that I directed. One result of his interest came to fruition recently in the volume *Paths to a Middle Ground : The Diplomacy of Natchez, Boukfouka, Nogales, and San Fernando de las Barrancas, 1791–1795* (Tuscaloosa: University of Alabama Press, 2005).

27. Although I am not certain of this, I suspect that I was invited to join on the advice of John Peterson.

28. Edited by William Brescia, published in 1982 by Choctaw Heritage Press, Philadelphia. The work was done under a grant from the U.S. Department of Education, Ethnic Heritage Studies Program. My essay was titled "French-Choctaw Contact, 1680s to 1763."

29. *Choctaw Anthology I* (1983), *Choctaw Anthology II* (1984), and *Choctaw Anthology III* (1985). As the introductions make clear these essays are certainly the work of high school students, but they are rich in traditional information for which the students became proxy speakers for their elder relatives.

30. Trigger, *The Children of Aataentsic: A History of the Huron People to 1660*

(Kingston: McGill-Queen's University Press, 1976), and *Natives and Newcomers: Canada's "Heroic Age" Reconsidered* (Kingston: McGill-Queen's University Press, 1985). It was helpful that I met Trigger early on at an ASE meeting.

31. James Taylor Carson and Greg O'Brien had both come to Jackson to carry out research during their time as students.

32. Patricia Galloway, *Practicing Ethnohistory: Mining Archives, Hearing Testimony, Constructing Narrative* (Lincoln: University of Nebraska Press, 2006).

33. Patricia Galloway, "Material Culture and Text: Exploring the Spaces Within and Between," in *Historical Archaeology*, ed. Martin Hall and Steven Silliman (Oxford: Blackwell, 2005).

34. See, for the leading project in this trend, "Aboriginal and Torres Strait Islander Protocols for Libraries, Archives and Information Services," www.alia.org.au/policies/atsi.protocols.html (accessed July 15, 2006). The 2006 meeting of the Society of American Archivists included a session on the work of North American Indian archivists in developing similar protocols, hosted by the newly created Native American Archives Roundtable (see www.archivists.org/saagroups/nat-amer).

35. Clara Sue Kidwell and I worked together in the 1980s on a grant from the National Endowment for the Humanities to study Choctaw landholding in Mississippi, which has had many repercussions for both of our work, and more recently we have partnered in writing entries on Choctaw for the *Southeast* volume of the *Handbook of North American Indians*, taking up the late John Peterson's draft chapter written long ago. The development of LeAnne Howe's novel *Shell Shaker* (San Francisco: Aunt Lute Books, 2001) allowed both of us fruitful discussions, and I continue to learn from her artist's vision of possibilities. Finally, I was pleased to be allowed to comment on the dissertation version of Michelene Pesantubbee's *Choctaw Women in a Chaotic World: The Clash of Cultures in the Colonial Southeast* (Albuquerque: University of New Mexico Press, 2005).

CHAPTER 4

Choctaw Factionalism and Civil War, 1746–1750

Patricia Galloway

> *This nation will not forget for a long time the civil wars which the projects of Red Shoe have caused it and which have been the source of the troubles that have prevailed among them for four years.*
> VAUDREUIL TO ROUILLÉ, JUNE 24, 1750, ARCHIVES DES COLONIES, SERIES C13A, 34:268v

Most previous treatments of the Choctaw intratribal war of 1747–50 have been brief, and few have gone further than to say that it took place and that it involved factions supported by the French and the English. The one really extended study of these events, a 1946 dissertation by William Paape, is an excellent analysis from the European point of view, but even this is generally unavailable as it has never been published.[1] In this essay I will not have the space to present a thorough analysis of every facet of the conflict, which is reserved for a longer treatment elsewhere, but I would like to present here and argue for the thesis that this civil war, as a response to the French version of the *lex talionis*, demonstrates Choctaw resistance to acculturation in the area of crime and punishment and their persistence in the belief that even an ally had to obtain justice through limited war.

The source materials for such a study, though of course they provide us with nothing obtained directly from Choctaw sources, are unusually rich for this period of Choctaw history. At the baseline is the French colonial correspondence contained in series C13A of the Archives des Colonies;[2] here we find not only Governor Pierre de Rigaud de Vaudreuil's official reports but also several field reports that he sent in to supplement his own. We are extremely fortunate that one of the volumes of Vaudreuil's private letterbooks, the one covering the Mobile District, also survives with the evidence for part of this period.[3] It contains all the letters written by Vaudreuil to his officers in the field in the Mobile District, which had jurisdiction over the Choctaw area. In most cases Vaudreuil acknowledges receipt of letters from his correspondents, and his answers permit one to reconstruct something of what the original reports must have contained.[4] Finally, there is an unusual abundance of English material, much of it of a polemic nature but still very useful. Edmond Atkin wrote a lengthy account of the Carolina traders' activities in the war in order to prove his own governor's self-interest,[5] and James Adair's account of the southeastern Indians contains much mention of his own part in the events of the war.[6] In addition, the surviving Carolina "Indian Books" have some material relating to the traders' activities (though only in the aftermath of the war); and the journals of the Upper House, the Commons House of Assembly, and the Royal Council log the official actions of the South Carolina colony that bear upon the Choctaws.[7]

There is much bias in these European reports of the Choctaw conflict, but fortunately for us the bias sprang from internal squabbles in the French and English colonies, so that in a sense the facts emerge as the bias cancels itself out. It is clear that the French were much more concerned than the English about the effects of the war on the Choctaws themselves, but the English sources permit us to have an exceptional view of the attempt by one Choctaw faction to manipulate one European ally in order to gain independence from another.

If all we wanted to know about the Choctaw civil war was what happened, it would be sufficient to relate the sequence of events as we have them from the European accounts and leave it at that. But this tragic conflict, which must have been the most momentous happening in Choctaw history from the beginning of European contact until removal, deserves rather closer scrutiny not only because of its importance in this light, but because of the fact that it represented the most serious stress that Choctaw society had had to face up to that point in the process of acculturation. Because of this, a closer examination of the events and the people who participated in them may permit us to learn more about the structure of Choctaw society before acculturation was too far advanced. By observing how the system performed under stress, we may be able to understand its structure better.

The Choctaw civil war looked momentous at the time not only to the Choctaws but probably also to everyone else in the Southeast. According to Vaudreuil, writing in 1751, more than eight hundred chiefs, honored men, and warriors of the Western faction had lost their lives, and the villages of Couëchitto, Nushkobo, and West Abeka were totally destroyed.[8] Thereafter he was wont to reiterate what an extraordinary mark of loyalty this had been on the part of the Choctaws. Edmond Atkin commented in 1753 on the unprecedented lengths to which the Choctaws went in undertaking civil war; James Adair called the war "bitter beyond expression."[9] We have little record of what other Indian groups thought of it, but we do know that the Abihkas, an Upper Creek tribe that one faction turned to for support, found it horrifying.[10]

Such a reaction, by the French and English as well as the Abihkas, cannot be justified by the number of dead alone. The Choctaws may have lost more lives in one year of the war to smallpox than to the hostilities of the whole of the civil war.[11] There is, however, much inferential evidence in the various accounts to suggest that the war was not simply a factional struggle, nor client warfare on behalf of French and English allies, but a conflict that cut far more shockingly into the fabric of Choctaw social life by involving the moieties of the tribe, eventually applying to them the sanctions of blood revenge usually reserved for external enemies. It is possible to show, however, that this was a situation into which the Choctaws were forced by the demands of their French allies for justice on the French model, and that it was not continued once the French had realized that their justice could not be done in Choctaw terms.

It is admittedly very difficult to make sense of this evidence, since in the first place it is made up of tiny scraps and in the second place Choctaw sociopolitical organization, which is so much at issue in understanding the problem, has never been well defined for the early contact period. For the latter reason it will be useful to review what is known about it on the several levels of village, division, and nation, and at the same time to outline the French attempts to make use of what they perceived the organization to be.

To the French the Choctaws looked like a confusion of small polities with no clear-cut chain of command. Generally speaking, each village had its chief, although some few villages had smaller dependent villages without independent chiefs, probably as a result of the budding-off of populations that could not be supported on the land of a single locality.[12] Each chief had his staff of officials, numbering about five. These men can be detected in the documents, where there is no clear statement about such an office, through the repeated occurrence of what the French took for personal names but which are clearly functional titles, though the function in question is sometimes unknown. The *tichou mingo* was apparently the master of ceremonies or "waiter" to the chief; the *taskanangouchi* was his speaker. Many if not all villages had a war chief, and often this office carried the title of *soulouche oumastabé* (red shoe killer) or simply *mingo ouma* (red chief). The frequently mentioned *hopaii mingo* (prophet chief; spelled variously *pahémingo, paemingo,* or *opayémingo*) was presumably the "war prophet," but this charismatic talent seems to have been a frequent attribute of the war chief as well. Finally, *fanimingo* (squirrel chief) is a name so often seen that it also seems to be a title, since it is nearly always qualified by village or other designation, but its function if it is a title is not known.[13]

Such a picture of a staff of men involved in village government is probably not so simple if Gearing's notion of different "structural poses" for different village activities can be said to apply in a general way to the Choctaws.[14] It does seem reasonable to apply this model at least to the activities of peace and war, and here we encounter the problem of the moieties and their function. There is solid evidence for the existence of "red" and "white" chiefs from the same village. They are referred to thus generically from time to time in the French documents and indeed in scattered reports of Indian speeches.[15] John Swanton has cited the evidence of a late English document to the effect that "war" and "peace" and hence "red" and "white" respectively do map onto the two moieties, called in the French documents the *Oulacta* (*Inholahta*) and *Immongoulacha* (*Imoklasha*) "races" or "castes."[16] There may be a problem with this mapping, since it is certain that the Choctaw moieties were traditionally ranked, the first-ranked being the Inholahta. If the Inholahta were the moiety of war, this would run counter to the very strong southeastern preference for wise deliberation over individual brilliance and abruptness of decision.[17] Whatever may be the correct assignment, and the events of the war do not provide an unambiguous answer, it is likely that in the village context the "red" and "white" leaders were conventionally chosen from the two moieties and that their powers were quite differentiated.[18] Certainly there are several instances in which the recorded speeches of such leaders do differ substantially in tone.[19]

There is also mention in the documents of "honored men" and "principal warriors," though we have no notion at all from these sources of what their roles were in Choctaw sociopolitical organization. It is likely that the honored men served as council to the white chief, and that they were older men; the principal warriors were probably leaders among the red chief's following, and were probably younger men—if we may assume an analogy with other southeastern tribes. The fact is that there was simply very little European observation of village government in action, and we are forced here to depend upon inference.[20]

The Choctaw villages were grouped into divisions. Swanton has discussed the number of divisions and the details of village membership in them, but there is now more evidence to which Swanton did not have access which allows us to assert that the number of three divisions was apparently constant throughout the historic period, though the village composition of the divisions might vary to some extent.[21] But in understanding the divisions it is necessary to distinguish between cultural/geographic and political aspects, since it seems to be the overlay of political factors that accounts for the shifting of villages from one division to another. The cultural/geographic divisions were pretty clearly based upon territories related to the three neighboring watersheds of the Pearl, Tombigbee, and Pascagoula rivers, and the cultural differences among them are reflected not only in stray references to oddities of dress and speech,[22] but also in the external alliances they maintained with other tribes: the Western Division with the Chakchiumas and Chickasaws, the Eastern with the Alabamas, and the Six Towns (including Chickasawhay and Yowani) possibly with the small coastal tribes and the Choctaw-related tribes of the Mobile River. The evidence of Henri de Tonti's journey among the Choctaws and the subsequent first French negotiations with them in 1702 shows that the three divisions existed by that time and could be represented in external negotiations by a single representative each.[23] Under Governor Etienne Périer the French tried to make use of this institution of representation by recognizing certain "division chiefs" as medal chiefs who would be granted large presents in order to strengthen their influence,[24] but some of the problems the French encountered with the institutionalization of the division chiefs probably stemmed from the fact that originally the division representatives were not permanently appointed to the job.

There are also problems with the relationship between the moieties and the divisions. Because the moieties were distributed through all the villages, it is very difficult to understand what is going on in terms of the influence of moiety affiliation upon political loyalty. It may, however, be possible to take an analogy from the white and red towns of the Creeks and to suggest that white and red towns were distributed among the divisions as the moieties were distributed among the villages. There is no evidence at all to prove that one or another of the divisions was dominated by either of the moieties, although it is possible to show that at least in the case of the civil war the leading men of the Eastern and Western divisions were members of opposite moieties.[25] And although the evidence is not conclusive, the Eastern Division, which proved firmly loyal to the French, may at least have been strongly influenced by the Inholahta moiety, whose members avowed a continuous adherence to the French alliance.[26]

There is little doubt that no supreme chief over the entire Choctaw Nation existed until Jean-Baptiste Le Moyne de Bienville created such an office for the purpose of establishing some kind of hierarchical accountability on the French model.[27] It is repeatedly obvious that the man recognized as supreme chief by the French held no such power in the nation; in fact, the apologetic tone taken by these chiefs in many of their public statements reported by the French suggests that they knew themselves to be a powerless anomaly.[28] Governor Vaudreuil himself was perfectly aware that this was the case with all the medal chiefs.[29]

The same thing is not true of the war chief of the nation. This seems to have been an office that existed at time of need and that was generally filled by some outstanding warrior whose charismatic qualities or luck in leading war parties made him able to gather large parties from the whole tribe under his leadership.[30] The fact that such an office should develop in advance of that of a supreme peace chief is not surprising if we consider that the historic tribes of the Southeast were born in the collapse of the Mississippian chiefdoms, which must have included warfare.[31] It was probably the current Choctaw war leader who was first recognized by Bienville as the supreme chief of the nation, and at least at first this created office seems to have devolved upon a lineage.[32] By contrast, the demand for charismatic qualities in a war leader made it certain that when the French-recognized supreme chief happened not to possess these qualities, a supreme war chief would be recognized separately in the nation. This is probably what made the French eventually recognize such a war chief.

It is not known with certainty how many medal chiefs were recognized by the French during the early years when their attempt at a system of governance was being built, but by 1732 five of them appear on the list made by Régis du Roullet,[33] and at later times there are repeated references to the number of six.[34] The distribution of the medals was never actually congruent with the power structure within the nation for reasons already discussed, but from the French viewpoint the medal was given to the supreme chief, the nation's war chief, and the three division chiefs. In addition, the medal was also held by the chief of Chickasawhay village where the Jesuit mission was established, and it was apparently granted for support of that mission.[35] We shall see that at the beginning of the Choctaw civil war the picture was more complex, since the medal was held by a Western chief, an Eastern chief, the chief of Concha villages, the Chickasawhay chief with authority over the Six Towns, the supreme chief, and the war chief.

It was through this superimposed system of medal chiefs and their subordinates that the French attempted to control the Choctaws by means of carefully graded and specified gifts. The largest gifts went to the medal chiefs, with the supreme chief distinguished especially above the others. Lesser gifts were given to the village chiefs and some of their officers. Finally, "extraordinary presents," which were one-time gifts ranked according to their correspondence with the permanently fixed gifts, were occasionally given to chiefs or warriors who had performed some unusual service. These gifts were intended not only to secure the loyalty of key men but to help them build their political power in the nation through redistribution of the gifts to their followers. By this means the French made a powerful if unknowing contribution to the spirit of factionalism among the Choctaws.[36]

At the time of the coming of Europeans, the Choctaw structural pose for war was a temporary seasonal change in the tribal structure, and even at first war leaders came and went with the fortunes of war. But possibly as early as the English slave-raiding period from before 1700 to about 1713, and certainly after the Natchez revolt of 1729, the Choctaws were encouraged to stay on a nearly permanent footing of war with their Chickasaw neighbors. The old patterns persisted in that the Choctaw enthusiasm for war was directly proportional to the season in which the French wished it to take place. Nor could the French medals prevent the emergence of successful division or village war leaders or the refusal of the majority of the nation to follow the French-recognized war chief. The real influence of the medal and substantial present granted to the war chief began to be felt when a war leader emerged who had the talents and persistence to hold the office through sheer force of personality over a period of years. When Red Shoe rose to this level of importance in the Natchez and Chickasaw wars of the 1730s,[37] he was able to hold the office permanently and thus to build a powerful enough faction that he was recognized as supreme chief by the English and was able with their support to make a bid for independence from the French, setting off the chain of events that led to the civil war.[38]

A major part of the function of war among the tribes of the Southeast was the execution of blood revenge on whatever enemy had caused loss to the aggrieved tribe.[39] Long years of this between neighbors had created "traditional enmities" by the time Europeans arrived, but the Europeans' concept of total war made them unable to understand how an enemy in time of war could become a relative connected by marriage ties and thus much reciprocal obligation at a time of peaceful negotiation. The French could not comprehend the notion that vengeance did not require the death of the person directly responsible, but could be satisfied by that of someone who could stand for him. But they had a perfectly lucid view of the meaning of the *lex talionis* as far as they themselves were concerned, and to give them credit it was two Frenchmen who were first put to death for the murder of two Choctaws in order to establish the principle in the French-Choctaw relationship.[40]

Among the Choctaws the principle of blood revenge as defined by the French was hedged around with difficulty. When a death occurred at the hands of another tribe, custom dictated that war was the answer, a limited engagement that could account for enough death to assuage the tears of the bereaved. Yet what the French asked, and demonstrated, was that the offending nation put its own culprits to death in order to *avoid* war, while on the Choctaw side there was no institutionalized way to do this. Worse, since there was no such person as an executioner who could be ritually freed from responsibility for his action, and no authority which could free him, whoever should undertake such a task would himself be subject to vengeance on the part of the relatives of the man executed. We shall see that the civil war did not solve this problem, since its dynamics were strongly influenced by an attempt to avoid killing Choctaws who had only been responsible for the deaths of non-Choctaws.

The history of the Choctaws during the whole of their alliance with the French is much too complex to more than summarize, but it is necessary to contextualize the events of the civil war by tracing something of this antecedent series of events. The Choctaws chose to ally themselves with the French in the first place because they were hard-pressed by gangs of Chickasaw and Creek slave-catchers, armed and instigated by the English traders who had extended their activities to the Mississippi River as early as 1698. To acquire firearms and to defend themselves, the Choctaws entered eagerly into a French alliance in 1702. Thus the French gained a powerful buffer to the east and north of their infant colony, and the Choctaws, in return, acquired guns and other trade goods. By and large they stuck with the French quite loyally until the complications of the Yamassee War in Carolina took some of the slave-raiding pressure off them, and when this persecution was not continued, a large obstacle to improved relations with the English was removed.

It was not the Choctaws who first took advantage of this possibility. The Natchez, who occupied what the French considered the best agricultural land in the Lower Mississippi Valley, were finally induced by French land-grabbing to break out in full revolt with the support of the Chickasaws and their English allies. This they did in 1729 by killing nearly all the men of the French fort and settlement at Natchez and by taking the women and children prisoner. The French called the Choctaws in to help pursue the Natchez and to recover French prisoners, and this the Choctaws did, though afterward they had a very hard time securing what they had understood as the promised reward for this action. The Natchez, however, managed to escape to take refuge among the Chickasaws, and at this point the French realized that the Mississippi River connection with the upper Louisiana colony in Illinois could never remain secure until the English-allied Chickasaws, who had been implicated in the Natchez rebellion, were subdued.

To this end Bienville pressed the Choctaws into service in two more campaigns in 1736 (via the Tombigbee River) and 1739–40 (via the Mississippi)—both of them abortive. Throughout the period of the Natchez revolt the French encouraged the Choctaws to attack the Chickasaws whenever the occasion presented itself. But these attacks, though they were favored by the young Choctaw warriors as a way to make a name for themselves, were not pursued with much enthusiasm unless Choctaw lives had been lost. And it should be noted that in the case of the Natchez rebellion and the French deaths it occasioned, the French themselves took the field in considerable force no less than three times.

Meanwhile, the French had established a missionary post near the southern border of the Choctaw Nation in 1728 and had built Fort Tombecbé as a supply base for the 1736 Chickasaw campaign. Both were to serve as bases for French trade activity among the Choctaws. The French colony had always, from its foundation, experienced a chronic shortage of goods from the mother country, and this presented a special problem for the Choctaw alliance because of the institution of annual presents given to the medal chiefs. This was an activity separate from the skin trade, which required merchandise within the nation throughout the year as well as on the occasion of the annual presents, when the Choctaws usually brought more skins to Mobile to trade. The shortage of trade goods became particularly acute in the late 1730s and early 1740s as more of French resources were bound up in continental wars and French shipping began to be preyed upon by British privateers. By then, however, the Choctaws had had time to become dependent upon European goods for certain comforts and especially for the powder and ball that they needed to make their hunt successful. When French supplies failed, the English traders to the Upper Creeks and Chickasaws were ready and willing to supply the Choctaws, and at lower prices than the French could offer.

It is obvious throughout the period leading up to the war and through the war itself that there was a set of several "national" priorities in operation providing the backdrop to events otherwise complicated by the conflicts of personal leadership and kinship claims among the Choctaws themselves. The Choctaws were a tribe of some fifteen thousand or more people, and to all intents and purposes they inhabited nearly the entire eastern border of the lower Louisiana colony at this period. To the French, especially in time of war with Britain, it was unthinkable that the Choctaws should be allowed to maintain a mixed allegiance; and to the French that was the import of any scale of trade with the English. To the English, who were too far away from their sources of supply in Carolina to have a realistic hope of becoming sole suppliers and allies of the Choctaws, the trade was a lucrative business with the added virtue of providing harassment of the French and keeping them too worried about events near home to intrigue with the Creek and Cherokee neighbors of the British colonies. The evidence suggests that the Choctaws themselves had no intention at all either of breaking completely with the French or of going over entirely to the English, and that generally they sought to emulate the neutrality of the Alabama tribe, which had been the Alabamas' key to the best of both trades and an enviable independence.[41]

The Chickasaws and their relationships with all three parties is a constant and important theme during the Choctaw civil war as during the rest of colonial history. In spite of Adair's romantic claims,[42] the Chickasaws had also managed a French-English balancing act from 1702 until 1729, when they took in the refugee Natchez; and even then a sizeable group, perhaps as much as half the nation, was prepared to go and live with the Choctaws rather than break with the French over this issue.[43] The real break came in 1736, when, in an even more extraordinary blunder than he was later accused of committing, Bienville had his force make its first attack on the village of Ackia—the very village of which the strongest French partisan, Imayatabé le Borgne, was chief.[44] The Chickasaws were closely related linguistically to the Choctaws, and stronger links are indicated both by the Choctaw migration legend and by some evidence of intertribal marriage alliance.[45] If they continued to pursue peace initiatives with the French, it was probably done because they wished to secure cessation of the continual Choctaw attacks urged by the French, who would not permit a treaty with the Choctaws alone. The English traders, knowing that the Choctaw trade could be more easily carried on from a safe base nearby, gave the Chickasaws such support that the French demand for their expulsion as a condition for peace would never be met.

There are several Choctaw leaders whose careers prior to the civil war are important because they tell us much about the roles that these men played both before and during the war. Red Shoe has already been mentioned as the man whose actions led to the outbreak of the war. What we know about him is little enough. When first met with in the French correspondence, he was living in Couëchitto and serving as the *porte-parole* (presumably taskanangouchi) for the supreme medal chief of the nation.[46] He was referred to several times as an "ordinary warrior" until in 1731 he led a highly successful raid against the Chickasaws and was rewarded with the medal, perhaps the medal of supreme war chief.[47] Beginning in 1734 he had an interest in the English trade through friends or possibly relatives through marriage alliance among the Chickasaws.[48] In 1738 his relationship with the English was formalized when he himself or an emissary speaking in his name went to Charleston and was recognized as supreme chief of the Choctaws with an English medal.[49] Doubtless he used the proceeds of both sides to build a faction, which is referred to by the French as consisting of members of his *famille* or his *race*; these expressions may refer to his moiety, since he found allies scattered throughout at least the towns of the Western Division, and one of his closest allies of this early period was the red shoe of Cushtusha village.[50] His general strategy in building power by benefiting from both French and English alliance was to make attacks on the Chickasaws during the late fall or early spring in order to secure his French present, while at other times he sought to establish peace with the Chickasaws to permit an English trade, sometimes even bringing English traders into his village of Couëchitto.[51] By 1739 he had been assigned control of ten villages by the authority of his French medal, since in that year he and the ten villages were actually cut off from the French present for his dealings with the English.[52]

Of equal importance in the politics of the Choctaw nation was the chief Alibamon Mingo of the Concha villages. His influence among the Choctaws was great, and in 1730 his harangue to the besieged Natchez Indians on the Red River secured the release of the French and Negro prisoners they had taken.[53] During the next few years he was active against the Chickasaws on behalf of the French, but in 1735 he joined with Red Shoe to bring the English traders into the nation, and in the following year he was deprived of the medal chief's present along with Red Shoe.[54] After this, however, he joined with the French in the first and second Chickasaw campaigns, and although at times he was reluctant to commit his people to breaking a peace with the Chickasaws established by Red Shoe, Alibamon Mingo's loyalties were pretty steadily committed to the French.[55] He stated several times that he belonged to the Inholahta moiety; he was also the medal chief of the Concha villages, which numbered at least ten.[56] His name and other circumstantial evidence attest to the fact that he enjoyed a special relationship with the Alabama tribe, which included some sort of alliance.[57]

Another chief, whose influence before his death in 1746 seems to have been greater than that of Red Shoe or Alibamon Mingo, is Choucououlacta. His name contains the *holahta* element, which implies membership in the Inholahta moiety. Never mentioned in the English documents, he is portrayed in the French sources as a nearly fanatically loyal ally. In 1739 he was described as the war chief of the Choctaw Nation and was said to control the ten easternmost villages nearest to Fort Tombecbé; in that year he was granted a French medal in the place of Red Shoe.[58] Also in that year and from then on he was closely allied with Alibamon Mingo in attacks on the Chickasaws, though he acted alone in leading the attack which killed a Chickasaw embassy and possibly precipitated Red Shoe's open rebellion.[59] In the year of that rebellion, 1746, he died, possibly of wounds suffered in the attack, possibly of the smallpox, which raged epidemically through the nation in the following year. Whatever the cause, the ceremonial treatment accorded his remains after death attested to his great importance in the nation, and the statement was made by a Choctaw leader that if he had lived he and Alibamon Mingo together could have averted the civil war.[60]

A further personality deserving of mention is the man frequently identified as one of Red Shoe's most trusted partisans, Mongoulacha Mingo. A member of the Imoklasha moiety, Mongoulacha Mingo was medal chief of Chickasawhay villages, with authority over the Six Towns. He was said to have been granted the medal for support of the mission of Father Michel Baudouin.[61] This position must have been one which he assumed after 1741, since before that date he was only listed as a subordinate to the chief of Chickasawhay and in that year the chief was killed in a quarrel.⁶² His resentment of the French, very vehemently expressed, was apparently caused by what he perceived as their discriminatory treatment of the moiety to which he belonged, and he remained so intransigent in his convictions that he was eventually killed by those in his village who opposed him.⁶³

It has already been suggested that the Choctaw civil war became an internecine struggle because the French demanded satisfaction from the Choctaws themselves for the deaths of three Frenchmen. The prelude to the war demonstrates vividly that the Choctaws would not find this kind of solution appropriate. In 1743 the Chickasaws had made elaborate overtures to the French to request peace, and at the annual presents in Mobile in December and January Vaudreuil announced an offer of peace to them if they would drive out the English. All the chiefs, honored men, and principal warriors of the Choctaw Nation who were present agreed to this, although the Eastern Division and Alibamon Mingo of the Conchas in particular were still disposed to make war on the Chickasaws for former losses, even attacking a peace embassy from the Chickasaws on its way to Fort Toulouse. Yet the Chickasaws persisted, sending a French prisoner to Mobile to plead for them. In answer the French sent him back with an old-time Chickasaw trader from pre-Natchez revolt days, but the expected reception at the Chickasaw villages were reversed when the warriors claimed that they had no desire for peace and had been sold out by their chiefs. By July Vaudreuil was urging the Choctaws back into war with the Chickasaws, but rumors that a peace was being arranged anyway in spite of French disapproval led to a more specific request of Choucououlacta and Toupaoumastabé (war chief of the Concha and "brother" to Alibamon Mingo) to put together a party to break the peace. It took until September for the French in Louisiana to receive word of the outbreak of war with England in the spring.⁶⁴

English documents show that in January of 1745 the Chickasaw "Blind King" (Imayatabé le Borgne, who had been so wronged by Bienville), together with the trader Campbell, had negotiated a peace with the Choctaws through Red Shoe, who was said to have won over all but one of the Choctaw medal chiefs to the plan. But the Chickasaws had apparently continued raids against the Choctaws, since soon after that the Choctaw captain of Boucfouca village led a party that recaptured Choctaw prisoners and brought in Chickasaws for torture. At the last minute before the presents in March, Red Shoe and Mongoulacha Mingo led small parties to take Chickasaw scalps for presentation in Mobile, and Red Shoe was not only received with gratitude but was treated in the Mobile hospital for wounds and eye trouble.⁶⁵

That Red Shoe's actions had been a facade became apparent when on July 20 at an assembly at Yanabé village he persuaded the medal chiefs to seek an English trade, doubtless aided in his persuasion by several intervening French actions: in the spring the French traders had closed a warehouse at Concha without the government's knowledge, and later the Choctaws of Chickasawhay had complained of a rape by a French soldier. After the Yanabé assembly Red Shoe sent an embassy made up of his son-in-law and two brothers-in-law (one of them possibly Mongoulacha Mingo) to negotiate with the Chickasaws. Soon afterward at an assembly held at Oni village, the full support of Alibamon Mingo and his district chiefs was secured by Red Shoe, and on August 24 a Chickasaw embassy addressed a group including all but one of the medal chiefs at Bouctoucoulou Chitto, opposed only by the Oni and Concha villages—though the character and strength of this opposition is not known.[66]

In an attempt to stiffen the resolve of the pro-French Choctaws and to gather additional intelligence on the happenings in the Choctaw Nation, the French sent the interpreter Roussève from Mobile into the nation with trade goods for the villages of Couëchitto, Concha, Yazoo, and Bouctoucoulou Chitto in early September. On September 15, probably as a result of this initiative, yet another assembly was held in Concha, and there Alibamon Mingo was scolded by his Concha subchiefs Toupaoumastabé and Offemeko, Red Shoe by his "brother" Tatoulimataha of Little Wood. By October 2 the village of Blue Wood had fielded a party that attacked an English convoy on its way to the Chickasaws and killed two English traders. Later on in the month the subalterns Chambly and de Verbois, the latter based at Red Shoe's village of Couëchitto, were accused of rape. On December 15 an embassy from the Chickasaws, consisting of a Choctaw woman from Cushtusha and Imayatabé's nephew, came to propose an English trade and the opportunity to ransom Choctaw prisoners. The Choctaw medal chiefs decided to send a party including the chief of Cushtusha to ransom captives and to fetch Imayatabé to confirm the peace. In spite of the fact that the Cushtusha chief turned back at the French-inspired rumor of a trap, Red Shoe, visiting at Fort Tombecbé in late December, assured the commander that a peace among the Choctaws, Chickasaws, Alabamas, Talapoosas, and Abihkas was imminent. At that time only four Choctaw villages were estimated to be loyal to the French.[67]

In late March and April the French presents were held at Mobile, and some 1,200 Choctaws attended, although Red Shoe and Mongoulacha Mingo did not appear and Vaudreuil humiliated another medal chief known to be allied with them. The Choctaw principal men and warriors demanded that the medal chiefs' presents be taken from them for their perfidiousness and divided among the other chiefs and warriors, but Vaudreuil did not do this. By April, faced with the actual loss of his present from the French, Red Shoe sent Imataha Pouscouche (his "brother," the "Little King" to the English) to negotiate the Chickasaw peace and thereby obtain an English trade, but apparently there was trouble with those chiefs whom Vaudreuil had rewarded, because later in the spring Red Shoe once more called an assembly and argued for the English alliance. He was opposed with some success by Choucououlacta, and in late May he set off for conferences with the Abihkas and the Cowetas. In June, at the urging of the English trader James Adair and the chiefs Pastabé and Pahemingo-Amalahta, the Chickasaws sent presents to Red Shoe with another offer of peace, having heard through Red Shoe's allies the Chakchiumas of the accusation of rape against de Verbois and the involvement of Red Shoe's wife. By that time Choucououlacta had begun to lead attacks on the Chickasaws with the support of the Eastern Division. In July Red Shoe sent an embassy to treat with Adair and offer a promise of death to several Frenchmen to avenge the deaths of the two English traders of the previous year at the hands of the Choctaws. A return embassy from the Chickasaws was attacked by Choucououlacta as it made its way from Bouctoucoulou Chitto to Couëchitto, and two important men and one woman were killed.[68]

Red Shoe and his allies, cut off from their French presents, had to have an English trade in order to maintain their influence, and to do that they had to have a Chickasaw peace. Yet two Englishmen and three Chickasaws had been killed by Choctaws, in both cases by parties composed of men of the Eastern Division. Red Shoe had to demonstrate good faith to the English and Chickasaws, but the solution he chose was to avoid vengeance on his own people, even though the responsible parties were not from his own division, were not his allies, and, at least in the case of Choucououlacta, were not of his moiety. What he chose to do was kill three Frenchmen; doubtless this solution was suggested by the personal injury he had suffered, but it is clear that it was not his solution alone, since two other important chiefs allied with him—Apekimataha of West Abeka and Opayéchitto of Immongoulacha, whose villages were bases for the two traders Petit and Replinque killed with de Verbois—were also involved in the deaths.[69] Thus we see a corporate decision taken by a faction composed of members of a single division: that corporate decision was to repay deaths from one European group with deaths from another even though Choctaws were responsible for the deaths to be avenged.

Red Shoe and his allies may still have though that it might be possible to make allies of the Eastern Division in a complete break with the French, and this may be taken to explain why they avoided killing their own people at this juncture; but it does not explain why this pattern continued on both sides long after such an assumption had been proved wrong.

On August 14, then, the three Frenchmen were ambushed and killed as they traveled along a path from one village to another. It is not known who killed them. Red Shoe and his two allies doubtless ordered the killings, and the suggestion is that they were carried out by men from all three towns, but the identities of these men were never known or indeed considered important, either by the French or apparently by the Choctaws. Both sides treated the killings as a corporate act for which the chiefs of the three villages, at least, were responsible. Such a view was doubtless reinforced as far as the French were concerned by the fact that after the killings the French warehouses in the Western Division were plundered. And Red Shoe himself represented the killings as an action of his faction when he sent portions of the Frenchmen's scalps both to the Chickasaws and their English traders and to the Abihkas and Talapoosas.[70]

The first English response to this action was from John Campbell, who sent two English traders into the Choctaw Nation from the Chickasaws; apparently the French deaths had been adequate recompense for those of the English traders. The French response, after recall of all traders from the nation and sealing of those warehouses that had not been plundered, was to send in an important officer with the French demand for three Choctaw lives in payment for the three French lives. On September 16 Jadart de Beauchamp, major of Mobile, was sent to the Chickasawhay village to deliver the French ultimatum. It is unfortunate that Beauchamp was not more perceptive in his understanding of the conventions of Choctaw diplomacy, but even though his observations do betray misapprehension, his journal of this mission, covering nearly a month, offers a day-by-day account of the developing loyalties in the Choctaw Nation as its leaders considered the French demand. What actually went on during Beauchamp's visit was a series of meetings with groups of leading Choctaw men, at which Beauchamp reiterated the French demand for vengeance and the chiefs argued the merits of the various courses they could take. In examining this account we must remember that though Beauchamp did not realize it at the time, the meetings he held were to the Choctaws a matter of external negotiation, and no real internal decisions were made in his presence. The value of the journal lies in the fact that many of the issues that were to influence Choctaw conduct in the course of the coming civil conflict did surface here.[71]

The assemblies were held in the Chickasawhay village where Beauchamp and his party—which included de Verbois's brother—stayed with Father Baudouin because they had been warned that their safety could not be guaranteed beyond that point. During the course of the meetings Beauchamp received and sent messages to and from Fort Tombecbé, Fort Toulouse, and Mobile, thereby receiving news of what was happening as the repercussions of the Choctaw act and the French response began to be considered by both the Choctaws and the Upper Creek groups to the east. The men who came to meet with Beauchamp did not all come at once, but in groups probably of allies. We have no way of knowing how representative they were of the opinions and loyalties of their villages.[72]

The first and second days of October were devoted to a meeting with the leading men of the Chickasawhay villages. All shades of opinion were offered. Mongoulacha Mingo, who appeared in an inebriated state, was virulently anti-French, partly because he had heard that the medal chiefs were to lose their medals to the red chiefs, and as medal chief of the Chickasawhays and the Six Towns he felt himself to be aggrieved. The Choctaw captain of Chickasawhay argued that the Choctaws needed French guns and ammunition, and would starve without them. The captain of Immongoulacha village and the taskanangouchi of Yowani were pro-French and felt that justice should be done, while Mingo Ouma of Chickasawhay urged that the French leave the Choctaws to solve the problem in their own way. On the second day of this conference it was reported that the Abihkas had rejected the French scalps and thereby an alliance with Red Shoe against the French.[73]

On October 3 Alibamon Mingo and his supporters from the Concha villages and the Eastern Division arrived. Alibamon Mingo spoke eloquently in favor of acceding to the French demand, but Toupaoumastabé and Quikanabé Mingo, also from Concha, argued that vengeance should be carried out by the Western Division, since the Frenchmen had been killed by their partisans. The taskanangouchi of Blue Wood urged calm deliberation to choose the best course of action. The next day the taskanangouchi of Yazoo pledged the support of the Eastern Division to Alibamon Mingo—who seems by now to have taken over the leadership of the Eastern Division in the power vacuum left by the death of Choucououlacta—and on October 5 the chiefs of Oni declared themselves pro-French.[74]

On October 6 the chief of the Six Towns arrived. The chiefs of Yellow Canes and Nachoubaouenya expressed pro-French sentiments, while the chief of Tala, Mingo Ouma of Nachoubaouenya, Imataha Pouscouche and Fanimingo Tchaa of Seneacha, the chiefs of Bouctoulouctsi and Toussana, and Pouchimataha of Toussana argued against taking the side of the French if it would mean civil war. In spite of what Beauchamp considered a very persuasive speech from Alibamon Mingo arguing the French position and the isolation of the Choctaws as a result of the horrified reaction of the Abihkas, Pouchimataha of Toussana replied for all of the Six Towns that they would refuse a civil war, though they would gladly take up the Chickasaw war again. The implication was that they felt that Chickasaw deaths should suffice as a reaffirmation of loyalty.[75]

Meanwhile at Fort Tombecbé, Paemingo of Cushtusha had brought in skins to trade, and though trade had been suspended for the whole nation pending restitution, he claimed a right to both trade and a reward for having led an attack on the Chickasaws. In private consultation with the fort commander, he proposed to kill Red Shoe himself with the aid of a picked party consisting of Taskaoumingo of Boucfouca, Pouchimataha of Toussana, Illetaska of Immongoulacha, and Tatoulimataha of Little Wood, Red Shoe's "elder brother." It is probable that this proposal had more to do with the individual jealousies of several leading men than with any intention to comply with the French notion of justice. In any case, the proposal was reported to Beauchamp by letter, giving him what seemed to be a possible solution which he could suggest in private talks if the occasion presented itself.[76]

On October 7 Alibamon Mingo departed to go and take part with other chiefs in the mourning for the death of Choucououlacta, who had died advising the Eastern Division to support the French in opposition to the action of Red Shoe. On the same day the French-recognized supreme chief of the nation, from the village of Oulitacha of the Eastern Division, arrived along with a chief of Chichatalaya and Imataha Mingo of Ibitoupougoula. The supreme chief expressed himself as unreservedly pro-French, but spoke of the very little authority he had and of an attack that had already been made on his life. He did promise to speak for the French at the tribal assembly that would be held for the ceremonies connected with the preparation of Choucououlacta's bones for interment. Imataha Mingo, however, was strongly opposed to civil war, for whatever reason. The supreme chief ordered Espaninantela, the only Six Towns representative still present, to command the Six Towns chiefs to apologize for the rudeness of their speeches. Through subsequent days there were promises from Sonakabetaska, perhaps from Couëchitto, to avenge de Verbois at the assembly for Choucououlacta, and from the chiefs of Immongoulacha to avenge their trader Petit, but these individual promises may have represented personal obligations to the dead Frenchmen rather than corporate commitment. The white chief of Okalusa proposed that the actual killers be punished, but Red Shoe spared; a chief of West Abeka felt that Red Shoe should be sacrificed for the sake of the nation. The red chief of Concha—perhaps Toupaoumastabé—warned that even self-defense against the more populous faction of Red Shoe might be difficult for the Conchas in case of civil war.[77]

Meanwhile, apparently some Choctaws had gone to the Chickasaws to seek English trade goods, for it was reported to Beauchamp that they had found no goods there. On October 12 an embassy from the Alabama tribe arrived to address the assembly, led by Tamatlémingo, war chief of the Conchatys Alabamas, and his Choctaw son, the nephew of the red shoe of Yanabé village. Tamatlémingo described the opposition of the Alabama, Talapoosa, Abihka, and Coweta tribes to Red Shoe's action and their demand for justice for the French. He warned that English goods were in short supply and that the English never offered presents on a regular basis as the French did. He also brought news of a pan-Indian peace being promoted by the Shawnees, which Choctaw actions would spoil. His Choctaw son (presumably the son of a Choctaw wife) assured the assembly that Tamatlémingo spoke the truth, and this assertion was supported by the red shoe of Tombecbé and Assetaoumastabé of Concha, who made up the rest of the accompanying party. As a result apparently of these speeches, the red shoe of Yanabé, who had argued against the killing of Red Shoe on the previous day, spoke in private with Beauchamp proposing to kill Red Shoe along with some picked men. Beauchamp, taking this opportunity to put together such a party, suggested as members Paemingo of Cushtusha, the Captain of Toussana, Illetaska of Immongoulacha, Tatoulimataha, and Taskaoumingo (captain?) of Boucfouca, the last of whom the red shoe of Yanabé rejected as untrustworthy because too ambitious.[78]

On the following day Beauchamp spoke with Tatoulimataha, since if he were involved in the death of Red Shoe it was said that his close relationship of blood might prevent civil war. Tatoulimataha responded that he could not take part in such an action against one so nearly related and that Red Shoe should be killed, if at all, not by the Choctaws but by the Abihkas or Talapoosas. He also offered an explanation of Red Shoe's revolt: abuse of his wives by the French, jealousy of the French trader given to Pouchimataha of

Toussana, and the English request for revenge for the Blue Wood attack on their traders. It is significant that Tatoulimataha clearly thought his last reason at least partly justified Red Shoe's action, at least as far as the Choctaws were concerned.[79]

By October 16 Beauchamp had seen all the chiefs he could and departed for Mobile, to be followed by a messenger bringing Choucououlacta's medal and a message from Attachimingo and Tchioulacta pledging the loyalty of the Eastern Division. Neither Beauchamp nor his superiors were particularly satisfied with the outcome of the meetings, since apparently they had expected an actual conclusion to be reached. Beauchamp was especially nettled by the failure of the groups of chiefs to reach consensus, since he had expected them to transact serious tribal business in his presence. It seems obvious to us with hindsight that they had no intention of doing so; that the use to which the Choctaw put the meetings was to assure the French of their loyalty in order to retain their presents while presenting all the arguments available against an internal war, which they anticipated as the inevitable outcome of the death of Red Shoe. At the same time, the evidence of several chiefs speaking with Beauchamp in private shows that many of the sentiments expressed were for public consumption, and that the Choctaws themselves had mostly adopted a wait and see attitude, waiting to see how events would develop—specifically to see how much support would be forthcoming to Red Shoe from the English and the Creeks—and also to see how the consensus of the Choctaw Nation itself would begin to shape. Beauchamp was quick to assume that sentiments were divided along moiety lines, and perhaps his assumption does reflect a strong impression that he received, but the nature of the evidence he has left us is not sufficiently unambiguous for us to accept that at this early stage such a division was completely inevitable.[80]

The French were not prepared to await Choctaw consensus in order to obtain satisfaction. Apparently the post commanders felt that the death of Red Shoe could bring a quick end to the problem, for on October 20 a party led by a Great Tohomé Indian long resident at Fort Tombecbé and another Indian called "Broken Leg" left the fort to try to kill him. On November 3 two young men not yet warriors, from Yazoo Iskitini and Chickasawhay, reported to the Tombecbé commander that in an attempt to kill Red Shoe they had burned his round house, though he had escaped. These two attempts at solution using both non-Choctaw and uninitiated young men were irregular enough that perhaps they would have stood a chance of success without substantial consequence had they succeeded, but they did not.[81]

Instead, Red Shoe's strength seemed to be increasing. By November 9 it was reported that his "brother," presumably Imataha Pouscouche, was escorting an English convoy to the Chickasaws, and Mingo Ouma of Ibitoupougoula was sent as his emissary to the Chickasaws to announce that he was coming to fetch the English goods. On November 12, at the Chickasaws, Red Shoe concluded a peace with the Chickasaws and the English, represented by the traders Adair, Campbell, Newberry, and Chinnery, who had come to meet him there. By December 11, twenty-five towns had declared in favor of Red Shoe, probably about half of the nation, though the Chickasawhays and the Conchas were still loyal to the French. Also by that date Red Shoe had sent Imataha Pouscouche with fifteen headmen to make a treaty in Charleston.[82]

In retrospect, the first six months of 1747 were the backdrop for a race against time, as Imataha Pouscouche attempted to reach Charleston and return with a sizeable quantity of English goods before the French could persuade the Choctaws to carry out their demand for retribution against Red Shoe. By January 14 the Choctaw embassy had reached Coosa, but in late February and March Vaudreuil was meeting with deputies said to represent all forty-two Choctaw villages, promising large rewards for Red Shoe's death and securing their promise to carry out his request. On March 24 Imataha Pouscouche's party had reached Fort Moore, and by March 28 an English trader, apparently coming independently from the Creeks, reached Fanimingo Tchaa at the Six Towns village of Seneacha with ten horse-loads of goods, thus helping shore up the English allegiance of the Six Towns. On the same day Taskaoumingo of Concha sent word to the chiefs and leading warriors to come to an assembly at Fort Tombecbé, and one of the young Choctaws who had previously attempted to kill Red Shoe set out to try it again. At the Tombecbé assembly on April 1 all the chiefs and principal men of twenty-three villages loyal to the French resolved to kill Red Shoe; the number is more than the villages of the Eastern Division plus the Conchas, and perhaps includes some of the Chickasawhays. Ten days later Imataha Pouscouche had reached Charleston, and by April 18 the English treaty was concluded. Governor James Glen chose Charles McNaire to carry presents and trade goods to the Choctaws, but it took him until June 10 to prepare his train of two hundred horses, and while he was still on the road, on the night of June 22, Red Shoe was killed while escorting the Creek trader Elsley to the Choctaws. In spite of Red Shoe's death, his faction was not to dissolve. Elsley's convoy continued on to Couëchitto, his village, and its contents were given out as presents to confirm Imataha Pouscouche as his successor.[83]

Meanwhile, Red Shoe's head and two English scalps were handed over to the French by their allies, clearly an attempt to answer the demand for three deaths. The French, however, not only continued to insist that two more Choctaw deaths were required, but apparently they now intended not just to have vengeance, but to destroy the leadership of Red Shoe's faction: instead of the chief of Immongoulacha, they demanded that Imataha Pouscouche be killed along with Apekimataha to make up the three required Choctaw deaths. The English scalps were dismissed as having nothing to do with the satisfaction that had been demanded.[84]

McNaire finally arrived in the Choctaw Nation on September 25, having left some of the goods he carried behind among the Creeks. Imataha Pouscouche called an assembly and once again presents were given out, reportedly binding forty-two Choctaw towns to the English, though this English report seems rather optimistic in counting only four towns as still loyal to the French. In a demonstration of strength, again avoiding direct aggression against other Choctaws, the English-supported group attacked settlements on the Mobile River, killing five French people and one Negro; shortly thereafter another band attacked the Natchez fort. In similar action again Europeans in October, Elsley was killed by the French-allied Choctaws while on his way back to the Creeks for more goods, and on October 25 the Great Tohomé leader and twelve Conchas attacked a convoy of five English traders carrying back sixty horse-loads of deerskins, killing one Englishman and the Choctaw chief who was escorting the party. Apparently in reaction to this Choctaw death, the Western Choctaws then attacked the Concha fortifications, and two were killed on each side before the attackers were driven off. Somewhat later four English traders, possibly the four who had escaped the Eastern attack, returned from the Creeks with powder and bullets, and in late November McNaire left the Choctaws with Imataha Pouscouche and Payamataha (Paemingo of Cushtusha?) to ask for more goods in Charleston, where they arrived at the end of the year.[85]

This sequence of events shows that the Choctaws had resisted becoming involved in internecine strife as long as it was possible. The documents do not tell us who it was that actually killed Red Shoe, and it is possible that in the stealth with which it was done no one really knew. Revenge for his death was certainly inflicted upon the French, not the Choctaws. The Western Choctaw did not attack the Eastern until after one of their chiefs had been killed by a Concha attack—a death that might well have been unintended, since it was plainly aimed at the English convoy. And even at that the Western attack on the Concha villages was not particularly violent or determined. One explanation for this lack of enthusiasm might be sought in the smallpox epidemic that had killed 1,000–1,200 Choctaws by the end of 1747, since although the victims would be predominantly very young and very old and hence noncombatants, Choctaw mortuary customs would have been a distinct hindrance to concerted military activity.[86] Certainly this massive mortality must have played a role, especially if Choucououlacta had been among the victims, and if many of the older men valued for their wisdom in council had died then it would be more likely for impulsive decisions to be able to prevail in Choctaw councils after 1747, as was apparently the case. It is also true, however, that the Choctaws were reluctant to kill one another in payment for foreign lives, when custom and the lesson of the Natchez wars licensed them to wonder why the French did not declare war to avenge their own dead.[87]

The French did not cease their demands, nor the English their support. By the end of March of 1748 McNaire had arrived back in the Choctaw Nation, but Imataha Pouscouche had stayed behind at the Creeks to await the coming of McNaire's partner Vann, who was actually bringing the convoy of goods. Using Campbell as his interpreter, McNaire gave out ammunition that he had taken from his storehouse at the Creeks. Meanwhile Louboey, commander at Mobile, was hosting twenty-eight loyal Choctaw villages for the French presents from April 9. These villages, which included six from the Western Division, pledged vengeance on Red Shoe's party, and Vaudreuil's offer of pardon to the Western Division in exchange for the three deaths previously demanded was passed on to be communicated to them officially by Imataha Mingo of Ibitoupougoula and the second chief of Chichatalaya, who must have been the only ones with enough authority—or perhaps sufficient connection with the Western leadership—to be convincing. But this was not done, and shortly after the presents there was another Western attack on the French colony, this time on the German Coast below New Orleans, where a man was killed, his wife scalped, and his daughter and five Negroes taken prisoner. An abortive French attempt to catch the perpetrators encountered Pahémingo of Immongoulacha and a small party in the woods near Lake Pontchartrain with what they claimed were six black and three Indian runaway slaves, but took no action; by June 15 it was reported that the leader of the raid on the Germans had been killed in his own village by his brother and chief. Also by that date Imataha Pouscouche and his Choctaw party were attacked in the vicinity of the Abihkas on the way back from Charleston, and the French spread the rumor that he had been taken away prisoner to Carolina.[88]

The summer of 1748 seems to have been the turning point when the Choctaws finally accepted the fact that the French would indeed not be satisfied with anything less than civil war, and strongly prosecuted attacks by Choctaws on Choctaw villages began. We may speculate that a more moderate course might have prevailed for even longer if the smallpox epidemic had not taken its toll of the more seasoned leadership, and it does seem to be the case that in the actions to follow some new names come to the fore. Yet neither the Choctaw perception of French determination nor a more impulsive leadership can account for the whole of the explanation for this turn of events, since there is an obvious—though not always explicable—political significance to the choice of villages attacked, and it seems to be clearly connected with prior events and loyalties. The first attack of this kind, made on July 14 by the Conchas and their allies of the Eastern Division led by Alibamon Mingo, was a raid on Couëchitto, Red Shoe's village, and Nushkobo (classified by Swanton as an Eastern village,[89] perhaps attacked for having deserted the Eastern cause). In this raid Tchicachas Ouma, chief of Nushkobo, was killed, along with two honored men of Couëchitto and ten others, among them six of Red Shoe's Chakchiuma allies. At this point the Chakchiumas living at Couëchitto fled to the Chickasaws and the two villages were abandoned.[90]

In August the second big English convoy from Charleston came as far as the accustomed waiting point on the Black Warrior River and then turned back after waiting three weeks for an escort. McNaire was forced to get ammunition from the traders at the Chickasaws, which he distributed before departing. Adair himself traveled through the Choctaw Nation after this, holding a large assembly at the Six Towns where he gave out extensive presents that included gorgets, bracelets, and earrings. Presumably on the strength of all this English support, the Western faction attacked Oulitacha, the village of the French-allied supreme medal chief, on August 16. More than a hundred were killed in this engagement, but the Western attackers seem to have had the worst of it, losing the captain of Boucfouca, the chief of West Abeka (perhaps Apekimataha, whose death was demanded by the French), Mongoulacha Oupayé of Immongoulacha (the original third of the demanded deaths), Pahémingo of Toussana, and more than eighty more. It is worth noting that the body of the probable leader of the attack, the Captain of Boucfouca, was terribly mutilated, a practice that the French said had been unknown among the Choctaws before. The Eastern defenders lost the chief of Chichatalaya, honored men of Ibitoupougoula and Boutoucoulou Chitto, and ten more.[91]

After this military failure the Western Choctaws sent to the Chickasaws for more ammunition, and at this juncture Vann finally arrived with Imataha Pouscouche and the pack train from Charleston. By October 4 there were sixteen Choctaws in Carolina, sent previously by Adair for more ammunition. On October 22 Red Shoe's Chakchiuma allies attacked the Natchez fort and killed a French soldier, but by October 24 Mongoulacha Mingo of Chickasawhay, the brother of Pahemingo of Toussana, and an honored man of West Yazoo had been killed by their own villages, and Red Shoe's "family" was said to have fled en masse to the Abihkas or Alabamas because the Western faction was out of ammunition. This must have been a rather specious explanation, since on November 8 a party of thirteen Choctaws attacked again at the German Coast and killed five people, losing five of their own.[92]

Although Imataha Pouscouche had not been killed, by now the Eastern Division had actually satisfied the original French requirements for vengeance, since Red Shoe, Pahémingo of Toussana, and perhaps Apekimataha had been killed. When we look at what happened at the French presents, however, something very different seems to be going on. Vaudreuil came to Mobile on November 26 and was met by a victorious party consisting of Alibamon Mingo, the chiefs of the Concha villages, the supreme chief, and all the chiefs and warriors of the Eastern Division, including Okalusa and Yanabé. They brought him more than a hundred Western scalps and the heads of three chiefs, and obviously they thought that French requirements would be satisfied. The heads they brought were those of chiefs from Couëchitto, of the West; Nushkobo, of the East, and West Abeka, of the West—the first two obviously obtained purposely in their attack in July, the third won in the battle against Western attackers in August. This point is worthy of note because it was in their power to present the other, originally demanded deaths for consideration.[93]

Yet the French still demanded that the attack on the Germans be avenged, and Alibamon Mingo handed out the weapons left behind by the attackers to the warriors of Yowani, Chickasawhay, and the Six Towns so that they too might prove their loyalty. The war chief of Yowani used them to attack Okeoulou, killing one man and taking three prisoners. It seemed that perhaps the violence could at last be concluded, and Vaudreuil offered a pardon to the villages of the Western Division through representatives from West Yazoo and West Immongoulacha.[94]

This much-desired conclusion was probably close to being reached, if only because the Western Division was in a desperate state for ammunition, which had apparently been in short supply in the pack trains that had arrived. In December the sixteen Choctaws sent by Adair arrived in Charleston and met with the Royal Council to ask for more munitions. On January 7, 1749, twenty more Choctaws arrived in Charleston with Campbell, among them Pouchimataha of Toussana and Paemingo of Cushtusha, claiming that all the chiefs of the Western Division were dead and their cause almost lost. Also in January an English trader was captured with a twelve-horse convoy near the Alabamas; in the spring Imataha Pouscouche died, apparently of natural causes; and on March 12 the English trader in West Yazoo village was shot. Also in March Fanimingo Tchaa of Seneacha brought in four English traders from the Chickasaws and then attacked a party from the Eastern Division in the plain of Seneacha. He and eight of his kinsmen were killed and the English traders were plundered, causing a split in the village. The pro-English group joined Oni, Tchanké, and Okéoulou villages in attacking Nachoubaouenya, killing twenty men and forcing the entire village to withdraw to Yowani. By mid-April, however, a party made up of forces from Chickasawhay, Yowani, Nachoubaouenya, Bouctoulouctsi, Yellow Canes, and the pro-French Seneachas attacked Oni, Tchanké, and Okéoulou, killing twenty to forty people.[95]

The split in the village of Seneacha must have been bitter, but again resentment was turned against the French when on July 1 ten Seneacha men killed three people near Mobile and withdrew to Seneacha. After the English trader at West Immongoulacha had been killed by the chief's nephew, an assembly was called at Fort Tombecbé by Grandpré, the commander, and Desilets, the leading French trader. At this assembly, presumably attended by the Conchas, the Eastern Division, and the Six Towns, the Choctaws agreed to end the war, and soon afterward what was supposed to be a definitive attack on Seneacha was made, killing nine of the ten men who had attacked the Mobile River settlement.[96]

Since war with the French in Europe had ended, the English were no longer particularly concerned to supply the Choctaws with anything that would not be paid for. However, there was still some support to be had. By August 3, three Choctaws who had come to Charleston with some Chickasaw chiefs claimed that all ammunition was gone; the trader Petycrou said that they were reduced to using glass beads for bullets. This lack may have been partially provided for when Pouchimataha arrived back in the nation on September 22 with three English traders, but the French were countering with gifts to Mingo Ouma and his warriors from Nachoubaouenya for the Chickasaw scalps they had started to bring in. Around October 6 Petycrou left Charleston with fresh supplies of ammunition, arriving at the Chickasaws on November 25 only to be told that the Choctaws had gone to Mobile to seek peace. This report was only partly erroneous, for Desilets brought fourteen leading men of Tchanké, Oni, Okéoulou, and Tala to New Orleans to talk peace and to see for themselves the supplies of trade goods then available. By December, however, Pouchimataha was in Caffetalaya with an English trader, and it was reported on December 20 that Caffetalaya and Cushtusha, supported by the English trader and the two chiefs Pouchimataha and Mingo Ouma, were still holding out against the French allies. Further, on January 1 a Choctaw guard fetched Petycrou from the Chickasaws to counter the influence of the French interpreter Faberie, who had been sent into the nation with a promise of French goods and a reward for British scalps. On January 12 Petycrou arrived in Pouchimataha's village Toussana and called an assembly to distribute presents; after that he claimed to have traded in twenty-four towns and to have bound 1,322 men to the English alliance.[97]

On April 14 the French presents began in Mobile, with all villages except Caffetalaya and Cushtusha represented, despite Petycrou's claims. Now the Six Towns made their final proof of loyalty, bringing 130 scalps from the raiders of the French settlement and their friends and relatives and claiming that they had themselves lost thirty killed and wounded. Representatives of the Western Division brought twelve Chickasaw and three English scalps, and apparently the French were willing to accept this as enough.[98]

The English supplies and resentments built up through the war continued to influence events, however. By June 24 a West Immongoulacha party killed a soldier at the Natchez fort, and by early July ten young men of the Eastern Division had been killed by the Western in revenge for a Western woman killed by an Eastern man. In September fourteen English traders came to the Choctaws, but were soon pillaged. The French must have realized that this kind of minor engagement could disrupt the nation indefinitely. Perhaps, too, they had grasped the fact that internal vengeance would be endless. At any rate, later in September Grandpré led a party from the Eastern Division with a detachment of French soldiers and a swivel-gun from Fort Tombecbé to attack Cushtusha and Caffetalaya, burning five forts and scalping twenty-five. This attack proved to be decisive; the French had at last at least symbolically taken the field on their own behalf, as the Choctaws had asked them to do in the first place. On November 15 the so-called Grandpré Treaty was entered into by the Choctaws at Tombecbé, by which they agreed to four points:

1. Any Frenchman killed by a Choctaw must be avenged by the Choctaws.
2. English traders and their Choctaw sponsors were to be killed by the Choctaws with no revenge obligation.
3. The Choctaws would pursue their Chickasaw war.
4. The Western villages would destroy their forts and exchange prisoners with the Eastern Division.

This treaty was ratified by Atakabé Oulacta, referred to as the former supreme medal chief of the Choctaws, and by Alibamon Mingo, in the name of the whole nation. A white feather flag and the English commissions of Pouchimataha and Mingo Ouma were sent to Vaudreuil. From November 15 until January of the following year the Choctaws took the field against the Chickasaws several times, killing fourteen Chickasaws and an Englishman and taking ten prisoners. Although the French continued to have problems in supplying the Choctaws, and although some chiefs—notably Pouchimataha of Toussana and Mingo Oumastabé of Cushtusha—remained unregenerate in appealing to the English, this was the end of the Choctaw civil war.[99]

It is obvious from the foregoing narrative that there is no simple explanation of the patterns of loyalties that emerged during the war, since the loyalties that were appealed to during its course were not only political, but also social and individual. We have, however, seen that the Choctaws did everything they could to avoid killing one another; that in spite of European demands (and just because the English sources do not indicate that such demands from them were continuously made, we cannot assume that they were not), the only times Choctaws were intentionally killed by other Choctaws were when Choctaw lives had been lost. It is true that during the second half of the war there was more fighting among the Choctaws themselves, but the French action that was required to end the war indicates that the principle of capital punishment *within* the tribe on behalf of an external complaint had not been adopted. What the Choctaws did do consistently was kill representatives of other *external* groups, and it is obvious that they expected this to serve as adequate retribution. This fact may suggest that here is an aspect of aboriginal intertribal warfare that deserves more investigation: the killing of mutual enemies as retribution for the unsanctioned death of an ally at the hands of the tribe.

Certainly there were numerous other factors involved in the war. We have indicated that moiety affiliation was an important influence on the composition of factions, and the very character of the moiety distribution may also account for much of the confusion of loyalties that has been observed. The relative availability of European goods and the effects of the smallpox epidemic also had their influence. The full story of the several charismatic personalities that emerged during the war and their role in the conflict has not been told here either. There are a number of such issues that will repay more detailed investigation than there has been space for in this essay. The rich potential of a study of this conflict has barely yet been assayed, but the above consideration of only one aspect shows that there remains a great mine of information on the problems of culture contact and change.

NOTES

This chapter originally appeared as "Choctaw Factionalism and Civil War, 1746–1750," *Journal of Mississippi History* 44 (November 1982): 289–327.

1. Charles William Paape, "The Choctaw Revolt, A Chapter in the Intercolonial Rivalry in the Old Southwest" (Ph.D. diss., University of Illinois, 1946).

2. Archives des Colonies, série C13A, Correspondence générale Louisiane (referred to hereafter as AC, C13A). Selections relevant to French-Choctaw relations are printed in Dunbar Rowland and A. G. Sanders, eds., *Mississippi Provincial Archives: French Dominion*, vols. 1–3 (Jackson: Mississippi Department of Archives and History, 1927–1932) (referred to hereafter as *MPAFD*).

3. Huntington MS Loudoun 9:III, Huntington Library (hereafter referred to as HMLO 9:III). For a calendar, see Bill Barron, *The Vaudreuil Papers* (New Orleans: Polyanthos, 1975).

4. See Patricia Galloway, "Louisiana Post Letters, 1700–1763: The Missing Evidence for Indian Diplomacy," *Louisiana History* 23, no. 1 (1981): 31–44.

5. Edmond Atkin, "Historical Account of the Revolt of the Chactaw Indians," 1753, Landsdowne MS 809, British Museum, London.

6. James Adair, *The History of the American Indians* (London: E. and C. Dilly, 1775).

7. What remains of the "Indian Books" has been edited in three volumes by W. McDowell, as the *Colonial Records of South Carolina*, ser. 2, vols. 1–3 (Columbia: South Carolina Department of Archives and History, 1955–70). Charles Lee and Ruth Green, in a series of articles in the *South Carolina Historical Magazine*, 67 (1966): 187–202; 68 (1967): 1–13, 85–96, and 165–83), have published useful guides to the remaining South Carolina records mentioned in the text.

8. Vaudreuil to Rouillé, January 12, 1751, AC, C13A, 35:65v.

9. Atkin, "Historical Account," 57; Adair, *History*, 330.

10. Beauchamp, Journal, September 16–October 19, 1746, AC, C13A, 30:226v (hereafter referred to only as Journal, with folio number[s]).

11. A total of 1,000–1,200 were said to have died of smallpox by the end of 1747:

Louboey to Maurepas, February 16, 1748, AC, C13A, 32:212v. According to my count of actual numbers of Choctaw dead mentioned in the documents, a maximum of 418 Choctaws lost their lives in the actual fighting of the civil conflict.

12. This seems to be the import of the common settlement pattern of daughter villages strung out along watercourses as observed by the French. Baudouin to Salmon, November 23, 1732, AC, C13A, 14:183.

13. For a discussion of these offices see John R. Swanton, *Source Material for the Social and Ceremonial Life of the Choctaw Indians*, Bureau of American Ethnology 103 (Washington, D.C.: U.S. Government Printing Office, 1931), 90–96. Swanton, who had access only to the French documents acquired up to that time by the Library of Congress and other American libraries (see H. P. Beers, *The French in North America* [Baton Rouge: Louisiana State University Press, 1958]), did not recognize the titular nature of the "soulouche oumastabe" and "fanimingo" appellations. It also seems, from the frequency with which the taskanangouchi appears rather than the village chief for external negotiations, that he and not the tichou mingo was the chief's speaker.

14. Fred Gearing, "Priests and Warriors: Social Structures for Cherokee Politics in the 18th Century," *AAA Memoir* 93 (1962).

15. Beauchamp, Journal, 232v.

16. Swanton, *Source Material*, 78.

17. Gearing, "Priests and Warriors," 47–54; Charles Hudson, *The Southeastern Indians* (Knoxville: University of Tennessee Press, 1976), 224–25. Compare Nassuba Mingo's statement in the 1765 Choctaw Congress with John Stuart, in Dunbar Rowland, ed., *Mississippi Provincial Archives: English Dominion* (Jackson: Mississippi Department of Archives and History, 1911), 241–42.

18. For the practice among the Creeks, see John R. Swanton, "Social Organization and Social Usages of the Indians of the Creek Confederacy," in *Forty-Second Annual Report of the Bureau of American Ethnology, 1924–1925, 1927* (Washington, D.C.: Smithsonian Institution, 1928), 249.

19. In general, "red" chiefs tend to speak more often and more assertively. Examples in Beauchamp, Journal, *passim*.

20. There are very few extant recorded observations even of Choctaw external negotiation. The only extant description for this period of Choctaw society in its domestic aspect that is worthy of mention is the "Anonymous Relation" printed in Swanton, *Source Material*, 243–58, and even this does not describe internal political activities. James Adair, close as he was to the Chickasaws, recorded very little about such activities for them, which suggests that inclusion of Europeans was very rare.

21. Compare the lists in the various sources summarized by Swanton in *Source Material*, 58–75. This summary table gives the erroneous impression that division membership was static, but a comparison of Régis du Roullet, Journal, April–August 1732, (Archives Hydrographiques, vol. 67^2, no. 14-1, portfolio 135, document 21) with Edmond Atkin, Treaty of Friendship and Commerce, July 18, 1759 (Lyttelton Papers, William L. Clements Library, Ann Arbor, Michigan), shows immediately that this was not the case.

22. Swanton, *Source Material*, 55–57.

23. See Patricia Galloway, "Henri de Tonti du village des Chactas, 1702: The Beginning of the French Alliance," in *LaSalle and His Legacy*, ed. Patricia Galloway (Jackson: University Press of Mississippi, 1982), 146–75. Four Choctaws came to the first negotiation with Iberville, but the Tonti documents make it clear that only three were actually sent as representatives.

24. *MPAFD*, 1:194–95.

25. Red Shoe was an Imoklasha (inferred from Vaudreuil to Maurepas, February 12, 1744, AC, C13A, 28:200–202v); Alibamon Mingo was an Inholahta (see his speech in the 1765 Choctaw Congress with John Stuart, in *MPAED*, 1:239); for other chiefs' moiety affiliations where known, see *infra*.

26. Beauchamp, Journal, speech of taskanangouchi of Yowani, an Inholahta; 227–227v.

27. Baudouin to Salmon, November 23, 1732, AC, C13A, 14:184; Bienville, Memoir, August 25, 1733, AC, C13A, 16:208–208v.

28. For examples, see Beauchamp, Journal, 231v; *MPAFD*, 1:32–33.

29. Vaudreuil to Baudouin, December 19, 1745; HMLO 9:III, 185.

30. Swanton, *Source Material*, 162–64; Hudson, *Southeastern Indians*, 225; Gearing, "Priests and Warriors," 50–51.

31. The rivalry and enmities observed by the Soto expedition among the neighboring chiefdoms of the Southeast, and especially of the Alabama-Mississippi area, manifested itself in concrete terms by the existence of fortified towns. Archaeological evidence shows that during the florescence of Mississippian cultures, fortification was seen at small villages only when they lay at considerable distance from the protection of a larger center, while during the "Mississippian decline" fortifications are seen on even very minor sites. See C. S. Peebles, "An Overview of Research in the Lubbub Creek Archaeological Locality," in *Prehistoric Agricultural Communities in West Central Alabama*, ed. C. S. Peebles (Ann Arbor: University of Michigan, 1981), 70–129.

32. The first supreme chief was created by Bienville in about 1708. This was Chicacha Oulacta, who was succeeded by his nephew. Baudouin to Salmon, November 23, 1732, AC, C13A, 14:186v–187.

33. *MPAFD*, 1:150–54.

34. Vaudreuil to Maurepas, February 12, 1744, AC, C13A, 28:199v.

35. Beauchamp to Maurepas, October 24, 1748, AC, C13A, 32:216.

36. Baudouin to Salmon, November 23, 1732, AC, C13A, 14:184–84v; Bienville Memoir, August 25, 1733, AC, C13A, 16:207v–208v.

37. As we have seen, soulouche oumastabé ("red shoe killer") was a functional title. The French version of the title is *soulier rouge*, or simply "red shoe." Here we shall capitalize the title and use it as a name to refer only to this particular man; others will be referred to as "the red shoe of . . . "

38. Red Shoe's motives will never be known with certainty, but clearly he wished to maintain neutrality and deal with both French and English. By disciplining him through cutting off his present at intervals, the French forced him to turn to the English to maintain the support of his allies.

39. Hudson, *Southeastern Indians*, 239.

40. The two young half-brothers Barthelemy, one sixteen and the other twenty-four years old, were put to death in 1738 for the murder of a Choctaw man and woman who had been employed in hunting for French settlers near Mobile. They were executed by order of the Superior Council of Louisiana, possibly under pressure from Bienville, in the presence of Choctaw witnesses. See AC, C13A, 23:200–205, 24:115–8v, 246–49.

41. The Alabamas, who had the French Fort Toulouse built in the midst of their lands, also traded quite happily with the English for whatever the French could not provide. They always refused absolutely to harm either French or English allies, and also to take the side of any other tribe that would. See Bienville, Memoir, 1726, AC, C13C, 1:371.

42. Adair, *History*, *passim*., categorically states on many occasions that the Chickasaws had always demonstrated unswerving loyalty to the English.

43. Régis du Roullet to Périer, February 21, 1731, AC, C13A, 13:177v.

44. Crémont to Maurepas, December 9, 1732, AC, C13A, 15:191.

45. Swanton, *Source Material*, 10–34; marriage alliances are indicated by several mentions of apparent wife exchanges (cf. AC, C13A, 13:177v).

46. *MPAFD*, 1:46, 110, 175.

47. Ibid., 1:187.

48. Ibid., 1:34.

49. Ibid., 1:371; Atkin, "Historical Account," 2.

50. *MPAFD*, 1:371.

51. Ibid., 1:224, 232.

52. Ibid., 3:725.

53. Ibid., 1:79.

54. Ibid., 1:289.

55. Ibid., 1:299, 338, 368.

56. Noyan to Maurepas, January 4, 1739, AC, C13A, 24:227.

57. Crémont to Maurepas, August 18, 1732, AC, C13A, 15:191v; Noyan to Maurepas, January 4, 1739, AC, C13A, 24:229v.

58. *MPAFD*, 3:724–26.

59. Vaudreuil to Maurepas, November 30, 1746, AC, C13A, 30:76v–77v.

60. Beauchamp, Journal, 229v.

61. Beauchamp to Maurepas, October 24, 1748, AC, C13A, 32:216.

62. *MPAFD*, 1:42. Baudouin to Loubouey, May 20, 1742, AC, C13A, 27:131v–131^4.

63. Beauchamp, Journal, 225. Vaudreuil to Rouillé, March 3, 1749, AC, C13A, 33:18v.

64. The primary sources for this narrative are AC, C13A; HMLO 9:III; and Atkin, "Historical Account." Adair's *History* would be very helpful if events of many different periods were not inextricably intertwined, undated, in his account; here it is only used as corroborative evidence. To reduce the thicket of footnotes, references will be simplified and grouped by paragraph under a single number. Because the events related will be chronological, it will be sufficient to reference blocks of manuscript material. AC, C13A, 28:199–211v, 260–261v, 29:196–200v; HMLO 9:III, 4036; HMLO 9:III, 23v; HMLO 9:III, 4–11, 36, 42, 48–51, 62–67, 81, 89–91, 99, 117, 119, 125–28.

65. Atkin, "Historical Account," 37–38; AC, C13A, 29:189–95v; 30:76–84.

66. AC, C13A, 29:189–95v, 196–200v; HMLO 9:III, 167, 178.
67. AC, C13A, 29:189–95v; 30:169–74; HMLO 9:III, 167, 180.
68. AC, C13A, 30:49–56, 76–84; Atkin, "Historical Account," 38; HMLO 9:III, 198, 201, 204; Adair, *History*, 313, 315.
69. HMLO 9:III, 125.
70. Beauchamp, Journal, AC, C13A, 30:76–84.
71. Beauchamp, Journal.
72. Ibid.
73. Ibid.
74. Ibid.
75. Ibid.
76. Ibid.
77. Ibid.
78. Ibid.
79. Ibid.
80. Ibid.
81. AC, C13A, 30:183–186v; HMLO 9:III, 242, 247.
82. AC, C13A, 30:183–186v; Atkin, "Historical Account," 2, 5, 36, 38; HMLO 4021.
83. Atkin, "Historical Account," 3–6, 36; HMLO 9:III, 521; HMLO 9:III, 266; AC, C13A, 19:11–12v, 31:17–23, 32:122–31, 210–13v.
84. AC, C13A, 31:98–102v; HMLO 9:III, 268.
85. Atkin, "Historical Account," 6–12; AC, C13A, 32:122–31, 210–13v.
86. AC, C13A, 32:210–13v; Swanton, *Source Material*, 170–93; cf. Beauchamp, Journal, 228v–229.
87. The Choctaws always asked for Frenchmen to accompany their external war parties.
88. Atkin, "Historical Account," 14–15; AC, C13A, 32:81–87v, 102–4, 33:12–27v.
89. Swanton, *Source Material*, 66.
90. AC, C13A, 32:122–31.
91. Atkin, "Historical Account," 15; Adair, *History*, 329–30; AC, C13A, 32:122–31.
92. Atkin, "Historical Account," 17–18; AC, C13A, 32:122–31, 137–44, 215–18.
93. AC, C13A, 33:12–27v.
94. Ibid.
95. Atkin, "Historical Account," 21, 29; AC, C13A, 33:49–54v, 79–88v.
96. AC, C13A, 33:79–88v; 34:251–58.
97. Atkin, "Historical Account," 29–33; AC, C13A, 33:79–88v, 34:251–58; HMLO 9:III, 508.
98. AC, C13A, 34:261–69v.
99. Ibid., 34:261–75, 315–17v; 35:61–69v, 354–60.

CHAPTER 5

Protecting Trade through War

CHOCTAW ELITES AND BRITISH OCCUPATION
OF THE FLORIDAS

Greg O'Brien

The conclusion of the Seven Years' War caused anxiety among Native Americans throughout eastern North America. As French troops withdrew from Canada, Louisiana, and the Ohio Valley, Indians wondered what a world with only one major European power would mean for them. In the Southeast, Britain occupied former French territory along the Gulf Coast and up the eastern shore of the Mississippi River (West Florida) in addition to Spanish territory in Florida (then called East Florida). Only New Orleans remained in non-British hands, although it became Spanish, rather than French, in 1766. French abandonment of the continent forced Indians to confront Britain as the sole supplier of trade.

Choctaws found this adjustment particularly difficult. Prior to 1763, they relied upon trade with France to supply many of their necessities. Few Choctaw leaders had met any British traders or officials until a major conference at Mobile in 1765. At that meeting, all of the Choctaw speakers alerted their new neighbors to the importance of supplying Choctaws with goods. For example, Nassuba Mingo appealed to John Stuart, the British Southern Indian superintendent: "I expect my people will receive presents in greater abundance, and if we do not, it must proceed from want of affection in their Father, & not from want of Ability, I do not speak for myself but for my Warriors, their

Wives & their Children, whom I cannot Cloathe, or keep in order without presents."[1] Britain failed, in the 1760s and 1770s, to equip Choctaw headmen with sufficient clothing, metal goods, paint, guns, and ammunition. This placed further strain on an already difficult relation and contributed to political instability.

By the 1760s, trade relations with Europeans affected Choctaw social stability directly. Since at least Mississippian times (ca. 1100–ca. 1600), southeastern Indian leaders maintained a level of noncoercive power and authority necessary to the preservation of social order by redistributing high-prestige items to their families and followers. France supported this ideal before 1763 by funneling presents through established leaders. French trade with the Choctaws occurred once a year at Mobile, at which time Choctaw chiefs gave deerskins to French officials and French governors reciprocated with ample gifts of their own. Thurs, trade took the form of an elaborate, ritualized gift-exchange that bolstered chiefly power through their control of goods which they redistributed according to the demands of kinship responsibilities and political needs.[2] The new British presence brought about a radically different trade relationship that centered on private enterprise and market values rather than diplomatic gift exchange. This threatened Choctaw chiefly authority.[3]

The problem for the chiefs was adjusting to a new set of rules. Independent British traders traveled directly to Choctaw villages and frequently bartered with nonchiefs for deerskins. Superintendent Stuart attempted to regulate the traders, but he faced stiff opposition as the southern colonies proved unwilling to relinquish their right to grant licenses freely. Stuart found that although every Choctaw village (numbering between forty and fifty) had white people who traded and lived in it, only three traders in the nation held licenses: "the rest were only authorized to trade by two or three Merchants in South Carolina and Georgia."[4] Abuses flourished as traders and their assistants assaulted Choctaw women, bartered with alcohol, and cheated Choctaws out of promised goods.[5]

At the same time, Choctaw chiefs no longer received annual presents as they had from the French. British officials understood perfectly well the difference between their system and that of France; West Florida Governor George Johnstone outlined the severe adjustments that would be necessary on the part of the Choctaws: "The French have accustomed both the Upper Creeks and Chactaws to such large Presents, that it will be difficult to break that Custom, until they are convinced of Our Superiority and their Dependence, which can only be done by Time, and a well regulated Trade restraining the general Licences; Or, by an immediate War."[6]

Market-driven, British trade did little to maintain chiefly authority. The state, in the form of the British imperial system, managed the distribution of gifts to Indians when they visited British officials at Mobile or Pensacola, but left the more mundane trading activities to private individuals and companies. Thus, trade with the British supplied necessities to the Choctaws, but it failed to obey customs that enabled chiefs to maintain power by controlling the flow of goods.

Since the trade remained unregulated, this new structure threatened the redistributive roles of the chiefs and rendered them politically weakened. Choctaw leaders explained to the British that their young men were virtually uncontrollable unless they received presents that enabled them to fulfill their redistributive function. As early as 1764, they alerted the British that gifts of trade goods would quiet the "young men at home [who] will think the English look upon them as friends."[7] But the British did not agree that the worth of such assemblies matched the huge expense.[8] Only two major gift-giving conferences were held before the American Revolution; one in 1765, the other during the winter of 1771–72.

Young men adapted by ignoring chiefly jurisdiction over the trade. Some of them circumvented British contact by trading with the Spanish and their French employees in New Orleans. Any man could acquire deerskins and exchange them directly with traders for the goods he desired. This loosening of control succeeded in putting more hunters in the woods in pursuit of deerskins. Whitetail deer supplied a vital source of food to Choctaws and their skins formed the basis of trade relations with Europeans. Also, Choctaw men hunted to gain prestige by showcasing their skills and proving their ability to contribute to a family's economic well-being. Successful hunting, as well as war exploits, further provided young men with the necessary accomplishments to acquire titles marking their transition from boys to men. Adult titles differentiated men from their mothers, who gave them their original boyhood names, and from women generally.[9] Direct participation in the trade gave nonelite males one way to handle a changed world, but there remained other options, such as preying upon British traders and outlying settlers.

Acts of violence and raids on European settlements escalated throughout the 1760s and the threat of armed conflict between the Choctaws and the British loomed ever larger. Both British and Choctaw leaders worked hard to avoid that scenario.[10] Choctaw headmen sought amicable trade relations in order to acquire the European manufactures on which Choctaws relied. War with the sole supplier of those goods promised disaster, but individuals and villages were entitled to behave as they saw fit to counteract the anguish engendered by the entrepreneurial system. Native groups throughout eastern North America felt these pressures owing to British ascendancy after the Seven Years' War. Several factors contributed to this, but "the withholding of gifts [by the British] must stand as one of the principal causes" of open tensions such as Pontiac's Revolt.[11]

British military and civil officials seized upon their own solution to the growing predicament. Their primary objective regarding southeastern Indians, after trade, aimed to prevent attacks on British settlers and traders. The numbers of potential Indian warriors in the Southeast, from the Creeks in the east to the Choctaws in the west, easily surpassed the sum of British troops in the Floridas.[12] Creeks expressed much displeasure at British occupation of the Floridas and had already killed British traders. British Indian policy initially sought to pacify them, with intimidation if necessary. At the same time, Britain could ill afford to enter into a war with a sizeable Native enemy. Consequently, British officials encouraged the Choctaws to do their dirty work for them.

General Thomas Gage, the British military commander for North America, encouraged Superintendent Stuart to prompt a conflict between the Creeks and Choctaws: "I therefore can't recommend it too strongly to you, so to foment the... bickering of the several tribes against each other and excite that jealousy so natural to all savages as shall be consistent with the peace security and welfare of His Majesty's subjects."[13] From the British point of view, an intertribal war solved the problem of potentially dangerous Indian men. When the Creeks and Choctaws obliged British designs by getting into such a war, Governor Johnstone displayed his satisfaction: "The present Rupture is very fortunate for us, more especially as it has been effected without giving them the least possibility of thinking we had any share in it. It was undoubtedly our Interest to foment the Disputes between those Nations... [and] I am of Opinion we should feed the war."[14] British officials congratulated themselves for starting the war and did their part to see it continue. Accordingly, most scholarly explanations of this war have focused on the British role as instigators.[15]

Choctaw and Creek reasons for fighting the war, however, did not include British meddling. In fact, with a few recent exceptions, scholars have overestimated the impact of European intruders, such as Gage and Johnstone.[16]

From the point of view of Choctaw elites, ongoing assaults between their warriors and the Creeks presented a solution to a society in turmoil. Instead of permitting revenge killings to remain localized, headmen chose to escalate the conflict into a full-fledged war. Quickly, they realized the potential of war with the Creeks to bridge the growing generational breach with their young men. Young men sought honor and prestige by participating in successful war parties, and they also needed an outlet for their antagonism toward trade abuses. Intertribal war offered an opportunity for headmen and warriors to pursue a common objective, while attempting to avoid violence toward Europeans in order to protect the trade relationship. War parties also required the power and expertise of established war leaders and therefore automatically reestablished a degree of chiefly authority. By promoting war, elites demonstrated that they were men of action, an essential characteristic for those who make claims to power.[17]

Choctaw reaction to the killing of a man named Suei Nantla by Creek Indians in the spring of 1766 supports this interpretation. Leaving no doubt of their identity, the Creek war party scalped the Choctaw and left "a Bloody War Stick and other hostile signals near [the body]."[18] The warclub produced its desired effect, for avenging Choctaw warriors soon killed six Creeks and captured a woman.[19] "Without doubt they'll have it Hot & Warm," John McGillivray, a British trader, predicted.[20] The warclub and a black bird's wing placed with Suei Nantla's body provided the needed spark. Choctaw leaders insisted the killing be punished in force:

> The Chactaws have sent a Challenge to Emistecigo [Upper Creek leader from the village of Little Tallassee] & they say they have lost above twenty Men at different Times, which makes them send this Challenge, as they are sure the Creeks have killed them. The Chactaws say they will send 100 Men to lye between Pensacola & the Upper Creeks to kill all they can find, & 100 Men against the Wolf Kings Town [Upper Creek leader from the village of Muccolossus] to destroy it, & 100 More against Paucana Talakasa [Little Tallassee] & have reserved 500 in the Nation to guard the women & Children, & told them that they would fight them in the Plains & not behind Trees like Cowards.[21]

That the Choctaws issued this threat of well-planned massive retaliation, involving numbers of warriors beyond the capacity of any single village, establishes intervillage agreement among elites. Because warriors from all three Choctaw political divisions, the Western, Eastern, and Six Towns, participated in the war from an early date, interdivisional cooperation existed as well.

Consensus between the Choctaw divisions rarely existed in practice and makes the Choctaw decision to wage war on the Creeks exceptional. However, the turbulent situation faced by all elites united them in common cause. They told the British that intertribal war enabled them to control aggressive warriors, "who not having done any feats during the War, think to gain Reputation and Name of Warrior by not consenting to make peace."[22] Chiefs earned respect from their fellow villagers by acquiring needed European goods, organizing hunting expeditions, conducting sacred rituals, leading war parties, and supervising relations with outsiders. The expanding conflict with the Creeks empowered chiefs to perform all of those roles.

Creek chiefs agreed that the war "will be a means of giving our young Men full exercise by which means the Chiefs expect to be the better able to govern them."[23] As the Creek leader Wolf King put it, "I am not sorry for it [war with the Choctaws], I will keep them [young men] at Home and from doing Mischief to the White people who I look on as Brothers."[24] Another Creek leader, Effatiskiniha, also known as "Mackay's Friend," told British agent David Taitt in 1772 that he led the first war party against the Choctaws and seized captives: "He says that he made war on purpose to keep his young people from falling out with the English, and as soon as his nation makes peace with the Choctaws he will spoil it again as he knows they must be at war with somebody." Such Creek sentiments describe the Choctaw position as well.[25]

Using war against the Creeks as the main method of protecting the trade relationship with Britain, Choctaw headmen never abandoned their lobbying efforts on behalf of gifts. Early in the war, all three Choctaw political divisions sent emissaries to Mobile. Mingo Houma Chito (Great Red Leader) from the village of East Imongoulasha (Eastern Division) pleaded in 1766 that lack of supplies threatened social stability: "My extreme poverty alone obliged me to come and trouble you this Day, particularly Ammunition, as for want of it I may have my head cut off in my own Town, and not be able to help myself ... [with] some ammunition to carry home; *I will send some work to my idle Warriors, who want it much.*"[26] Tomatle Mingo ("Leader who finishes or destroys") from Seneacha (Six Towns Division) promised that he could prevent contact between his young men and New Orleans traders if the British furnished supplies.[27] Shulustamastabé ("Red Shoes"), from the village of West

Yazoo (Western Division) recalled the British promise to keep them well supplied: "But I am sorry to find I am poor for ammunition, while I am surrounded with Enemies who are supplied it by the English toward the rising Sun [traders from Georgia and South Carolina], which gives them [Creeks] every Advantage they can wish for over us."[28]

Once having decided that war with the Creeks was both unavoidable and advantageous, Choctaw chiefs, warriors, and young men who wished "to gain Reputation and name of Warrior,"[29] manipulated the war toward several purposes. In order to succeed, war parties required sufficient ammunition and guns from the British. British officials proved quite willing to dispense the necessary weapons to Choctaws who promised to use them against the Creeks, but many warriors desired the supplies in order to hunt and thus participate more fully in the trade.[30] Choctaw men rationalized that either use of the weapons would allow them to prove "that all the Chactaws are not old Women."[31] Success in either hunting or war awarded Choctaw men the "abi" (or "abé") suffix to their name, designating them as "killers" or "slayers," giving them higher status.[32] At times, the two methods of procuring rank overlapped one another and resulted in tragedy.

In the autumn of 1767, for instance, hundreds of Choctaw men from all three divisions flooded the British posts at Tombeckby, Pensacola, and Mobile asking for guns and ammunition. Choctaws started their annual deer hunts in the autumn, but the British insisted that they use the supplies to attack the Creeks. One chief, Red Captain, of the village of Shatalaya in the Eastern Division, heeded the call and paid the ultimate price.[33] Out of a reported eight hundred Choctaws who traveled to Tombeckby to get ammunition, only Red Captain and a force of forty-two warriors stayed to strike the Creeks. Approximately 150 Creeks ambushed the party, killed twenty-four Choctaws and tortured Red Captain, skinning him alive.[34] Red Captain had a long record of working in the interest of the British, making his loss doubly profound. Most troubling from the British point of view, however, was the reluctance of other Choctaws to fight. Even the supposedly pro-British Shulustamastabé fled the battle soon after it began.[35] Although the deaths of twenty-five Choctaw warriors, including Red Captain's son and twelve others from his village, provoked cries for revenge, little retaliation took place. Prospective leaders were more interested in acquiring Red Captain's position as a British Great Medal Chief, which entitled them to extra gifts and greater access to trade goods.[36]

Young men certainly desired war titles and honors, but it seems that they often attempted the least dangerous method of attaining that higher status. In Red Captain's case, too few young men chose to attack the Creeks. In another instance, young men attacked a lone traveler too readily.

In February 1767, a war party led by the Small Medal Chief Chocoulacta, from the village of "Ebitabougoula ouchy" in the Eastern Division, accidentally killed a British settler while on the path from South Carolina to Natchez. Confused by the dark of night, Chocoulacta and "young men greedy of war names had flown to the man & scalped him before they knew him to be a white man."[37] The killing sparked an immediate reaction from divisional headmen. Several Eastern Division chiefs, including Olacta Houma, of "Iteokchakko," who was the "landlord" of Chocoulacta and his village, confirmed the killing and met to decide on punishment. Divisional chiefs, who were most responsible for overseeing relations with outsiders, perceived the murder as a serious threat to the maintenance of a mutually beneficial attachment to the British. Evidently, they had the authority to kill Chocoulacta in order to appease the British and prevent a rift from forming which jeopardized the trade relationship. Because he had admitted his mistake and reported it to Olacta Houma, the chiefs decided that Chocoulacta need not die.

Instead, Chocoulacta promised to bury the scalp and return the traveler's saddle and gun to the British commander at Fort Tombeckby. But the headmen remained extremely concerned about what the effects on the British might be, "in particular Olacta Houma his landlord, that he charged [Chocoulacta] to give no credits to the men that had been sent out to war with [him]."[38] Not only did the young men and warriors involved not receive recognition for a war exploit, but Olacta Houma confiscated Chocoulacta's British medal and even threatened to make him wear animal skins instead of his high-status manufactured clothing.[39] The Eastern Division headmen remained so concerned about this killing of an innocent British man that they sent a horse and deerskins to Superintendent Stuart as atonement, three years later. When it came to war and the honors to be gained by taking part, divisional headmen, even those like Olacta Houma who held no obvious recognition of status from the British, controlled the reins of power.[40]

The Choctaw division involved in the incidents concerning Red Captain and Chocoulacta (the Eastern Division) and the Western Division were the first to regard war with the Creeks as perhaps more harmful than beneficial. For five years war between the Choctaws and Creeks had continued, "in their manner, very few killed, but all in perpetual apprehension on both sides."[41] The Creeks were by far the more militant side, even going to the extreme of attacking the Chickasaws and the occasional British trader. Despite Chickasaw involvement on the side of the Choctaws and a Creek congress with the British in 1768 (during which they were resupplied with guns and ammunition), by 1770 both sides extended peace overtures. In particular, the Western and Eastern divisions of the Choctaws and the Upper Towns of the Creeks (the Creek political division located along the Coosa and Tallapoosas rivers and closest to the Choctaws) sought peace. They exchanged tobacco, pipes, strings of white beads, and white swans' wings, and the negotiations produced real progress. Yet, although most people of both sides desired peace, there were "a few fellows excepted on both sides, who not having done any feats during the War, think to gain Reputation and Name of Warrior by not consenting to make peace."[42] In particular, men from the Choctaw Six Towns Division and the Creek Lower Towns (the political division of Creek villages located on the Chatahoochee River), who had largely avoided participation in the war to this point, hoped to gain prestige through success in battle. Both Choctaws and Creeks viewed an attack by any member of the other as a renewal of the war, and when the Creeks murdered four Choctaws and kidnapped the niece of Mingo Houma Chito, a Great Medal Chief, peace dissolved in an outburst of revenge.[43] Once again the autonomy of divisions and young men proved decisive in circumventing the chiefs' attempts at cooperation.[44]

Other circumstances worked against the peace as well. John Stuart insisted, and the Creek Upper Towns and Choctaw Western and Eastern divisions accepted, that he act as a mediator to end the war. The use of neutral third parties to end conflicts was a common feature of southeastern Indian diplomacy.[45] Stuart attempted to bring about reconciliation until he received instructions from London that British imperial ambitions would be better served by keeping the two groups at odds. Because Britain had removed most of its troops from West Florida in the late 1760s to cut expenses, the government of West Florida feared that peace between Choctaws and Creeks would increase Indian visits and depredations. Additionally, Shawnee efforts to recruit Creeks into an anti-British confederacy increased British desires to see the Creeks occupied with an intertribal war. By December 1770, Stuart applauded himself for preventing the peace, notwithstanding the case that "Both Nations, with great reason, consider us as the Incendiaries who kindled the war."[46]

Choctaw leaders realized that peace was impossible as long as their destiny was so inextricably tied to British goals. Britain lacked the military capacity to defeat the Choctaws had they desired to do so, but they could disrupt relations between the Choctaws and Creeks and threaten to withhold the trade. Choctaw elites shifted their strategy after the peace failed; Eastern Division leaders abandoned the peace efforts, whereas chiefs of the Western Division preserved an open line of communication through the Chickasaw to the Creek Upper Towns. Leaders of both Choctaw divisions used the leverage of thousands of potentially uncontrollable warriors to chastise the British for supplying the Creeks while not doing the same for them. They demanded another gift-giving congress with which to reassert their redistributive authority and consequently keep young warriors in line.[47]

This time the pressure worked. Britain acquiesced finally in the winter of 1771–72, holding a conference more than six years after the previous one. Several medal chiefs had died in the meantime, some like Red Captain at the head of war parties against the Creeks, and the rise of new contenders to chiefly status needed to be verified with medals. This, plus the necessary gift exchanges and ceremonies, reaffirmed the Choctaw-British relationship. Contingents from each village left Mobile in January 1772, well supplied with guns, ammunition, cloth, and other merchandise.[48]

Although they continued to pursue peace with the Creeks, Western Division leaders simultaneously sent war parties against them. The other two divisions also continued to war, largely unsuccessfully, with the Creeks. In one battle during 1772, for instance, Creeks killed fifteen Choctaws while losing none of their own. Even Emistisiguo, who in the past had been very receptive to Choctaw peace overtures, led a party which scalped seven Choctaws. Two Choctaw Great Medal Chiefs, Tattoully Mastabé from Coosas and Cholko Oulacta from Ayanabe, and one Small Medal Chief, Yasi Mattaha from East Yazoo, lost their lives in the ongoing fighting. Despite the guns and other gifts received at the 1771–72 congress, Choctaw fortunes in the war seemed only to worsen.[49]

Suddenly, in 1773, Choctaw prospects in the eight-year-old war reversed. Well supplied and probably incensed at the loss of more medal chiefs, they began to defeat large Creek war parties. For the first time in the war, Choctaw chiefs seemed to recognize that the conflict must be brought to a favorable conclusion, rather than merely allowing it to fester without a decisive end. Their aggressive pursuit of Creeks garnered still more material support from the British and in turn strengthened their position as leaders. Britain helped further, in 1774, by cutting off trade with the Creeks in response to the killing of Georgia settlers. British officials failed to employ that strategy earlier out of fear the Creeks would react violently. But attacks on settlers required immediate and drastic actions, and the war with the Choctaws weakened Creek retaliation. The beneficiaries, as expected, were the Choctaws. Knowing the Creeks were poorly armed, Choctaws assailed them with large numbers. Choctaw leaders, such as Taska Oumastabé from the Western Division and Captain Houma from the Six Towns, journeyed to Mobile specifically offering their assistance to the British to punish the Creeks for killing Georgians. For the next two years they enjoyed stunning victories. They severely wounded Emistisiguo in an ambush, boldly attacked stragglers on the outskirts of Creek villages, and, most impressively, killed the staunchly anti-British Creek leader "The Mortar" and several of his men. Soon the Creeks suffered severe deprivation as they were unable to hunt safely. They appealed to the Chickasaws to help end the war once and for all.[50]

It so happened that a British imperial crisis aided the peace efforts. In 1775 instructions from General Gage and London urged Superintendent Stuart to promote peace between all of the southern Indian groups in order to enable their possible deployment against American "rebels." Western Division Choctaws and Upper Towns Creeks began negotiations, with the Chickasaws acting as intermediaries. Realizing that the two groups "are intent on making peace,"[51] John Stuart initiated mediating efforts of his own.[52]

Stuart's efforts reached fruition in October 1776. Choctaw and Creek peace delegations, dominated by the Choctaw Western and Eastern Divisions and the Creek Upper Towns, met in Pensacola and performed an elaborate diplomatic ritual to signify the end of fighting. Both groups, displaying white flags and white swans' wings, marched into an open area, stopping three hundred yards apart. The chiefs sang "peace songs" while waving eagles' and swans' wings over their heads. In a clever acknowledgment of the part that warriors and would-be warriors played in starting and continuing the war, a "false battle" was performed by the Choctaw and Creek young men. Then the two groups met, joined hands, and presented two red warclubs to Stuart to signify laying down their arms.[53] Further negotiations lasted two days. Final reconciliation took place the following July when a Choctaw delegation, headed by Western Division leaders, traveled to Emistisiguo's village of Little Tallassee and invited Creek chiefs to visit and assure the nation, the "young people" in particular, that peace was a reality.[54] Headmen from both sides clearly dominated the peace proceedings, but British generosity made internal social cohesion possible as both groups enjoyed frequent and plentiful gifts. The influx of guns and other items helped ensure a degree of Indian loyalty to the British as the War for American Independence began and, more importantly, bolstered the position of Native leaders within their respective societies.[55]

Choctaw chiefs weathered a nearly two-decade-long storm before they saw the return of gift-giving congresses on an annual basis. Spain, after defeating Britain in West Florida during the American Revolution, continued the annual congresses and regulated traders in Choctaw villages by giving the British Panton, Leslie and Company a monopoly on the Indian trade.[56] During the 1780s and 1790s, chiefs, especially those from the Western Division who came of age during the years of war with the Creeks, sought to establish additional trade relationships with Georgia and the United States, in part to satisfy disgruntled young men. Choctaws also continued to war with other native groups, especially those on the western side of the Mississippi River, as a way to channel animosities and provide opportunities for young men to acquire status.

Changed economic relations brought about by British occupation of the Floridas destabilized Choctaw political and social norms. Young men caused the anxiety which their chiefs, and many British traders and administrators, experienced. By attacking European property, they forced their chiefs to become more aggressive with the British and the Creeks. They ignored chiefly authority by interacting with British traders on their own initiative. Moreover, the power and authority that headmen exercised depended upon other Choctaws perceiving them as leaders. As abuses related to the trade relationship continued unabated, who were young men to turn to but themselves? Young men traveled to New Orleans to trade with the Spanish and French, and hunted ever greater numbers of deer to participate more effectively in the British trade. Choctaw elites demonstrated an inability to control their fellow villagers unless they acquired the presents of trade goods which made redistribution possible.

Nevertheless, headmen such as Olacta Houma, whose status did not rest upon British recognition, maintained their authority as the only legitimate decision makers and granters of war titles. The authority of such men rested in a sphere which originated solely within Choctaw culture. These men recognized the potential of an intertribal war to alleviate internal stress through a bonding of purpose with their young men. For some elites, such as Red Captain who did enjoy British recognition of his status, that bonding resulted in a fatal sacrifice to the goal of cross-generational cohesion.

We know that Native American intertribal warfare sometimes acted to remove competitors for trade resources or to replace population losses through adoption of war captives, as with the "Beaver Wars" between the Iroquois and Hurons.[57] Still others fought to conquer new lands, such as Lakota Sioux expansion on to the Plains.[58] In the Choctaw-Creek war, however, we are faced with reasons for fighting based upon generational conflict, the need to gain higher status, and the desire to transfer anxieties caused by changing economic relationships on to non-European targets, thus protecting access to value-laden goods. What is most striking is the sense that this solution to diverse predicaments by the Choctaws was not at all new. Archaeological evidence shows us that there was intertribal warfare throughout the Southeast before European arrival.[59] The reasons for those conflicts are perhaps forever obscure, but it is tempting to view Choctaw and Creek actions toward each other in the 1760s and 1770s as a manifestation of precontact notions of the proper way to handle a society-threatening crisis.

When Nassuba Mingo lost the power to "control" his "Warriours, their Wives & their Children,"[60] he and other elites preserved their authority by the best means available; they deflected tensions away from one source of authority and used them to bolster another. By so doing, they exhibited the resourcefulness necessary for preservation in an altered and rapidly changing world.

NOTES

This chapter originally appeared as "Protecting Trade through War: Choctaw Elites and British Occupation of the Floridas," in *Empire and Others: British Encounters with Indigenous Peoples, 1600–1850*, ed. Martin Daunton and Rick Halpern (Philadelphia: University of Pennsylvania Press, 1999), 149–66.

1. Dunbar Rowland, ed., *Mississippi Provincial Archives: English Dominion, 1763–1766* (Nashville, Tenn.: Brandon Printing, 1911), 242 (hereafter cited as *MPAED*).

2. Small numbers of French traders ventured to Choctaw villages and affiliated themselves with village leaders, thus preserving chiefly control. See Patricia Galloway, " 'The Chief Who is Your Father': Choctaw and French Views of the Diplomatic Relation," in *Powhatan's Mantle: Indians in the Colonial Southeast*, ed. Peter H. Wood, Gregory A. Waselkov, and M. Thomas Hatley (Lincoln: University of Nebraska Press, 1989), 271. For eighteenth-century references to Choctaw leaders' authority resting upon persuasion and redistributive abilities, see Jean Bernard Bossu, *Travels through That Part of North America Formerly Called Louisiana* (London, 1771), 294–95; Bernard Romans, *A Concise Natural History of East and West Florida* (1775; repr., Gainesville: University Press of Florida, 1962), 76; and "Memoir on Indians by Kerlerec [French Governor in New Orleans]," December 12, 1758," in *Mississippi Provincial Archives: French Dominion*, 5 vols. (hereafter cited as *MPAFD*); vols. 1–3, ed. Dunbar Rowland

and A. G. Sanders (Jackson: Mississippi Department of Archives and History, 1927–1932); vols. 4–5, ed. Dunbar Rowland, A. G. Sanders, and Patricia K. Galloway (Baton Rouge: Louisiana State University Press, 1984), 5:214.

3. The disruptions of the Seven Years' War prevented the French from holding annual congresses in the early 1760s, contributing further to Choctaw social disruption and exposing their utter dependence upon certain European goods. See Kerlerec to Berryer, June 8, 1761, Kerlerec to Choiseul, February 10, 1762, *MPAFD*, 5:271–2, 273; d'Abbadie to Farmar, October 14, 1763, and "a Counsel Held with the Tchaktaw Nation, 14 Nov. 1763," Great Britain Public Record Office, War Office (Library of Congress photostat copy), v. 49; Kerlerec to Major Robert Farmar, October 4, 1763, and George Johnstone and John Stuart on 1765 Mobile Congress, June 12, 1765, both in *MPAED*, 35, 187.

4. John Stuart to John Pownall, August 24, 1765, Great Britain Public Record Office, Colonial Office, Class 5, America and the West Indies, vol. 66 (hereafter cited as CO5/vol. no.).

5. Choctaw complaints about these conditions are sprinkled throughout British, French, and Spanish records, but the most accessible are found in the transcripts of British-Choctaw conferences in 1765 and 1771. See "Congress with the Chickasaws and Choctaws at Mobile, 26 March 1765," *MPAED*, 216–55, also in CO5/66; and "1771–1772 Congress with the Chickasaws and Choctaws," in "Peter Chester: Third Governor of the Province of British West Florida under British Dominion, 1770–1781," Eron O. Rowland, ed., *Publications of the Mississippi Historical Society*, centenary series, 5 (1925): 134–59; also in CO5/73. For increased use of alcohol by traders after 1763, see also Peter C. Mancall, *Deadly Medicine: Indians and Alcohol in Early America* (Ithaca, N.Y.: Cornell University Press, 1995), chap. 7.

6. Johnstone and Stuart on the 1765 Congress, June 12, 1765, *MPAED*, 187.

7. "The talk of the head warrior of the Choctaws [unnamed]," in "A congress held at Pensacola with several Indian chiefs of the Creek nation and chiefs of other nations, 10 Sept. 1764," General Thomas Gage Papers, American Series, William L. Clements Library, University of Michigan, Ann Arbor, v. 24 (hereafter cited as Gage Papers).

8. René Roi [interpreter to Indians] to John Stuart, August 11, 1769, CO5/70.

9. Edmund J. Gardner Papers, Gilcrease Institute of American History and Art, Tulsa, Oklahoma, "Choctaw People File"; and Amelia R. Bell, "Separate People: Speaking of Creek Men and Women," *American Anthropologist* 92 (1990): 336–37.

10. Daniel H. Usner Jr., *Indians, Settlers, and Slaves in a Frontier Exchange Economy: The Lower Mississippi Valley before 1783* (Chapel Hill: University of North Carolina Press, 1992), 127–30, discusses the acts of banditry committed by Choctaws against outlying European settlements, but does not consider the Choctaw-Creek War and its potential to lessen the severity of these confrontations.

11. James A. Brown, "The Impact of the European Presence on Indian Culture," in *Contest for Empire: 1500–1775*, ed. John B. Elliott (Indianapolis: Indiana Historical Society, 1975), 12.

12. Circa 1775, Choctaw and Creek total populations numbered approximately 14,000 each, with warrior populations estimated at slightly more than 4,000 each; see

Peter H. Wood, "The Changing Population of the Colonial South: An Overview by Race and Region, 1685-1790," in Wood, Waselkov, and Hatley, *Powhatan's Mantle*, 38, 72. British troops in West Florida, on the other hand, numbered just over 1,000 men in 1766; see "An estimate of the expense of provision... [1766]," Earl of Shelburne Papers, William L. Clements Library, University of Michigan, Ann Arbor, v. 50, "Indian trade" (hereafter cited as Shelburne Papers).

13. Gage to Stuart, January 27, 1764, Gage Papers, v. 13. Similarly, Gage remarked to the Northern Superintendent of Indian Affairs, William Johnson, that "it's my Opinion as long as they [Creeks and Choctaws] Quarell with one another we shall be well with them all[.] And when they are all at Peace, It's the Signal for us to have a good look out," in *The Papers of Sir William Johnson*, ed. Alexander C. Flick (Albany: University of the State of New York, 1921–65), 4:304 (hereafter cited as *Johnson Papers*).

14. Johnstone to Shelburne, May 19, 1766, CO5/67. See also "Governor Johnstone's report to Mr. Conway, 23 June 1766," *MPAED*, 511–12; Johnstone to John Stuart, May 19, 1766, Gage Papers, v. 55; Governor Wright [of East Florida] to John Stuart, July 10, 1766, CO5/67; and Robin F. A. Fabel, *Bombast and Broadsides: The Lives of George Johnstone* (Tuscaloosa: University of Alabama Press, 1987), 54–57.

15. Clarence E. Carter, "The Beginnings of British West Florida," *Mississippi Valley Historical Review* 4, no. 3 (1917): 337–38; Angie Debo, *The Rise and Fall of the Choctaw Republic* (Norman: University of Oklahoma Press, 1934), 31; John R. Alden, *John Stuart and the Southern Colonial Frontier* (Ann Arbor: University of Michigan Press, 1944), 224–28; Robert S. Cotterill, *The Southern Indians: The Story of the Civilized Tribes Before Removal* (Norman: University of Oklahoma Press., 1954), 33–34; David H. Corkran, *The Creek Frontier, 1540–1783* (Norman: University of Oklahoma Press, 1967), 254–55; James H. O'Donnell III, "The Southern Indians in the War for American Independence, 1775–1783," in *Four Centuries of Southern Indians*, ed. Charles Hudson (Athens: University of Georgia Press, 1975), 49–50; Richard White, *The Roots of Dependency: Subsistence, Environment, and Social Change among the Choctaws, Pawnees, and Navajos* (Lincoln: University of Nebraska Press, 1983), 76–79; and Jesse O. McKee, *The Choctaw* (New York and Philadelphia, 1989), 30.

16. Current thinking on the causes of the war have taken seriously Choctaw and Creek motivations. Historian Kathryn Braund, in *Deerskins and Duffels: Creek Indian Trade with Anglo-America, 1685–1815* (Lincoln: University of Nebraska Press, 1993), 133–34, placed the onus of starting the war on the Creeks who acted to prevent Choctaw access to British trade. Clara Sue Kidwell follows this interpretation in *Choctaws and Missionaries in Mississippi, 1818–1918* (Norman: University of Oklahoma Press, 1995), 12. But Braund does not resolve why Choctaws willingly continued the war when British occupation of Mobile brought them unimpeded access to European trade. In the late seventeenth and early eighteenth centuries, Creeks often obstructed Choctaw access to British traders on the Atlantic Coast, but the British occupation of the Gulf Coast from Pensacola to the Mississippi River made their blockade ineffectual. Superintendent Stuart informed two Choctaw leaders as early as 1763 that traders could soon be expected from Mobile, thus circumventing the creeks (see Governors of Georgia, Virginia, Carolinas, and John Stuart on Southern Indian Relations, No-

vember 10, 1763, CO5/65). Sociologist Duane Champagne, *Social Order and Political Change: Constitutional Governments among the Cherokee, the Choctaw, the Chickasaw, and the Creek* (Stanford, Calif.: Stanford University Press, 1992), 72–73, offered a scenario in which Choctaws and Creeks fought over hunting resources along the Choctaws' eastern boundary on the Tombigbee River. But at least one third of the Choctaws (the Western Division, which constituted one of three geographic and political divisions) held no claim to those lands, and they participated in the war as enthusiastically as any other group of Choctaws. Additionally, all Choctaws responded to a declining deer population by hunting in the west across the Mississippi River. See Lt. John Ritchey to Brig. Gen. Taylor, December 27, 1767, British Museum: Additional Manuscripts, Library of Congress photostat copy, no. 21671, part 3 (hereafter cited as BMAM); and Lawrence and Lucia B. Kinnaird, "Choctaws West of the Mississippi, 1766–1800," *Southwestern Historical Quarterly* 83 (April 1980): 349–70.

17. Mary W. Helms, *Craft and the Kingly Ideal: Art, Trade, and Power* (Austin: University of Texas Press, 1993), 136.

18. Elias Legardee to Governor Johnstone, March 27, 1766, BMAM, no. 21671, part 1.

19. William Tayler to General Thomas Gage, June 1, 1766, Gage Papers v. 52. Warclubs served as the main symbol of war and south-eastern Indians repeatedly left them at the scene of a killing in order to incite their enemies: see Charles Hudson, *The Southeastern Indians* (Knoxville: University of Tennessee Press, 1976), 245–47, and Wayne William VanHorne, *The Warclub: Weapon and Symbol in Southeastern Indian Societies* (Ph.D. diss., University of Georgia, 1993).

20. John McGillivray to Charles Stuart [Deputy Superintendent to the Choctaws and Chickasaws], May 10, 1766, Shelburne Papers, v. 60, "Indian trade," 81.

21. S. Forrester to Johnstone, May 25, 1766, BMAM, no. 21671, part 1. See also William Struthers to Johnstone, May 20, 1766, *MPAED*, 522. British military officers mistakenly interpreted the "black wing" as a call for the Choctaws to join the Creeks in alliance against the English and expressed relief that war between them broke out instead. See Colonel Taylor to Gage, September 18, 1766, BMAM, no. 21671, part 2.

22. Charles Stuart to John Stuart, June 12, 1770, Gage Papers, v. 94.

23. Talk by "Molten" [the Mortar?], quoted in James Germany to Johnstone, June 28, 1766, BMAM, no. 21671, part 1.

24. Wolf King to Johnstone, June 28, 1766, enclosed in James Germany to Johnstone, June 28, 1766, BMAM, no. 21671, part 1.

25. "David Taitt's Journal To and Through the Upper Creek Nation, 1772," in *Travels in the American Colonies*, ed. Newton D. Mereness (New York: Macmillan, 1916), 532–34, also in *Documents of the American Revolution, 1770–1783*, ed. K. G. Davies, 21 vols. (Shannon: Irish University Press, 1972), 5:265–66 (hereafter cited as *DAR*).

26. "Mingo Houma Chito of Imongoulasha in the East. His talk to the deputy superintendent, 27 July 1766," CO5/67, emphasis added.

27. "Tomatle Mingo, Great Medal Chief of Seneacha, his talk to the deputy superintendent, 12 July 1766," CO5/67.

28. "Shouloustamastabe, alias Red Shoes, his talk to the deputy superintendent, 4 July 1766," CO5/67.

29. Charles Stuart to John Stuart, June 12, 1770, Gage Papers, v. 94.

30. Lt. John Ritchey of Fort Tombeckby complained about this situation in a letter to Brig. Gen. Taylor dated December 27, 1766, BMAM, no. 21671, part 3.

31. "Shouloustamastabe, alias Red Shoes, his talk to the deputy superintendent, 4 July 1766," CO5/67.

32. Cyrus Byington, *A Dictionary of the Choctaw Language*, Bureau of American Ethnology Bulletin 46, ed. John Swanton and Henry S. Halbert (Washington, D.C.: U.S. Government Printing Office, 1915), 73; Henry C. Benson, *Life among the Choctaw Indians, and Sketches of the Southwest* (1860; repr., New York: Johnson Reprint Co., 1970), 53; and John R. Swanton, *Source Material for the Social and Ceremonial Life of the Choctaw Indians*, Bureau of American Ethnology Bulletin 103 (Washington, D.C.: U.S. Government Printing Office, 1931), 119–24.

33. Patricia Galloway, "'So many little republics': British negotiations with the Choctaw Confederacy, 1765," *Ethnohistory* 41, no. 4 (1994): 519, 528, and n. 37, lists Red Captain's village as "Chicktalaya" with no divisional designation. This is probably a version of "Shatalaya" as found in "Conferences with 73 Chactaw Head Warriors, 1 Nov. 1759" (William Henry Lyttelton Papers, William L. Clements Library, University of Michigan, Ann Arbor), when Red Captain attended negotiations with the British at the Creek village of Okfuskee. At that time, Red Captain was listed as the "Chief Leader of the Great Red Mingo of Betapoucoulou's Men." Betapoucoulou was an Eastern Division village. The Eastern Division affiliation is also evident from trader James Adair's description (*History of the American Indians*, ed. Samuel Cole Williams [1775; repr., Johnson City, Tenn.: Watauga Press, 1930], 292–93) of Red Captain's home as being in a "northern barrier town" that was within one day's ride from Fort Tombeckby on the eastern Choctaw boundary. This material further clarifies one of Galloway's arguments in the above article that most Eastern Division leaders (except Red Captain and another leader named Alibamon Mingo) wavered about whether to meet with the British in 1765. For maps of the Choctaw homeland, see esp. "Part of the Purcell Map [by John Stuart] 1760s," reprinted as plate 7 in John R. Swanton, *Early History of the Creek Indians and Their Neighbors*, Bureau of American Ethnology Bulletin 73 (Washington, D.C.: U.S. Government Printing Office, 1922); and Henry S. Halbert, "Bernard Roman's map of 1772," *Mississippi Historical Society Publications* 6 (1902): 415–39.

34. Trader James Adair's well-known *History of the American Indians* (pp. 312–14) offers a compelling portrayal of Red Captain's last days which concurs with other documentary sources (listed below) including the statement that two white traders betrayed the Choctaw war party's whereabouts. Only ten Creeks died in the battle. See James Hewitt (trader to the Choctaws) to McGillivray and Struthers (Trading Co.), October 16, 1767; Charles Stuart to John Stuart, October 29, 1767; and John Stuart to Gage, November 27, 1767, all in Gage Papers, v. 72; Roderick MacIntosh (commissary in the Creek Nation) to John Stuart, November 16, 1767, and John Stuart to Gage, December 26, 1767, both in Gage Papers, v. 73; John Stuart to Earl of Shelburne, May 7, 1768, CO5/69; John Stuart to Gage, May 17,1768, Gage Papers, v. 77; and John Stuart to Hillsborough, December 28, 1768, CO5/70.

35. This probably happened because Shulustamastabé and Red Captain were war leaders from different divisions and therefore probably unwilling to serve under the other's command in a war party.

36. European governments recognized southeastern Indian leaders on three levels: Great Medal, Small Medal, and Captains (warriors with commissions).

37. "Deposition of John Farrell, packhorseman in the Choctaw Nation, 4 March 1767," BMAM, no. 21671, part 4.

38. Ibid.

39. Trader Nathanial Folsom reported that late eighteenth-century Choctaws wore European clothing when buried if they were an important person or chief, while others were buried in blankets or "sum other old worn out [animal] skin": "Discussion of Choctaw history by Nathaniel Folsom, [1798?]," Peter Pitchlynn Papers, Gilcrease Institute of American History and Art, Tulsa, Okla., hereafter cited as "Folsom Discussion."

40. Chocoulacta regained his Small Medal Chief status at the 1771–72 Mobile Congress at which he supplicated to Stuart while painted in white clay and accompanied by four Great Medal Chiefs and about a thousand other Choctaws. See Ritchey to Elias Legardére, March 4, 1767, and Legardére to Charles Stuart, March 4, 1767, both in BMAM, no. 21671, part 4; Taylor to Gage, March 22, 1767, Gage Papers, v. 63; Charles Stuart to John Stuart, June 12, 1770, Gage Papers, v. 94; and John Stuart to Hillsborough, February 7, 1772, CO5/73.

41. Taylor to Gage, March 4, 1767, BMAM, no. 21671, part 4.

42. Charles Stuart to John Stuart, June 12, 1779, Gage Papers, v. 94.

43. Ibid. Mingo Houma Chito ("Great Red Leader") hailed from the village of East Imongoulasha in the Eastern Division.

44. See Upper House of Assembly [of West Florida] to Earl of Hillsborough, August 24, 1768, in *The Minutes, Journals, and Acts of the General Assembly of British West Florida*, ed. Robert R. Rea and Milo B. Howard Jr. (Tuscaloosa: University of Alabama Press, 1979), 146; John Stuart to Hillsborough, June 8, 1770, CO5/71; Emistisiguo to Charles Stuart (July–August) 1770, CO5/72; Charles Stuart to John Stuart, June 17, 1770, August 26, 1770, September 27, 1770, and December 26, 1770, CO5/72; Elias Durnford to Hillsborough, July 8, 1770, DAR, 1:139; Charles Stuart to the Creeks, December 12, 1770, CO5/72; and Gage to Hillsborough, January 16, 1771, in *The Correspondence of General Thomas Gage*, ed. Clarence E. Carter, 2 vols. (New Haven, Conn.: Yale University Press, 1931), 1:289 (hereafter cited as *Gage Correspondence*).

Richard White (*Roots of Dependency*, 78) contended that, rather than fighting to gain war titles, the Six Towns and Lower Creeks fought over hunting resources on the lower Tombigbee River. This is confirmed by Nathaniel Folsom who, at the end of the eighteenth century, cited an aged Choctaw man named "Osha humah" (a.k.a. "the Irish Man") who stated that the Creeks wanted too much Choctaw hunting territory ("Folsom Discussion"). However, both views are likely correct since it was access to hunting and the status it provided, as well as war and the rank it bestowed on successful warriors, that were at issue. Neither the Choctaws nor Creeks sought to occupy the disputed territory; rather they both sought to preserve a boundary area that would continue to support game. Mississippian ancestors of the Creeks and Choctaws rarely fought to conquer territory. See Jon L. Gibson, "Aboriginal Warfare in the Southeast: An Alternative Perspective," *American Antiquity* 39, no. 1 (1974): 130–33.

45. See David H. Dye, "Feasting with the Enemy: Mississippian Warfare and Prestige-Goods Circulation," in *Native American Interactions: Multiscalar Analyses and Interpretations in the Eastern Woodlands*, ed. Michael S. Nassaney and Kenneth E. Sassaman (Knoxville: University of Tennessee Press, 1995), 300–301.

46. John Stuart to Hillsborough, December 2, 1770, CO5/72. See also Gage to Hillsborough, July 7, 1770, *Gage Correspondence*, 1:262; Charles Stuart to John Stuart, June 12, 1770, CO5/71; John Stuart to Hillsborough, July 16, 1770, CO5/71; Governor James Wright [Georgia] to Hillsborough, December 8, 1770 and July 20, 1771, *DAR*, 1:225, 2:151; Charles Stuart to John Stuart, August 26, 1770, September 27, 1770, and December 26, 1770, CO5/72; Hillsborough to Gage, September 28, 1770, *Gage Correspondence*, 2:117; John Stuart to Head Warriors of Upper Creeks, November 25, 1770, CO5/72; John Stuart to Haldimand, January 23, 1771, BMAM, no. 21672, part 1; Hillsborough to John Stuart, February 11, 1771, *DAR*, 1:267; Governor Peter Chester [West Florida] to Hillsborough, March 9, 1771, *DAR*, 3:64–67; and Gage to Johnson 1 April 1771, *Johnson Papers*, 8:58. For insistence that the war adversely affected trader's profits, see [Anonymous], "Survey of West Florida, 1768," in *Colonial Captivities, Marches, and Journeys*, ed. Isabel M. Calder (New York: Macmillan, 1935), 230; and "Memorial of traders to Creek and Cherokee nations to Governor James Wright June 1771," *DAR*, 3:126.

47. Peter Chester to John Stuart, September 10, 1771, in Rowland, "Peter Chester," 102.

48. John Stuart to Hillsborough, February 7, 1772, CO5/73; John Stuart to Gage, February 16, 1772, Gage Papers, v. 109; and "A list of towns in the Chactaw nation with the names of the Indians in each town receiving presents at the Congress, 1771–1772," CO5/73.

49. John Stuart to Gage, May 15, 1772, and May 23, 1772, Gage Papers, v. 111; Charles Stuart to John Stuart, March 17, 1773, Gage Papers, v. 118; and Gov. Sir James Wright [Georgia] to Earl of Dartmouth, June 17, 1773, *DAR*, 6:157.

50. Robert Mackay to John Stuart, November 30,1773, David Taitt to John Stuart, January 3,1774, January 12, 1774, and January 24, 1774, Wright to John Stuart, January 27, 1774, all in CO5/75; John Stuart to Haldimand, February 3, 1774, *DAR*, 8:34–37; John Stuart to Earl of Dartmouth, February 13, 1774, *DAR*, 8:49; Charles Stuart to John Stuart, May 12, 1774, Gage Papers, v. 119; same to same, May 19, 1774, CO5/75; John Stuart to Gage, July 3, 1774, Gage Papers, v. 120; John Stuart to Earl of Dartmouth, August 2, 1774, CO5/75; John Stuart to Gage, November 19, 1774, Gage Papers, v. 124; Charles Stuart to John Stuart, December 12, 1774, CO5/76; John Stuart to Gage, January 18, 1775, Gage Papers, v. 125; "Letters from West Florida, 6 Jan. 1775," in *American Archives: A Documentary History*, 4th series, ed. Peter Force (Washington, D.C., 1837), 1:1099; and *South Carolina Gazette*, May 24, 1773. See also note 46.

51. John Stuart to Germain, June 6, 1776, Lord Germain Papers, William L. Clements Library, University of Michigan, Ann Arbor, v. 5.

52. Gage to John Stuart, September 12, 1775, CO5/76; John Stuart to Gage, October 3, 1775, National Archives Microfilm Publications, *Papers of the Continental Congress, 1774–1789* (M247, r65, i51, v1, p. 159); David Taitt to John Stuart, October 20, 1775, Niaha Thlaco [Creek] to John Stuart, October 20, 1775, John Stuart to Earl of Dartmouth, January 6, 1776, John Stuart to Maj. Gen. Henry Clinton, March 15, 1776, same to same, August 23, 1776, and same to same, September 16, 1776, all in CO5/77; and Germain to John Stuart, September 5, 1776, Lord George Germain Papers.

53. The "false battle" was likely performed as a ritualized hand-to-hand combat with warclubs, rather than with guns or bows and arrows. The warclub was absolutely vital to the prowess of a warrior in battle and provided a direct link to precontact Mississippian times during which skill in hand-to-hand fighting was far more important than proficiency in killing from a distance. See VanHorne, *The Warclub*, esp. 49, 105.

54. David Taitt to John Stuart, August 3, 1777, CO5/78.

55. John Stuart to Germain, October 26, 1776; John Stuart to Brig..Gen. Augustin Provost, July 24, 1777, John Stuart to William Knox, July 26, 1777; Taitt to John Stuart, August 3, 1777, and John Stuart to Germain, August 22, 1777, all in CO5/78; and Charles Stuart to John Stuart, March 7, 1778, in Guy Carleton, Lord Dorchester Papers, 1747–83, microfilm copy, University of Michigan Libraries, Ann Arbor.

56. See William S. Coker and Thomas D. Watson, *Indian Traders of the Southeastern Borderlands: Panton, Leslie & Company and John Forbes & Company, 1783–1847* (Gainesville: University Press of Florida, 1986).

57. Daniel K. Richter, "War and Culture: The Iroquois Experience," *William and Mary Quarterly* 40, no. 4 (1983): 528–59.

58. Richard White, "The Winning of the West: The Expansion of the Western Sioux in the Eighteenth and Nineteenth Centuries," *Journal of American History* 65 (September 1978): 319–43.

59. See, for example, David H. Dye, "Warfare in the Sixteenth-Century Southeast: The de Soto Expedition in the Interior," in *Columbian Consequences*, vol. 2, *Archeological and Historical Perspectives on the Spanish Borderlands East*, ed. David Hurst Thomas (Washington, D.C.: Smithsonian Institution Press, 1992), 211–22.

60. *MPAED*, 242.

CHAPTER 6

The Choctaw Defense of Pensacola in the American Revolution

Greg O'Brien

Authors of history textbooks sometimes forget that the world war that resulted from the American Revolution manifested itself in part on the North American coast of the Gulf of Mexico. Two British colonies, East Florida and West Florida, had existed there since the Seven Years' War ended in 1763. Those colonies remained loyal to the mother country during the Revolution and found themselves in a desperate fight against enemies determined to remove the British military presence from the area. To students of Florida and Gulf South history, the basic setting is familiar: Spain, which possessed New Orleans and territory west of the Mississippi River, declared war on Britain in June 1779. By March 1780 Spanish forces under the governor of Louisiana, Bernardo de Gálvez, had captured the British posts of Manchac, Baton Rouge, and Natchez along the Mississippi River, as well as Mobile on the Gulf Coast. The only remaining major British position on the Gulf Coast was Pensacola, the capital of West Florida. Gálvez's forces, including French and African Louisianans, the French navy, a brigade of Irish troops, and some Indians, prepared for the siege of Pensacola for over a year, while British forces similarly prepared to defend Pensacola with British regulars, Hessian mercenaries, Maryland and Pennsylvania loyalists, local citizens, Africans (slave and free), and American Indians. Eventually, after a two-month-long naval blockade and siege of Pensacola, Spanish artillery found its mark, hitting the British gunpowder magazine at Fort George on May 8, 1781. The British immediately surrendered, abandoning the Gulf Coast and, after the Treaty of Paris in 1783, the entire Florida peninsula to the Spanish.[1]

Perhaps because the Gulf Coast has been historically overlooked in discussions of the American Revolution, studies examining the Pensacola battle between Spain and Britain say little about the role and motivations of Indian people in the conflict.[2] The scarcity of scholarly attention to Indian perspectives exists even though thousands of Creek, Chickasaw, Choctaw, and other Indians fought in and around major battle sites like Mobile and Pensacola from 1779 to 1781. Another reason that the significance of Indian involvement at Pensacola and other Revolutionary-era battles in the Gulf South has gone largely unnoticed is that no Americans were involved in the fighting. Though Britain lost these battles, Spanish efforts on the side of the United States have been viewed more as a sideshow than as crucial to victory in the war. Conceivably Indian participation in these Revolutionary War battles has been underemphasized because most Indian forces aided Britain, and the British ultimately failed to hold either Mobile or Pensacola. Thus, defeat contributed to the seeming insignificance of Indian involvement, though some Indian peoples—including a significant number of Choctaws—aided Spain's victorious military actions in the Revolutionary Gulf South. The majority of Indian allies, however, executed the bulk of offensive maneuvers against the Spanish and enabled Britain to keep Pensacola through May 1781. As British Indian Superintendent Alexander Cameron claimed in June 1780, "Our being still possessed of [Pensacola] is entirely owing to the great number of Indians that speedily repaired hither to our assistance" after the fall of Mobile.[3]

Over sixteen hundred Indians journeyed to Pensacola to support the British after the fall of Mobile in March 1780. The British military commander at Pensacola, Major General John Campbell, counted 1,235 Creeks, 236 Choctaws, and 31 Chickasaws at Pensacola in April and credited them with deterring the enemy from attacking at that time.[4] Initially, the Creeks supplied the largest force, but by May most of them abandoned the Pensacola area when it was obvious that a Spanish attack was not imminent.[5] The threat of exposure to deadly diseases may have also encouraged the Creeks to leave Pensacola hurriedly, since some of them had contracted smallpox there the year before and the disease had spread throughout their villages.[6] Choctaws comprised the greatest number of Indians who remained in Pensacola to defend British positions for the long term. As the Spanish began to implement their siege of Pensacola in February 1781, 744 Choctaws from twenty villages could be counted among the British defenders, out of 788 total Indians in the town.[7] These Indian forces comprised between one-third and one-half of all military defenders of Pensacola, but Campbell, mistakenly thinking that the Spanish attack was not imminent, sent about three hundred Choctaws home just before the Spanish fleet arrived to establish a blockade. When the Spanish ships showed up in Pensacola Bay in February, about 150 Choctaws returned to join the four hundred or so who remained there, and other Creek and Chickasaw forces arrived in small numbers throughout the following three months.[8]

Choctaws had already proven themselves one of the most versatile military forces available to the British in the Revolutionary-era Gulf South. After full-scale war erupted between some of Britain's American colonies and the mother country, British officials in Mobile held a conference with the Choctaws in 1777 to cement their alliance.[9] Since 1777 the British Southern Indian Department, under the leadership of Superintendent John Stuart, paid Choctaws and Chickasaws to patrol the Mississippi River and to report and confront any American expedition that journeyed from the north. In 1778 one such American expedition led by Captain James Willing got through when the Choctaws coincidentally abandoned their posts to return to their villages to visit family members. With only handfuls of troops stationed along the lower Mississippi River, the British response to the raid was to urge and pay the Choctaws to pursue the Americans. By the time Choctaws from the Western Division, one of three politically and geographically distinct groupings of Choctaw villages, reached the area's most important European settlement at Natchez, the American expedition had already arrived in Spanish New Orleans, but the Choctaws occupied Natchez for weeks and convinced residents there to remain loyal to Britain.[10] In April and May 1779 the British held a meeting with Choctaw and Chickasaw representatives at Mobile at which a thousand guns and numerous other items were distributed to the Choctaws in order to firm up their friendship and willingness to fight for the British.[11] In Mobile in late June 1779, the British Southern Indian Department loaded Indian agent Farquhar Bethune with gifts to take to the Choctaw villages to again reinforce the British-Choctaw alliance.[12] In July 1779 another British agent, Robert Tait, brought gifts in payment for the Choctaw expedition to Natchez the previous year. The Western Division town of West Yazoo received the most merchandise, as it was one of the town's war leaders, Franchimastabé, who organized the Choctaw expedition to Natchez.[13] At least 239 Choctaw warriors responded to British pleas to defend Mobile as the Spanish quickly occupied British posts along the lower Mississippi River in late 1779.[14] In Mobile the fight was primarily in the form of a Spanish naval blockade and bombardment, leaving little opportunity for Britain's Indian allies to respond and stop the Spanish takeover of the town. During the Spanish siege of Mobile in February and March 1780, groups of Choctaws journeyed to Pensacola to smoke the calumet with Superintendent Cameron and receive gifts to maintain their alliance with Britain.[15] After the fall of Mobile in March 1780, Choctaw groups who traveled to Pensacola chided the British for being "frightened" of the Spanish, and one Choctaw chief advised the Hessian forces in Pensacola that "if the whites would be as good warriors as the reds, he was certain that they would defeat the enemy."[16] Before the Pensacola campaign began, Choctaws had proven their willingness to come to Britain's aid when compensated, but Choctaws were not necessarily pro-British.

Choctaw foreign relations never followed a single national course through the time of the American Revolution or for many decades beyond. Choctaw politics and diplomacy were largely carried out at the village or, at most, the divisional level. Eighteenth-century Choctaw society was divided into three primary politically and geographically distinct divisions that also reflected ethnic differences among the people calling themselves "Chahtas." Each division, called the Western, Eastern, and Six Towns (or Southern) divisions by the British, encompassed several to dozens of villages and thousands of people with a total population somewhere between fifteen thousand to twenty thousand persons. The equivalent Choctaw terms for the three divisions reflected the ethnic distinctiveness and unique origins of each one: with the Western Division being known as *Okla falaya* (people who are widely dispersed), the Eastern Division referred to as *Okla tannap* (people from the other side), and *Okla hannali* (people of six towns). In such a noncentralized leadership structure decisions about whether or not to participate in a war involving European powers, and about which side to support, rested with divisional and village elites and war chiefs rather than with any national or confederation-level political body. It is incorrect to speak of the Choctaws as being pro-British, pro-Spanish, or pro-American since there was no national policy; in fact, Choctaws could and did support more than one side at the same time. We can generalize that Western and Eastern division leaders and warriors tended to act on behalf of Britain while Six Towns combatants tended to assist Spain. From the fall of Mobile in 1780 to the Battle of Pensacola in 1781, Choctaws from different divisions could be found aiding both Spain and Britain. To Choctaws, there was no contradiction for some to interact and ally with one European country while other Choctaws maintained contact with the opposing European nation. Choctaw people had always constructed relationships with as many European entities as possible to get access to trade and enhance their status. Only once, in the Choctaw civil war of 1746–50 when Choctaws disagreed over whether to support France or Britain, did this divisional and village independence result in Choctaws attacking each other. In that civil war, Eastern Division warriors burned Western Division villages to the ground, and hundreds died on both sides. The lessons of that deadly civil war had been learned by the 1770s, however, and no Choctaws fought against each other during the American Revolution, even though Choctaw people supported both sides. Unlike the destruction and permanent split that happened to the Iroquois Confederacy during the Revolution, when Oneidas and Tuscaroras supported the American side and fought against other Iroquois allied with Britain at the Battle of Oriskany, Choctaws never allowed themselves to become so devoted to either the cause of Britain or Spain that they would spill the blood of other Choctaws.[17]

Though some Six Towns Choctaws allied with Spain, it is a stretch to say that Choctaws supported the Americans during the Revolution. Other than opposing Willing's raid down the Mississippi River, the Choctaws had no concern one way or the other for the Americans. The United States was too new and too distant to be a known entity to Choctaws, until the first diplomatic meeting between the Choctaws and the United States after the Revolution at Hopewell, South Carolina, in the winter of 1785–86.[18] Nevertheless, a son of missionaries sent to minister to the Choctaws in the early nineteenth century, Horatio B. Cushman, insisted, in a rambling and at times demonstrably incorrect book, that the Choctaws had in fact supported the Americans during the Revolutionary War with Choctaw scouts serving in several American armies.[19] This single claim of Choctaw support for American aims in the Revolution has been repeated by some subsequent historians to the point that it is now considered by many to be conventional wisdom.[20] By uncritically accepting and repeating a mistaken assertion as fact without properly investigating the claim, adherents of the notion that the Choctaws directly assisted the United States in the American Revolution have propagated one of the greatest myths in Choctaw history. Choctaw scholar Anna Lewis wrote in her generally well-researched biography of Pushmataha that "there is little or no record" of the Choctaws supporting the United States in the American Revolution, but she then proceeded to say that "there is no doubt" that they did so. Lewis went so far as to repeat Cushman's assertion that the "Choctaw war whoop struck terror" in the hearts of the British and Cherokees.[21] The rhetoric of the American and Choctaw delegates at the Hopewell meeting, however, makes it clear that these two powers had never before interacted with one another. Moreover, there are no records to my knowledge of Choctaws supporting American military efforts until the war between the United States and the Ohio Valley Indians erupted in the early 1790s, whereas Choctaw actions in support of Britain or Spain during the American Revolution are clearly demonstrated in countless published and archival documents. Cushman may have confused the later Choctaw support of the Americans in the 1790s, or the still later Choctaw alliance with the United States against the Red Stick Creeks during the War of 1812, with the Revolutionary era. Or perhaps Cushman had other motives for portraying the Choctaws as pro-American since the Revolution. Regardless of the reason for Cushman's mistake, his assertion has further muddied the waters surrounding the role the Choctaws played in the American Revolution.

The diffused political structure of the Choctaws frustrated both Spanish and British authorities in the lead-up to the Pensacola campaign. British Indian agent Alexander Cameron called the Choctaws "the most mercenary of Indians" in July 1780, and he feared that they would soon fight a civil war as chiefs jockeyed for position and sought access to whichever Europeans could supply them with the most manufactured goods. Cameron had reason to worry because Spanish officials had aggressively courted the Choctaws even before the capture of Mobile and had increased their overtures since then.[22] In 1779 Spanish officials hosted seventeen Choctaw chiefs and 480 warriors at a conference in New Orleans where they exchanged their British commissions, medals, and other symbols of authority for Spanish ones.[23] Adding to Cameron's worries was the lack of gifts in Pensacola to distribute to potential Indian allies. Cameron criticized Major General Campbell for only wanting to dole out munitions and other merchandise to Indians when the British expected an attack from Spanish forces rather than keeping the Choctaws constantly supplied and friendly to British interests.[24] Campbell referred to his Indian allies as "Barbarians" and considered them unreliable, even as he depended on their support to counter the Spanish. He cited the example of a group of Choctaws who had arrived in Mobile in December 1779 to aid in its defense only to join the Spanish after the fighting began.[25]

Viewed from another perspective, what these examples demonstrate is that the American Revolution was not a Choctaw fight. They worried to some degree about who won the war and how the changing geopolitical situation would impact preexisting trade relationships, but as a group they harbored no blind allegiance or ideological commitment to either side. To varying degrees, groups of Choctaws used the war to gain material largesse and enhance their own status. When British agent and resident of the Chickasaw Nation James Colbert talked to Six Towns Division Choctaws in November 1779 to counter Spanish contacts with them, some chiefs told him that "two People loves us[,] whoever gives us the most [trade goods] will be the most regarded[.] So I would advise you to give presents superior to the Spaniards."[26] The Choctaws did not worry that Europeans or Americans might try to take their lands or attack their villages because all of the dominant powers in the Gulf South at that time were Indian. Their commitment to fight on one side or the other or remain neutral was contingent on a number of factors, including, as Cameron, Campbell, and Colbert suggested, on which Europeans could offer the most payment. Other factors also shaped Choctaw responses to the American Revolution, such as the history of the relationship between individual Choctaws and Europeans and cultural imperatives to participate in war and gain higher societal standing.

All of these motivations came into play during the competition among chiefs for access to Spanish and British goods in the year between the Spanish capture of Mobile and the Battle of Pensacola. In late August 1780, British agent Bethune traveled to the Choctaw villages to try to counter Spanish pleas for Choctaw assistance. He found that the Western and Eastern Division chiefs preferred the British alliance, and some of them sent war parties against the Spanish at Mobile in response to Bethune's granting of gifts and his insistence that they prove their allegiance to Britain. In the Six Towns Division Bethune confronted a very different situation, much like the one James Colbert had encountered nine months before. Six Towns villages were located along the Chickasawhay River northwest of Mobile and along the path from Mobile to the rest of the Choctaw villages. As the closest Choctaw division to Spanish-held Mobile, many of their chiefs had journeyed to Mobile after the Spanish takeover seeking trade and confirmation of their high status, as well as looking for a source of goods distinct from their cohorts among the Western and Eastern divisions who still traded with Britain. Spanish officials obliged by giving Six Towns chiefs military officers' coats, Spanish flags, and medals that entitled them to special gifts and publicly displayed their high status and ties with Spain. Bethune received a chilly reception when he later met with five hundred Six Towns Choctaws and listened to several of their chiefs. Some Six Towns chiefs adamantly supported Spain and warned that

Spain was about to capture Pensacola, thus removing the British presence from the Gulf South. Others publicly regretted having renounced the British and forged an alliance with Spain but blamed the lack of British attention to their needs for forcing their hand. Still other Six Towns chiefs remained firmly in the British alliance and threatened with violence their colleagues who had reached out to the Spanish. Bethune reported that the debate among Six Towns chiefs about which European power to trade with lasted from eight o'clock in the morning to six o'clock in the evening on August 21. He insisted that most Six Towns Choctaws, including women and warriors, desired to remain allied with Britain, with the exception of certain chiefs who sought Spanish trade but neutrality in the war. Ultimately, whether an individual chief interacted with Spain or Britain depended on whether or not they perceived personal or communal advantage in talking with one European nation or the other. Bethune, writing to Superintendent Cameron in Pensacola, claimed that an immediate distribution of British goods and British medals among the Six Towns Choctaws would reattach them firmly to the British cause. There is no doubt that access to European merchandise played a role in some Six Towns Choctaws' decision to talk to the Spanish, but pride and a spirit of independence and honor also pervaded their talks with Bethune and further explain their willingness to interact with the Spanish. Choctaws and other Indian peoples insisted on gifts and confirmation of their high status from European powers as a basic condition of asking for their help in fighting a war. Bethune eloquently summarized this situation among the Six Towns Choctaws in his appeal to Cameron to send supplies:

> Human Nature is the same whether savage or Civilized[.] [E]very man thinks himself possessed of some abilities and nothing arouses resentment in the human heart more than the Idea of neglected merit. [R]evenge of the imagined neglect immediately succeeds and where we might make a friend we ensure an enemy. [A]t all events it is better to risk a little expence & trouble in hope of an uncertain friend than by a refusal ensure an inveterate enemy. . . . I must further begg leave to observe that neither abilities or address will long support any man's influence in an Indian Nation unless strengthened by presents. Reason & Rhetoric will fall to the Ground unless supported by Strouds and duffels. Liberality is alone with Indians true Eloquence without which Demosthenes & Cicero, or the more modern Orators Burke & Barre might harangue in vain.[27]

Just one week after writing the above passage, Bethune had heard nothing from his superiors in Pensacola and faced Six Towns Choctaws sent from Mobile with instructions from Spanish officials to kill him. Moreover, Choctaws siding with Britain found themselves without ammunition or gunpowder because of the lack of trade, and they too grumbled about the deceitfulness of the British. Though he was residing in the Western Division village of West Yazoo, whose chiefs had acted strenuously on Britain's behalf in the past, Bethune wrote that he feared daily for his safety. Somewhat ironically, he encouraged Superintendent Cameron to not let the private British fur traders in Pensacola send goods to the Choctaw Nation because that would encourage the Western and Eastern division men to leave the towns for their annual deerskin hunts, leaving their villages vulnerable to attack from the disaffected Six Towns Choctaws. He instead pleaded for ammunition sent on behalf of the British government with the stipulation that the Choctaws use it to fight the Spanish. Whether Cameron had the power to enforce such action, even in a time of war, is questionable, and Bethune's ideas are more indicative of his fear than of any realistic British strategy. Choctaws conducted months-long annual deerskin hunts to acquire meat for food and deerskins that were exchanged for a multitude of European manufactured items that Choctaws had become dependent on. Choctaws needed to acquire the merchandise through either trade or as gifts and payment for service in the war. Even with gifts there was no guarantee that Choctaws or other Indians would behave exactly as the British or other Europeans wanted them to.[28]

Spanish and British officials had accused each other of encouraging the Choctaws and other Indians to commit atrocities against civilians and soldiers since the war began, but in August 1780 Spanish accusations reached a crescendo in response to the killing of several Spanish soldiers by a group of Choctaws. Warriors belonging to a British-allied Eastern Division military patrol led by Mingo Pouscouche of Concha village encountered four European soldiers while scouting for Spaniards between British Pensacola and Spanish Mobile. The Europeans had set up camp in an isolated house near the Perdido River and invited the Choctaws to join them for a meal, which they did. When Mingo Pouscouche arrived some time later he realized that the four Europeans were Spaniards, and he ordered his men to seize them to take back as prisoners to Pensacola. In fear for their lives, the Spanish soldiers resisted and fought back fiercely, wounding a few of the Choctaws. The Choctaws then killed the outnumbered Spaniards, thinking they had done what was expected of them, given it was their mission to intercept and capture or kill any Spaniards trying to reach Pensacola by land. The Choctaws in this patrol viewed killing the enemy as part of their job, for which they were to be compensated by the British, and the men participating in the attack gained prestige for successfully dispatching a known enemy. The Choctaws scalped the Spaniards and brought the scalps to Pensacola, shouting and yelling in celebration as they approached the British town. Scalps served as visible symbols of prowess and accomplishment in war and had been a standard trophy of war for southeastern Indians for hundreds of years. A Chickasaw war leader visiting Pensacola explained the role of scalps while acknowledging that Europeans viewed scalping differently, "He was well aware," recorded Hessian Chaplain Philipp Waldeck, "that taking scalps was not customary among the white folks, but one should not deny them the right to retain this custom, because they would earn the praise and especially the name of warrior in the tribe only when they brought the scalps of their enemies back home in triumph."[29] Participating in triumphant war parties offered Choctaw males the chance to prove they were men who could access spiritual power to protect their society. In fact, they remained mere boys until they participated in a successful war party. This cultural imperative served as a potent motivation for Choctaw warriors to join patrols like the one led by Mingo Pouscouche.[30]

What Mingo Pouscouche and his warriors did not know was that they had violated a basic principle of eighteenth-century European warfare. The Spanish sergeant and three soldiers greeted the Choctaws with openness initially because they were awaiting escort to Pensacola under a flag of truce to exchange official messages between the Spanish commander of Mobile, Lieutenant Colonel José de Ezpeleta, and General Campbell. The Spanish soldiers likely viewed the Choctaw patrol as that escort or perhaps as Choctaws friendly to Spain, and panic ensued when Mingo Pouscouche revealed the truth. One severely wounded Spanish soldier survived and limped back to Mobile to tell Ezpeleta what had happened. Ezpeleta denounced the apparent British role in ordering the Choctaws to attack this peaceful delegation. Ezpeleta wrote Campbell that the Choctaw actions constituted murder, and he demanded that the British cease using Indians to commit deeds that would be deemed by Europeans to be uncivilized. By European definitions some forms of killing in a time of war were not justifiable and constituted murder. Campbell's response to Ezpeleta's accusations mirrored this understanding when he blamed the incident on the confusions inherent in a time of war and added that the Spanish had ordered Indians to rob and plunder British citizens in West Florida and thus broke the same unwritten rule about how to employ Indians. Superintendent Cameron added that the Spanish had paid Creek Indians to attack innocent British farmsteads around Mobile and Pensacola. Campbell also insisted that Mingo Pouscouche's group had once supported Spain and only changed their minds when denied goods by the Spanish and after Campbell had "sent them away" from Pensacola because he did not trust them; thus, Ezpeleta was to blame for the mood of Mingo Pouscouche's men. Mingo Pouscouche lived in the Eastern Division town of Concha and therefore was more likely to support the British, but before encountering the Spanish patrol he had tried to get trade goods from the British at Pensacola by claiming that the Spanish had given them inferior merchandise. Mingo Pouscouche's claim was likely a ruse, and he and his men did receive some gifts from the British, but the claims of prior contact with the Spanish had caused the British to question his motives. General Campbell condemned the actions of Mingo Pouscouche and his men in killing the Spaniards and ordered Cameron to reprimand them and not compensate them for their effort.

Campbell, who had little respect for his Indian allies anyway, needed to distance himself from Indian actions that all Europeans viewed as barbarous and regain Ezpeleta's trust in order to prevent the Spanish from ordering reprisal attacks on British diplomatic missions or civilians. Campbell's stance became clearer as the Spanish navy approached and blockaded Pensacola in the spring of 1781. Spanish and British officials exchanged several letters promising not to mistreat prisoners or civilians during the siege and to direct attacks at military targets like Fort George rather than the town of Pensacola proper. The Battle of Pensacola, as with most battles between European powers at this time, was conducted according to an elaborate set of rules that left certain potential targets off limits and prevented "total war" tactics of annihilation from being employed.[31]

For Choctaws such distinctions between "murder" and justifiable killing and cooperation with one's enemies made little sense; when a person or group identified as an enemy fought back it was expected that they would be killed as part of the ongoing war. This group of Choctaws had no real relationship with the Spanish, so all Spaniards were theoretically enemies and subject to attack, especially since the British had promised to compensate Mingo Pouscouche for killing or capturing Spanish soldiers. Such cultural differences between Choctaw and European notions of proper conduct in war caused confusion and rancor for all involved. Mingo Pouscouche explained that he tried to arrest the Spaniards first and only ordered their deaths when the Spaniards wounded some of his men. The chief reacted angrily to the criticism levied at him by Campbell and Cameron and responded pointedly that he, not the British or the Spanish, was in charge of his actions. Cameron recorded his complaint:

> If I wanted to kill these [Spaniards] I could have done it without the least risk to myself or any of my Party, but you may observe that my intention was to take them Prisoners, otherwise I would not have suffered by them so much. Since my arrival [back in Pensacola] the [British] seem very cool and cross with me, and it seems to me, that they love the Spaniards; I was told that some of the Warriors here said that I knew the Spaniards came from Mobile to see some of the English safe to Pensacola; but if they said so they told a lye [*sic*]. I have thrown away the Spaniards, and if the English throw me away for killing their Enemy, I can go away to some other Nation who hates them as well as myself. While I was out [on patrol] I have seen Men[,] Women and Children which I believe were French or Spaniards and whom I might have killed if I had a mind [to do so]. But I have been always told by the English, never to be guilty of killing People who did not trouble them or me, and who lived Peaceably at home. But as the English seem now cross with me, I will for the future kill every Man[,] Woman or child belonging to [the Spanish] that I shall come across.[32]

Mingo Pouscouche further explained that, as Campbell had informed Ezpeleta, he had gone to Mobile before initially coming to Pensacola. Spanish officials told him that the British were soon to abandon Pensacola and disappear from the Gulf Coast, which encouraged him to accept their gifts. When he arrived in Pensacola to find the British still in charge, he was relieved and eager to patrol on behalf of Britain in order to protect the one place where Choctaws could still come to meet with the British and receive their superior goods. He told Cameron that he feared the Spanish takeover of Pensacola since they already occupied Mobile, as that change would place Choctaws in a severe bind as British traders and British merchandise moved away. For this reason, Mingo Pouscouche insisted, he hated the Spanish. Though disapproving of his actions in killing the Spanish soldiers, Cameron smoothed over Mingo Pouscouche's bitterness by giving him supplies and having him renounce his pledge to kill innocent civilians.[33]

This incident soon passed, but the British remained uncomfortable with their reliance on Indians as military allies because of the cultural misunderstandings that frequently arose. In September 1780 Campbell summarized his attitude toward his Indian allies to his superiors in London, writing that "I sincerely regret the Necessity of ever employing Savages, or being obliged to court them to War." He predicted "horrid Scenes of Cruelty and Barbarity besides the loss of Property" that would occur if, as Bethune had warned, sizable portions of Choctaws chiefs and warriors decided to support Spain rather than Britain.[34] Bethune and Cameron urgently requested that fifty horse-loads of ammunition and other supplies be sent to the Choctaws under armed escort by Choctaws friendly to the British.[35] In this instance Campbell relented slightly and dispersed some commodities in Pensacola to keep at least some of the Choctaws on good terms with Britain. Cameron despised employing Indians as allies, no matter how necessary such an arrangement was for Britain's hope of holding on to Pensacola and a presence on the Gulf Coast; he also viewed the post of Pensacola as insignificant to the British empire and complained constantly about the conditions in the town and lack of military reinforcements. Campbell's arrogance and naïveté in regard to Indian affairs served repeatedly to estrange Choctaws who might otherwise have supported Britain even more forcefully.[36]

Cameron reported at this time that the Choctaws seemed anxious to give proof of appreciation and attachment to the British. Choctaw patrols headed to the outskirts of Mobile and attacked any Spaniard who ventured too far from fortified settlements. In addition, because of the dispersal of supplies to the Choctaws, Indian agent Bethune was able to return to the Gulf Coast in October.[37] In early October a group of Choctaw warriors killed three people—a Frenchman named Trouillett, his female Indian servant, and an African American—and captured fourteen others near Mobile and brought them to Pensacola. British officials again condemned the Choctaw actions because the victims were a French family and their slaves, whom the Choctaws attacked without provocation. The treatment of the captives shocked Chaplain Waldeck, who wrote that it "is a frightening experience to fall into the hands of these savage people. . . . The members had been stripped nearly naked and even the children were not left with even a shirt. The Indians dragged them through the wilderness for three days."[38] According to Waldeck, the British paid the Choctaw party with goods, not to reward them, but rather to encourage them to turn over the French family, who then moved in with acquaintances in Pensacola. Still, Cameron insisted to his superiors in London that the Choctaws realized their mistake and turned over the prisoners for free at his insistence. Given Choctaw willingness to do as they please unless compensated by the British, as Mingo Pouscouche had demonstrated, it is likely that Cameron did offer them some provisions in order to secure the safety of the French family. Cameron could not afford, however, to give the appearance of rewarding Indians for behavior that all Europeans viewed as unacceptable.[39]

Cameron more willingly criticized General Campbell for being "ignorant" of Indian customs. The supplies sent to the Choctaws in early October had produced positive effects in the fight against Spain, and Cameron argued that constant gifts to the Choctaws must be maintained by the British to keep the Choctaws in the field. Choctaw chiefs reminded Cameron that they had sacrificed their annual deer hunt in order to fight for Britain and must receive the merchandise that they would normally have bought with deerskins. They also insisted on having a large congress with the British since the British had invited the Creeks and Cherokees to one at Augusta. Thousands of Choctaws attended weeks-long congresses sponsored by Britain or other European nations in order to acquire gifts, food, medals, and commissions. The practice of annual or semiregular conferences between European countries and the Choctaws had begun in the early eighteenth century, with France's annual meeting at Mobile, and persisted into the early 1760s. When Britain assumed French territory after the Seven Years' War, it too held congresses but much less often than the French had done. But in November 1780 Campbell announced that no more gifts should be given to the Choctaws. The high expense was offered as the reason for the new policy, but it could not have come at a worse time from Cameron's or the Choctaws' perspective. Western and Eastern division leaders complained loudly that the Six Towns Choctaws had just received a load of goods from Britain despite their flirtations with a Spanish alliance, and now the more reliable British supporters among the rest of the Choctaw confederacy were being penalized. These Choctaws suggested that the British supply them with ammunition and other provisions so they could live and patrol along the Tombigbee River northwest of Pensacola rather than send supplies over hundreds of miles to their villages. From the Tombigbee the Choctaws could more easily harass the Spanish around Mobile, steal Spanish cattle for food, and be readily available to respond to any Spanish movement on Pensacola. Campbell denied gifts to the Choctaws in early November despite Cameron's warning that "at present our principle [*sic*] dependance is on the Indians for the protection of this place in Case of a Visit from the Spaniards" and that "Refusing presents to the Indians at so Critical a Conjuncture may be very hurtfull to his Majesty's Interest."[40] Campbell remained unconvinced despite the bravery shown by another Choctaw war party that had attacked Spanish positions near Mobile.

In early November 1780 a British trader and interpreter named John Pitchlynn and an officer and seven soldiers of the West Florida Royal Forresters joined a Choctaw war party of at least two hundred men in an attack on Spanish positions at Mobile Village (also called Frenchtown) on the east side of Mobile Bay (nearer Pensacola than the town of Mobile). Initial word back in Pensacola was that the effort had failed and that the Spanish repulsed the attack. But on November 6 the Choctaws returned to Pensacola with several Spanish scalps and explained that what caused the attack to fail was a lack of ammunition and insufficient support from the British participants. The fortified Spanish position employed two four-pound artillery pieces that fired grapeshot at the Choctaws who attacked on foot. The Choctaws quickly adjusted their advance by moving to the left and then to the right to get out of the cannons' line of fire. When a few Spaniards made a small charge on the attackers' position, "the Officer and Men of the Royal Forresters as well as Mr. Pitchlin [sic] ... mounted their Horses which they kept at a little distance and made the Best of their way home [to Pensacola] leaving their Baggage behind." Despite the retreat of their British comrades, the Choctaws continued to advance on the Spanish position and came close enough to set fire to some of the buildings within the entrenchments before breaking off the attack. Cameron reported that they had killed four Spanish soldiers including "an Officer whose Regimentals they brought [to Pensacola] as well as his Scalp," while suffering only one Choctaw warrior wounded. Not only did the Choctaws prove they could adjust battle tactics when faced with artillery fire, they embarrassed their British allies with their superior bravery. Upon returning to Pensacola, these Choctaws asked that a new party of regular British troops who "would not be afraid to fight the Spaniards" be sent back with them to attack the Mobile Village. They also stated that they knew there was more than enough ammunition stored in Pensacola and that Campbell simply needed to release it in order to keep the Choctaws on the offensive against the Spanish. General Campbell refused the offer, thanked the Choctaws for their brave service, and sent them home without further provisions.[41]

Word that the Spanish navy was about to initiate an attack on Pensacola and the arrival of hundreds more Choctaws in Pensacola in November nevertheless kept the Choctaws close by. When word of Campbell's policy of refusing gifts to the Choctaws and sending them home to their villages became known among the British troops and citizens in Pensacola they appealed to Campbell to change his mind. Campbell relented and ordered Cameron to send runners to the Choctaws to request more Choctaw warriors to defend Pensacola. He refused, however, Cameron's request to outfit several parties of Choctaws, accompanied by British agents and fur traders, to continually harass the Spaniards in and around Mobile in an effort to keep the Spanish occupied with the Indian attacks and interupt their planning of an offensive against Pensacola. Campbell, citing the inordinate expense, also refused to send ammunition into the Choctaw villages unless the Choctaws themselves provided the horses and protection to transport the material. Cameron explained that only a few Choctaws possessed sufficient numbers of horses, and they were not willing to contribute them to public use on behalf of the British. An exasperated Cameron wrote his superiors in London that he feared that Campbell's contradictory statements and policies would alienate the Choctaws rather than inspire them. "With regard to Indians," Cameron wrote about Campbell, "He certainly takes the Wrong Steps to make them Useful to Government." The Choctaws were not stupid, counseled Cameron, and they perceived the lack of respect inherent in Campbell's actions. Cameron urged Campbell to keep the Choctaws satisfied by arming them and encouraging their attacks on the Spanish, whether or not an attack on Pensacola seemed imminent.[42]

Campbell authorized one final attack on the Mobile Village in early January 1781 with a force of three hundred Choctaws and some British regulars, Hessian mercenaries, and Maryland and Pennsylvania loyalists comprising one hundred infantrymen and eleven cavalrymen. The force commander, Colonel Hanxladen of the Hessian unit, died in the attack, and his second in command, Captain Baumback, was wounded, leaving Captain Key of the Loyalist troops in charge. Key proved unable to keep the combined force on the offensive, especially since he did not speak German or Choctaw, and the Choctaws provided the majority of troops. The attack had again reached the Spanish entrenchments, as in November 1780, but failed to press the advantage. Five Hessians died and eight were wounded, along with an unknown number of Choctaws and other participants dead or wounded. This action closed the fighting until the Spanish navy and army forces approached Pensacola in March.[43]

Spanish forces initiated the siege of Pensacola on March 9, 1781, when Spanish ships entered Pensacola Bay and General Gálvez landed with Spanish troops on Santa Rosa Island. Detailed descriptions of the months-long siege by both Spanish and British participants and their accounts of frequent skirmishes between Indians and Spanish forces make clear that Choctaw forces aggressively fought the Spanish, supplying the primary offensive power for the British during the siege. Just four days before the siege began Campbell had once again ordered the seven hundred or so Choctaws in Pensacola home, but on the very next day, March 6, he pleaded with them to return as the Spanish fleet had been sighted. One of the primary Choctaw chiefs in Pensacola at this time, Franchimastabé from the Western Division village of West Yazoo, complained that they had been called to many false alarms before and did not receive many provisions for their efforts. So he left it up to individual Choctaw warriors whether or not they wanted to heed Campbell's latest entreaty for their assistance, though he stayed in Pensacola awaiting opportunities to lead attacks against the Spanish. Thus, only about four hundred Choctaws remained in Pensacola when Gálvez's troops first appeared. Another few hundred Choctaws arrived during the siege, along with a couple of hundred other Chickasaw and Creek Indians, which brought the Indian force defending the town to about one thousand. Those Choctaws who chose to help the British defend Pensacola continued to grumble about the insufficient supplies of ammunition and basic provisions provided by Campbell. The pack train of horses loaded with merchandise that had been promised them months before had still not materialized, and they suggested instead that the goods be stored in a safe place near Pensacola in order to protect the items from Choctaws who had allied themselves with Spain.[44]

Just weeks before the Spanish fleet began arriving in Pensacola Bay, a large contingent of Choctaws, most likely from the Six Towns Division, showed up in Mobile to talk to Spanish commander Ezpeleta. Their demands of him highlight their desire to maintain their honor, enhance their status, and gain material largesse. On February 19 the trader and interpreter accompanying them, named Juzan, informed Ezpeleta that the Choctaws had five demands. They wanted to conduct official diplomacy with the Spanish, or "to dance the calumet and to strike the stake" and thus forge an official bond between the two peoples. Such a formal diplomatic meeting that consisted of smoking pipes together, performing the eagle's tail dance, recounting war exploits, turning the Spanish into fictive kin, and negotiating for trade would obligate these Choctaws and the Spanish to support each other.[45] If the Spanish planned to attack Pensacola within a month, these Choctaws promised to remain in Mobile awaiting orders, but if the Spanish intended on waiting, the Choctaws needed to return to their villages to plant crops for the year. They asked that a Talapoosa Creek Indian being held prisoner by the Spanish be released as that would remove the motivation of the Creeks to fight against Spain. When Pensacola fell to the Spanish they wanted Spain to punish other Choctaws who aided Britain by denying them gifts and forcing them to turn over the scalps and other war trophies taken from Spanish victims. If implemented, such actions on the part of Spain—especially renouncing the war trophies—would certainly enhance the prestige of these Six Towns chiefs and embarrass their competitors among the other divisions, who would not receive the culturally defined recognition as successful warriors and war leaders that war trophies graphically demonstrated. Last, the eleven chiefs participating in the delegation felt insulted that they had not been invited to dine at Ezpeleta's table and treated with the respect their position accorded them. Ezpeleta responded cautiously and hoped to see verifiable proof of their allegiance to Spain before making any significant promises to these Choctaws. Yet, it was clear that Choctaws had remained divided, or rather had maintained their divisional and village autonomy, in choosing to forge relationships with Britain and Spain at the same time. Chiefs, warriors, families, and whole towns sought their own best advantage when they chose how to respond to the crisis and opportunities offered by the American Revolution.[46]

It was the Choctaws in Pensacola aiding Britain, as had been the case for months, who actually engaged in combat. From March 9, when the Spanish established a presence in Pensacola Bay, Indian forces (mostly Choctaws) harassed and fired upon Spanish positions constantly. On March 17 the Spanish attempted to land at the mouth of the Perdido River but a "number of Indians in sight prevented them."[47] A British resident of West Florida and former British Army Major named Robert Farmar reported that a British captain and "a body of Indians" attacked a Spanish party of eleven men on March 20, killing ten and taking the remaining one prisoner.[48] On March 22 Gálvez reported that Indians fired on Ezpeleta's army as it marched overland from Mobile and that night killed three Spaniards and wounded four more.[49] An Indian ambush of Spanish soldiers on March 25 resulted in the capture of two Spanish scalps and twenty-three horses. Indians turned back an attempted landing of Spanish troops on March 27, and then killed and wounded several Spanish soldiers encamped that evening.[50] The following day an estimated four hundred Indians "approached the [Spanish] camp and made an intensive attack on the advanced guard units" that killed and wounded "a few" before being repulsed by militia from New Orleans composed of white and black soldiers.[51]

That group of four hundred Indians was likely the same group of Choctaws led by Franchimastabé who nearly overran Spanish lines on March 30. Spanish forces numbering over one thousand men marched to within a mile of Fort George in order to move their siege artillery within range of the fort. The Choctaws, under cover of trees, directed rifle and musket fire at the Spanish for over four hours until British reinforcements with two cannons reached the area. The blistering Choctaw attack temporarily broke the Spanish front lines. Spanish infantry units accompanied by field artillery counterattacked and forced the Indians to retreat and the British forces to flee back to Fort George leaving their artillery pieces in the field. Despite being forced to retreat, the Choctaws had captured four Spanish drums, "a number of scalps," and one entire head of a Spanish soldier, while losing only one killed and two wounded. The Spanish reported three men dead and twenty-eight wounded in this engagement. The Spanish spent the night entrenching their position and making it nearly impregnable to future attack. This battle marked a major turning point in the siege campaign and the Choctaws, especially their primary war leader Franchimastabé, reacted with a combination of resignation and fury.[52] Franchimastabé met with Superintendent Cameron two days later on April 1 to outline his grievances, and Cameron recorded his speech:

> Since our arrival here [in Pensacola], and the landing of the Spaniards the Indians have behaved well[;] they have done all that has been done without being supported, as was promised them by the troops. [H]ad [the British] advanced the day before yesterday we would have drove the Enemy off but when they begun to run the Troops retreated, cou'd we manage the Great Guns (artillery) ourselves we wou'd have drove off the Spaniards. But without any support we find ourselves overpowered, and the Spaniards are so numerous that we do not miss those we Kill or it looks as if they came again to life. We have done every thing in our power, we find it in vain to make any further attempts; and I now put you in mind of your promise at the Saw Mill, you promised me large presents, and it is time you should perform your promise.[53]

Franchimastabé highlighted some of the key reasons why Choctaws aided Britain in fighting the Spanish. As various Choctaws, whether speaking to Spanish or British officials, had long noted, the expectation that they would be paid for their services acted as a significant motivation to engage in the fighting. Chiefs who received large gifts of European merchandise for their followers and families earned higher sociopolitical prestige as providers and as generous givers who could then expect deference in return. Acquiring foreign-made items held an important traditional significance, for individuals who interacted successfully with the outside world and non-Choctaw people were accorded special status and deemed to be spiritually powerful people who acted on behalf of the wider community. The ability to acquire gifts from Europeans enabled chiefs to exercise a degree of political power, as they could reward warriors for their support and services with valuable items. As one chief, perhaps Franchimastabé, explained to Cameron after the Spanish siege of Pensacola had begun, unless Britain gave generous presents the chiefs "cannot prevail with their young men to remain or fight any longer."[54] Manufactured goods served more of a status role than a purely economic function for chiefs and other elites in Choctaw society, and thus the maintenance of social standing supplied a major reason for chiefly willingness to fight on behalf of Europeans in war.[55]

However, warriors or young males who had yet to become warriors viewed participation in the war from another angle. Participation in war for young men was a cultural necessity. A Chickasaw chief in Pensacola clarified this imperative when he said that "the older warriors had not wanted to make this long journey, but they, the young men, still had to earn their good names in war."[56] Only through participation in a successful war party could a young man perform deeds that would result in his being granted an adult title that described in some way his accomplishment or new higher status. Until such a time, the young man remained culturally a boy with a name given to him by his mother after he was born. War provided a basic marker of Choctaw masculinity and thus explains the willingness of young men to engage in battle, especially against a European enemy that would not seek familial revenge in the way that a Native enemy might. When European wars ended, all killing in the war was essentially forgiven; when Indian people killed an enemy Indian the context did not matter, for revenge from the victim's family against the killer or the killer's family was expected. All of these culturally defined motivations lay behind Choctaw actions on behalf of Britain in defending Pensacola from the Spanish.[57]

Franchimastabé headed the single largest contingent of Choctaw forces at the Pensacola siege, and his desire to receive payment and head home by April 1 signaled the beginning of the end for the British presence in the region. Though Indians continued to arrive in Pensacola, including another group of ninety Choctaws from the Western Division accompanied by the British traders Benjamin James and Alexander Frazer who arrived on April 15, and small-scale Choctaw attacks on Spanish positions persisted, no attack matched the ferocity of either Franchimastabé's or Mingo Pouscouche's earlier efforts.[58] Britain surrendered Pensacola on May 10, 1781, after Spanish artillery struck the powder magazine in Fort George on May 8. Many Choctaws regretted the loss of Pensacola and its British occupiers, but ties with the British in Georgia remained until the end of the American Revolution in 1783, and the Choctaws, including Franchimastabé and other chiefs formerly allied with Britain, soon created new relationships with Spain, the United States federal government, and individual states. The actions of Choctaws in the Battle of Pensacola, though small in the overall context of the American Revolution, loomed large in Spanish accounts of the conflict. As historian Thomas Chávez has recently argued, the Indian "benefit to the British defenders had become painfully evident. Without them, there would not have been counterattacks and the fighting would not have been as fierce. Pensacola would have been a much easier and less costly victory."[59]

NOTES

1. For studies that focus on some aspect of the fighting between Spain and Britain on the Gulf Coast in the American Revolution, see John Walton Caughey, *Bernardo de Gálvez in Louisiana, 1776–1783* (Berkeley: University of California Press, 1934); N. Orwin Rush, *Spain's Final Triumph over Great Britain in the Gulf of Mexico: The Battle of Pensacola, March 9 to May 8, 1781* (Tallahassee: Florida State University, 1966); J. Leitch Wright Jr., *Florida in the American Revolution* (Gainesville: University Press of Florida, 1975); J. Barton Starr, *Tories, Dons, and Rebels: The American Revolution in British West Florida* (Gainesville: University Press of Florida, 1976); William S. Coker and Hazel P. Coker, *The Siege of Pensacola, 1781* (Pensacola, Fla.: Perdido Bay Press, 1981); the collected essays in William S. Coker and Robert R. Rea, eds., *Anglo-Spanish Confrontation on the Gulf Coast During the American Revolution* (Pensacola, Fla.: Gulf Coast History and Humanities Conference, 1982); David J. Weber, *The Spanish Frontier in North America* (New Haven, Conn.: Yale University Press, 1992); and Thomas E. Chávez, *Spain and the Independence of the United States: An Intrinsic Gift* (Albuquerque: University of New Mexico Press, 2002). For thorough Spanish-language monographs, see F. De Borja Medina Rojas, *José de Ezpeleta: Gobernador de la Mobila, 1780–1781* (Seville: Escuela de Estudios Hispano-Americanos de Sevilla, 1980); and Carmen de Reparaz, *Yo solo: Bernardo de Gálvez y la toma de Panzacola en 1781* (Madrid: ICI, 1986). For a bibliographical guide, see James A. Servies, *The Siege of Pensacola, 1781: A Bibliography* (Pensacola, Fla.: John C. Pace Library, 1981).

2. Works that discuss to some degree the Indian involvement in these actions include James H. O'Donnell III, *Southern Indians in the American Revolution* (Knoxville: University of Tennessee Press, 1973); Michael D. Green, "The Creek Confederacy in the American Revolution: Cautious Participants," in Coker and Rea, *Anglo-Spanish*

Confrontation, 54–75; Kathryn Holland, "The Anglo-Spanish Contest for the Gulf Coast as Viewed from the Townsquare," in Coker and Rea, *Anglo-Spanish Confrontation*, 90–105; and Colin G. Calloway, *The American Revolution in Indian Country: Crisis and Diversity in Native American Communities* (New York: Cambridge University Press, 1995).

3. Alexander Cameron to Gen. Henry Clinton, July 18, 1780, Guy Carleton, Lord Dorchester Papers, 1747–1783 (hereafter cited as Dorchester Papers), microfilm copy, University of Michigan Libraries, Ann Arbor.

4. Maj. Gen. John Campbell to Lord George Germain, August 6, 1780, in *Documents of the American Revolution, 1770–1783*, ed. K. G. Davies, 21 vols. (Shannon, Ireland: Irish University Press, 1972), 16:377 (collection hereafter cited as *DAR*); letter also in *Mississippi Provincial Archives: English Dominion*, microfilm collection (Jackson: Mississippi Department of Archives and History), 9:317 (collection hereafter cited as *MPAED*).

5. Campbell to Germain, May 15, 1780, *DAR*, 18:93–94; and Green, "The Creek Confederacy in the American Revolution," 69–70.

6. Elizabeth A. Fenn, *Pox Americana: The Great Smallpox Epidemic of 1775–82* (New York: Hill and Wang, 2001), 114–15.

7. "Return of Chactaw, Chickasaw, Alabamas, and Creek Indians Remaining at Pensacola," February 1, 1781, British Public Record Office, Colonial Office, class 5: America and the West Indies, vol. 82 (collection hereafter cited as CO5/vol. no.).

8. Cameron to Germain, May 27, 1781, *DAR*, 20:149–50; and E. A. Montemayor, *The Battle Journal of Bernardo de Gálvez during the American Revolution* (New Orleans: Polyanthos, 1978), 16, 25, 30.

9. Reference to this conference is in Robert Tait's report of his journey to the Choctaw villages, August 5, 1779, CO5/81.

10. Greg O'Brien, "'We Are Behind You:' The Choctaw Occupation of Natchez in 1778," *Journal of Mississippi History* 64 (Summer 2002): 107–24.

11. "List of Presents Necessary for a Chactaw Congress," November 23, 1778, CO5/80; and "A General Account of Presents issued to Chactaw & Chickasaw Indians from the 1st of April to 31st May 1779," CO5/81.

12. "Return of Presents Supplied Farquhar Bethune, Esqr. For the Chactaws," June 26, 1779, CO5/81.

13. Robert Tait's report of his journey to the Choctaw villages, August 5, 1779, CO5/81.

14. "Account of Provisions Issued to Indians," December 31, 1779, Dorchester Papers.

15. Bruce E. Burgoyne, ed., *Eighteenth Century America: A Hessian Report on the People, the Land, the War: As Noted in the Diary of Chaplain Philipp Waldeck, 1776–1780* (Bowie, Md.: Heritage Books, 1995), 149.

16. Burgoyne, *Eighteenth Century America*, 158–59.

17. Greg O'Brien, *Choctaws in a Revolutionary Age, 1750–1830* (Lincoln: University of Nebraska Press, 2002), 10, 13–20; and Patricia Galloway, "Choctaw Factionalism and Civil War, 1746–1750," *Journal of Mississippi History* 44 (November 1982): 289–327, and reprinted in this volume. On the Oneida split with the Iroquois Confederacy during the American Revolution, see Joseph T. Glatthaar and James Kirby Martin,

Forgotten Allies: The Oneida Indians and the American Revolution (New York: Hill and Wang, 2006).

18. Greg O'Brien, "The Conqueror Meets the Unconquered: Negotiating Cultural Boundaries on the Post-Revolutionary Southern Frontier," *Journal of Southern History* 47 (February 2001): 39–72, and reprinted in this volume.

19. Horatio B. Cushman, *History of the Choctaw, Chickasaw, and Natchez Indians*, ed. Angie Debo (1899; repr., Norman: University of Oklahoma Press, 1999), 238–42.

20. For repetition of Cushman's error, see Angie Debo, *The Rise and Fall of the Choctaw Republic* (1934; repr., Norman: University of Oklahoma Press, 1961), 31; Anna Lewis, *Chief Pushmataha, American Patriot: The Story of the Choctaws' Struggle for Survival* (New York: Exposition, 1959), 30–32; Arthur H. DeRosier Jr., *The Removal of the Choctaw Indians* (Knoxville: University of Tennessee Press, 1970), 17; Jesse O. McKee and Jon A. Schlenker, *The Choctaws: Cultural Evolution of a Native American Tribe* (Jackson: University Press of Mississippi, 1980), 36; and Jesse O. McKee, *The Choctaw* (New York: Chelsea House, 1989), 30.

21. Lewis, *Chief Pushmataha*, 32.

22. For Spanish overtures to the Choctaws before the capture of Mobile in March 1780, see Henry Atkins to Charles Stuart, September 7, 1778, *MPAED*, 8:177–78; Charles Stuart to John Stuart, September 15, 1778, *MPAED*, 8:179–80; and James Colbert to Cameron, November 19, 1779, Dorchester Papers and CO5/81.

23. Jack D. L. Holmes, "Juan De La Villebeuvre and Spanish Indian Policy in West Florida, 1784–1797," *Florida Historical Quarterly* 58 (1980): 388.

24. Cameron to Sir Henry Clinton, July 18, 1780, Great Britain Historical Manuscripts Commission, *Report on American Manuscripts in the Royal Institution of Great Britain*, 4 vols. (London: H.M. Stationery Office, 1904), 2:159–60.

25. Campbell to Germain, August 6, 1780, *MPAED*, 9:317.

26. Colbert to Cameron, November 19, 1779, Dorchester Papers and CO5/81.

27. Bethune to Cameron, August 27, 1780, CO5/82.

28. Bethune to Cameron, September 4, 1780, CO5/82.

29. Burgoyne, *Eighteenth Century America*, 163.

30. Rojas, *José de Ezpeleta*, 326; Burgoyne, *Eighteenth Century America*, 168; José de Ezpeleta to Campbell, June 8, 1780; same to same, August 26, 1780; in "Correspondence between General Campbell and Lieut. Col. Joseph [José] de Ezpeleta, June 8, 1780–September 14, 1780," Record Group 26, Mississippi Department of Archives and History, Jackson (hereafter cited as Campbell Correspondence); and Cameron to Campbell, August 29, 1780, *MPAED*, 7:346–50. For the role of warfare in Choctaw masculine identity and the purpose of scalps and other war trophies, see O'Brien, *Choctaws in a Revolutionary Age*, 27–49.

31. Burgoyne, *Eighteenth Century America*, 168–69; Ezpeleta to Campbell, August 26, 1780, Campbell Correspondence; Cameron to Campbell, August 29, 1780, *MPAED*, 7:346–50; and Cameron, "Superintendent's Report," August 29, 1780, Campbell Correspondence.

32. Cameron, "Superintendent's Report," August 29, 1780, Campbell Correspondence.

33. Ibid.; Burgoyne, *Eighteenth Century America*, 169.

34. Campbell to Germain, September 22, 1780, *DAR*, 18:175–76.
35. Cameron to Campbell, September 19, 1780; and same to same, September 20, 1780, CO5/82.
36. Rush, *Spain's Final Triumph*, 18–20.
37. Cameron to Germain, October 31, 1780, *DAR*, 18:219–22.
38. Burgoyne, *Eighteenth Century America*, 170.
39. Cameron to Germain, October 31, 1780, *DAR*, 18:219–22; and Campbell to Germain, October 31, 1780, Campbell Correspondence.
40. Cameron to Campbell, November 8, 1780, CO5/82. See also Cameron to Germain, October 31, 1780, *DAR*, 18:219–22.
41. Cameron to Germain, November 30, 1780, CO5/82; see also Cameron to Germain, October 31, 1780, *DAR*, 18:219–22; Burgoyne, *Eighteenth Century America*, 171; and Cameron to Campbell, November 8, 1780, CO5/82.
42. Cameron to Germain, November 30, 1780, CO5/82.
43. Campbell to Germain, January 5, 1781, and same to same, January 7, 1781 in Campbell Correspondence; Rush, *Spain's Final Triumph*, 24–25; and Burgoyne, *Eighteenth Century America*, 173.
44. "Return of Chactaw, Chickasaw, Alabamas, and Creek Indians Remaining at Pensacola," February 1, 1781, CO5/82; Cameron to Campbell, March 20, 1781, CO5/82; Cameron to Germain, May 27, 1781, *DAR*, 20:149–51; and Burgoyne, *Eighteenth Century America*, 173.
45. For diplomatic protocol, see O'Brien, *Choctaws in a Revolutionary Age*, 56–63.
46. Juzan to Ezpeleta, February 19, 1781, and Ezpeleta to Juzan, February 19, 1781, in *Spain in the Mississippi Valley, 1765–1794*, ed. and trans. Lawrence Kinnaird, 3 vols. (Washington, D.C.: U.S. Government Printing Office, 1949), 1:419–21.
47. Robert Farmar, "Journal of the Siege of Pensacola," Peter Force Collection, series 7E, item 33, Library of Congress, Washington, D.C.
48. Farmar, "Journal of the Siege of Pensacola."
49. Maury Baker and Margaret Bissler Haas, "Bernardo de Gálvez's Combat Diary for the Battle of Pensacola, 1781," *Florida Historical Quarterly* 56 (1977): 181.
50. Farmar, "Journal of the Siege of Pensacola"; and Montemayor, *Battle Journal of Bernardo de Gálvez*, 14.
51. Montemayor, *The Battle Journal of Bernardo de Gálvez*, 15; and Baker and Haas, "Bernardo de Gálvez's Combat Diary," 182.
52. Farmar, "Journal of the Siege of Pensacola"; Montemayor, *Battle Journal of Bernardo de Gálvez*, 16; Baker and Haas, "Bernardo de Gálvez's Combat Diary," 182–83; Cameron to Germain, May 27, 1781, *DAR*, 20:149–51; and O'Donnell, *Southern Indians in the American Revolution*, 113.
53. "Talk by Frenchumastabie, Great Medal Chief of the Choctaw Nation," April 1, 1781, CO5/82.
54. Cameron to Campbell, March 20, 1781, CO5/82.
55. O'Brien, *Choctaws in a Revolutionary Age*, 72–75.
56. Burgoyne, *Eighteenth Century America*, 163.
57. O'Brien, *Choctaws in a Revolutionary Age*, 28–30. For a focused discussion of

the role of masculinity within eighteenth-century Choctaw society, see Greg O'Brien, "Trying to Look Like Men: Changing Notions of Masculinity among Choctaw Elites in the Early Republic," in *Southern Manhood: Perspectives on Masculinity in the Old South*, ed. Lorri Glover and Craig Friend (Athens: University of Georgia Press, 2004).

58. Farmar, "Journal of the Siege of Pensacola."

59. Chávez, *Spain and the Independence of the United States*, 192.

CHAPTER 7

The Conqueror Meets the Unconquered

NEGOTIATING CULTURAL BOUNDARIES ON THE POST-REVOLUTIONARY SOUTHERN FRONTIER

Greg O'Brien

On December 26, 1785, a group of 127 bedraggled Choctaw Indians arrived at Hopewell, Andrew Pickens's home on the Keowee River in South Carolina. They had trekked for over two months and traveled hundreds of miles from their central Mississippi homeland to represent the Choctaw people in a meeting with representatives of the U.S. government. Several days of negotiations resulted in the first treaty between these two powers. This encounter in the southern backcountry (which was the second in a series of three consecutive meetings at Hopewell during the winter of 1785–86 between the United States and the Cherokees, Choctaws, and Chickasaws, respectively) reveals several issues vital to an understanding of intercultural relations in the post–Revolutionary War South.[1]

Since the extant transcripts of these negotiations have never been published, previous accounts of the Choctaw Hopewell Treaty have relied exclusively on the written and signed treaty as the basis for what each side agreed to and tried to accomplish.[2] Such accounts have told an accordingly simplistic story of Indian acquiescence to American demands.[3] A close examination of the talks and the rituals that accompanied them reveals a picture different from that presented by the treaty itself, including what each side tried to accomplish at Hopewell, their attempts to accommodate one another, and the diversity of diplomatic expression and language employed by American Indians and Euro-Americans in the post-Revolutionary South. An analysis of the Hopewell Treaty negotiations from the perspectives of both participants exposes two societies acting in accordance with inherited tradition and utilizing new approaches arising from their Revolutionary War experience. Such reconsideration also calls into question whether the model of a "middle ground" of interaction between Native Americans and Europeans—which has been employed by some recent scholars to describe a zone where different peoples borrowed certain cultural practices from one another in the interest of civility and peace—can be applied uncritically.[4]

The years between the end of the Revolutionary War and the establishment of a new U.S. government under the Constitution were a crucial, albeit brief, period of transition during which many Indian groups east of the Mississippi River still operated according to centuries-old notions of proper behavior and the United States had not yet established hegemony over the lands supposedly under its jurisdiction. Scholars using twenty-twenty hindsight from a later time when Americans had militarily defeated most of the eastern Indians too easily forget that reality. In order to fully appreciate the diverse motivations, tactics, and happenings at play in the post-Revolutionary southern backcountry, the Indian side to the equation and a sense of uncertainty about the eventual outcome must be restored to the historical record.[5]

Choctaw relations with Europeans underwent several permutations in the years preceding the Hopewell Treaty. France supplied the bulk of trade goods and was the main European ally for the Choctaws living in present-day east-central Mississippi from the early eighteenth century until the end of the Seven Years' War in 1763. Britain also made sporadic inroads into the Choctaw trade before 1763, often at the request of Choctaw chiefs, and served as the principal trade ally for the Choctaws from that year until 1781. Spain occupied New Orleans in 1766, holding occasional meetings with various Choctaws and allowing Choctaw deerskin traders to conduct business there, despite British wishes that the Choctaws trade with them alone. In June 1779, during the turmoil of the American Revolution, Spain declared war on Great Britain, and military forces under Governor Bernardo de Gálvez promptly defeated British soldiers along the east bank of the Mississippi River at Manchac, Baton Rouge, and Natchez. Mobile fell to Spain in March 1780, and Pensacola followed in May 1781. For the remainder of the century Spain and the United States vied for control of the southeastern Mississippi Valley.[6]

This simple Eurocentric account of military and diplomatic events masks an underlying complexity: Choctaw society was divided into three distinct political and geographic divisions, a reality that lends an added, and often disregarded, dimension to Choctaw diplomacy. During the American Revolution some Choctaw warriors, primarily from the Western and Eastern divisions, fought in support of British forces protecting Mobile and Pensacola. In 1778 a Western Division war party of about 150 men, along with a handful of British officers and traders, occupied Natchez in the late spring and early summer. The group hoped to prevent additional American raids down the Mississippi River like the one that had been carried out by Captain James Willing in February of that year. The Choctaw war leader Franchimastabé warned the citizens of Natchez to remain pro-British, putting them on notice that "should you offer to take the rebels by the hand or enter into any treaty with them, remember also that we are behind you and that we will look on you as Virginians and treat you as our enemies."[7] Choctaw warriors from the Six Towns Division, on the other hand, assisted the Spanish in taking Mobile and Pensacola from the British, although, presumably by design, no Choctaw warriors fought against each other.[8]

Such divisional autonomy made Choctaw governance more akin to a confederacy than a "nation." It also made it easier for them to "play off" one European country against another in diplomacy, since Europeans could never be sure exactly where Choctaw loyalties lay. While the country that supplied the Choctaws with the greatest quantity and quality of gifts could often feel assured of their influence over Choctaw military actions, their loyalty was never guaranteed.[9] As the British presence in the South diminished to nothing by 1783, with the abandonment of posts in Charleston, Savannah, and St. Augustine, Choctaws searched creatively for way to reestablish the play-off system and the flow of trade goods. Three potential sources of trade existed for the Choctaws: Spain and their British-operated trading companies (such as the Mather and Strother Company and Panton, Leslie and Company), individual American states such as Georgia and South Carolina, or the new national government of the United States.[10]

Choctaw chiefs responded to the post-Revolutionary situation by seeking to increase trade with all of these groups. In July 1784 separate Choctaw delegations representing all three divisions met simultaneously with Spain at Mobile and with the Georgia government in Savannah to establish peaceful relations and resume trade.[11] European manufactured goods provided an essential part of Choctaw material life, as they did for Indians throughout eastern North America by the late eighteenth century. In the Southeast, Euro-American traders and officials offered guns, bullets, hatchets, hoes, brass and tin kettles, needles, knives, scissors, woolen cloth, shirts, blankets, paint, earrings, armbands, buttons, rum, and even Jew's harps in return for deerskins, bear fat oil, and other animal products.[12] Manufactured commodities made hunting, warfare, agriculture, domestic chores, rituals, and beautification easier for Indians. Many of these items—such as kettles that were cut up and used as arrowheads, knives, and adornment—were altered from their original form and used in ways more congruent with native views of practicality or even cosmology.[13] Since at least Mississippian times (ca. 1000–1600), Choctaws and their predecessors had expected their chiefs to acquire rare, prestige-laden foreign goods for the use of the community. Acquisition of such items bolstered the authority of chiefs because it required them to negotiate with the outside world and foreign peoples, which only diplomatic specialists who had mastered spiritual power could accomplish. Furthermore, a chief secured reciprocal obligations by redistributing trade items to his family and supporters. Distributing foreign manufactured items also bolstered leaders' status within Choctaw society, and demands for trade may have been motivated as much or more by their desire to accrue status as by material needs.[14] Beginning in the 1760s, however, unregulated British trade increasingly democratized the barter system among southern Indians because traders exchanged their products with any Indian who had skins rather than obeying Indian custom by acting through established chiefs. As a result, Choctaw chiefs sought new ways to funnel goods through their own hands, and treaty negotiations offered them just such an opportunity.[15]

In the summer of 1785 two American delegations arrived in the Choctaw village of West Yazoo in the Western Division. The first contingent came from Georgia to assert that state's claim to lands all the way to the Mississippi River, while also promising trade and "commissions" to Choctaw warriors. The principal chief of West Yazoo, Franchimastabé (the same man who had led the Choctaw military force to Natchez in 1778), welcomed the Georgians and was glad to "hear a good talk from his old friends."[16] Coming on the heels of the previous summer's trade mission to Savannah—which Franchimastabé had organized—it appeared to the Choctaws that the Americans might actually fulfill their promises of trade goods. This perception was further confirmed when another American, trader John Woods, reached West Yazoo with an invitation from the U.S. government to meet during the coming winter. Understanding the potential for restoring the play-off system and the flow of merchandise, Franchimastabé and other chiefs seized the opportunity to establish relations with this third source of commodities. In the late eighteenth century Franchimastabé and other Choctaw chiefs used relations with European officials and traders to amass large reservoirs of reciprocal obligations by means of distributing manufactured goods. From the time of initial British occupation of West Florida in 1763, Franchimastabé earned payments in guns and other items by militarily supporting British aims in the South. These actions and his acquisition of goods pushed his status well beyond that of other chiefs. In 1784 Spain officially recognized Franchimastabé as the principal leader of the entire Choctaw Western Division. In the post-Revolutionary era, Franchimastabé and other chiefs viewed the new U.S. government as a source of economic, political, and even spiritual aggrandizement, not as a former enemy confronted on the field of battle. The Choctaws felt aloof from the conflict between the eastern seaboard colonies and Great Britain, telling the governor of Georgia, John Houston, in 1784 that "we have always Been friends to both the English and Americans long before the late Divisions between them and in the time of their Contest have never taken an Active part on Either side against the other." Having never attacked the United States, the unconquered Choctaws brought an elaborate and hopeful strategy to Hopewell that focused on establishing mutually beneficial trade relations with the new nation.[17]

However, flushed with victory and a peace in Paris that ended the war but neglected Indian land claims, representatives from the Continental Congress asserted their right to dictate postwar realities to Indians. In the South, all of the larger Indian groups—the Cherokees, Creeks, Chickasaws, and Choctaws—had aided Great Britain's military efforts in some fashion. Thus, according to European definitions of warfare, those Indians "lost" the war when their ally surrendered at Yorktown. "The United States in these first treaties after the Revolutionary War," writes historian Francis Paul Prucha, "thought it was dealing with conquered tribes or nations," even though Indian peoples "had no idea that they were to be treated as conquered peoples."[18] The U.S. government built upon the treaty system established by Great Britain in more than a century of interacting with Indians. Initiating this strategy first in the Old Northwest through the treaties of Fort Stanwix (with the Iroquois in October 1784), Fort McIntosh (with the Delawares, Wyandots, and others in January 1785), and Fort Finney (with the Shawnees in January 1786), the United States adopted a policy of imposing terms upon Indians and seizing their lands where possible and desirable. Negotiations with Indians who lived south of the Ohio River, which began in the fall of 1785, also entailed a heavy-handed, though less land-hungry, approach on the part of the young government.[19]

Based upon its jurisdiction over foreign relations and its authority to make treaties and manage Indian affairs, in March 1785 the Continental Congress appointed commissioners to treat with the southern Indians. Of the original five commissioners, South Carolinian Andrew Pickens, Virginian Joseph Martin, and North Carolinian Benjamin Hawkins accepted their appointments and journeyed southward. The young United States found it harder to develop and implement a cohesive Indian policy in the South than in the North, partly because southern states opposed congressional control over Indian affairs. Virginia, North Carolina, Georgia, and South Carolina had all raised their own armies against Indian enemies (particularly the Cherokees) during the war, and the first three held claims, dating from their colonial charters, to Indian lands in the West. All of the southern states viewed it as their right to handle Indian affairs and manage their western land claims. The Continental Congress and its designated commissioners recognized southern sensitivity to Indian issues and invited each southern state to send its own representative to the proposed treaty councils. For example, William Blount of North Carolina, one of the principal participants in the Hopewell negotiations, joined the delegation specifically to ensure that his state's land claims in Cherokee territory remained valid.[20]

The American commissioners met first with the Creek Indians in late October 1785. Although Georgia protested Congress's authority to negotiate with the Creeks, resistance to subjugation on the part of Creek chiefs contributed more to the failure of their treaty with the United States than did Georgia's protests. The Creeks showed up at their appointed meeting place in Galphinton, Georgia, in insufficient numbers to represent the entire nation. Upper Creek leader Alexander McGillivray had prevented many Creek towns from sending representatives, and the congressional commissioners refused to negotiate a treaty with the few who did appear. McGillivray blocked American ambition whenever possible during the 1780s in part because of Georgia's confiscation of his Tory father's land holdings and other property during the Revolution. In addition, McGillivray had a close business relationship with Panton, Leslie and Company, which was employed by Spain to conduct the deerskin trade with southern Indians. Nevertheless, agents from Georgia concluded a treaty with the small group of Creek Indians at Galphinton. Most other Creeks renounced the land cessions in this treaty and used it as an example of why Americans of all types could not be trusted.[21]

Cherokee Indians met first with representatives of the United States and North Carolina at Hopewell in late November 1785, and they offered little resistance to U.S. demands. The Cherokee Hopewell Treaty, however, reflected more the American government's concern with a lasting peace and improved trade relations than with securing land cessions. Officials from North Carolina, like William Blount, opposed the Cherokee treaty from the outset because it failed to recognize the validity of prior Cherokee cessions to their state. North Carolina refused to adhere to the particulars of the Cherokee treaty, and, since the Continental Congress failed to hold a vote on the treaty, a new round of treaties commenced after adoption of the Constitution.[22] Such jurisdictional conflicts between the states and the national government help to explain the lack of a cohesive Indian policy in the South prior to the establishment of the new federal government in 1789, but even afterward, Georgians would challenge federal authority in Indian affairs and press their western land claims until 1802.[23]

The Chickasaws had gained notoriety for their hostility to the new United States during the Revolutionary War. Allies of Britain throughout the eighteenth century, the Chickasaws responded to the threat of a Virginia wartime military expedition by warning Virginians to "take care that we dont serve you as we have served the French before with all their Indians, [and] send you back without your heads."[24] The Chickasaws who met with the U.S. commissioners at Hopewell in early January 1786 (after the Choctaws had finished their treaty meeting) sought to establish trade relations with the United States, just as they had with Spain a year and a half earlier. The U.S. commissioners backed away from dictating terms to the Chickasaws, asking for no land cessions and promising a trading post at the Muscle Shoals on the Tennessee River, but they did insist that the Chickasaws accept the sovereignty of the United States "and of no other sovereign whatsoever." State opposition to the Chickasaw treaty was minimal—other than a protest lodged by Blount—since their homeland in present northern Mississippi and southern Tennessee was distant from American settlements.[25]

These meetings with the southern Indians highlighted the disarray of U.S. Indian policy in the post-Revolutionary, pre-Constitution South, reflecting, in the words of historian Reginald Horsman, "a most confused and precarious state."[26] State goals, federal goals, individual goals, and Indian goals all contributed to the lack of a cohesive policy on the part of the United States. Within a year after the Hopewell treaties, the national government underwent, what historian Dorothy Jones called a "major policy retreat" whereby it recognized Indian occupation and title to lands in the West.[27] The encounter with groups like the Choctaws increased American awareness that native powers operating in the Southwest met or exceeded American strength. However, the Hopewell Treaty proceedings reveal that U.S. officials, while recognizing the tentative nature of their authority in the southern backcountry, nonetheless assumed an air of superiority, dictated terms, insisted on the inclusion of phraseology crafted before negotiations even took place, and probably deceived the Choctaws about the land cessions found in article three of the treaty document (which will be discussed below). Americans may have been conquerors in their own minds, but members of the Continental Congress and other American officials encountered, rather unexpectedly, the reality of Indian sovereignty and Indian control in vast regions east of the Mississippi River. Throughout the talks at Hopewell, Choctaw participants constantly reminded their hosts about Choctaw power and expectations.

Hopewell provided the first formal forum for the United States and the Choctaws to meet. Creating peaceful relations with a foreign people required the Choctaws to manipulate supernatural powers and employ political-religious specialists who could establish the sacred atmosphere necessary for incorporating strangers into the Choctaw kinship system. This requirement existed because there were essentially two types of people in Choctaw eyes: relatives and enemies. Turning enemies into kin was a serious business fraught with spiritual overtones, and accordingly, Franchimastabé appointed a chief named Taboca, who "had always been sent by the Nation as their representative in all their important Negotiations," to lead the expedition to Hopewell.[28] Taboca and Franchimastabé had teamed up before to represent the Choctaws in meetings with foreigners: in 1784 Taboca had led the diplomatic mission to Savannah that Franchimastabé coordinated. The two possessed close marriage ties as well, for at least one of Taboca's daughters was also a niece of Franchimastabé.[29] Taboca's importance in diplomacy derived from his extensive command of spiritual power. His unique name designated "midday," "the [sun's] highest point," or "all sunshine," either connecting him directly with the energy of the sun, the most important manifestation of power in southeastern Indian cosmology, or with openness and honesty, for Choctaws believed that the sun observed their words and actions and punished those who committed transgressions. He held two additional titles, Hopaii Mataha and

Mingo Hopaii, denoting "priest," "prophet," "war-prophet," or someone who could control events from afar. Taboca told the U.S. commissioners at Hopewell, "I am a headman in my Nation to receive and to give out talks [with foreigners]," and the interpreter for the Choctaws at Hopewell, John Pitchlynn, characterized Taboca as "the ablest speaker of all the chiefs." Taboca's presence thus ensured the safety of the mission and the likely success of the treaty meeting.[30]

Cognizant of the spiritual as well as physical dangers inherent in travel abroad, the Choctaw diplomatic mission to Hopewell traveled slowly, probably to preserve a deliberate and ritualistic air.[31] Native Americans in the Southeast and elsewhere customarily journeyed long distances from home to trade, fight, or meet with other people. Doing so, however, required adherence to strict rules governing proper behavior and the presence of proven spiritual leaders, like Taboca, who could ensure the group's success. Accompanying Taboca, and just as vital to the success of the treaty expedition, were ten women, several lower-ranked chiefs, and nearly a hundred warriors. Leaving their homeland in central Mississippi for Hopewell brought the Choctaw delegates into contact with potentially dangerous people, especially the Creek Indians, who had a history of warring against the Choctaws, and equally dangerous supernatural beings, such as the "Hoklonotéshe" who could "assume any shape he desires and is able to read men's thoughts."[32]

Upon arriving on the treaty grounds at Hopewell on December 26, 1785, after over two months of walking in the early winter cold, the Choctaws began trying to educate the American representatives about the correct way to construct a bond between two peoples. Trader John Woods escorted the Choctaws to Hopewell, and he sent a letter when the party was but a few days from the meeting site, warning the Americans of their imminent arrival. When they reached Hopewell, the Choctaws looked miserable and waited for the Americans to mollify their discomfort. Clothed in animal skins and appearing impoverished, they expected to be supplied with new garments by the people who had invited them to Hopewell and insisted that they journey so far. They wanted gifts of clothing, food, and other items from their hosts as a gesture of goodwill and honesty. As with many, if not all, American Indian groups, the Choctaws considered gifts fundamental to the establishment of a social environment in which peaceful relations could take place. The Americans did not understand Choctaw etiquette and were disappointed with the Indians' insistence on gifts, calling them "the greatest beggars, and the most indolent creatures we ever saw." Expectation of gifts is a pervasive feature of Native

American diplomacy, and refusing to provide them threatened harmonious relations.[33] The Choctaw delegates, perhaps aware of their host's dismay, explained that the Creek Indians had stolen their horses and supplies and declared that negotiations could not begin without proper clothing from the U.S. commissioners. Following the Choctaws' compelling—but maybe less than honest—explanation, the Americans agrees to provide the Choctaws with clothes and other supplies, including eighteen army coats, but they resented doing so, complaining that the Choctaws' "strong hankering for presents could not be abated."[34]

The U.S. commissioners opened official talks on December 30 with a speech calling for peace between the two peoples and for Choctaw acknowledgment of American sovereignty in the region. Before adjourning for the day (and again on January 2), the Americans attempted to demonstrate the size of U.S. territory, including the Choctaw homeland, on a map. Either the Choctaw representatives misunderstood the American claim to all land east of the Mississippi River or they intentionally feigned confusion. "Their knowledge of maps was not equal by any means to the Cherokees," complained Joseph Martin, "and it was difficult to make them comprehend the extent of territory within the United States of America." Just as the tale of Creeks stealing Choctaw supplies persuaded the American commissioners to abide by Choctaw definitions of diplomatic protocol, the Choctaw's ignorance of maps permitted them to disregard another nation's claims to their lands. The Choctaw delegates probably wondered why the land where they lived, and for which no land cession had ever been negotiated, fell within the jurisdiction of the United States. Conversely, the Americans insisted on printed documents such as maps as the legitimate record and sought Choctaw adherence to the authority of these pieces of paper. Throughout the meeting, however, Choctaws reminded their hosts that they were in control of their own destiny and that diplomacy must proceed according to their rules and wishes, regardless of what a paper map might indicate.[35]

When their talks resumed on December 31, Choctaw speakers emphasized the importance of the weather. Although it mattered little, beyond basic comfort, to the Americans, for the Choctaws the weather during the talks was very significant. According to Choctaw belief, the sun observed their words and deeds and guaranteed that everyone spoke honestly. Talks conducted in cloudy conditions might result in dishonesty or in a lack of trust that could undermine the goal of creating kin out of strangers. The Choctaw chief Yockonahoma announced on the first day of talks that "this is a clear sunshiny day and I hope it will be emblematical of but future Happiness and that nothing will happen to cloud or obscure our Talks." Similarly, another chief, Mingohoopoie, noted three days later that "this is a Clear and Sunshiny day on which we have met and it is to us as the promise of length of years."[36] This feature of Choctaw diplomacy probably explains the three days during the conference when the Choctaws refused to negotiate: December 29, January 1, and January 4. Only when the sun shone did talks proceed.

Under a sunny sky on December 31, the Choctaw delegation began by excusing Franchimastabé's absence. The Continental Congress had sent Franchimastabé the original invitation to the Hopewell meeting, thinking that he ruled the Choctaws. A letter from Franchimastabé explained that he chose the members of the Choctaw mission and authorized Taboca to treat with the United States. Presumably, Franchimastabé declined attendance at Hopewell because he had received official recognition as the leading chief of the Western Division, in addition to medals, flags, clothing, and other merchandise, from Spain at the 1784 Mobile Conference. Conceivably, Choctaws chose their representatives at Hopewell based on their not having attended the 1784 treaty negotiations with Spain, rather than because they were the principal leaders of their divisions. None of the Choctaw speakers from Hopewell appear in a detailed list of principal men recognized by Spain at the 1784 Mobile Treaty.[37] What is clear is that the speakers at Hopewell did not reflect the highest ranking chiefs of the three divisions. Most of the Choctaw speakers expressed anxiety about their lack of high status. Yockonahoma claimed that Franchimastabé "ordered me to come but not to make the talk long."[38]

Yockehoopoie cautioned that "I am not a principal headman of our Nation but what I do here is valid."[39] Shinshomastabé similarly excused himself: "There are others to speak who have greater abilities than I have—and as I am a young hand I will not say anything more. . . . I am not a leading man of the Nation."[40] Not all Choctaw speakers at Hopewell were novices in diplomacy, but the presence of so many lower-ranked chiefs playing a prominent role in the proceedings and their absence in the extant records of the 1784 treaty with Spain suggests that the Choctaws purposely avoided individual chiefs forming personal alliances with more than one Euro-American nation at a time.

This diplomatic principle caused Taboca to ceremonially disavow his allegiance with Spain. He had received a Spanish medal at Mobile just months before the Hopewell meeting, and other Choctaw speakers exposed his apparent conflict of interest. According to Martin, "[Taboca] was now ordered to be disgraced for his impudence before the Commissioners of the United

States by making him speak last," normally the place of those with the lowest status.[41] Nevertheless, Taboca performed an indispensable role in Choctaw diplomacy, making his presence essential to the success of the Hopewell conference and the Choctaw rituals performed there, and his attendance demonstrated the elasticity of diplomatic and cultural rules.

Taboca ended the first day of talks on December 31 in the mode of educator: "It is not usual to finish our talks in one day—I have brought up the headmen—they have talked—we will now shake hands with you and take these talks back to camp [for further deliberations]."[42] The treaty council proceeded two days later with the smoking of a calumet at the insistence of the Choctaws, another device meant to foster honesty and openness. Taboca and the other Choctaws assured the Americans that they were "the friends of white people whenever in their power," and that they would not let past alliances with Britain prevent the establishment of peaceful relations with the United States.[43]

West Yazoo's two leading chiefs, Franchimastabé and Taboca, supervised the outcome of this conference with the United States, but they organized the Hopewell mission with an eye toward representing all Choctaws. They selected headmen and warriors, and presumably the ten women, from each of the three Choctaw political divisions. Of the seven Choctaw men who spoke at Hopewell, Taboca and Yockanahoma represented the Western Division, Yockehoopoie, Mingohoopoie, and Tuscoonohopoia lived in the Eastern Division, Pooshemastubie resided in the Six Towns Division, and Shinshomastabé came from either the Western or Six Towns Division. Pooshemastubie pointed out how closely allied his Six Towns Division—the grouping of Choctaw villages closest to the Gulf Coast—was to the Spanish: "The part of our Nation where I live have never had any talks but from people on the Sea Shore [Spaniards] and when the chiefs of our nation [evidently Franchimastabé and Taboca] received your talks they sent for me because I was always firmly united with them." The speakers at Hopewell also demanded three American flags—one for each division—to demonstrate that all three divisions recognized the new relationship with the United States, which would enable all three groupings to share any material largesse from the new nation. Despite apparent difficulties in finding eligible representatives from all three divisions, doing so ensured that an agreement with the Americans would benefit everyone and avoid conflict.[44]

Choctaws displayed a sophisticated understanding of the new political realities among Euro-Americans in post-Revolutionary North America. The

United States comprised a completely new nation and people in Choctaw eyes. Although Taboca had led a Choctaw delegation to Georgia in 1784 and thus had met "Americans," the U.S. commissioners at Hopewell represented Americans of a different sort. Choctaws called the Americans present at Hopewell "Virginians," which Joseph Martin explained was "the term they use to express the citizens of the United States."[45] These "Virginians" may have spoken English, but Choctaws differentiated them from the British or from those Americans utilizing a state identity, such as the Georgians. Choctaws recognized political identities readily and classified peoples according to the manner that such foreigners described themselves. Thus, Yockanahoma, who surely had encountered English-speaking persons before 1786, could say to the Americans at Hopewell, "I have never heard of you White People and our forefathers may have heard of you but I never saw you till now and I never heard that [our forefathers] ever did see you."[46]

Of course, very few Americans—and certainly not the delegates sent by the Continental Congress to Hopewell—knew much about the Choctaws either. They knew only that Britain served as the Choctaws' closest European ally since the early 1760s and that Spain had signed a treaty with these Indians in 1784. Consequently, they met with the Choctaws in the manner that an immigrant approaches his neighbors after moving into a new home. Civility and decorum characterized all the speeches and public actions undertaken by Pickens, Hawkins, and Martin at the treaty negotiations. They especially wanted to impress upon the Choctaws and other Indians "the humane views of Congress towards all the tribes of Indians within the United States of America." Although they detested certain Choctaw rituals, actions, and words used at the meeting, they only expressed those thoughts—so far as we know—in private correspondence. Martin took pain to write down what the two sides said to each other and to describe in detail the Choctaw rituals, and Hawkins later transcribed and edited Martin's journal, which suggests that the Americans wanted a detailed record of the proceeding to educate other U.S. officials about this unfamiliar group of American Indians and to demonstrate their fairness and honesty in conversing with the Choctaws. Despite their professional behavior toward the Choctaws, the American delegates found little to praise and much to condemn when describing these "honest, simple" people who were still "the most indolent creatures we ever saw."[47]

Lack of familiarity rarely breeds tolerance and appreciation. American officials held preconceived and unflattering notions about who Indians were and what they were like, and these images stayed in the minds of the commissioners as they negotiated with the Choctaws. Revealing their ignorance of the Choctaws' mores, the Americans found their "passion for gambling and drinking is very great; we have had instances of their selling blankets at a pint of rum each, and gambling them away, when they had no prospect of replacing them." Choctaws and other southeastern Indians frequently wagered goods—especially European manufactured items—at diplomatic meetings and at celebratory activities such as their ball games. Gambling served to redistribute valuable goods throughout the confederacy, and Choctaws viewed it as a perfectly acceptable way to exchange an item they had for something they wanted. Notwithstanding their barely hidden ethnocentrism, the Americans tolerated some Choctaw customs—at least superficially—in their attempt to construct genuine bonds between the two societies.[48]

Initiating relations with a hitherto unknown polity required an elaborate collection of rituals that created a sacred atmosphere for the Choctaws to convert foreigners into fictive kin. When the sun reached its highest point in the sky on January 3, the day the treaty was signed, six Choctaws covered themselves in white clay, the color of peace and openness among southeastern Indians, and led the others in performing a series of formal ceremonies, including the eagle tail dance. Amid music, singing, and dancing, the Choctaw chiefs set up a twelve-foot-long white pole, establishing a sacred area in front of the bower constructed for the treaty meetings. Yockonahoma explained the pole's purpose: "I have set up a white pole—our token of peace—it is but a short pole but the peace will be long and lasting." Three chiefs carried shorter poles with deerskins attached to the tops, while two others carried white calumet pipes and fire to light the pipes. The 121 other Choctaw men and women wore the clothes that the commissioners had given them a few days earlier and marched to the area where the larger pole stood. The congressional representatives lined up across from the Choctaws and distributed more presents of clothing and pipes. Taboca then laid at the base of the pole sacred fire carried all the way from the Choctaw homeland and lifted hot coals from the American fire to take home. In this way, people of two fires—or two distinct families—merged together. A warrior told his war exploits and then the chiefs on one side and commissioners on the other joined hands, exchanged lighted pipes, and walked under the bower to the meeting table.[49]

Under the bower, "the master of ceremonies Taboca applied the eagle tail to the breasts of the Commissioners, the agent, and some respectable Gentlemen, then covered the seat of the Commissioners with two [white] deerskins and laid them under their feet." Taboca explained that "these feathers of the

Eagle tail we always hold when we make peace."[50] Bald eagles appear repeatedly in southeastern Indian iconography as a symbol of peace. Eagles represented the Upper World of the sun because they traveled between the earth and sky, thus making their feathers appropriate symbols of honesty and openness since Choctaws thought that the sun observed their actions and punished those who spoke falsely or acted deceitfully.[51] Placing prominent foreigners in a seat covered with white deerskins during diplomacy was a demonstration of tremendous respect. "The [southeastern] Indians cannot shew greater honour to the greatest potentate on earth, than to place him in the white seat . . . and dance before him with the eagles tails," observed British trader James Adair in the mid-eighteenth century.[52]

In addition to ceremonies with eagles' tails and white deerskins, smoking the calumet sanctified agreements between peoples. Calumets carried inherent spiritual power and guaranteed that a treaty was sacred because it was sealed by the smoking of the pipe. An eighteenth-century French eyewitness of other Choctaw diplomatic meetings clarified the pipe's role: "When they have concluded the peace the master of ceremonies lights this calumet and has all those who are in the assembly smoke two or three whiffs," after which "the treaty is [considered to be] concluded and inviolable." The smoke metaphorically carried everyone's words upward to the sky and sun, ensuring honesty and commitment to the agreements reached during the meeting. The host then gave the leading chief of the foreign group the calumet, "which is a hostage of their good faith, and the fidelity with which they wish to observe the articles on which they have agreed."[53]

The Hopewell Treaty with the United States involved far more than a simple agreement. Because the Choctaws had no prior relationship with the Americans, one more crucial element was needed for them to complete the alliance rituals. After the women painted themselves with white clay, sang and danced as part of the eagle tail dance, and exchanged gifts with the Americans, Taboca informed the commissioners, "You see our women are painted white—an emblem of peace and of their hopes of being able to raise up their Children in peace." The final ritual on January 3 required the women to approach the U.S. commissioners and embrace them.[54] The embrace of the women almost certainly meant that they metaphorically adopted the Americans into their lineages. The ten women adopted the American commissioners as fictive kin, something only they could do in Choctaw matrilineal society. Although there are few descriptions of the role of eighteenth-century

Choctaw women in diplomatic missions as detailed as this one, it seems likely that women always accompanied men to diplomatic meetings and participated in the rituals there. Their absence from many other records of Choctaw diplomacy with Europeans likely reflects more the Euro-American emphasis on men as political leaders and negotiators than Choctaw realities.[55] In the absence of the bonds of kinship, Choctaws did not know how to relate to other people; for them, a person who had no place in the kinship system stood outside the boundaries of normal human interaction. Adoption rituals and the mediation of women, therefore, were essential to conducting diplomacy according to Choctaw rules. After the women's embrace of the commissioners, the music stopped and the participants took their seats to continue talks.

This extraordinary day ended in the same instructive tone with which it began. Yockehoopoie reminded the Americans that the peace just established "is not for ourselves alone, we are now making peace for the people of all our respective nations and their posterity."[56] Taboca added that "the object of the Great men who Employed you and the Great man who sent us is accomplished as with out mouths we have locked our hands."[57] In Choctaw eyes, U.S. citizens and the Choctaw people now regarded one another as fictive kin. Having completed that vital task, the Choctaws adjourned for the day and rested comfortably knowing that subsequent days would bring the negotiations around to the issue they most wanted to discuss: trade.[58]

Two days later, the U.S. commissioners presented the written treaty to the Choctaws. Believing that the Choctaw delegates "comprehended the whole perfectly," the Americans declared the Choctaws "satisfied with every part" of the treaty.[59] The Choctaws and Americans signed two copies of the treaty, one for each party. After the treaty was signed, the Americans considered their business over and looked forward to their impending meeting with the Chickasaws. The Choctaw delegates viewed the signing of the treaty as less climactic, regarding it instead as simply the one major ritual that the Americans required. Yockonahoma suggested that he was not even sure what had been agreed to when he said that he "shall take John Pitchlynn the interpreter with me [so] he can tell us all our talks over again." According to the Choctaws, the negotiations had just begun. The treaty established peaceful relations between fictive kin, but "we will after this day talk of something else."[60]

That "something else" was trade, which was the real motive underlying the Choctaws' arduous journey to Hopewell. Although "we have ended all peace talks," Mingohoopoie explained that "our Nation is much in Want of

Match Coats[,] powder[,] and lead and I wish they could be supplied by your traders.... I hope the [Choctaw] Nation will be supported with necessaries as early as possible. We are much in want of guns[,] amunition[,] and clothing." He further insisted that trade goods formed a basic part of diplomacy between Choctaws and whites: "It was formerly a custom when I was at peace talks for the Indians to receive such guns as the white people made to carry to our nation."[61] Taboca reiterated this sentiment, declaring that "our Nation is much in want of clothing, arms, & ammunition and it is my desire that Capt. John Woods should be in a situation to see that our situation is remembered." John Woods had escorted the Choctaws to Hopewell, and they expected him to serve as the official American representative to their towns. A prominent feature of eighteenth-century Choctaw diplomacy, the exchange of ambassadors gave Choctaw chiefs a person to whom they could appeal in order to ensure a consistent and plentiful supply of trade goods. Taboca, who referred to himself as the "Great Traveler," offered in turn to visit the U.S. Congress, thus demonstrating Choctaw willingness to maintain direct contact with the American government now that kin relations had been established between the two peoples.[62] For the Choctaws, trade would provide an equal basis for their future interactions with the United States.

In addition to trade, Mingohoopoie focused on two other issues about which he cared deeply. Article 1 of the Hopewell Treaty called on the Choctaws to release any prisoners or African slaves taken during the Revolutionary War. Since the Choctaws held no such prisoners, this article's inclusion suggests that the Americans arrived at Hopewell with a document already prepared for the signatures of Britain's former Native American allies, and thus it should come as little surprise that Choctaw attempts to actually negotiate would meet with frustration. Nevertheless, Mingohoopoie called on the Americans to abide by the first article, protesting that some Americans had kidnapped one of his wives and a niece when they were visiting a Creek town. He asked the commissioners to look into the matter and return the women if possible. Articles 4, 5, and 6 of the treaty covered persons committing crimes within Choctaw territory, specifying that Americans who trespassed on Choctaw lands forfeited their right of protection from the U.S. government; that Indian or white criminals who harmed Americans and took refuge among the Indians were to be turned over to the United States for punishment; and finally that the United States would punish any of its citizens who committed crimes against the Choctaws. Mingohoopoie responded favorably to these articles and revealed a perceptive understanding of possible conflicts between Choctaws and Euro-Americans that had existed from the earliest days of contact:

> The article respecting the mode of punishment of villains &c I am exceedingly pleased with and it will prevent the commission of evil. [Y]ou are not the first men I have treated with on this subject. [F]ormerly when I treated with the British we did something like it and I always punished accordingly thereto. We here are headmen and it is as impossible for us to be responsible for all the warriors as it is for you to become responsible for the disorderly people of your nation. We have bad people in our nation and there are good and bad of all nations.... I have received your talks and I love your talks and if there should be any violation of the articles we will punish immediately in the Nation.[63]

The Choctaw delegates thus agreed with certain aspects of the written and signed treaty, but they strongly disagreed with the second and third articles. Article 2 placed the Choctaws "under the protection of the United States of America, and of no other sovereign whosoever."[64] From the Choctaw perspective, the full implications of such a stipulation were unthinkable; they intended to preserve their sovereignty and maintain relations with whomever they chose. Just one year later, an emissary of the Spanish government, Juan de la Villebeuvre, visited Franchimastabé at West Yazoo and reaffirmed the Choctaw-Spanish alliance of 1784.[65] In the meantime, the Choctaws continued to welcome sporadic traders and agents from the southern states, such as Benjamin James from Georgia.[66] White the Choctaws failed to protest Article 2 directly, they probably interpreted it in light of reciprocal kinship and trade relations between the two nations rather than as an acknowledgment of U.S. jurisdiction over Choctaw territories and peoples. Otherwise, their subsequent unilateral actions to establish relations with as many Euro-American polities as possible would make little sense.

It is doubtful that anyone explained the precise implications of Article 3 to the Choctaw delegation during the treaty negotiations. Despite a stated goal on the part of the United States not to want "more of your lands or anything else which belongs to you," Article 3 of the Hopewell Treaty called for the establishment of three trading posts, six square miles each, within Choctaw territory. Furthermore, the United States claimed sole right to choose the locations of these posts.[67] Had the Choctaws known that the United States intended to build three trading posts within their territory, it would not have been necessary to request traders and insist on supplies of trade goods. However, it was the fine print of Article 3, in which these American trading posts were said to consist of six square miles each, that caused an uproar among the Choctaws. After learning of this provision upon the delegation's return, Franchimastabé offered to send his warriors to fight with the Creeks against the Americans—a clear indication that he strongly rejected the notion that the Choctaws had ceded any of their lands to the United States. He also employed a trader among the Choctaws to write to the Cherokees' American agent chiding U.S. representatives for not establishing a consistent trade (without occupying Choctaw lands) and warning them about possible attacks from his warriors.[68] Other Choctaw chiefs further condemned American actions at Hopewell in meetings with Spanish officials in 1787 and 1788. Yockonahoma, one of the principal speakers at the Hopewell negotiations, eloquently argued the Choctaw position and defended his actions:

> You, my father, have reproached me several times for having gone to the Americans. That is correct, I have, but without intending to bring them into the nation, or to give them lands, like they say. It simply is poverty. As all red men are poor and do not know how to make anything, they are obliged to go see the white nations that make everything, in order that they may give them presents, and we went, believing that we would receive them. They began by asking us for lands, to which we said that we were not authorized by the nation to give lands to anyone. Nevertheless, they drew up a document, without telling us what it contained, and we thought it was for the purpose of giving us presents. They had us make some marks on it without our knowing what we were doing. Afterward they told us what it was. Then I seized the paper and I burned it. After this they had us drink strong water, or fire water, which intoxicated us, and when they saw us in this condition, they made us again make marks on the paper.[69]

Six square miles multiplied by three, or 11,520 acres, may seem diminutive from the standpoint of the eventual Indian land cessions to the United States, but Choctaws perceived a potential conflict if the United States ever sought to occupy the three areas of their choosing. Although Choctaws wanted traders to visit their villages, they refused to accept permanent settlers with the livestock and large-scale agriculture that inevitably accompanied the construction of trading posts. Just a few years later, the Spanish governor of Natchez, Manuel Gayoso de Lemos, confronted this problem when construction of a fort, post, and outlying buildings began at Nogales along the Mississippi River (present-day Vicksburg), which was within Choctaw territory. After the conclusion of the Revolution, Americans had flooded into Spanish-controlled lands around Natchez along the boundary with the Choctaws, and now they began moving to Nogales as well. Some of these newcomers killed game animals in Choctaw hunting lands, stole horses within the confederacy, traded large quantities of alcohol to Choctaw warriors, and otherwise seriously strained constructive intercultural relations and local social control. Choctaw warriors and chiefs, especially Franchimastabé and Taboca, vehemently opposed the Nogales construction, and Gayoso spent two years attempting to placate them until the issue was finally settled. The Choctaws found it almost impossible to tolerate Americans living among them unless they were traders living in Choctaw villages, married to Choctaw women, and working under the purview of chiefs.[70] Such difficulties with permanent white settlements caused the Choctaws to agree with the Chickasaw desire for a trade store on the Muscle Shoals of the Tennessee River, still accessible to but outside the territory of both groups.

As Yockonahoma admitted in the passage quoted above, the Choctaws drank alcohol provided to them by the Americans throughout the meeting at Hopewell (and the U.S. commissioners complained about their crude behavior when drunk), but it is not at all clear that they were inebriated at the time of the treaty signing; no such references exist in the proceedings as recorded by Joseph Martin. Many Choctaws blamed interpreter John Pitchlynn's supposed illiteracy and his inability to read Article 3 for their ignorance of the land cessions. That would mean that the U.S. delegates failed to verbally explain Article 3, something they explicitly denied in their descriptions of the negotiations. However, Pitchlynn was not illiterate, at least not in later life. Interpreters between American Indians and Euro-Americans, as James Merrell has demonstrated, brought their own fallibilities and motivations to treaty councils and often caused the imperfect communications that developed there. Pitchlynn's qualifications seemed adequate enough: his trader father had introduced him to the Choctaws as a young boy, and he was raised among them, prospering materially in the confederacy and eventually taking a Choctaw wife by whom he fathered several children. As the U.S. commissioners at Hopewell noted of Pitchlynn, "He is a very honest sober young man, and has lived twelve years in the nation and is much respected by the Chiefs as an Interpreter." It is impossible to ascertain whether Pitchlynn misled the Choctaw delegation at Hopewell (either through intention or incompetence), but if the meaning of Article 3 became lost in translation, then he certainly played a role in that confusion.[71]

Yockonahoma had denied that the Choctaws ceded any lands at Hopewell, telling Spanish agents in January 1788 that the delegation at Hopewell did not have the authority to grant lands.[72] That contention seems confirmed by the generally low-ranking status of most of the Choctaw chiefs at Hopewell, as well as the fact that they only partially represented each of the three divisions. The Americans, Spanish governor Esteban Miró insisted, "certainly know that the cited chiefs did not go to [Hopewell] on behalf of the entire nation, because the great chiefs had not convened in order to send them, and therefore they did not have the necessary authority to grant lands and make treaties." Miró also alluded to the divergence of views between the Americans and the Choctaws about what constituted a treaty; the Americans "had all [the Choctaw speakers at Hopewell] make a mark on the paper, which among the whites gives full authority to a treaty."[73]

Despite the controversy over Article 3, U.S. officials, especially General Henry Knox (who was appointed secretary of war in 1789), emphasized all of the articles—and Choctaw agreement with them—when explaining the importance of the Choctaw Hopewell Treaty in following years. In 1790 Knox recommended that the U.S. Senate further extend trade to the Chickasaws and Choctaws in order to counter the anti-American actions of the Creek Indians and the machinations of the Spanish; their allegiance, he said, should be pursued "agreeably to the Treaty of Hopewell." Around the same time, President George Washington called on American citizens to abide by the principles of the Hopewell Treaty in dealings with the Choctaws and Chickasaws. Conveniently unaware of Choctaw objections to key portions of the written treaty, for years afterward American officials continued to issue misleading pronouncements that took for granted a decisive acceptance of the treaty's terms by both parties to it.[74]

The U.S. government also paid little attention to the specific Choctaw demands made at Hopewell. For example, they responded negatively to the Choctaw request for an American representative to live among them. No official agent of the federal government would live among the Choctaws for another decade. John Woods, who owned property around Natchez and had escorted Taboca and other Choctaw negotiators to Savannah, Hopewell, Philadelphia, and New York in the mid-1780s, lost his bid to gain authorization from the Continental Congress to be the official Indian agent to the Choctaws. Pickens, Hawkins, and Martin had questioned Woods's loyalties at

Hopewell, calling him "a man of some enterprise and ability, but much addicted to strong drink. He came in with the Indians, and has been at much trouble [drinking] with them."[75]

The U.S. commissioners at Hopewell tried to discourage Taboca from visiting Congress, but he journeyed to Philadelphia and New York anyway, arriving during the busy Constitutional Convention summer of 1787. Accompanied by a Choctaw warrior, a Chickasaw chief named Piamingo, and his wife, Taboca met with Benjamin Franklin, Henry Knox, George Washington, and other American officials before returning home by boat down the Ohio and Mississippi rivers.[76] Although he did convey the specific request for the establishment of a U.S. trading post at the Muscle Shoals on the Tennessee River, Taboca was interested in more than material benefits from his contact with the United States. His prestige and authority within Choctaw society reached new heights as he demonstrated his command over spiritual forces by traveling to distant lands and meeting foreign people. The Choctaws, like other cultures, accorded special status to those who gathered knowledge of foreign places and foreign people. Travel beyond the bounds of Choctaw civilized society carried mystical significance and designated one as a spiritual specialist. Years after Hopewell, Taboca would continue to display the tools of his power, all of which were based on the accumulation of esoteric knowledge from foreign travel. When the Spanish government official Stephen Minor paid the venerable chief a visit outside West Yazoo in 1792, Taboca "took out a small box in which he had his Papers and told me to read them all. I examined them and found an English Patent, and another in Spanish, a letter from an English delegate and another from the Americans of Philadelp[h]ia as to his conduct, one thing and another. . . . He also had Portraits of General Washington, his wife, Governor Penn, and various others."[77] Taboca's journeys had helped him to gain access to this esoteric source of power based on contact with foreign peoples and the accumulation of knowledge, and such spiritual forms of power still resonated loudly as a basis of authority within late-eighteenth-century Choctaw society.

Other Choctaws also traveled within the seaboard states in subsequent years. For example, a small delegation of Choctaws (most likely from the Eastern Division) traveled to Charleston, South Carolina, within two month of the Hopewell meetings. Like Taboca, they also requested that trade be increased as soon as possible, and they offered to assist the Americans in their ongoing conflicts with the Creeks as an additional incentive. The Choctaws knew that the southeastern states worried constantly about Creek intentions and feared their frequent small-scale attacks on American settlers. Although the Choctaws attempted to play on these fears in order to secure a more plentiful trade, more trade from South Carolina was not forthcoming.[78]

Indeed, increased trade, which was the primary reason that the Choctaws traveled to Hopewell in the first place, generally failed to materialize at all. No steady American trade with the Choctaws developed until the Choctaw Trading Factory was established at St. Stephens in 1802. Even as the Choctaw delegation prepared to leave Hopewell on January 6, 1786, they registered their disappointment with the undersupplied Americans. "The Indians appeared perfectly satisfied with everything except the Guns," wrote Joseph Martin, "as instead of Musquets they had been promised before they left the Nation that they should receive some Guns of the Manufacture of the United States of America . . . that . . . were rifles."[79] Of the Choctaw delegation to Hopewell, only Yockonahoma received a rifle; the other chiefs received muskets, with which they were understandably less than satisfied. Led to believe that the United States was a new and powerful nation capable of providing large quantities of trade goods, they discovered instead that the young republic was financially poor. The commissioners spent $1,181 on their meeting with the Choctaws at Hopewell, a sum that far exceeded what they had intended to spend. Since rifles were in short supply in the United States and the national government suffered from perpetual lack of money, it seems unlikely that the American delegation to Hopewell ever intended to initiate a consistent trade relationship with the Choctaws. Only when confronted with intractable Indian groups who refused to accept their role as conquered peoples did the United States look to trade (and the consequent debts that it caused) as a tool to better influence Indian actions.[80]

Although southern states threw up roadblocks to the federal management of Indian affairs, these are an inadequate explanation for the obstacles that the United States encountered in their meetings at Hopewell. Southern Indians, as the Choctaw example demonstrates, resisted efforts by the United States to redefine their status as something other than sovereign. In their assumed role as conquerors, U.S. officials expected Indians in the post-Revolutionary era to realize—even if not to fully accept—their subordinate role in the new North American order. However, most Indian groups east of the Mississippi River never lost a battle, much less a war, to the Americans, and, beginning in the 1780s, their goals appeared to clash fundamentally with those of the United States. Many Indian groups responded to American arrogance and encroachment on their lands with violence, as in the recurrent warfare between Creek Indians and Georgians, and the Miami war chief Little Turtle's multitribal war against American settlements in the Ohio Valley during the 1790s. Increasingly aware that Indians from the Great Lakes to the Gulf of Mexico rejected the role that the United States preferred them to play and that the world was casting a critical eye on the new republic's bullying tactics, government officials such as Henry Knox insisted that the United States try to work with Indians rather than simply impose terms on them. By 1789 the United States had renounced its claims of absolute sovereignty over the territory it had acquired from Great Britain, thus converting Indian affairs from a domestic problem to a foreign policy issue.[81] In other words, the United States acknowledged Indian autonomy and sovereignty in areas like the Old Southwest because there was little alternative. In subsequent decades, new American strategies developed concurrently to remove Indians from lands east of the Mississippi River, including negotiating with Indians for land cessions; warring against them to acquire undisputed title to new territory; promoting trade relations to encourage financial indebtedness; and insisting that Indians adopt the tenets of "civilization."[82]

Stubborn Choctaw adherence to a centuries-old diplomatic style drove home the message that, despite its desires, the U.S. government could not dictate terms to Indians who refused to accept passively the notion of a new order that placed them on the losing side. Euro-Americans of different types may have lived all around them, but the Choctaws would make their own decisions about how to handle this rapidly changing universe. Native groups still constituted the dominant powers in the late-eighteenth-century southeastern Mississippi Valley, a notion that the Choctaws accepted as a matter of fact and that the Hopewell negotiations did little to change. Rather than bringing the two peoples closer together as Taboca, the other Choctaw dignitaries, and even the American delegates had hoped, the treaty council and its aftermath drove home the point that, for the foreseeable future, the southern backcountry frontier would comprise a contested zone with little room for compromise or intercultural cooperation between the United States and Indian groups. The possibilities suggested by the joining together of fictive kin crashed on the rocky shore of cultural misunderstanding and obstinacy. One side would need to yield and accept portions of the other culture's values before true collaboration and harmony could have any chance of success.

Careful analysis of the ceremonial and diplomatic context in which the

Choctaw Hopewell Treaty was negotiated thus reveals a very different picture than does an analysis based on the treaty document alone. The Choctaw delegation made demands, conducted rituals, educated the U.S. representatives about their culture, and left Hopewell unsatisfied. The U.S. commissioners complained about Choctaw ignorance and also worried that little of value had resulted from the meeting. Both sides adhered to a rigid agenda and resisted compromise at Hopewell.

Viewing the treaty through the eyes of both sets of participants, however, reveals two societies acting in accordance with inherited tradition as well as employing new approaches borne out of the Revolutionary War experience. Even though neither side had the power to coerce concessions from the other, the Choctaws insisted that their American counterparts act according to Choctaw notions of proper diplomatic conduct. Although they had conducted diplomatic meetings with Europeans for nearly a century and accepted the Euro-American insistence on written documents as a formalized record of any treaty proceeding, the Choctaws were more concerned to uphold their own rituals, speeches, and sacralized objects as the true record of negotiations. And even though American officials recognized the need to accommodate Indian notions of diplomatic procedure, they did so in a largely perfunctory manner that caused misunderstanding, misinterpretation, and disagreements about the meaning of the Hopewell Treaty in later years. In that sense, U.S. acquiescence to Choctaw rituals was merely a grease to lubricate the machinery that produced a written, legally binding document and thus lacked the sincerity needed to make the agreement work.

Hence the "middle ground" of Indian-European interaction emphasized by recent scholars did not always consist of an area where different peoples enacted a "vision of peaceful coexistence and creative accommodation." Instead, as Richard White insisted in his seminal work, frontier zones comprised contested spaces where the meanings of rituals and words were argued over and contentions over power persisted.[83] As an analysis of the Hopewell Treaty proceedings between the Choctaws and the United States demonstrates, peaceful meetings could just as easily be characterized by intransigence and miscommunication. In this case, the Choctaws dominated the process of treaty making and assumed the continuation of their absolute sovereignty and control over their own destiny; the Americans, however, arrived at Hopewell believing in their own cultural superiority and left thinking that all of the components of their preplanned treaty had been agreed upon. But the historical realization of the character and outcome of intercultural encounters like Hopewell can only stem from a sensitive reading of the entire context in which such negotiations—or contests—occurred.

NOTES

This chapter originally appeared as "The Conqueror Meets the Unconquered: Negotiating Cultural Boundaries on the Post-Revolutionary Southern Frontier," *Journal of Southern History* 68 (February 2001): 39–72.

1. William H. Masterson, *William Blount* (Baton Rouge: Louisiana State University Press, 1954), 107. For background on Pickens and his home see Alice Noble Waring, *The Fighting Elder: Andrew Pickens, 1739–1817* (Columbia, S.C.: University of South Carolina Press, 1962). Estimates of the Choctaw population in the late eighteenth century range from around 14,000 up to 30,000; see Peter H. Wood, "The Changing Population of the Colonial South: An Overview by Race and Region, 1685–1790," in *Powhatan's Mantle: Indians in the Colonial Southeast*, ed. Peter H. Wood, Gregory A. Waselkov, and M. Thomas Hatley (Lincoln: University of Nebraska Press, 1989), 38, 72; Richard White, *The Roots of Dependency: Subsistence, Environment, and Social Change among the Choctaws, Pawnees, and Navajos* (Lincoln: University of Nebraska Press, 1983), 5; and Daniel H. Usner Jr., *American Indians in the Lower Mississippi Valley: Social and Economic Histories* (Lincoln: University of Nebraska Press, 1998), 35. I wish to thank Michael Green, Theda Perdue, Daniel Richter, Nancy Shoemaker, and the anonymous reviewers from the *Journal of Southern History* for commenting and making valuable suggestions on earlier drafts of this essay.

2. Joseph Martin was Virginia's designated representative to the Hopewell meetings, and his handwritten "Journal of the Hopewell Treaties, 1786" is in the Draper Manuscript Collection (State Historical Society of Wisconsin, Madison), series U, vol. 14, pp. 56–92, which is also available on microfilm (Madison, 1944–1949, reel 65) (hereafter cited as Martin Journal). Benjamin Hawkins, North Carolina's representative to the negotiations, transcribed a copy of Martin's journal, and it resides in the Joseph Vallance Bevan Papers, series 7E, item 11 of the Peter Force Collection (Manuscript Division, Library of Congress, Washington, D.C.).

3. See Walter H. Mohr, *Federal Indian Relations, 1774–1788* (Philadelphia: University of Pennsylvania Press, 1933), 151–56; Waring, *The Fighting Elder*, 135; Reginald Horsman, *Expansion and American Indian Policy, 1783–1812* (East Lansing: Michigan State University Press, 1967), 29–30; W. David Baird, *Peter Pitchlynn: Chief of the Choctaws* (Norman: University of Oklahoma Press, 1972), 8; John D. Guice, "Face to Face in Mississippi Territory, 1798–1817," in Carolyn Keller Reeves, ed., *The Choctaw before Removal* (Jackson: University Press of Mississippi, 1985), 164; Samuel J. Wells, "Federal Indian Policy: From Accomodation to Removal," in Reeves, *Choctaw before Removal*, 183; Robert B. Ferguson, "Treaties between the United States and the Choctaw Nation," in Reeves, *Choctaw before Removal*, 214–15; Francis Paul Prucha, *The Great Father: The United States Government and the American Indians*, 2 vols. (Lincoln: University of Nebraska Press, 1984) 1:46; and Prucha, *American Indian*

Treaties: The History of a Political Anomaly (Berkeley: University of California Press, 1994), 62–63.

4. For the original concept of the "middle ground," which emphasized cultural competition and violence as much as cultural borrowing and civility, see Richard White, *The Middle Ground: Indians, Empires, and Republics in the Great Lakes Region, 1650–1815* (Cambridge: Cambridge University Press, 1991). More recent works have advanced an "alternative vision of peaceful coexistence and creative accommodation" between Europeans and Indians; see Andrew R. L. Cayton and Fredrika J. Teute, eds., *Contact Points: American Frontiers from the Mohawk Valley to the Mississippi, 1750–1830* (Chapel Hill: University of North Carolina Press, 1998), 9. For an essay critical of such revisionism, see Daniel J. Herman, "Romance on the Middle Ground," *Journal of the Early Republic* 19 (Summer 1999): 279–91. Other recent works that analyze in greater detail the contrasting meanings of metaphors and actions utilized by Indians and Europeans in colonial and early national America include several of the essays in Cayton and Teute, *Contact Points*. On the importance of analyzing treaty council proceedings to observe the "clash of two idea systems" between Indians and Euro-Americans, see Raymond J. DeMallie, "Touching the Pen: Plains Indian Treaty Councils in Ethnohistorical Perspective," in *Ethnicity on the Great Plains*, ed. Frederick C. Luebke (Lincoln: University of Nebraska Press, 1980), 38–40; and James H. Merrell, *Into the American Woods: Negotiators on the Pennsylvania Frontier* (New York: Norton, 1999).

5. By contrast, see the promotion of the official American line in Prucha, *American Indian Treaties*, 65–66, where he wrote: "The Indians agreed to a considerable diminution of their autonomy [in 1786] when they accepted peace given by the United States, agreed to be under its protection, and acquiesced in the treaty provisions that Congress would have 'the sole and exclusive right of regulating the trade with the Indians, and managing all their affairs in such manner as they think proper.'"

6. Greg O'Brien, "Choctaws in a Revolutionary Age: A Study of Power and Authority, 1750–1801" (Ph.D. diss., University of Kentucky, 1998), 108–10; and O'Brien, "Protecting Trade through War: Choctaw Elites and British Occupation of the Floridas," in *Empire and Others: British Encounters with Indigenous Peoples, 1600–1850*, ed. Martin Daunton and Rick Halpern (Philadelphia: University of Pennsylvania Press, 1999), 149–66. Spain's defeat of British forces in the Southeast is summarized neatly in David J. Weber, *The Spanish Frontier in North America* (New Haven, Conn.: Yale University Press, 1992), 265–70.

7. Farquhar Bethune to John Stuart [British Superintendent of Southern Indian Affairs], June 16, 1778, in *Documents of the American Revolution, 1770–1783*, ed. K. G. Davies, 21 vols. (Shannon: Irish University Press, 1972–81), 15:143–45 (quotation on p. 145); see also Davies's description of the events of 1778, pp. 12–15. The Choctaw confederacy was composed of three principal ethnic and geographical groupings called the *Okla falaya* (people who are widely dispersed), *Okla tannap* (people from the other side), and *Okla hannali* (people of six towns). Eighteenth-century Europeans and subsequent scholars have simplified this terminology into the Western, Eastern, and Six Towns (or Southern) Divisions, respectively. See White, *Roots of*

Dependency, 37–38, 106–8; Patricia Galloway, "Confederacy as a Solution to Chiefdom Dissolution: Historical Evidence in the Choctaw Case," in *The Forgotten Centuries: Indians and Europeans in the American South, 1521–1704*, ed. Charles Hudson and Carmen Chaves Tesser (Athens: University of Georgia Press, 1994), 408–9; Galloway, *Choctaw Genesis, 1500–1700* (Lincoln: University of Nebraska Press, 1995), 338–60; and John R. Swanton, *Source Material for the Social and Ceremonial Life of the Choctaw Indians*, Bureau of American Ethnology Bulletin 103 (Washington, D.C.: U.S. Government Printing Office, 1931), 55–56.

8. For Choctaw assistance to Spain see Caroline Maude Burson, *The Stewardship of Don Esteban Miró, 1782–1792* (New Orleans: American Printing Company, 1940), 48; for Choctaw aid to the British see James H. O'Donnell III, *Southern Indians in the American Revolution* (Knoxville: University of Tennessee Press, 1973), and O'Brien, "Choctaws in a Revolutionary Age," 108–10.

9. European officials used the term "nation" to refer to Indian societies such as the Choctaws for decades before the 1780s, but "confederacy" or the more ambiguous but less misleading "group" offers a more accurate assessment of Choctaw political realities, while also avoiding the sometimes pejorative "tribe." On the Choctaw "play-off" system see White, *Roots of Dependency*, 34–68.

10. For the British-operated trading companies hired by Spain see William S. Coker and Thomas D. Watson, *Indian Traders of the Southeastern Spanish Borderlands: Panton, Leslie & Company and John Forbes & Company, 1783–1847* (Pensacola: University of West Florida Press, 1986).

11. For the Spanish treaty see "Tratado de alianza entre España y los indios Chactas y Chicasas o Chicachas, 14 de Julio de 1784," in Manuel Serrano y Sanz, *España y los Indios Cherokis y Chactas en la Segunda Mitad del Siglo XVIII* (Seville: Tip. de la "Guia oficial," 1916), 82–85. On the meeting with Georgia see John Woods to [Georgia Lieutenant Governor] John Habersham, June 12, 1784, and "Talk Delivered by Habersham to Mingahoopa the Second Chief of the Choctaw Nation, July 17, 1784," in *Creek Indian Letters, Talks, and Treaties, 1705–1839*, ed. Louise Frederick Hays, 4 vols. (Atlanta: Georgia Department of Archives and History, 1939), 1:56, 59–60.

12. For analysis of the Creek deerskin trade see Kathryn E. Holland Braund, *Deerskins and Duffels: The Creek Indian Trade with Anglo-America, 1685–1815* (Lincoln: University of Nebraska Press, 1993).

13. Christopher L. Miller and George R. Hamell, "A New Perspective on Indian-White Contact: Cultural Symbols and Colonial Trade," *Journal of American History* 73 (September 1986), 311–28. For lists of the items being traded to the Choctaws see Helen Louise Shaw, *British Administration of the Southern Indians, 1756–1783* (Lancaster, Pa.: Lancaster Press, 1931), 70, 166–72; White, *Roots of Dependency*; and Daniel H. Usner Jr., *Indians, Settlers, and Slaves in a Frontier Exchange Economy: The Lower Mississippi Valley before 1783* (Chapel Hill: University of North Carolina Press, 1992), 260, 270–72.

14. Jon D. Muller, "The Southeast," in *Ancient Native Americans*, ed. Jesse D. Jennings (San Francisco: W. H. Freeman, 1978), 281–325; Alex W. Barker and Timothy R. Pauketat, eds., *Lords of the Southeast: Social Inequality and the Native Elites of Southeastern North America* (Washington, D.C.: American Anthropological Association,

1992); Patricia B. Kwachka, ed., *Perspectives on the Southeast: Linguistics, Archaeology, and Ethnohistory* (Athens: University of Georgia Press, 1994); Timothy R. Pauketat and Thomas E. Emerson, eds., *Cahokia: Domination and Ideology in the Mississippian World* (Lincoln: University of Nebraska Press, 1997); John F. Scarry, ed., *Political Structure and Change in the Prehistoric Southeastern United States* (Gainesville: University Press of Florida, 1996); and Thomas E. Emerson, *Cahokia and the Archaeology of Power* (Tuscaloosa: University of Alabama Press, 1997).

15. Tom Hatley, *The Dividing Paths: Cherokees and South Carolinians through the Era of Revolution* (New York: Oxford University Press, 1993), 10; and O'Brien, "Protecting Trade through War," 149–60.

16. Nicholas Long Jr., William Davenport, and Nathaniel Christmas to Governor Samuel Elbert [of Georgia], September 13, 1785, in Edmund C. Burnett, comp., "Papers Relating to Bourbon County, Georgia, 1785–1786, [Part] II," *American Historical Review* 15 (January 1910), 337.

17. Letter from the Choctaw Nation to [Governor of Georgia] John Houston, May 8, 1784, File II, RG 4-2-46, Loc. 1543-01, box 74, folder 2 (Georgia Department of Archives and History, Atlanta) (quotation). All quotes by the Choctaws contained in this article were translated and transcribed by Euro-Americans and therefore should not be considered entirely literal statements. Nevertheless, the quotations selected should give the reader a reasonably accurate idea of what the Choctaws were trying to say and accomplish. On Franchimastabé see O'Brien, "Choctaws in a Revolutionary Age," chap. 5.

18. Prucha, *Great Father*, 1:45; cf. his similar statement in Prucha, *American Indian Treaties*, 41.

19. For summaries of post-Revolutionary relations between American Indians and the U.S. government see Colin G. Calloway, *The American Revolution in Indian Country: Crisis and Diversity in Native American Communities* (New York: Cambridge University Press, 1995), esp. 272–91; Dorothy V. Jones, *License for Empire: Colonialism by Treaty in Early America* (Chicago: University of Chicago Press, 1982), esp. 151–53; James H. Merrell, "Declarations of Independence: Indian-White Relations in the New Nation," in *The American Revolution: Its Character and Limits*, ed. Jack P. Greene (New York: New York University Press, 1987), 197–223; and Kenneth M. Morrison, "Native Americans and the American Revolution: Historic Stories and Shifting Frontier Conflict," in *Indians in American History: An Introduction*, ed. Frederick E. Hoxie (Wheeling, Ill.: Harlan Davidson, 1998), 87–104.

20. Edmund C. Burnett, *The Continental Congress* (New York: Macmillan, 1941), 628; Benjamin Hawkins, Andrew Pickens, and Jos[eph]. Martin, Commissioners, to Governor Patrick Henry of Virginia, June 10, 1785, in *Calendar of Virginia State Papers*, ed. William P. Palmer, 11 vols. (Richmond, Va., 1875–93), 4:33; and William Blount to Governor Richard Caswell [of North Carolina], July 3, 1785, William Blount Papers (McClung Historical Collection, Knox County Public Library System, Knoxville, Tennessee).

21. Alexander McGillivray to Carlos Howard, August 11, 1790, in *McGillivray of the Creeks*, by John Walton Caughey (Norman: University of Oklahoma Press, 1938), 274–

75; Mohr, *Federal Indian Relations*, 143–51; Prucha, *American Indian Treaties*, 60; Michael D. Green, "Alexander McGillivray," in *American Indian Leaders: Studies in Diversity*, ed. R. David Edmunds (Lincoln: University of Nebraska Press, 1980), 41–63; Thomas D. Watson, "Strivings for Sovereignty: Alexander McGillivray, Creek Warfare, and Diplomacy, 1783–1790," *Florida Historical Quarterly* 58 (April 1980), 400–414; Randolph C. Downes, "Creek-American Relations, 1782-1790," *Georgia Historical Quarterly* 21 (June 1937), 142–84; Benjamin Hawkins and Andrew Pickens to Charles Thomson, January 1786, Henry Knox Papers (microfilm; Gilder Lehrman Collection, Pierpont Morgan Library, New York), reel 47; and Treaty of Galphinton, November 12, 1785, Knox Papers, reel 18.

22. Mohr, *Federal Indian Relations*, 147–51; Calloway, *American Revolution in Indian Country*, 208–9; and Jones, *License for Empire*, 134.

23. North Carolina ceded its western claims to the federal government in 1789. See Mohr, *Federal Indian Relations*, 141–43; and Horsman, *Expansion and American Indian Policy*, 24. The Cherokee Hopewell Treaty is reprinted in *Indian Affairs: Laws and Treaties*, vol. 2, ed. Charles J. Kappler (Washington, D.C.: U.S. Government Printing Office, 1904), 8–11, and the treaty council in *American State Papers: Documents, Legislative and Executive, of the Congress of the United States... March 3, 1789–March 3, 1815*, class II, vol. 4, *Indian Affairs* (Washington, D.C.: Gales and Seaton, 1832), 40–43.

24. Calloway, *American Revolution in Indian Country*, 226.

25. Ibid., 235–36; William L. Saunders and Walter Clark, eds., *Colonial and State Records of North Carolina*, 25 vols. (Raleigh, N.C.: P. M. Hale, 1886–1914), 18:493–95; Prucha, *American Indian Treaties*, 63; the treaty in Kappler, ed., *Indian Affairs*, 14–16; and the treaty council in *American State Papers*, 4:50–54.

26. Horsman, *Expansion and American Indian Policy*, 30.

27. Jones, *License for Empire*, 147.

28. Martin Journal, 64.

29. O'Brien, "Choctaws in a Revolutionary Age," 111–45, 170–73.

30. Martin Journal, 73, 64 (quotations). For more detail on Taboca as a political-religious specialist see O'Brien, "Choctaws in a Revolutionary Age," 111–45. On the translation of Taboca see Cyrus Byington, *A Dictionary of the Choctaw Language*, ed. John R. Swanton and Henry S. Halbert, Bureau of American Ethnology Bulletin 46 (Washington, D.C.: U.S. Government Printing Office, 1915), 336; and Horatio B. Cushman, *History of the Choctaw, Chickasaw, and Natchez Indians* (Stillwater, Okla.: Redlands Press, 1962), 47. On the translation of other titles see Byington, *Dictionary*, 165, 190, 525; Swanton, *Source Material*, 122–23; and James Adair, *Adair's History of the American Indians* (Johnson City, Tenn.: Watauga Press, 1930), 71. On the sun as an expression of power see John R. Swanton, "Sun Worship in the Southeast," *American Anthropologist*, n.s., 30 (April–June 1928), 208–9; and Charles Hudson, *The Southeastern Indians* (Knoxville: University of Tennessee Press, 1976), 126–27.

31. For other examples of Native American trade missions see Mary W. Helms, *Ulysses' Sail: An Ethnographic Odyssey of Power, Knowledge, and Geographical Distance* (Princeton, N.J.: Princeton University Press, 1988), 84–85.

32. Swanton, *Source Material*, 198 (quotation). The Creeks and Choctaws fought

a protracted war from 1766 to 1777; see O'Brien, "Protecting Trade through War," 149–66.

33. U.S. Commissioners [Benjamin Hawkins, Andrew Pickens, and Joseph Martin] to John Hancock [President of Congress], January 4, 1786, in *Early American Indian Documents: Treaties and Laws, 1607–1789*, ed. Colin G. Calloway, vol. 18 of *Revolution and Confederation*, Alden T. Vaughan, gen. ed. (Bethesda, Md.: University Publications of America, 1994), 415–16 (quotation on p. 416). See also Usner, *Indians, Settlers, and Slaves*, 212; Daniel K. Richter, *The Ordeal of the Longhouse: The Peoples of the Iroquois League in the Era of European Colonization* (Chapel Hill: University of North Carolina Press, 1992), 47; Elizabeth Vibert, *Traders' Tales: Narratives of Cultural Encounter in the Columbia Plateau, 1807–1846* (Norman: University of Oklahoma Press, 1997), 145–49; and Mary Black-Rogers, "Varieties of 'Starving': Semantics and Survival in the Subarctic Fur Trade, 1750–1850," *Ethnohistory* 33 (1986), 367–70.

34. U.S. Commissioners to John Hancock, January 4, 1786, in Calloway, *Early American Indian Documents*, 416 (quotation). From at least November 4, 1785, the Choctaw mission waited among the Creek Indians before journeying all the way to Hopewell. Probably, they toured various Creek villages, reinforcing old ties and establishing new ones. See Luke Mann to the Governor of Georgia Samuel Elbert, November 4, 1785, in Hays, *Creek Indian Letters, Talks, and Treaties*, 1:101; Martin Journal, 56–58; and Benjamin Hawkins and Andrew Pickens to Charles Thomson, January 1786, Knox Papers, reel 47. The Choctaws returned to their homeland through Creek territory as well, something they likely would not have attempted (especially laden with new supplies from the Americans) if the Creeks had indeed stolen their horses and supplies, though it is possible that certain Creek towns disrupted the Choctaw delegation on their journey to Hopewell and that the Choctaws chose a different route home through different Creek villages. The Chickasaws met the Americans at Hopewell immediately following the Choctaws and presented themselves in the same impoverished situation—perhaps demonstrating a ploy common to southeastern Indian diplomacy.

35. Martin Journal, 59–63, 75 (quotation).

36. Ibid., 66, 81 (quotations). Spellings of Choctaw chiefs' names and titles, other than Franchimastabé and Taboca, are as found in Martin's journal.

37. Martin Journal, 64–67. The list of Choctaw men receiving recognition from Spain is in "Tratado de alianza entre España y los indios Chactas y Chicasas o Chicachas, 14 de Julio de 1784," in Serrano y Sanz, *España y los Indios*, 82–83.

38. Martin Journal, 65.

39. Ibid., 81.

40. Ibid., 69–70.

41. Ibid., 64.

42. Ibid., 73.

43. Ibid., 74–76.

44. Ibid., 71. See also U.S. Commissioners to John Hancock, January 4, 1786, in Calloway, *Early American Indian Documents*, 416.

45. Martin Journal, 75.

46. Ibid., 79–80.

47. U.S. Commissioners to John Hancock, January 4, 1786, in Calloway, *Early American Indian Documents*, 416.

48. Ibid., 416 (quotation). On southeastern Indian gambling see Hudson, *Southeastern Indians*, 418, 423; and Swanton, *Source Material*, 140, 155. On the importance to American government officials of civility when dealing with Indians in the early republic period see Andrew R. L. Cayton, "Noble Actors' upon 'the Theatre of Honour': Power and Civility in the Treaty of Greenville," in Cayton and Teute, *Contact Points*, 235–69. On American images and perceptions of Indians see Robert F. Berkhofer Jr., *The White Man's Indian: Images of the American Indian from Columbus to the Present* (New York: Knopf, 1978), esp. 134–45.

49. Martin Journal, 76–82 (quotation on p. 80). On the significance of the color white see Hudson, *Southeastern Indians*, 132.

50. Martin Journal, 79, 82.

51. Adair, *History of the American Indians*, 32; and Hudson, *Southeastern Indians*, 163–65.

52. Adair, *History of the American Indians*, 176–77; spellings are as contained in the original document.

53. John R. Swanton, "An Early Account of the Choctaw Indians," *American Anthropological Association Memoirs* 5 (1918): 67, also printed in *A Choctaw Source Book*, ed. John H. Peterson Jr. (New York: Garland, 1985). Swanton dated this anonymous document to 1755. See also Robert A. Williams Jr., *Linking Arms Together: American Indian Treaty Visions of Law and Peace, 1600–1800* (New York: Oxford University Press, 1997), esp. 44, 47, 75–76; and Robert L. Hall, "Calumet Ceremonialism, Mourning Ritual, and Mechanisms of Inter-Tribal Trade," in *Mirror and Metaphor: Material and Social Constructions of Reality*, ed. Daniel W. Ingersoll Jr. and Gordon Bronitsky (Lanham, Md.: University Press of America, 1987), 30–32.

54. Martin Journal, 82 (quotation), 79.

55. See O'Brien, "Choctaws in a Revolutionary Age," chap. 4.

56. Martin Journal, 80–81.

57. Martin Journal, 82.

58. For further analysis of the purpose of establishing kin-like associations see Mary W. Helms, *Craft and the Kingly Ideal: Art, Trade, and Power* (Austin: University of Texas Press, 1993), 190; and William N. Fenton, "Structure, Continuity, and Change in the Process of Iroquois Treaty Making," in *The History and Culture of Iroquois Diplomacy: An Inter-disciplinary Guide to the Treaties of the Six Nations and Their League*, ed. Francis Jennings and William Fenton (Syracuse, N.Y.: Syracuse University Press, 1985), 12–14.

59. Martin Journal, 84.

60. Ibid., 86 (first quotation), 85 (second quotation).

61. Ibid., 87–88.

62. Ibid., 90. On Choctaw exchanges of permanent ambassadors with other nations see Patricia Galloway, " 'The Chief Who is Your Father': Choctaw and French Views of the Diplomatic Relation," in Wood, Waselkov, and Hatley, *Powhatan's Mantle*, 254–78.

63. Martin Journal, 89.

64. Choctaw Hopewell Treaty of 1786, repr. in Kappler, *Indian Affairs*, 11–14 (quotation on p. 12). The Choctaw Hopewell Treaty is also reprinted in appendix B of this volume.

65. Manuel Serrano y Sanz, *Spain and the Cherokee and Choctaw Indians in the Second Half of the Eighteenth Century*, trans. Samuel Dorris Dickinson (Idabel, Okla.: Potsherd Press, 1995), 26–28; and Reply of Franchimastabé after the speech of Captain Don Juan de Villebeuvre, November 1, 1787, *Mississippi Provincial Archives: Spanish Dominion* (Jackson: Mississippi Department of Archives and History) (hereinafter cited as *MPASD*), vol. 3, reel A521.

66. On James's appointment as Georgia agent to the Choctaws see Mohr, *Federal-Indian Relations*, 154–55; "An Ordinance for Appointing Agents to Reside in the Indian Nations [1786]," in *The Colonial Records of the State of Georgia*, ed. Allen D. Candler (Atlanta: C. P. Byrd, 1911), 19:532–33; and Colonel Joseph Martin to Governor [Edmund] Randolph of Virginia, March 25, 1787, in Palmer, *Calendar of Virginia State Papers*, 4:261 (Martin mistakenly refers to James as "Jones").

67. Martin Journal, 63 (quotation). Article 3 of the Choctaw Hopewell Treaty, as reprinted in Kappler, *Indian Affairs*, 12, reads as follows: "The boundary of the lands hereby allotted to the Choctaw nation to live and hunt on, within the limits of the United States of America, is and shall be the following, viz. Beginning at a point on the thirty-first degree of north latitude, where the Eastern boundary of the Natches district shall touch the same; thence east along the said thirty-first degree of north latitude, being the southern boundary of the United States of America, until it shall strike the eastern boundary of the lands on which the Indians of the said nation did live and hunt on the twenty-ninth of November, one thousand seven hundred and eighty-two, while they were under the protection of the King of Great-Britain; thence northerly along the said eastern boundary, until it shall meet the northern boundary of the said lands; thence westerly along the said northerly boundary, until it shall meet the western boundary thereof; thence southerly along the same to the beginning: saving and reserving for the establishment of trading posts, three tracts or parcels of land of six miles square each, at such places as the United [States] in Congress assembled shall think proper; which posts, and the lands annexed to them, shall be to the use and under the government of the United States of America." The treaty is also reprinted in Fredrick E. Hosen, ed., *Rifle, Blanket and Kettle: Selected Indian Treaties and Laws* (Jefferson, N.C.: McFarland, 1985), 29–32; and Calloway, *Early American Indian Documents*, 413–15. See also appendix B of this volume.

68. Alexander McGillivray to Estevan Miró, May 1, 1786, in D. C. Corbitt and Roberta Corbitt, trans. and eds., "Papers from the Spanish Archives Relating to Tennessee and the Old Southwest, 1783–1800," *East Tennessee Historical Society Publications* 10 (1938): 134–35.

69. Speech of Yagane-huma (Yockonahoma) to Governor Estevan Miró, January 3, 1788, in Serrano y Sanz, *Spain and the Cherokee and Choctaw Indians*, 30. See also John Pittslaw to Captain William Davenport, September 5, 1786, in Hays, *Creek Indian Letters, Talks, and Treaties*, 1:136.

70. Documentation on the Nogales affair is extensive; the following works provide an introduction into the diplomatic wrangling that took place. Sarah J. Banks and Charles A. Weeks, *Mississippi's Spanish Heritage: Selected Writing, 1492–1798* (Jackson, Miss.: State Department of Education, 1992), 112–80; Christopher J. Malloy and Charles A. Weeks, eds., "Shuttle Diplomacy, Eighteenth-Century Style: Stephen Minor's First Mission to the Choctaws and Journal, May–June, 1791," *Journal of Mississippi History* 55 (February 1993): 31–51; and Edward Hunter Ross and Dawson A. Phelps, eds., "A Journey over the Natchez Trace in 1792: A Document from the Archives of Spain," *Journal of Mississippi History* 15 (October 1953): 252–73. For Choctaw and Chickasaw efforts to have a trading post established at the Muscle Shoals see "A Talk for Colo[nel] Joseph Martin—From Piomingo, One of the Chiefs of that Tribe," February 15, 1787; and Colonel Arthur Campbell to Governor Edmund Randolph, April 15, 1787, both in Palmer, *Calendar of Virginia State Papers*, 4:241–42, 268.

71. U.S. Commissioners to John Hancock, January 4, 1786, in Calloway, *Early American Indian Documents*, 416 (quotation). On Pitchlynn's early life see Baird, *Peter Pitchlynn*, 5–8; see also Merrell, *Into the American Woods*, 210–15. On Pitchlynn's supposed illiteracy see McGillivray to Miró, May 1, 1786, in Corbitt and Corbitt, "Papers from the Spanish Archives," 135.

72. Speech of Yagane-huma (Yockonahoma) to Governor Estevan Miró, January 3, 1788, in Serrano y Sanz, *Spain and the Cherokee and Choctaw Indians*, 30.

73. Serrano y Sanz, *Spain and the Cherokee and Choctaw Indians*, 27.

74. The treaty was entered into the journals of the Continental Congress on April 16, 1786, and printed in the Philadelphia *Pennsylvania Gazette* on May 9, 1786. See also Henry Knox to the President of the United States, July 7, 1789, *The New American State Papers: Indian Affairs: Southeast* (Wilmington, Del.: Scholarly Resources, 1972), 6:59–60; U.S. Commissioners to Choctaw Nation, September 13, 1789, in *The Papers of Panton, Leslie and Company* (microfilm; Woodbridge, Conn., 1986), reel 5, 595–96; Recommendation to the Senate, April 1, 1790, Knox Papers, reel 26; and "By the President of the United States of America, A Proclamation," n.d., Knox Papers, reel 53.

75. U.S. Commissioners to John Hancock, January 4, 1786, in Calloway, *Early American Indian Documents*, 416 (quotation). See also May Wilson McBee, comp., *The Natchez Court Records, 1767-1805: Abstracts of Early Records* (Greenwood, Miss.: M. W. McBee, 1953), 2:164-67; Thomas P. Abernathy, *The South in the New Nation, 1789–1819* (Baton Rouge: Louisiana State University Press, 1961), 76; Joseph Martin to Gov. Edmund Randolph of Virginia, March 16, 1787, in Palmer, *Calendar of Virginia State Papers*, 4:256; William Blount to John Gray Blount, July 19, 1787, in *Letters of Members of the Continental Congress*, ed. Edmund C. Burnett, 8 vols. (Washington, D.C.: Carnegie Institution, 1921–36), 8:624; and John Woods to C. Griffin, February 21, 1788, and May 10, 1788, in *Papers of the Continental Congress, 1774–1789* (microfilm; Washington, D.C., 1959), M-247, reel 56, vol. 8, item 42, pp. 402, 406.

76. On Taboca's trip see Governor John Sevier [of Tennessee] to Governor George Matthews [of Georgia], March 3, 1787, in J. G. M. Ramsey, *The Annals of Tennessee to the End of the Eighteenth Century* (1853; repr., Knoxville: East Tennessee Historical Society, 1967), 385; Colonel Arthur Campbell to Governor Edmund Randolph [of

Virginia], March 9, 1787, and April 15, 1787; and "John Woods, Indian Interpreter," May 25, 1787, all in Palmer, *Calendar of Virginia State Papers*, 4:254, 268, 290; Henry Knox to "Chamby" [Chickasaw Chief], June 27, 1787; and Knox to Frenchemastubie [*sic*] June 27, 1787, both in Josiah Harmar Papers, William L. Clements Library, University of Michigan, Ann Arbor; "Choctaw Chief [Taboca] to Benjamin Franklin, June 19, 1787," American Philosophical Society Library, Philadelphia, Pennsylvania; William Blount to John Gray Blount, July 19, 1787, in Burnett, *Letters of Members of the Continental Congress*, 8:624; Carlos de Grand-Pré to Estevan Miró, October 26, 1787, in *Spain in the Mississippi Valley, 1765–1794*, ed. Lawrence Kinnaird, vols. 2–4 of *Annual Report of the American Historical Association for the Year 1945* (Washington, D.C., 1946), 3:236–37; and Alexander Fraser to Miró, April 15, 1788, *East Tennessee Historical Society Publications* 14 (1942): 99.

77. Ross and Phelps, "A Journey over the Natchez Trace in 1792," 261 (quotation); Helms, *Craft and the Kingly Ideal*, 109–10, 128–31; and O'Brien, "Choctaws in a Revolutionary Age," chap. 4. For further general analysis of esoteric knowledge as a basis of elite authority in native societies, see Helms, *Ulysses' Sail*.

78. Antonio Pace, trans. and ed., *Luigi Castiglioni's Viaggio: Travels in the United States of North America, 1785–1787* (Syracuse, N.Y.: Syracuse University Press, 1983), 132–34; and *Gentleman's Magazine* (London), 78 (May 1786): 433–34.

79. On January 6 the U.S. commissioners directed interpreter John Pitchlynn "to hurry the departure of the Indians as early tomorrow as possible"; however, for reasons unknown, the Choctaws did not depart until January 12. See Martin Journal, 92 (quotations); Hawkins's transcription of Martin's Journal [n.p., 18]; and *American State Papers*, 4:50.

80. Martin Journal, 92; Hawkins's transcription of Martin's journal, [n.p., 18]; and *American State Papers*, 4:50. For the government's promotion of debt among Indians in the early republic period see Braund, *Deerskins and Duffels*, 178. On the shortage of guns in the United States during this period see Michael A. Bellesiles, "The Origins of Gun Culture in the United States, 1760–1865," *Journal of American History*, 82 (September 1996), 425–55.

81. Jones, *License for Empire*, 147–55; and Merrell, "Declarations of Independence," esp. 204–5.

82. Horsman, *Expansion and American Indian Policy*, 171–73; Wiley Sword, *President Washington's Indian War: The Struggle for the Old Northwest, 1790–1796* (Norman: University of Oklahoma Press, 1985); Bernard W. Sheehan, *Seeds of Extinction: Jeffersonian Philanthropy and the American Indian* (Chapel Hill: University of North Carolina Press, 1973); Michael Paul Rogin, *Fathers and Children: Andrew Jackson and the Subjugation of the American Indian* (New York: Knopf, 1975); and Ronald N. Satz, *American Indian Policy in the Jacksonian Era* (Lincoln: University of Nebraska Press, 1975).

83. Cayton and Teute, *Contact Points*, 9; White, *Middle Ground*, ix–xv.

CHAPTER 8

Native Americans, the Market Revolution, and Culture Change

THE CHOCTAW CATTLE ECONOMY, 1690–1830

James Taylor Carson

The market revolution has emerged as an important interpretive paradigm for the study of cultural, economic, and social change among societies around the world. However, Charles Sellers, the preeminent historian of the American market revolution, excluded Native Americans from his study.[1] The early-nineteenth-century cattle economy of the Choctaw Indians offers a striking example of how Native Americans responded to the revolution. Generally speaking, students of the cattle economy of the Old Southwest have either overlooked the involvement of Native Americans, or as Richard White and Daniel Usner have done, considered it solely as an economic innovation without examining its cultural ramifications. Contrary to Sellers's argument that land was the most conservative force opposed to the American market revolution, culture proved to be an even more conservative force because it structured the Choctaws' adaptation to and participation within the market economy. Men adapted by incorporating cattle herding into their warfare and hunting traditions, and women exploited cattle and expanded their economic roles too without transgressing the cultural conventions that had patterned their lives well before the first cattle ambled into the Lower Mississippi Valley.[2]

Cattle and the cattle trade first became important in the Lower Mississippi

Valley when the French settled the region at the end of the seventeenth century. Tribes like the Houmas, Tunicas, Chitimachas, Pascagoulas, Natchez, Avoyelles, and Attakapas valued European trade goods, and they incorporated the French into what historian Daniel Usner has termed a frontier exchange economy. These tribes, the *petites nations*, traded, among other goods, cattle, which they had acquired as early as 1650 from tribes who traded with the Spanish in New Mexico, to the beef-starved French. In return these tribes received guns, ammunition, and other manufactured items. The commercial success of the petites nations was, however, short lived. By the mid-eighteenth century, disease, dependency, and European political and demographic expansion had reduced their remnants to economically and politically marginal groups. Moreover, by the 1740s French settlements at Opelousas and Natchitoches had begun to produce enough cattle to satisfy much of the Louisiana colony's needs.[3]

Only the Choctaws withstood colonial pressures and remained a forceful presence in the Lower Mississippi Valley throughout the eighteenth and early nineteenth centuries. Among the region's tribes, the Choctaws were by far the most numerous and politically influential. They numbered around twenty thousand throughout the period, inhabited several towns in present-day east-central Mississippi, and practiced a mixed economy of horticulture and hunting. Women directed domestic life and oversaw farming. They fabricated clothing and tools from animal skins and bones, manufactured earthen containers, prepared food, and sowed and harvested crops. Their expansive fields of corn, pumpkins, beans, and squash provided two-thirds of the Choctaws' diet and made the Choctaws what British surveyor Bernard Romans termed a "nation of farmers." Men, on the other hand, oversaw vitally important public ceremonies, but hunting, trading, and warfare were equally important occupations, and their social prestige depended on their success in these endeavors. Together men and women fashioned a surplus subsistence economy predicated on a sexual division of labor. Thus, when the frontier exchange economy made itself felt among the Choctaws in the eighteenth century, women traded foodstuffs, baskets, clothing, and firewood, and men offered deerskins and military service to the French in exchange for manufactured goods. Whether or not the Choctaws, like the petites nations, traded cattle in this economy is unclear, but linguistic evidence indicates they may have done so.[4]

Choctaws and other Indians of the Lower Mississippi Valley had conceived of cattle as a trade good since their first contact with the animals in the late seventeenth century. Jesuit priest Jacques Gravier visited them in 1701 and reported their use of the word *waka*, derived from the Spanish *vaca*, for cow. *Waka* is one of the few European loanwords Choctaws incorporated into their language. They typically named European goods with indigenous words that reflected their conception of the good's function or from. For example, Choctaws called horses *isuba*, deer-resembler, and guns were *tanampo*, from the verb *tanampi*, to fight. The use of the Spanish loanword was a regional phenomenon because the languages of many tribes that bordered the Lower Mississippi Valley and that had extensive contacts—belligerent and peaceful— with the Choctaws also included derivatives of *vaca*. The Mobilian trade dialect that served as a regional lingua franca employed *waka* as well. Linguistically, *waka* constructed cattle in such a manner that they became inseparable from the European colonial presence, and their use as a trade good conformed to Spanish expectations of regional trade and alliance. Moreover, the incidence and prevalence of the loanword suggests that the Choctaws and other tribes may not have integrated cattle into their daily lives like they had horses and guns.[5]

Frenchman Régis du Roullet visited the Choctaws in 1732, and he recorded evidence that reveals the extent to which cattle were becoming an integral part of what historian James Merrell has called the "Indians' New World." While traveling westward from Mobile to the Choctaw Nation, du Roullet crossed a small river about eight miles outside of Mobile, the Choctaw name of which translated to "bayou where cattle pasture." In contrast, the French name for the river, Mill River, reflected an altogether different conception of the river's utility. Perhaps this was the site where Choctaws raised cattle for trade with the French colonists. Regardless, by the 1730s cattle had become a feature of the postcontact landscape.[6]

Inferences drawn from toponyms are far from conclusive, but artifactual evidence substantiates the links between Choctaws and cattle in the early eighteenth century. Warriors and hunters used powder horns made of cattle horn; buffalo horn may also have been used. Native doctors used horns, open on both ends, to bleed their patients in a cupping fashion, and women fabricated winter cloaks from cowhides.

The impact of cattle on Choctaw place-names and material culture signaled an acceptance of the animals that allowed for more important and farreaching innovative uses of cattle in community and individual life later in the century.[7]

By the last half of the eighteenth century Choctaws certainly had begun to raise cattle, and they altered their settlement patterns to accommodate their herds. In the early 1770s many Choctaws abandoned the towns and moved out to unsettled land that had been previously reserved for hunting and warfare. Here they dispersed along the Yazoo and Tombigbee rivers to take advantage of the thick stands of cane and rich fields of grass that proliferated in the river bottomlands.[8]

The expansion of the Choctaws collided with the expansion of the United States. In other parts of the continent such conflict usually led to war, but the United States and the Choctaws signed the Treaty of Hopewell on January 3, 1786, to ensure peace on the frontier. The treaty, and the wane of imperial rivalries in the region, brought an end to the intertribal and imperial wars that had characterized the Lower Mississippi Valley throughout much of the eighteenth century. Consequently, the peace imperiled the social and political prestige of Choctaw warriors. The Hopewell Treaty, however, reserved for the Choctaws the right to punish illegal American squatters "as they please," and "rouguish young men," coming of age in a society where the traditional forms of social advancement were no longer present, took to raiding the cattle of American squatters as a substitute for warfare. In 1803, eight warriors, for example, raided Daniel Grafton's farm outside of Natchez and killed one of his work steers and wounded the other. Other Americans who lived closer to Natchez complained to the territorial governor incessantly about Choctaw depredations against their herds. The young men so valued cattle raids that they incorporated *waka* into their war names. By the early nineteenth century several men named Wakatubbee, which means "cow-killer," bore testimony to the juxtaposition of an innovative mode of warfare within the broader persistence of a more ancient tradition.[9]

The federal government had failed to foresee the "problems" that resulted from Choctaw enforcement of the punishment clause, and President Jefferson sought to end the cattle raids without resort to hostilities. In the early 1800s the trading firm of Panton, Leslie and Company, a company run by Englishmen that operated out of Spanish Mobile and Pensacola, began to demand from the Choctaws repayment of debts incurred by their purchase of bullets, guns, and powder on credit. By 1803 the debt exceeded $46,000, and the firm demanded a Choctaw land cession to retire it. Opposed to the cession of Indian land to private individuals, and wary of Spanish and British intrigues in the Lower Mississippi Valley, Jefferson intervened and federal commissioners held treaty talks with the Choctaws. The resulting 1805 Treaty of Mount Dexter ceded a substantial portion of southeastern Mississippi to the

United States for $50,000, and the federal government extinguished the Choctaw debt owed to the company with most of the cash settlement. The federal government earmarked what cash remained after paying off Panton, Leslie and Company to compensate citizens who had suffered depredations committed "on stock, and other property by evil disposed persons of the said Choctaw nation." Holding the Choctaws corporately liable for the legal livestock raids and punishing them collectively for such actions brought an end to the raids.[10]

In addition to cattle's vital place in male warrior culture, the animals emerged as an important part of its counterpart, hunter culture. Although deerskins overwhelmingly dominated the Choctaw skin trade throughout its duration, cowhides and beef tallow became important exchange commodities by the early 1800s. In 1802 the federal government built a trading factory on the banks of the Tombigbee River in present-day western Alabama to facilitate trade with the Choctaws, and it flourished. (At a later date the factory was moved upriver closer to the Choctaw towns.) Though the quantities of cowhides brought to the factory were small in relation to the amounts of other skins, in terms of value they rivaled bear skins as the second most important skin traded. Unlike the deer, bear, fox, and wildcat skins and beaver pelts, cowhides were not destined for consumption in distant markets. Instead, American factors, that is, government traders and their slaves, cut the hides into strips and used them to tie up the bundles of deerskins and other furs for shipment. The factors also used cowhides to shield the decks and crews of the factory's two boats from balls and arrows shot by hostile Indians. Another important trade commodity was beef tallow, but it never overtook its rival, beeswax, which was used in the manufacture of candles and was worth twice as much per pound. Cowhides and tallow obtained an important but secondary position in the vast array of skins, peltries, and other products that the Choctaws traded at the U.S. factory, but this trade allowed hunters, like warriors, to establish a relationship with the animals that comported with cultural norms.[11]

By the 1810s the Choctaws had become entirely dependent on the deerskin trade. Never able to trade enough skins to pay off their debts, they had mortgaged their economic and political independence first to the French, then to the British, and then to the United States. This decline, as Richard White has written, further undermined their society and degraded their environment. When the United States trading factory closed its doors in 1822, the Choctaws lost perhaps the only source of credit available to them, as well as the guaranteed prices that had been set by the federal government. Left on their own to cope with an emerging market economy that set prices according to demand and had little need for deerskins, the Choctaws for the most part abandoned commercial hunting. As Usner and White have argued, cattle raising offered an alternative to the increasingly impracticable deerskin trade.[12]

After over a century of contact with cattle, Choctaw warriors and hunters laid down their rifles, saddled their horses, strapped on spurs, unfurled their rawhide whips, and began to herd livestock as their primary economic endeavor. How they managed their herds, beyond free-ranging them, is unclear because there is no evidence to indicate that they selectively bred animals or culled their herds, or that they used traditional land management techniques like burning to manage their cattle and the cattle range.

As Terry Jordan has argued, other features of the nineteenth-century Choctaw cattle complex bore a strong Anglo-American imprint. English traders and cattlemen from Georgia and the Carolinas had settled in Mississippi in the late eighteenth and early nineteenth centuries, and they imparted much of their knowledge to the Choctaws. At round-up times, Choctaw herdsmen, *wak apistikeli*, summoned their cattle from the canebrakes, pastures, and forests with loud cracks of the whip, herded the cattle on horseback, and enclosed them in cow pens. Once penned cattle could be driven down innumerable cow trails, *wak aiitanowa*, to markets in surrounding American communities. To distinguish between herds, they branded their animals, as was common practice among non-Indians of the region. Choctaw cowboys like Mushulatubbee, Puckshenubbee, Mastubbee, and Indian countrymen John Pitchlynn and Charles Juzan bartered deerskins and cowhides for, among other things, saddles, bridles, spurs, whips, cow bells, and salt. (Salt was essential for the cattle's nutrition, and they would never venture far from a secure source of it.) Although Choctaw men retained deeply rooted hunting and warfare values in their relationship to cattle, they nevertheless also had learned how to use the accoutrements and techniques of the Anglo-American cattle economy.[13]

Cattle raising was an innovative economic behavior that fit perfectly within the regional market economy. Choctaws could raise cattle with ease, and the demand for beef in the Old Southwest remained constant because the region's plantation and subsistence economies depended to a large extent on cattle. Indeed, federal Indian agent William Ward remarked that the Choctaws "generally supplied (in part) the neighboring whites with . . . beef." The average price for a cow in Mississippi in the 1820s was between eight and ten dollars, and the price of fresh beef was four cents a pound. In the late 1820s, when the Choctaw herd numbered over 43,000 head, it had a maximum market value of almost four hundred thousand dollars on the hoof and a half million dollars when converted into fresh beef. In addition to its value, the Choctaw herd's size was comparable to that of non-Indian herds in the region.

In 1828 there were 2.07 cattle per capita in the Choctaw Nation. In Spanish Natchez, for example, the same ratio was obtained in 1784, and in 1840 the state of Mississippi had a much lower ratio of 1.8 cattle per capita. The size of the Choctaw cattle economy meant that unlike their cotton economy it was not concentrated in the hands of a few entrepreneurs.[14]

Whether they owned herds of several hundred head or only a few animals, by all accounts most Choctaws participated in the cattle economy. Families would have had access to approximately 1,290,000 pounds of beef annually, or just under three ounces per capita per day, and incalculable quantities of milk and butter. Whereas formerly adults had taught boys to hunt and girls to farm, the Choctaws began impressing on the young the value and importance of stock raising. Sons and daughters received from their families, if possible, a cow and calf, a sow and piglet, and a mare and colt. As the child grew older, his or her herd multiplied and provided the owner with a sound source of income and subsistence in adulthood. The recognition of cattle as the key for future generations' prosperity prompted Choctaw leaders to attempt to control strictly the trade of cattle with Americans.[15]

American cattle traders frequently ventured into the nation to buy and trade for Choctaw cattle. Mushulatubbee, one of the nation's principal leaders, often entertained buyers from Alabama at his home. With what such men bought Choctaw cattle is unknown, but the most noteworthy, and hence recorded, transactions between Choctaws and American buyers involved midnight swaps of cattle for alcohol. Indians took whisky from the traders and exchanged it with other Choctaws for their cattle, blankets, and guns and then traded these items back to the Americans. Failing this, some tribesmen simply stole their fellow Choctaws' cattle for trade with the Americans, and this drew the ire of reform-minded leaders such as Hwoolatahoomah, who banned livestock stealing and whisky trading in his district. Despite the trouble caused by the whisky trade, most Choctaws seem to have adapted to the market economy by raising livestock.[16]

But not all uses of cattle reflected market concerns. Choctaws also incorporated them into rituals that affirmed kin and community relationships and obligations. When a Choctaw died, kinfolk shot and killed the deceased person's cattle, horses, and dogs for the funeral ritual. Choctaws reasoned that the animals "would be equally useful and desirable in the state of being which they enter at death." Of use to the deceased in the afterlife, the meat of the slain animals served the kinfolk as well. Relatives feasted on the meat to honor the passage of the deceased and to reaffirm symbolically the bonds of kinship and community, and life and death.

Such a ritual use of cattle found further expression in another form of social behavior, reciprocity. At a council held in August 1819, Choctaw headmen donated eighty-five cows and calves for the support of the Boston-based American Board missionaries, who had begun building the Elliot missionary station and school in the western part of the Choctaw Nation. When the missionaries accepted this gift, they unwittingly committed themselves to the system of reciprocal social relations and obligations that characterized Choctaw society.[17]

Adam Hodgson, an Englishman who visited the Elliot mission in 1820, witnessed firsthand the juxtaposition of tradition and innovation among the Choctaws, for he recorded both the use of cattle in traditional funerals and the prosperity of the new cattle economy. During his journey through the Choctaw Nation, Hodgson stopped and visited two Choctaw brothers who raised cattle for a living. The size of their herds, the lushness of their range, and the sturdy prosperity of their farmsteads impressed him, and he decided to spend the night at their home. As the sun set their cattle ambled in from the forest for milking, and Hodgson's host shot one of the cows for supper just as, a half century earlier, he might have killed a deer or turkey. That evening the Englishman sat down with the family for a meal of fresh beefsteaks. What escaped Hodgson's normally observant eyes, however, were the women who had milked the cows and who had cooked the steaks.[18]

The infrequent mention of Native American women in historical sources makes any study of their lives difficult and any conclusions reached tenuous, but linguistic evidence can open new lines of inquiry and illuminate what otherwise would be overlooked or incomprehensible. Anthropologists Mary Haas and Amelia Rector Bell have shown that the Muskogee language family, to which the Choctaw language belongs, contains grammatical structures and vocabulary that differentiate in subtle ways the language that the men spoke from the language that the women spoke. By drawing on the Choctaw language and the few references to women and cattle in the documentary sources, a number of suggestions about Choctaw women and cattle may be offered.[19]

Gendered social structures historically have exerted a considerable influence on different societies' development of a cattle complex and their participation in a market economy. Among patrilineal peoples such as the Marakwet and Nambi of Kenya, men controlled property like cattle and, consequently, entry into the market economy. Women could own cattle, but what animals they owned were added to the men's herds. More importantly, men had the final say in whether cattle owned by women would be sold, traded, or left in the men's herds. Women's participation in the market economy was thus limited to the marketing of vegetable produce and sex. In early-nineteenth-century New England a similar process occurred whereby women were cordoned off into "separate spheres" and hindered by law and custom from participating in the male-dominated economy.[20]

Unlike the Marakwet and Nambi of Kenya and the Americans of New England, Choctaws were matrilineal. Descent was traced through the mother, and children belonged to the mother's family. Moreover, they were matrilocal. Families lived grouped in matrilineages that further enabled Choctaw women to have a considerable if not decisive say in the distribution and control of land, property, and labor. Matriliny, therefore, differentiates the Choctaws' experience from that of their Kenyan and American counterparts.[21]

Just as men's relationship to cattle was conditioned by their warrior and hunter traditions, so too was women's relationship with the animals structured by their link to the home and horticulture. Like male Choctaws, females incorporated *waka* into their names, and the names reveal much about the complex intersection and discrete segmentation of Choctaw gender structures. According to Amelia Rector Bell, the Creek language differentiates gender distinctions according to definitions of male behavior. Thus, the woman "food maker" can only be understood in secondary opposition to the primary male "warrior." One of the translatable female names that incorporated *waka*, Wakaihoner, means "cow cooker." When contrasted to the male name Wakatubbee, which means "cow killer," the names bear a striking resemblance to the pattern described by Bell. For women, it seems cattle could define them in relation to men insofar as women performed a gendered function like food preparation that was predicated upon a male behavior like hunting. But cattle could also be defined in terms that were predicated upon distinctly feminine activities like farming.[22]

Another Choctaw term for cattle—*alhpoa*—means literally "fruit trees such as are cultivated" and suggests a uniquely feminine construction of the value and utility of livestock. The fruit trees that proliferated among Choctaw towns offered a sensible linguistic construction of cattle for several reasons. Just as women tended plum or peach trees for their fruit, so too could they care for cattle and obtain milk. The association of women with the formidable power of fertility also may have created a special relationship between them and cattle because, like fruit trees, the annual reproduction of cattle was what made the animals particularly valuable. Above all, orchards were an integral part of the town landscape, and other cattle-related terms derived from *alhpoa* suggest this held true for cattle as well. For example, *alhpoa aiimpa* meant pasture, and *alhpoa imilhpak* meant fodder. Both terms imply the careful tending and close proximity to the towns that characterized women's farming as opposed to the neglect that characterized the free-range herding practiced by the men.[23]

The linguistic construction of cattle as fruit trees may have allowed women to adapt to changing Choctaw settlement patterns. When the Choctaws abandoned their towns in the 1770s, relocated in the borderlands that had once been reserved for hunting and fighting, and began to raise cattle, the women had to abandon the orchards that had been a part of their land holdings and subsistence cycle. Once settled in the borderlands, they would have been unable to reconstitute immediately their orchards because native fruit trees took at least three years before they started to bear fruit. But, in a cognitive sense, women could have taken their cattle, as fruit trees, into the previously unsettled and uncultivated borderlands that had been reserved for male hunting and fighting and reconstitute immediately what had been an integral part of village life.[24]

The cognition and exploitation of cattle as fruit trees further facilitated women's entry into the market economy. Early in the contact period Choctaw women had welcomed explorers, travelers, and traders with gifts of food and shelter, but newer market sensibilities pervaded this ethic and transformed it by the 1800s. Women obtained scarce hard cash from travelers who were beholden to their Choctaw hosts by selling them milk, beef, corn, fodder, peaches, and other foods. This hospitality economy allowed women both to participate in the wide range of opportunities made possible by the market economy and to obtain hard cash for further participation in it. What the women purchased with this money is impossible to discover, but cloth, sewing necessities, and agricultural implements constituted the bulk of purchases made by women at the U.S. trading factory. Although the hospitality economy grew out of an older ethic of reciprocity, its transformation reflected the extent to which custom had given way to innovation, and reciprocity and subsistence had given way to sale and profit.[25]

Whereas selling beef or milk had precedent in the hospitality economy, the selling of livestock as animals did not. Nevertheless, *alhpoa* constructed cattle so that women like men could trade or sell cattle. However, as a result of the *alhpoa* construct, women, like men, could trade or sell cattle. In July of 1820 a thirteen-year-old Choctaw girl tried to enter the Elliot missionary school, located in present-day west-central Mississippi. The missionaries, however, denied her request for admission because the school was already overcrowded. Reluctant to crush the girl's hopes of going to the school, her friends told her that because she lacked a school uniform, she could not enter the school. Undaunted, the girl determined to sell her cow for cash to buy a uniform. Touched by her resolve, the missionaries agreed to take the girl in, and her uncle offered to pay any expenses to cover the cost of her schooling.[26]

What the missionaries mistook for youthful precocity, and what some might mistake for an everyday occurrence in the Old Southwest, in fact revealed the juxtaposition and interplay of Choctaw culture and new market sensibilities. The girl's conception of the cow as a good that could be sold for cash suggests the prevalence of a distinctly market-oriented mindset. Furthermore, selling the entire cow rather than its milk or meat represented an elaboration of the feminine hospitality economy that was nevertheless sanctioned by the language of the Choctaws' gendered economy and culture.

The Choctaws' transition from the early-eighteenth-century frontier exchange economy to the nineteenth-century market economy failed to upset the gendered economic structures of their culture. By killing, hunting, raising, trading, and selling cattle, they adjusted to the new world wrought by European colonization and American settlement. Moreover, Choctaw women avoided the economic marginalization and social subjugation that had characterized women's experiences in New England and Kenya by drawing on their traditional roles and responsibilities to sanction innovative economic activities. Contrary to Charles Sellers, market revolutions are not contests of impersonal forces but struggles waged by individuals within a changing world economy, and language and culture are crucial elements in understanding how different peoples have managed the fight.

NOTES

This chapter originally appeared as "Native Americans, the Market Revolution, and Culture Change: The Choctaw Cattle Economy, 1690–1830," *Agricultural History* 71 (1997): 1–18.

1. Charles Grier Sellers, *The Market Revolution: Jacksonian America, 1815–1846* (New York: Oxford University Press, 1991). The Indians in Sellers's study vanish from the scene before the market economy emerges. Among other studies of the market's impact, Nancy Cott's *The Bonds of Womanhood: "Woman's Sphere" in New England, 1780–1835* (New Haven, Conn.: Yale University Press, 1977) was the first to argue that women's "separate spheres" and a "cult of domesticity" emerged to segregate women from the market revolution in New England. In contrast to Cott, Catherine Clinton's *The Plantation Mistress: Women's World in the Old South* (New York: Pantheon Books, 1982) argues that southern women did not necessarily experience the same changes that had occurred in the North. Nancy Hewitt's *Women's Activism and Social Change: Rochester, New York, 1822–1872* (Ithaca, N.Y.: Cornell University Press, 1984) has broadened further the debate in American historiography on the market economy's impact on gender by examining women from different social classes and their responses to social and economic change.

Anthropologists Henrietta L. Moore (*Space, Text, and Gender: An Anthropological Study of the Marakwet of Kenya* [Cambridge: Cambridge University Press, 1986]) and Regina Smith Oboler (*Women, Power, and Economic Change: The Nandi of Kenya* [Stanford: Stanford University Press, 1985]) have argued that in Kenya the patriarchal structure of the Marakwet and Nandi peoples structured their responses to colonialism and the market revolution in ways that perpetuated men's dominance and weakened the position of women. Their work and that of Cott, Clinton, and Hewitt suggest that far from exerting a uniform influence, the market revolution caused disparate, culturally conditioned changes in economic production and gender segmentation.

2. Lewis Cecil Gray, *History of Agriculture in the Southeastern United States to 1860*, 2 vols. (Washington, D.C.: Carnegie Institution of Washington, 1933); Jack D. L. Holmes, "Joseph Piernas and the Nascent Cattle Industry of Southwest Louisiana," *McNeese Review* 17 (1966): 13–26; Jack D. L. Holmes, "Livestock in Spanish Natchez," *Journal of Mississippi History* 23 (October 1961): 15–37; John Hebron Moore, *Agriculture in Antebellum Mississippi* (New York: Octagon, 1971); John Hebron Moore, *The Emergence of the Cotton Kingdom in the Old Southwest: Mississippi 1770–1860* (Baton Rouge: Louisiana State University Press, 1988); Kenneth D. Israel, "A Geographical Analysis of the Cattle Industry in Southeastern Mississippi from its Beginnings to 1860" (Ph.D. diss., University of Southern Mississippi, 1970); John D. W. Guice, "Cattle Raisers of the Old Southwest: A Reinterpretation," *Western Historical Quarterly* 8 (April 1977): 167–87; Terry Jordan, "The Origins of Anglo-American Cattle Ranching in Texas: A Documentation of Diffusion from the Lower South," *Economic Geography* 45 (January 1969): 63–87; Terry Jordan, *North American Cattle-Ranching Frontiers: Origins, Diffusion, and Differentiation* (Albuquerque: University of New Mexico Press, 1993); Lauren C. Post, "The Old Cattle Industry of Southwest Louisiana," *McNeese Review* 9 (1957): 43–55; Richard White, *The Roots of Dependency: Subsistence, Environment, and Social Change among the Choctaws, Pawnees, and Navajos* (Lincoln: University of Nebraska Press, 1983).

See also Michael F. Doran, "Antebellum Cattle Herding in the Indian Territory," *Geographical Review* 66 (January 1976): 48–58, for a discussion of cattle raising among the Choctaws in Indian territory; and Louise Spindler, *Culture Change and Modernization* (New York: Holt, Rinehart and Winston, 1977) for an overview of cultural change and adaptation.

3. Charles W. Arnade, "Cattle Raising in Spanish Florida, 1513–1763," *Agricultural History* 35 (July 1961): 116–24; William Beer, ed., *Early Census Tables of Louisiana*, vol. 5 of *Publications of the Louisiana Historical Society* (New Orleans: Tulane University Press, 1911), 79–104; David I. Bushnell Jr., "Drawings by A. DeBatz in Louisiana, 1733–35," *Smithsonian Miscellaneous Collections*, vol. 80, no. 5 (Washington, D.C.: Smithsonian Institution, 1927); Heloise H. Cruzat, trans., "Louisiana in 1724: Banet's Report to the Company of the Indies, Dated Paris, 20 December 1724," *Louisiana Historical Quarterly* 12 (January 1929): 121–33; Gary Dunbar, "Colonial Carolina Cowpens," *Agricultural History* 35 (July 1961): 125–30; M. de Rémonville, "Memoir, addressed to Count de Pontchartrain, on the importance of Establishing a colony in Louisiana"; André Pénicault, *Annals of Louisiana*, vol. 1 of *Historical Collections of Louisiana and Florida, Including Translations of Original Manuscripts Relating to Their Discovery and Settlement with Numerous Historical and Biographical Notes*, new series, ed. Benjamin French (New York: J. Sabin & Sons, 1869), 2–14, 62, 144; Gray, *History of Agriculture*, 1:79; Pierre Margry, *Découvertes et Établissements des Français dans l'Quest et dans le Sud de l'Amérique Septentrionale (1614–1754)*, vol. 6 (Paris: D. Jouaust, 1888), 245–46; Antoine Simon Le Page du Pratz, *The History of Louisiana Translated from the French of M. Le Page du Pratz*, ed. Joseph Tregle Jr. (Baton Rouge: Louisiana State University Press, 1975), 166; Lauren C. Post, "The Domestic Animals and Plants of French Louisiana as Mentioned in the Literature with References to Sources, Varieties, and Uses," *Louisiana Historical Quarterly* 16 (October 1933): 560–63; Lauren C. Post, "Some Notes on the Attakapas Indians of Southwest Louisiana," *Louisiana History* 3 (Summer 1962): 233–34; Dunbar Rowland and A. G. Sanders, eds. and trans., *Mississippi Provincial Archives, 1729–1740: French Dominion*, vol. 3 (Jackson: Mississippi Department of Archives and History, 1932), 268; Nancy M. Surrey, *The Commerce of Louisiana during the French Regime, 1699–1763* (New York: Columbia University Press, 1916), 253–55; Reuben Gold Thwaites, ed., *The Jesuit Relations and Allied Documents*, 73 vols. (Cleveland: Burrows Brothers, 1900), 57:257; Daniel H. Usner Jr., *Indians, Settlers, and Slaves in a Frontier Exchange Economy: the Lower Mississippi Valley before 1763* (Chapel Hill: University of North Carolina Press, 1992), esp. chaps. 1–3.

4. Bernard Romans, *A Concise Natural History of East and West Florida; a Facsimile Reproduction of the 1775 Ed.* (1775; repr., Gainesville: University of Florida Press, 1962), 71, 76; White, *Roots of Dependency*, chaps. 2, 4; Jean-Bernard Bossu, *Travels in the Interior of North America, 1751–1762*, ed. and trans. Seymour Feiler (Norman: University of Oklahoma Press, 1962), 169–70; John Swanton, ed., "An Early Account of the Choctaw Indians," in *Memoirs of the American Anthropological Association*, vol. 4, no. 2 (Lancaster, Penn.: American Anthropological Society), 59, 67–68; Patricia K. Galloway, "Choctaw Factionalism and Civil War, 1746–1750," *Journal of Mississippi History* 44 (November 1982): 289–327.

5. Marc de Villiers du Terrage, "Notes sur les Chactas d'aprés les journaux de voyage de Régis du Roullet (1729–1732)," *Journal de la Société des Américanistes de Paris*

15 (1923): 234; Cyrus Byington, "A Dictionary of the Choctaw Language," Bureau of American Ethnology Bulletin 46 (Washington, D.C.: U.S. Government Printing Office, 1915).

Besides the Choctaw language and the Mobilian trade language, the Wichitas, Biloxis, Cherokees, Creeks, and Chickasaws used some form of *vaca* for cattle. David S. Rood, *Wichita Grammar* (New York: Garland, 1976), 295; John Owen Dorsey and John R. Swanton, eds., *A Dictionary of the Biloxi and Ofo Languages*, Bureau of American Ethnology Bulletin 47 (Washington, D.C.: U.S. Government Printing Office, 1912), 301; Durbin Feeling, *Cherokee-English Dictionary* (Talequah: Cherokee Nation of Oklahoma, 1975), 187; Henry Frieland Buckner, *A Grammar of the Masjwke [Muskogee], or Creek Language: to Which Are Prefixed Lessons in Spelling, Reading, and Defining* (Marion, Ala.: Domestic and Indian Mission Board of the Southern Baptist Convention, 1869), 35; James M. Crawford, *The Mobilian Trade Language* (Knoxville: University of Tennessee Press, 1978), 4, 76, 83; Kenneth H. York, "Mobilian: The Indian Lingua Franca of Colonial Louisiana," in *La Salle and His Legacy: Frenchmen and Indians in the Lower Mississippi Valley*, ed. Patricia K. Galloway (Jackson: University Press of Mississippi, 1982), 139–45.

For a discussion of the diffusion of Spanish loanwords in the Gulf Coast region see J. L. Dilliard, "The Maritime (Perhaps Lingua Franca) Relations of a Special Variety of the Gulf Corridor," *Journal of Pidgin and Creole Languages* 2 (1987): 244–49. For discussions on the development of pidgins and incorporation of loanwords see Terry Crowley, *An Introduction to Historical Linguistics* (Oxford: Oxford University Press, 1992), 267, 308; Theodora Bynon, *Historical Linguistics* (Cambridge: Cambridge University Press, 1977), 256–61; M. Mosha, "Loan-words in Luganda: A Search for Guides in Adaptation of African Languages to Modern Conditions," in *Language Use and Social Change*, ed. W. H. Whiteley (Oxford: Oxford University Press, 1971), 288–308; and Florian Coulmas, ed., *Language Adaptation* (Cambridge: Cambridge University Press, 1989), 6. The river was named "Bouk ouaka apouka" (Bok wak hopohka). Villiers du Terrage, "Notes sur les Chactas," 234–35; James Merrell, *The Indians' New World: Catawbas and Their Neighbors from European Contact through the Era of Removal* (Chapel Hill: University of North Carolina Press, 1989).

7. Bushnell, "Drawings by A. DeBatz"; Swanton, "An Early Account of the Choctaw Indians," 71, describes a Choctaw medicine man using a horn in his treatments but does not specify whether it was a cow or buffalo horn. The use of buffalo wool in the treatment suggests it may have been a buffalo horn, but, like powder horns, Choctaws could have used both types.

8. White, *Roots of Dependency*, 102–5; *Missionary Herald* 25 (November 1829): 350; Horatio B. Cushman, *A History of the Choctaw, Chickasaw and Natchez Indians* (Greenville, Tex.: Headlight Printing House, 1899), 389–91, 403; Francis Armstrong to Lewis Cass, September 21, 1831, Letters Received by the Office of Indian Affairs, 1824–1880, Choctaw Agency, 1824–1876, reel 169, microfilm series M234, Bureau of Indian Affairs, record group 75, National Archives (hereafter RG 75); Adam Hodgson, *Letters from North America Written during a Tour in the United States and Canada*, vol. 1 (London: Hurst, Robinson, 1824), 224.

9. John McKee to Choctaw Headmen, December 11, 1815, Letters Received by the Secretary of War Relating to Indian Affairs, 1800–1823, reel 1, microfilm Series M271, War Department, RG 75; Dunbar Rowland, ed., *Official Letter Books of William C. C. Claiborne, 1801-1816*, vol. 1 (Jackson: Mississippi Department of Archives and History, 1917), 13, 60; Dunbar Rowland, ed., *The Mississippi Territorial Archive, 1798–1803*, vol. 1 (Nashville, Tenn.: Brandon Printing, 1905), 32, 350, 393, 527–29; Lawrence Kinnaird, ed., "Spain in the Mississippi Valley, 1765–1794," *Annual Report of the American Historical Association*, (Washington, D.C.: Smithsonian Institution Press, 1949), 26; Roster of Choctaws claiming to have lost horses during removal, October 8, 1837, Letters Received by the Office of Indian Affairs, 1824–1880, reel 184, microfilm series M234, Choctaw Agency West, 1825–1838, Bureau of Indian Affairs, RG 75; Treaty of Hopewell, January 3, 1786, Articles 4 and 5, reel 2, microfilm series M668, Ratified Indian Treaties, 1722–1869, Bureau of Indian Affairs, RG 75.

10. William Simpson, Abstract of debts owed to Panton, Leslie and Company, August 20, 1803, Letters Received by the Secretary of War Relating to Indian Affairs, 1800–1823, reel 1, microfilm series M271, War Department, RG 75; Article 2, Treaty of Mount Dexter, 16 November 1805, Ratified Indian Treaties, 1722–1869, reel 3, microfilm series M668, Bureau of Indian Affairs, RG 75.

11. Indent Books, December 14, 1805, January 24, 1809, February 6, 1809, and Miscellaneous Accounts, April 3, 1816, reels 1–3, microfilm series T500, Records of the Choctaw Trading House, under the Office of Indian Trade, 1803–1824, RG 75; Deborah A. Hay, "Fort St. Stephens and Fort Confederation: Two U.S. Factories for the Choctaw, 1802–1822" (master's thesis, Auburn University, 1979), 39–43, 88–93, 112.

12. White, *Roots of Dependency*, chaps. 4, 5; Daniel H. Usner Jr., "American Indians on the Cotton Frontier: Changing Economic Relations with Citizens and Slaves in the Mississippi Territory," *Journal of American History* 72 (September 1985): 297–98; Michael F. Doran, "Antebellum Cattle Herding in the Indian Territory," *Geographical Review* 66 (January 1976): 102–4.

13. Jordan, *North American Cattle-Ranching Frontiers*, 182–83; *Missionary Herald* 18 (May 1822): 150; *Panoplist and Missionary Herald* 15 (October 1819): 460, 463; Hodgson, *Letters from North America*, 1:23, 241, 253; Byington, *Dictionary of the Choctaw Language*, 74, 77, 361–62; Francis Baily, *Journal of a Tour in Unsettled Parts of North America in 1796 and 1797* (London: Baily Brothers, 1856), 373; Israel, "A Geographical Analysis of the Cattle Industry," 26, 65; Harry Toulmin, comp., *Digest of the Statues of the Mississippi Territory* (Natchez, Miss.: Territorial Publisher, 1807), 403; Dunbar, "Colonial Cowpens," 125–30; Guice, "Cattle Raisers of the Old Southwest," 167–87; Forrest McDonald and Grady McWhiney, "The Antebellum Southern Herdsmen: A Reinterpretation," *Journal of Southern History* 41 (May 1975): 147–66; Daybook entries, August 18, 1808, September 16, 1808, May 22, 1809, July 13, 1809, October 9, 1809, April 18, 1810, March 8, 1811, and February 19, 1813, Daybooks, 1803–24, reel 4, microfilm series T500, Records of the Choctaw Trading House, under the Office of Indian Trade, RG 75; Henry Halbert, "Origins of Mashulaville," *Publications of the Mississippi Historical Society* 7 (1903), 393; André Michaux, "Travels to the West of the Allegheny Mountains in the States of Ohio, Kentucky, and Tennessee . . . , " in *Early*

Western Travels, 1748–1846, ed. Reuben Gold Thwaites (Cleveland: Arthur H. Clarke, 1904), 246.

14. *Niles' Weekly Register* 38 (July 3, 1830): 345; Gray, *History of Agriculture*, 2:812, 1042; United States Bureau of the Census, *The Statistical History of the United States from Colonial Times to the Present* (New York: Basic Books, 1976), 30. In 1828 the American Board missionaries took a census of the Choctaw cattle herd in the eastern district of the nation and counted 5,627 people and 11,661 cattle, yielding a ratio of 2.07 cattle per capita. Using this ratio I have reconstructed the Choctaw herd for a total population of 21,000 Choctaws in 1828 to be over 43,000 animals. *Missionary Herald* 25 (February 1829): 51, 153; *Missionary Herald* 17 (April 1821): 110.

15. U.S. Senate, *Report on Indian Tribes*, 20th Cong., 2nd sess., 3 January 1829, vol. 1, S. Doc. 27, 6; Guice, "Cattle Raisers of the Old Southwest," 175–77; Israel, "A Geographical Analysis of the Cattle Industry," 5–7, 79; Thomas L. McKenney, *Memoirs, Official and Personal . . .* , vol. 1 (New York: Paine and Burgess, 1846), 323.

In the absence of figures that might reveal how much of their herds Choctaws consumed annually, I have used Leonard Brinkman's estimates for cattle weight and Harold K. Schneider's figure of 10 percent of the herd annually as a maximum for consumption, coupled with his estimation that a cow yields half of its body weight in meat. Choctaw cattle probably weighed about six hundred pounds. Harold K. Schneider, *Livestock and Equality in East Africa* (Bloomington: Indiana University Press, 1979), 62, 101; Leonard W. Brinkman Jr., "The Historical Geography of Improved Cattle in the United States to 1870" (Ph.D. diss., University of Wisconsin, 1964), 38.

16. William A. Love, "Moshulitubbee's Prairie Village," *Publications of the Mississippi Historical Society*, vol. 7 (Oxford, Miss.: Mississippi Historical Society, 1903), 375; *Missionary Herald* 17 (March 1821): 74; *Missionary Herald* 19 (January 1823): 9–10; Samuel Brown, *The Western Gazetteer; or Emigrant's Directory Containing a Geographical Description of the Western States and Territories* (Auburn, N.Y.: H. C. Southwick, 1817), 242.

17. *Panoplist and Missionary Herald* 15 (October 1819): 461; *Panoplist and Missionary Herald* 15 (December 1819): 535; Louis LeClerc de Milford, *Memoir or a Cursory Glance at My Different Travels and My Sojourn in the Creek Nation*, ed. John Francis McDermott, trans. Geraldine de Courcy (Chicago: R. R. Donnelly and Sons, 1956), 204; White, *Roots of Dependency*, 105.

For further discussions of Choctaw funeral rites, see Hodgson, *Letters from North America*, 1:216; Henry Frieland Buckner, "Burial among the Choctaws," *American Antiquarian and Oriental Journal* 2 (July–September 1879): 55–58.

18. Hodgson, *Letters from North America*, 1:224, 241, 253. Hodgson does not state that women milked the cows and cooked the steaks. In the absence of documentary evidence, I have used the methodology of ethnohistory and my own interpretation of what we know about the Choctaws to infer that it was women who did this.

19. Mary Haas, "Men's and Women's Speech in Koasati," in *Language in Culture and Society*, ed. Dell Hymes (New York: Harper and Row, 1964), 228–33; Amelia Rector

Bell, "Separate People: Speaking of Creek Men and Women," *American Anthropologist* 92 (June 1990): 332–45.

20. Moore, *Space, Text, and Gender*, 66–67, 144; Oboler, *Women, Power, and Economic Change*, 9–11, 25–28, 153–55, 191, 229, 243; Cott, *The Bonds of Womanhood*.

21. John R. Swanton, *Source Material for the Social and Ceremonial Life of the Choctaw Indians*, Bureau of American Ethnology Bulletin 103 (Washington, D.C.: U.S. Government Printing Office, 1931), 139–40; Henry Clark Benson, *Life among the Choctaw Indians* (Cincinnati: L. Swormstedt and A. Poe, 1860), 31–32.

22. Amelia Rector Bell, "Separate People," 332–35. The Choctaw names come from a roster of Choctaws claiming to have lost possessions during removal, October 8, 1837, Letters Received by the Office of Indian Affairs, 1824–1880, Reel 184, Microfilm Series M234, Choctaw Agency West, 1825-1838, RG 75.

23. Du Pratz, *History of Louisiana*, 234; Post, "The Domestic Animals and Plants of French Louisiana," 560; U. P. Hedrick, *The Peaches of New York* (Albany: J. B. Lynn, 1917), 44–45.

24. White, *Roots of Dependency*, 103–5, 130–37; *Missionary Herald* 25 (November 1829): 350; Hedrick, *The Peaches of New York*, 44–45.

25. Baily, *Tour in Unsettled Parts of North America*, 373; Eron Opha Rowland, "Peter Chester, Third Governor of the Province of West Florida under British Dominion, 1770–1781," in *Publications of the Mississippi Historical Society* 5 (1925): 83–84; Lists of travel expenses, George Gaines, March 31, 1811, and September 30, 1811, Miscellaneous Accounts, 1811–1815, reel 2, microfilm series T500, Records of the Choctaw Trading House, under the Office of Indian Trade, 1803–1824, RG 75.

26. *Panoplist and Missionary Herald* 16 (July 1820): 320.

CHAPTER 9

Choctaws and Missionaries in Mississippi before 1830

Clara Sue Kidwell

I n the northeastern corner of Winston County, Mississippi, rises an oval mound that covers about an acre and is approximately forty feet in height. Its name is Nanih Waiya, the sacred mound of the Choctaws. Various origin traditions of the tribe center around the mound. According to one story, the great spirit, Hushtahli, created the Choctaw in the center of the mound, and they emerged into the light from its top.[1] "Old Hopankitubbe (Hopakitobi) . . . was wont to say that after coming forth from the mound, the freshly-made Choctaws were very wet and moist, and that the Great Spirit stacked them along on the rampart, as on a clothes line, so that the sun could dry them."[2]

As if the great spirit had indeed made the Choctaws out of wet earth, the missionaries who first came into their territory to Christianize them felt that they were like malleable clay, ready to be shaped into the likeness of the Christian god and to become good Christians and Americans. However, it soon became obvious that the Choctaws were not ready to be molded to the will of the missionaries. Indeed, the missionaries often found themselves being bent to the will of tribal leaders even as they tried to bring the Choctaws to spiritual salvation. They were drawn into the secular and political concerns of the tribe as much as they were able to bring Christian conversion to tribal members.

Christianity and civilization went hand in hand as American moved out across the frontier. The Protestant Christian ethic of bringing God's will and order into being in this world was a strong inventive to clear and tame the wilderness and make it productive. The rhetoric of westward expansion claimed that Indian use of the land was unproductive, that the Indians raised only a few crops, and that they roamed in small numbers over vast territories that could and should support vastly larger populations.

The role of Christianity on the American frontier was important not only because it endowed attitudes toward the unknown wilderness with intellectual content. It was also important because the church generally represented the only true source of order in the lives of people who had moved beyond the pale of organized community life. Very little governmental regulation or organization existed in the wilderness to enforce law and social order. Churches stood for decency and order, and they brought discipline and stability to groups of people who found disorder and temptation at every turn.[3]

Missionary activity on the American frontier was an important concern of religious groups. In good part it was aimed at serving those church members who were venturing into the wilderness to establish new homes.[4] But concern about making new converts among the Indians was also strong. In 1787, the American Society for Propagating the Gospel Among the Indians and Others in North America, which had existed for twenty-five years as a voluntary organization, was given legal status by an act of the Massachusetts legislature.[5]

The American Board of Commissioners for Foreign Missions was established in 1810 as an interdenominational organization, founded upon the bedrock of New England Presbyterian Calvinism and Congregationalism. It was one of the first and most important of the missionary organizations working with Indian tribes on the frontier. Initially, the American Board directed its efforts to overseas missions since other missionary attempts with the Indians in North America had "been attended with so many discouragements." By 1817, however, the American Board was concerned that if the Indians were not civilized, they would soon become extinct.[6]

The aims and purposes of Christian missionary societies fit quite well with the intent of the federal government to establish its own sense of civilization and authority on the frontier. It was a simple step for the government to enlist the aid of churches. The Civilization Act that was passed in 1819 was only one of several acts that had, over the years, given financial assistance to churches to promote the civilizing of Indians through education and their conversion to Christianity. Church and state were to work closely together to promote the ends of decency and order in the uncivilized wilderness.[7]

In 1818, the Prudential Committee of the American Board advised the missionary group at Brainard, the establishment among the Cherokees, that "such a disposition should be made as would best serve the purposes of that establishment and promote the object of a similar establishment in the Choctaw Nation." On the advice of the missionaries at Brainard, Cyrus Kingsbury and Mr. and Mrs. Loring S. Williams were deemed best suited for the work to be undertaken.[8] Kingsbury sought the advice of the Choctaw agent, Colonel John McKee, about an appropriate location for a mission and was advised that a site on the Yalobusha River should be used, and that the government would provide the same support there that it had provided at the Cherokee mission at Brainard.[9]

The missionaries set off on the four-hundred-mile trek over land into the Choctaw country in May of 1818.[10] The country was described as fine, and the Choctaws as possessed of considerable wealth and having strong tendencies toward a civilized state. Their agent, John McKee, was in favor of missionary work and would use his influence with the tribe to support the missionaries' design.[11] Despite the fact that panthers lurked in the woods and roads were difficult to navigate, the missionaries began their work with a positive feeling.[12]

Thus began the long relationship between the Choctaw Nation and the American Board of Commissioners, a relationship that was to prove often troubling and frustrating for missionaries and Choctaws alike, but whose impact on the tribe was profound. Kingsbury and other missionaries lived with the Choctaws throughout the difficult period of treaty making, the ultimate removal of the majority of the tribe to the Indian Territory west of the Mississippi River, and the reestablishment of the nation there. Although the missionaries struggled valiantly to bend the Choctaws to the will of God, they as often as not found themselves submitting to the will and desires of tribal leaders. The hardships that they suffered in their attempts to tame the wilderness were severe, far more than anything endured by the Choctaws in their settled and peaceful communities. They fell ready prey to illnesses induced by environmental conditions to which their Choctaw neighbors were long accustomed. They suffered for their faith in many ways and were sustained primarily by their belief in their God, and secondarily by the U.S. government.

Despite the fact that missionaries gave little credence to Native beliefs, they did not move into a spiritual vacuum. Although ethnographers have given the Choctaws little credit for religious activities, Horatio B. Cushman, the son of a missionary who grew up among them and learned the language, described their personal religious beliefs in some detail. One of the earliest records in the journal of the first Choctaw mission also described the beliefs of the Choctaw in spirits who gave them special protection and abilities.[13] Their tribal dances and stickball games had both social and religious connotations.

They also had an inherent suspicion of the *alikchi* and *ishti ahullos*, men who had special spiritual powers and were recognized as healers and clairvoyants. In the long origin story related to Gideon Lincecum by a Choctaw man in the 1830s, the ishti ahullos set themselves up as leaders of the tribe during the migration toward their homeland in Mississippi, but the people resisted their leadership and feared their powers. Although they were held in awe because of their special abilities, people distrusted them because they were different and asserted control over the group. This distrust of people who asserted authority over others might have led the Choctaws to suspect the motives of missionaries, both because they were outsiders and because they claimed religious powers of a special sort.

The Choctaws definitely had their own religious beliefs. And as it turned out, they were not as interested in Christian salvation as they were in education. Christian missionary activity did not replace Native beliefs; primarily, it was turned to the purposes of the Choctaws, and that was to remain the case throughout the history of contact between Christian missionaries and Choctaw people. The early relationship between tribal and Christian beliefs was based upon the desire of missionaries to bring salvation to the savages and the desire of Choctaw leaders to learn the ways of white men.

Kingsbury and the Williamses arrived at the site of their new mission station on the Yalobusha River in late June of 1818. The name chosen for the station was Elliot, a tribute to John Elliot, the famous missionary to the Algonquians of the East Coast in 1636. There was support from influential full-blood chiefs. Pushmataha and Mushulatubbee wrote to the president saying, "Father, we thank you for the kind assistance you are affording to the Foreign Mission Society in establishing schools among us."[14] In a letter to Samuel Worcester dated July 30, 1818, Kingsbury reported that the reception by the half-bloods and those who understood their object was kind, but he also noted that "there are not wanting those who look upon all white people with a jealous eye."[15]

The work of building the mission and gathering souls proceeded. Kingsbury preached on Sundays to a mixed audience of half-bloods, white people, blacks, and occasionally, some of the Natives. And on Sunday, March 26, 1819, after solemn preparation by fasting and prayer, a church was organized at the mission house. However, its members included only the missionaries themselves.[16] No converts had been made yet.

The Choctaws wanted schools, and Kingsbury expressed his frustration over the situation in a letter to Samuel Worcester of the American Board: "We wish we could say that as much has been done to enlighten & save the souls of these perishing people as to make preparations for the instruction of their children. But, alas, as yet we have been able to accomplish but little towards this most important object. It is impossible for us to express our feelings on this subject. The expectation of this people has been that all our efforts would be directed toward the commencement of a school."[17] Although the mission was still under construction, the Choctaws were anxious to have the school begin operating. Around the middle of April, eight promising children were presented at the mission by their parents, who had traveled some 160 miles to bring them there. They had heard that the school was ready; it was not, but Kingsbury accepted the children rather than risk alienating their parents and other members of the nation. On April 19, the first Choctaw school officially opened.[18]

Kingsbury persisted in his efforts to persuade the Choctaws to give up their traditional ways and adopt those of the white man. On August 11, 1819, in a letter addressed to them as "Chiefs, Brothers and Warriors," he said, "You see that you can no longer live by hunting. You must raise corn & cattle & cotton that your women & children may have plenty to eat & to wear."[19]

So that the Choctaws could learn a new way of life, plans were made for three new establishments to be built with government assistance, and local schools in Choctaw communities were contemplated.[20] However, Kingsbury still had occasion to despair of accomplishment. On October 5 he wrote in the mission journal: "But we know not what to do; we are here in the wilderness more than $12.00 in debt, without money, without the necessary conveniences for a large family, a number of sick to take care of, provisions for 80 or 100 to procure for a year to come, & not a single cable from the Treasurer of the Board for almost eleven months. At times, we feel as tho' we should sink into the grave & no one come forward to raise the smouldering ruins."[21]

Plans for new missions continued despite the physical and financial hardships that had been encountered in establishing the first mission. The Elliot journal for April 4, 1820, recorded a resolution that Mr. Kingsbury go to Ook-tib-be-ha to attend to the concerns of mission establishment there, and on April 6, Kingsbury left Elliot to visit the new post.[22]

The missionary school at Elliot had the support of two important chiefs,

Puckshanubbee and Mushulatubbee, full-bloods, who wrote to Dr. Samuel Worcester of the American Board on June 4, 1820. They had visited the school and were impressed with what they saw.

> Brother, out hearts are made glad to see our children improving so fast. We are pleased to see our boys go into the woods with their axes, and into the field with their hoes, under the care of their teacher to learn to work, that they may know how to clear and cultivate our land; for we cannot expect to live any longer by hunting. Our game is gone; and the missionaries tell us, the Good Spirit points out to us now this new and better way to get our meat, and provide bread and clothes for ourselves, women and children. And we are very glad to see our daughters learning to cook, and to make and mend clothes, and do all such things as the white women do.[23]

In order to assist the school, the two chiefs announced that they had recently agreed to give the sum of $6,000 per year to the mission from their treaty annuities. Additional support for the school came from an annual appropriation of $1,000 from the Civilization Fund.[24]

The support of another prominent leader, Pushmataha, can be inferred from the fact that his son, a youth of about fifteen, became a student at the school. It was reported that the young man spoke English fluently and had a good knowledge of grammar and some acquaintance with geography. He had obtained his knowledge from some white men at the trading station at St. Stephens.[25]

In 1820, the government negotiated the Treaty of Doak's Stand with the Choctaws. By the terms of the treaty, the tribe ceded its lands in central Mississippi in exchange for a tract of land west of the Mississippi River. The treaty negotiations gave the missionaries of the American Board an opportunity to seek support from the government for their establishments. Kingsbury laid before Jackson and Hinds an ambitious plan for building schools, explaining that "a large number of the children must be fed and clothed, all must be initiated in habits of industry, and a portion taught the Mechanics Arts." He proposed that in 1821 the government would provide $5,000 for the school at Elliot, $12,000 for construction of a school at Ook-tib-be-ha, and $10,000 for the establishment of five small schools. In the succeeding years through 1828, the missionaries would establish two more major schools, and twenty-eight more small schools in Choctaw communities. The total costs entailed by Kingsbury's plan would be $358,500, or an average of $44,812 per year. The large schools would be boarding schools to serve 80–100 children at an average cost of $15,000 per year, and the small schools would be day schools to serve 20–40 children at an average cost of $2,000 per year.[26]

The treaty provided support for education. Article 7 agreed that fifty-four sections, each one square mile, should be laid out and sold to raise funds for the support of schools—three-fourths designated for schools in Mississippi and one-fourth for schools to be established in the Arkansas Territory.[27]

The missionaries stood to get support, but at the expense of Choctaw lands, and the amount that would be provided by the sale of the fifty-four sections at the prevailing rate of $1.25 for public lands would be only $43,200, far short of the expenses projected in Kingsbury's grand scheme for the establishment of schools. However, the treaty provision and continuing support from the Civilization Fund gave evidence of the federal government's commitment to education for the Choctaws.

The school at Elliot meanwhile was increasing its enrollment. Kingsbury reported to the secretary of war that thirty-eight new students had been admitted to the school. The enrollment was seventy-four, of whom six were home on vacation. Fifty of those students had not been able to speak English on their arrival, but all were learning it and some were now fluent in it. Of sixty-five children who began learning the alphabet, twenty-eight now read the New Testament with facility. Ten had made progress in arithmetic, and two students who were considered advanced when they entered had learned some grammar and geography. Also, some fifty thousand bricks had been made, and a number of new buildings had been erected.[28]

A second mission was established on Ook-tib-be-ha Creek in 1820. Kingsbury took up residence there and named the new station Mayhew, in honor of another early missionary.[29] The numbers of the mission family continued to increase, and new leaders came to assist Cyrus Kingsbury. The person who was to have probably the greatest impact of any of the missionaries to the Choctaws, Cyrus Byington, arrived at Elliot in April of 1821.[30]

Byington, who had graduated from Andover Theological Seminary in September of 1819, had been assigned by the Board to raise funds for missionary efforts, and had been asked to accompany the missionary contingent that left Goshen, Massachusetts, for the Choctaw missions in 1820.[31] If Kingsbury was the spiritual leader of the Choctaw missions and the man most singularly responsible for their secular concerns of hiring laborers and dealing with the government agents, Byington was the teacher whose influence on the Choctaws was the most lasting. In their respective roles, Kingsbury and Byington represented the conflicts that the missionaries of the American Board faced in dealing with both their spiritual responsibilities and the secular forces of tribal and federal politics.

The Choctaws wanted schools near their homes, and in 1822 Moses Jewell traveled from Elliot to the Six Towns Division to follow up on Kingsbury's visit to locate a school. Loring S. Williams went to French Camps, a settlement that had grown up around the tavern and trading post established by the LeFlore family on the Natchez road in the southern part of Choctaw country. The community was primarily one of mixed-bloods. There he established the station that ultimately became known as Bethel.[32]

The importance of the Choctaw language as a means of communicating Christian doctrine to the Natives was apparent to the missionaries. Alfred Wright undertook to learn the Choctaw language by going to live with the family of Captain David Folsom at the Pigeon Roost, Folsom's tavern and trading post on the road from Elliot to Mayhew.[33] And the school at Elliot introduced the translation of English words into Choctaw and vice versa into its curriculum.[34]

It was apparent that the mission schools could serve the ends of conversion by educating their students to read and write and understand the Bible, and there were some encouraging signs regarding conversions. The journal at Elliot for February 16, 1822, reported that Tus-eam-i-ub-by and his son visited and expressed an interest in hearing more about Christianity.[35] And every so often, a workman at the mission or a student at the school would appear genuinely concerned or even show the distress of mind that accompanied the question, "What must we do to be saved?" These were occasions of the greatest joy to the missionaries.

But there were also the secular concerns of the schools, and on March 15, 1822, Kingsbury left Mayhew for the Choctaw agency to attend the payment of the tribal annuity and to discuss with leaders of the Six Towns Division the possibility of a school there.[36]

Missionaries were not the only influence changing the lives of some Choctaws. A group of about one hundred who had no clan affiliation and hence no settled place of residence or claim on the tribal annuities took up residence near Captain Folsom's home. Folsom encouraged them to give up drinking and to lead a settled life, and he also explained the missionaries' aims. Since Alfred Wright resided at Captain Folsom's house, he had an opportunity to preach to this group.[37]

Influential Choctaw leaders continued to support the efforts of the missionaries to establish new schools, even if the support did not always come in quite the way the missionaries would have liked. In April of 1822 Major John Pitchlynn, a mixed-blood leader who was the chief interpreter for the Choctaws in their negotiations with the U.S. government, gave a donation of $1,000 by forgiving a note that he held for that amount. He said that although he did not consider himself a pious man, he was glad that his children would be educated by the missionaries.[38]

The school at the mission station at Mayhew opened on April 30, 1822. Twelve children, eight Choctaws and four children of missionaries, comprised the student body. The Indian children had their Native dress exchanged for clothing donated to the missions, with the fervent wish that "these previous little immortals may be clothed in robes washed, and made white, in the blood of the Lamb."[39]

Despite the expressed desires of some of the Choctaws for education, there was still strong suspicion of the intentions of the missionaries. The journal of Mayhew mission for June 10, 1822, mentions this suspicion. "Many of them cannot believe that we possess that disinterested benevolence which we profess.... Wicked white people are not wanting, who endeavor to persuade the Indians that our object is gain."[40]

These aspersions did not dissuade some Choctaws from bringing their children to the school and speaking in its support. Mushulatubbee came to a conference at Mayhew in July with fifteen to twenty captains from his division and two of his sons and a nephew to put in the school. Another elderly Choctaw man brought his daughter and his grandson. Of the grandson he said, "I wish you to take him by the arm and the heart, and hold him fast. I shall hereafter only hold him by the end of his fingers."[41] Given the strong sense of relationship between grandfathers and grandchildren, the old man's statement represents a significant commitment to the education of his grandson.

Major John Pitchlynn and Captain David Folsom visited the school and spoke to the children, saying that they must learn the ways of the white people who were settling and becoming so numerous. The missionaries could teach them to read and write and cultivate crops and deal with mechanical things. Nothing was said about the religious import of what the missionaries had to teach.[42] The next day, Kingsbury addressed the council of Choctaws that had assembled at the school. He pointed out that the Choctaws themselves had contributed $4,000 toward the school; the president of the United States had contributed $1,275, and the American Board had contributed $8,000. He stressed that the white man did not owe anything to the Choctaws but gave of his own free will. The white people came to the Indians, he argued, to save them from ruin. He continued: The fate that had befallen other tribes could be avoided. The white man had prospered because of the Good Book, and if the Choctaws would accept its teachings, they too could have good things. But the children must accept discipline, since that was part of the teaching of the Good Book, and parents must not object if their children were punished for disobedience. The children must not take the clothes they were given away from the mission. The parents must be prompt in returning their children to school after vacation periods.[43]

A major objective of the talk was to impress on the Choctaws the obligation Kingsbury thought they owed the white people and that "they must expect [the schools] to be managed in all respects, not according to their own views, but according to the views of the President, and the good people who established them."[44] The tone of Kingsbury's sermon did not sit well with the assembled Choctaws, although they did not object openly. Although Kingsbury emphasized white supremacy and Choctaw dependence, the Choctaws themselves wanted the school, and the efforts of the missionaries were being directed to a large extent by their desires.

Had Kingsbury had his way, the missionaries' efforts would have been devoted primarily to preaching and conversion, and education would have been a secondary concern. The actual situation was the opposite. It would continue to be, and leaders of the missionary families would continue to debate the relative importance of preaching versus teaching among the Choctaws. Kingsbury and Cyrus Byington were the main spokesmen for the opposing points of view. Kingsbury laid plans for the schools but always resented the burdens of secular life that they imposed. Byington devoted his efforts to developing texts in the Choctaw language for use in the schools to educate the children in reading, writing, and arithmetic, but he believed that this facility would ultimately make it easier for them to learn the Christian doctrine. Preaching and teaching were both directed at the same end, but they were the objects of considerable controversy among the missionaries.

The influence of Christian ideals on individual Choctaws as a result of missionary efforts was apparent. The American Board received a letter from Hwoo-la-ta-hoo-mah, chief of the Six Towns, dated October 18, 1822, describing laws that he had passed for his people. The *Missionary Herald* noted that it was possible that the letter had been dictated by some white person, but that the handwriting was definitely that of the chief. Among the laws were ones calling for the destruction of any whiskey brought into the nation by any

Choctaw who had traded with white people, punishment for infanticide, for stealing hogs or cattle, and for polygamy and adultery. For those who went to Mobile and New Orleans and neglected their crops, their corn was to be burned.

The chief concluded his letter with the remark, "We have made the above laws, because we wish to follow the ways of the white people. We hope they will assist us in getting our children educated." Kingsbury noted in a letter to the Board that "some active and well disposed young half-breeds, particularly Joel Nail," were instrumental in procuring these laws.[45]

However well-disposed some of the Choctaws leaders were toward the missionary schools, there was also dissatisfaction among some students and parents. The mission journal of Mayhew reported on January 12, 1821, that four parents had come to investigate unfavorable reports circulating about the schools. The reports began, according to the journal, when some young boys who wanted to go home complained about their treatment. Kingsbury and the other missionaries were able to convince the parents that the discipline to which their children were subjected was necessary. The woman in the group expressed her desire to become a student but Kingsbury reluctantly denied her wish. Already the school could not accommodate all the children who might attend.[46]

The emphasis of the missionaries upon manual labor for the children and physical discipline went counter to the very permissive ways of Indian parents. Choctaw children learned by example, by emulating their parents in their daily chores, and the ethics and values of the tribe were passed down by grandparents who sat the children down in the evening for lectures about what was right and what was wrong. Children had a great deal of freedom in their own society because they were constantly involved in the world of adults, observing and mimicking them. Discipline was enforced by teasing or ridiculing children who were acting inappropriately. The system of formal instruction, organized work details, and sometimes physical punishment was quite foreign to Choctaw child-rearing and education practices, and the complaints of children would continue to be heard with sympathy by Choctaw elders and would be a continuing cause of discontent with the mission schools.

In 1825, the U.S. government and the tribe negotiated another treaty of land cession. This treaty established a boundary between the Choctaw lands west of the Mississippi and the Arkansas Territory. In consideration of the cession, the United States agreed to pay to the Choctaw Nation an annuity of $6,000 forever. For the first twenty years, however, the annuity was to be applied by the president to support schools in the nation, "and extending to it the benefits of instruction in the mechanic and ordinary arts of life." The government also agreed to survey and sell the fifty-four sections of land that had been set aside for the support of schools in the Treaty of Doak's Stand.[47]

This annuity for education did not go to the schools of the American Board but to the Choctaw Academy in Kentucky. Choctaw discontent with the missionaries and their schools was expressed in part by their support of the academy, which was to play an important part in the education of future tribal leaders.

The existence of the academy predated the treaty, but its impact on the nation up to 1825 was slight. It had originally been established in 1818 by the Baptist Mission Society of Kentucky at Great Crossings, and it admitted its first class of eight boys in the spring of 1819. Its initial success was short-lived, and missionary contributions dropped off during the 1820–21 school year. However, Elias Cornelius of the American Board expressed concern about its existence to Kingsbury in a letter of March 8, 1820. But the Baptist Mission Society decided to close the school in 1821.

The academy was reopened, however, at the request of the Choctaw leader Mushulatubbee in 1825. The man who was responsible for the reopening was Richard Johnson, a rather flamboyant military man and Kentucky politician whose political fortunes rested in part on his claims that he had been the man who killed the great Shawnee leader Tecumseh at the Battle of the Thames in 1813. The financial support came from the $6,000 annuity provided by the Choctaw Treaty of 1825.[48]

The first class consisted of twenty-six Choctaw pupils and ten young men from the surrounding area. The curriculum included "reading, writing, arithmetic, grammar, geography, practical surveying, astronomy, and vocal music," and the equipment included a pair of elegant artificial globes, a variety of atlases, two surveying compasses, one orrery, an octant, a quadrant, and a telescope.[49]

Although the expense of the academy was relatively great, Greenwood LeFlore wrote to Secretary of War Barbour on January 9, 1828, to approve its location and assert his support. "I am perfectly Satisfyed with the Establishment in its present form. And although it is probable that we could get our children Taught Something cheaper yet we do not wish to put out their Education to the Lowest Bidder."[50]

The list of students in the school for 1827 shows the names of most of the prominent mixed-blood families in the Choctaw Nation—Folsom, Pitchlynn,

Nail, Juzon, Harkins, Garland, Perry, Durant, LeFlore.[51] There were also students who were probably full-bloods. We can infer this fact from the names reported and the custom of the missionaries to give recognizable names to students who came with traditional Choctaw names. Thus we find in the list Alexander Pope and Samuel Worcester. We also find William Ward, the son of the Choctaw agent William Ward, evidence that the school served some of the sons of white settlers in the region. It was necessary for a student to have a certificate from a school in the Choctaw Nation before he could be admitted to the academy.[52]

The success of the Choctaw Academy depended upon the education that students received at the schools of the American Board, and the requirement that they have a certificate for those schools represents a triumph for interdenominational education. However, the academy drew away the young men who might otherwise have gone to the Board's missionary school in Cornwell, Connecticut. The Board report of 1826 noted that "there is at present no disposition, either among the Cherokees or Choctaws, to send their young men to Cornwall."[53] The Choctaw Academy was becoming the preparatory school of the Choctaw Nation, and the education there was secular rather than religious.

The academy had the support of Choctaw leaders. LeFlore and Mushulatubbee both visited. But one of its students was highly critical of certain nonacademic aspects of the school. Peter Pitchlynn charged that, among other things, the food was bad, the linen dirty, and the coffee weak. Richard Johnson responded vigorously in a letter of September 12, 1828, to David Folsom refuting the charges. His letter was accompanied by the signatures of Pierre Juzan, George W. Harkins, Selas D. Fisher, Samuel Worcester, Samuel Garland, and Robert Jones. Thomas Henderson, headmaster of the school, wrote to the Indian Office that the school had very good food and provided adequate clothing and footwear. He did not comment on the quality of the coffee.[54]

Despite this criticism from a student, Choctaw leaders continued to support the schools. Mushulatubbee, Oklabbee, Ispiahhomah, Charles King, James M. King, Hiram King, and Peter King wrote to Andrew Jackson on December 23, 1830, to complain bitterly that "we have employed and payed those Yankee Missionarys for twelve years.... We have never Recd. a Scholar out of their Schools that was able to keep a grog shop Book when we found that we could get nothing from them we Established an academy in Kentucky... from which we have Recd. a great number of first Rate Scholars."[55]

The American Board was also facing competition from another denomination. In December of 1823, Methodists appeared in Choctaw territory. Although the organization of the Missionary Society of the Methodist Episcopal Church on April 5, 1819, coincided closely with the passage of the Civilization Act, it was not until December of 1823 that a missionary was appointed to the Choctaws by the Mississippi Conference.[56]

The bishop of the conference, William Winans, held very low opinions of the competing denominations among the Indians. He wrote to a fellow clergyman in July of 1824 that "if there is anything more ridiculous, in the religious world, than every thing else, it is the Baptist domestick Missions; and the Presbyterian Missions among the Indians especially, are oppressive; and, if not quite unprofitable, are of but little value."[57]

Wiley Ledbetter was appointed to ride the circuit among the Choctaws, and after he began, Winans reported that he was "still flourishing greatly among the Indians," although he needed money.[58] And in December of 1824, at a session of the conference in Tuscaloosa, Alabama, Ledbetter produced tangible evidence in his efforts. He introduced to the bishop of that conference some converted Choctaw Indians. Bishop Soule's soul "was deeply stirred within him. Standing erect in all his imposing stature, eyes filled with tears of joy, he cried out; 'Brethren, the Choctaws are ours. No, I mistake; they are Christ's.'"[59]

Whoever laid claim to the Choctaws—the Methodists, Jesus Christ, or the American Board who had been working among the tribe since 1819—it appears that Choctaw souls were viewed as trophies by several competing parties. The competition between Presbyterians and Methodists hinted at in Winans's statement regarding rival denominations became overt during 1824 when Ledbetter attempted to lay a claim to Bethany, a school that had been established by the American Board.

It is not clear whether the rather general Choctaw disaffection with the schools was a result of the new Methodist influence or whether the Methodists simply benefited from it. Ledbetter had approached Captain Robert Cole about taking over the mission school named Bethany near his house, and had offered to board and clothe the children there. His action was taken without any consultation with Dr. William Pride, the teacher at the school, or with Kingsbury, who complained vigorously to Evarts about the action. Cole had delegated to one of his subordinate chiefs the task of telling Pride that his services were no longer needed.[60]

Kingsbury also complained to Bishop Winans about Ledbetter's action.

The takeover of the school represented the loss of an investment of over $1,000 by the Board. Kingsbury pointed out to Winans that the school was under the patronage of the U.S. government, and Secretary of War John C. Calhoun wrote to the Choctaw delegation that was in Washington for treaty negotiations, pointing out to them that the school in question was under Kingsbury's supervision.[61]

Despite the importuning, Ledbetter evidently retained control of the school, and it was only his failure to fulfill his promise to board and clothe the pupils that led to the abandonment of the school altogether.[62] Ledbetter's success among the Choctaws came to an abrupt end after this failure. In 1825 it was noted by the conference that Ledbetter had failed to convert a single Indian, and he was finally "located" by the Mississippi Conference, that is, moved to a different site.

After his departure the Methodist effort among the Choctaws languished until 1827, when Alexander Talley, a physician, was appointed missionary.[63] He began his work in the spring of 1828, and he evidently found a welcome at the home of Greenwood LeFlore, since several of his letters were written there. He rode his circuit for the first two months without an interpreter, but he reported success in a council that LeFlore had arranged and at which he had interpreted Talley's words.[64] LeFlore was to remain the most important proponent of Methodism among the Mississippi Choctaws before removal. He also laid the groundwork for several schools in Choctaw communities.

Continuing discontent among the Choctaws with the schools of the American Board missionaries may have contributed to the success of Talley's efforts. Kingsbury wrote to Evarts in the summer of 1827 that "the Missionaries & the schools in the nation are in very low estimation among the people generally in the nation."[65]

Part of the problem was the existence of the Choctaw Academy. Part was ongoing disaffection. But an incident at the American Board school at Bethel probably contributed to the level of Choctaw discontent. In June of 1828 Zeddock Brashears wrote to Kingsbury to charge that Stephen McComber, the teacher at Bethel, had impregnated his granddaughter, Susan Lyle.[66] Under questioning, the girl reported that McComber had seduced her, and McComber admitted the charges. Although LeFlore demanded a money payment to the girl's family, Kingsbury was willing to concede only that the missionary family would contribute monetarily to the support of the girl and her child.[67]

McComber was removed from the station at Bethel and ultimately dismissed from missionary service. Alexander Talley mentioned the incident to Winans early on, and although he indicated that he was still in favor of the missionaries, he also said, "I have taken such a course as to keep our work and standing distinct."[68]

Talley's influence among the Choctaws was primarily centered on his relationship with the LeFlore family. Because the LeFlore residence was a center of political activity, and Talley was often there, he was able to reach a number of leaders. Three chiefs who appeared at LeFlore's home on business stayed for a prayer meeting conducted by Talley and "at the close of the first prayer a deep seriousness appeared on every countenance." The chiefs "humbled themselves in the dust" with other potential converts at the end of the meeting and showed signs of true conversion.[69] At the same meeting LeFlore's wife and mother showed signs of conversion to Methodism, and eventually Talley converted LeFlore himself, when he was grieving over the death of his wife.[70]

Talley realized the conflict with the Presbyterians that Methodist conversions presaged, especially so significant a conversion as that of LeFlore, one of the most important Choctaw leaders. "We have been on friendly terms with the Presbyterians, but I fear this will not last much longer. We are beginning to admit persons into society, around Elliot, which I think likely to produce a breach, but if the people wish it we shall go fearlessly forward." He also complained that a Choctaw youth who had been at a school in Kentucky (the Choctaw Academy) and had been educated as a Baptist preacher was trying to baptize Methodist converts without telling them that he represented a different denomination.[71]

The impact of missionary activity from 1827 to 1829 came primarily in the form of large-scale conversions at camp meetings for the Methodists. Talley reported in 1829 that some 1,300 persons, most of them Choctaws, were reported to have experienced the very emotional state associated with conversion. Indeed, during one meeting the attentions of Brother Smith and several Choctaw chiefs were attracted to the son of a prominent chief, "who had retired to his fire, and was now so much affected that we were apprehensive he would fall into the fire by which he was standing. From these feelings we were soon relieved by his falling a different course."[72]

The missionaries of the American Board saw the results of the camp meeting among the Choctaws. They noted in the late summer of 1828 a more than ordinary interest among the Choctaws in the public preaching of the gospel. But where the Methodists would claim about 1,300 conversions as a result of camp meetings between 1828 and 1829, the efforts of the American Board in the period from July 1, 1828, to July 1, 1829, produced only twenty-eight additions to their membership.[73] The American Board adopted the technique of camp meetings held in the woods near Choctaw villages.[74]

The difference in rates of conversion was as much a function of the definitions of conversion and the interpretation of its manifestation as it was a result of any specific efforts by the missionaries. The American Board demanded signs of complete conversion over a period of time before they would accept the evidence as real. Those who came forward to sit on the anxious seats at Presbyterian meetings had to do so for long periods of time, and had to demonstrate in their behavior the fact of submission to God's will. The Methodists were willing to accept the highly emotional behavior apparent in a single episode as evidence that a person had been moved by God. The Presbyterians expressed strong skepticism about Methodist conversions, and the Methodists knew that they were a real threat to the hold that the American Board was trying to establish over the Choctaws.

The appeal of the Methodists in converting Choctaws is understandable in light of traditional Choctaw beliefs in individual visionary experiences, which were highly emotional, and in traditional patterns of ceremonial activity that brought together large groups of people. The camp meeting allowed Choctaws to express both the highly emotional aspect of their own religious life and their own traditional social predilections. The Presbyterians, in their stress upon personal unworthiness, personal guilt, and individual conversion, went very strongly counter to traditional Choctaw ideas of collective identity.

The missionaries of both denominations had their greatest impact on the mixed-blood members of the tribe, and they came under harsh criticism from the full-blood chiefs. The schools that they started served the children of mixed-blood families more often because they were located primarily around the communities that grew up around the establishments of mixed-blood leaders such as the Folsoms and LeFlores. Their influence measured in the number of conversions they reported is slight. By the end of 1830, the Board could report only about 360 converts in the Choctaw Nation, of which we can estimate that approximately 250 were Choctaws.[75]

Choctaw leaders, both full-bloods and mixed-bloods, wanted education that would allow their children to deal with the white men on their own terms. And missionaries found themselves offering education to Choctaw children when many of them would rather have been preaching the gospel. It is ironic that the most tangible and possibly the most lasting result of missionary activity among the Choctaws in Mississippi was the preservation of the Choctaw language. The translations that Cyrus Byington made of biblical texts and school books introduced Choctaws to literacy. Even today in the Choctaw communities in central Mississippi, there are many who maintain that the published version of the Bible in Choctaw prepared by Cyrus Byington is the definitive version of Choctaw orthography. By teaching the reading and writing of the language, missionaries helped to make possible the continuation of language in Choctaw communities and to preserve the sense of identity that has sustained those communities to the present.

NOTES

This chapter originally appeared as "Choctaws and Missionaries in Mississippi before 1830," *American Indian Culture and Research Journal* 11 (1987): 51–72.

1. John R. Swanton, *Source Material for the Social and Ceremonial Life of the Choctaw Indians*, Bureau of American Ethnology Bulletin 103 (Washington, D.C.: U.S. Government Printing Office, 1931), 195.

2. H. S. Halbert, "Nanih Waiya, the Sacred Mound of the Choctaws," *Publications of the Mississippi Historical Society* 2 (1899): 230.

3. William Warrent Sweet, *Religion on the American Frontier*, 4 vols. (New York: Henry Holt, 1931–46), 2:60, 64.

4. Ibid.

5. Wade C. Barclay, *History of Methodist Missions: Part One, Early American Methodism, 1769–1844; Part Two, The Methodist Episcopal Church, 1845–1939; Part Three, Twentieth Century Perspectives; Methodist Episcopal Church, 1896–1939* (by J. Tremayne Copplestone), 4 vols. (New York: Board of Missions and Church Extension of the Methodist Church), 1:165.

6. American Board of Commissioners for Foreign Missions, *First Ten Annual Reports of the American Board of Commissioners for Foreign Missions, with Other Documents of the Board* (Boston: Crocker and Brewster, 1834), 18, 57. See also the manuscript copies of reports filed in the National Anthropological Archives, Smithsonian Institution, Washington, D.C., MS 3153.

7. U.S. Statues at Large, 3, chap. 75, March 3, 1819.

8. Ibid.

9. Kingsbury to McKee, March 18, 1818, Papers of the American Board of Commissioners for Foreign Missions (hereafter ABCFM), MS 18:3:4, folder 1, Houghton Library, Harvard University.

10. Horatio B. Cushman, *History of the Choctaw, Chickasaw, and Natchez Indians* (Greenville, Tex.: Headlight Printing House, 1899), 135.

11. American Board, *First Ten Annual Reports*, 199.

12. Ibid.
13. Cushman, *History of the Choctaw, Chickasaw, and Natchez Indians*, 92–93; ABCFM, 18:3:4, vol. 1, folder 1, Journal of Elliot Mission, 7–8.
14. Pushmataha and Mushulatubbee to the President, Choctaw Trading House, October 20, 1818, National Archives, Record Group 75, Letters to the Secretary of War—Received, microfilm series 271, roll 2; American Board, *First Ten Annual Reports*, 209; ABCFM, vol. 2, folder 5.
15. American Board, *First Ten Annual Reports*, 209; ABCFM, vol. 2, folder 5.
16. American Board, *First Ten Annual Reports*, 243; ABCFM, 18:3:4, vol. 1, folder 1; Joseph Tracy, *History of the American Board of Commissioners for Foreign Missions* (New York: M. W. Dodd, 1842), 78–79.
17. American Board, *First Ten Annual Reports*, 243.
18. Ibid., 242; ABCFM, 18:3:4, vol. 1, folder 1, Journal of Elliot Mission.
19. Kingsbury to Choctaw chiefs, August 11, 1819, ABCFM, 18:3:4, vol. 2, folder 33.
20. Ibid.
21. Ibid., vol. 1, folder 1, 10.
22. *Missionary Herald* 12 (1821): 48, 49.
23. *Missionary Herald* 16, no. 8 (August 1820), 187.
24. *Missionary Herald*, 17, no. 1 (January 1821), 5.
25. Ibid.
26. Cyrus Kingsbury to Andrew Jackson and Thomas Hinds, Treaty Ground, Choctaw Nation, October 18, 1820. National Archives, Record Group 75, Letters to the Secretary of War—Received, microfilm series 271, roll 3.
27. Charles J. Kappler, ed., *Indian Affairs: Laws and Treaties*, 5 vols. (Washington, D.C.: U.S. Government Printing Office, 1904–41), 2:193–94.
28. *Missionary Herald* 17, no. 4 (April 1821): 108–9.
29. *Missionary Herald*, 17, no. 5 (May 1821): 152.
30. Tracy, *History of the American Board*, 338.
31. *Missionary Herald* 18, no. 1 (January 1822): 5.
32. Ibid., 9.
33. *Missionary Herald* 18, no. 3 (March 1822): 82–83.
34. Ibid., 181.
35. Ibid.
36. Ibid., 18, no. 7 (July 1822): 222.
37. Ibid.
38. Ibid., 18, no. 12 (December 1822): 373.
39. Ibid., 374.
40. Ibid.
41. Ibid., 376.
42. Ibid., 378.
43. Ibid.
44. Ibid.
45. Ibid., 19, no. 1 (January 1823): 10–11.
46. Ibid., 17, no. 9 (September 1821): 288.

47. Kappler, *Indian Affairs*, 2:212.
48. Walter Brownlow Posey, *The Baptist Church in the Lower Mississippi Valley 1776–1845* (Lexington: University of Kentucky Press, 1957), 83–84; *American Board of Commissioners for Foreign Missions Compiled from Documents Laid Before the Board, at the Seventeenth Annual Meeting*... (Boston: Crocker and Brewster, 1826), 64.
49. Shelley D. Rouse, "Colonel Dick Johnson's Choctaw Academy: A Forgotten Educational Experiment," *Ohio Archaeological and Historical Quarterly*, 25, no. 1 (January 1916), 97; Carolyn Foreman, "The Choctaw Academy," *Chronicles of Oklahoma* 6 (1928): 460.
50. Foreman, "The Choctaw Academy," 461.
51. National Archives, Record Group 75, Choctaw Removal Records, entry 267, box 8.
52. Ibid.
53. *American Board of Commissioners for Foreign Missions Compiled... Seventeenth Annual Meeting*, 105.
54. Foreman, "The Choctaw Academy," 468, 471.
55. Ibid., 475.
56. Barclay, *History of Methodist Missions*, 2:114; John G. Jones, *A Complete History of Methodism as Connected with the Mississippi Conference of the Methodist Episcopal Church, South*, 2 vols. (Nashville, Tenn.: Publishing House of the Methodist Episcopal Church, 1908), 2:34; *Minutes of the Annual Conferences of the Methodist Episcopal Church, 1773–1845*, 3 vols. (New York: T. Mason and G. Lane, 1840–45), 1:429.
57. William Winans to Rev. Zechariah Williams, Wilkinson, Mississippi, July 2, 1824, Papers of William Winans, microfilm, Mississippi State Department of Archives and History, Jackson, Mississippi (hereafter cited as Winans Papers).
58. Winans to Bishop R. R. Roberts, August 6, 1824, Winans Papers.
59. Jones, *History of Methodism*, 2:34.
60. Kingsbury to Evarts, October 8, 1824, ABCFM, vol. 3, folder 1.
61. Kingsbury to William Winans, ABCFM, vol. 3, folder 5; John C. Calhoun to Choctaw Delegation, December 3, 1824, ABCFM 18:3:4, vol. 4, folder 25.
62. Barclay, *History of Methodist Missions*, 2:135.
63. Ibid., 135–36.
64. Talley to Winans, box 1, folder 10, Alexander Talley Papers, Millsaps College, Jackson, Mississippi (hereafter cited as Talley Papers).
65. Kingsbury to Evarts, Mayhew, June 21, 1827, ABCFM, vol. 3, folder 24.
66. Zeddock Brashears to Kingsbury, June 21, 1828, ABCFM, vol. 3, folder 26.
67. Kingsbury to LeFlore, Mayhew, July 30, 1828; LeFlore to Kingsbury, N.W. District, August 8, 1828; Deposition by Susannah Lyles, ABCFM, vol. 3, folder 26.
68. Talley to Winans, box 1, folder 10, Talley Papers.
69. Talley to Winans, box 1, folder 10, Talley Papers.
70. Talley to Winans, Choctaw Nation, Big Land, October 28, 1829, Talley Papers.
71. Ibid.
72. Smith to Winans, at Captain Cobb's, Choctaw Nation, November 3, 1828, box 1, folder 10, Winans Papers.

73. Talley to Winans, Choctaw Nation, July 1, 1829, Talley Papers; American Board of Commissioners for Foreign Missions, *Report of the American Board of Commissioners for Foreign Missions, Compiled from Documents Laid Before the Board at the Twentieth Annual Meeting*... (Boston: Crocker and Brewster, 1829), 74–75.

74. Cyrus Byington to J. Evarts, Yaknokchaya, July 13, 1829, ABCFM, vol. 3, folder 92.

75. American Board of Commissioners for Foreign Missions, *Report of the American Board of Commissioners for Foreign Missions, Read at the Twenty-Second Annual Meeting*... (Boston: Crocker and Brewster, 1831), 80.

CHAPTER 10

Greenwood LeFlore

SOUTHERN CREOLE, CHOCTAW CHIEF

James Taylor Carson

In an 1843 interview Greenwood LeFlore spoke of his regret over taking part in the removal of most of the Choctaws from Mississippi. At the time, he was well on his way to accumulating the fifteen thousand acres, four hundred slaves, and an elegant mansion that he would leave behind when he died.[1] But his prosperity came at a steep price. In 1830 he had been the principal chief of the Choctaw Nation and the lead negotiator of the Treaty of Dancing Rabbit Creek that ceded to the federal government the Choctaws' remaining land in Mississippi. In the interview he looked back sorrowfully on the treaty. He was, he admitted, "sorry to say that the benefits realized from [the treaty] by my people were by no means equal to what I had a right to expect, nor to what they were justly entitled."[2]

Historians have not been kind to Greenwood LeFlore. Historian Grant Foreman once characterized the chief as "shrewd" and "ambitious."[3] Several decades later Ronald Satz echoed Foreman's sentiments, referring to LeFlore as a "shrewd mixed-blood" out for pecuniary gain at the expense of his people.[4] More recent ethnohistorical interpretations of LeFlore and the Mississippi Choctaws offer similar conclusions. LeFlore has been called at various times a member of a "new elite" that "led an assault on Choctaw customs," a man who "practiced duplicity," and a member of a "small but thriving Choctaw landed aristocracy" who "spoke publicly against removal because of their elected positions, but . . . favored it privately in order to consolidate their political positions."⁵

The historiographical verdict that "mixed-bloods" like LeFlore were duplicitous cheats can be traced, oddly enough, to one of LeFlore's principle antagonists, Andrew Jackson. Old Hickory's experience in the 1810s as a frontier warrior and treaty negotiator led him to see men like LeFlore as exploiters of "real" and "true" Indians. During negotiations with the Cherokees in 1817, for example, Jackson remarked, "Halfbreeds . . . have been and are fattening upon the annuities, the labours, and folly of the native Indians." Such assumptions informed his later presidential policy objectives. In communications with the Choctaws in 1830 on the eve of the Dancing Rabbit Creek talks, Jackson hoped he could convince leaders who opposed LeFlore to come to Washington to discuss removal and thus "leave the halfbreeds . . . disappointed."⁶

By casting their interpretations of people like LeFlore in terms that echo Andrew Jackson's own cramped worldview and by perpetuating Old Hickory's conflation of mixed blood, character, and behavior, historians have imported early-nineteenth-century notions of blood and behavior into recent and current writing on the history of the Native South. While ideas about race were important in LeFlore's day, they cause problems when historians use them to interrogate that same past. If the language we use to write history derives from the language of race as it was used in the American past, then we can never really escape the ways of thinking that gave rise to the idea of mixed bloodedness in the first place. Interpreting the lives and deeds of people like LeFlore based on an alleged relationship between blood and behavior cannot move beyond, and indeed has not moved beyond, Andrew Jackson's own observations during his career as a soldier against the South's Native people.

Mixed bloodedness, or its more neutral incarnations of biraciality and biculturality, is moreover problematic because of the way it constructs the individuals it proposes to study.⁷ Such terms imply that LeFlore's heritage and upbringing were somehow fractured and deny the wholeness of the world as he inhabited it. Neither the language of biraciality nor of biculturality can really capture the subtlety and complexity of what made Greenwood LeFlore both a southern Creole and a Choctaw chief. Scholars need to recognize that, although native southerners, enslaved southerners, and settler southerners looked and often behaved differently, their world could on some level be seen as whole and integrated. They could be said, in fact, to constitute together, through their many common day-to-day practices and beliefs, a kind of southern culture.⁸

Creole theory offers a way out of the trap of race that has had such a stranglehold on the writing of southern history. The term *Creole*, derived from the Latin verb *creare*, to create, was used by both the Spanish and the Portuguese to denote the animals, plants, and people born in the Americas from contact between the Old World and the New. In southern history *Creole* is often associated with the descendants of early French, Spanish, and African inhabitants of Louisiana.[9] Creole theory, as it developed in the hands of Caribbean scholars and writers, however, focuses not on the identity of particular people but on the processes whereby people who came to the Americas drew from the cultures of the people they encountered to weave together New World societies.[10] The degree to which Americans, Africans, and Europeans resisted one another, borrowed from one another, or simply found cultural consonances among one another and the conditions under which they coexisted varied from place to place and from time to time. But the Creole people who emerged did so not as characters who were half this and half that but rather as whole people who carried within them, albeit to differing degrees, the multicultural environments in which they had grown up.

LeFlore was then on one level a Creole, and to call him this is not intended to distance him from his "Choctawness" but rather to overlay it. My use of the term is an attempt to suggest that, while he identified himself as a Choctaw, he shared much with the broader world the Choctaws inhabited. Indeed, much of the racist rhetoric of the nineteenth-century South was designed to undermine the cultural ties that were being forged everywhere among Native people, settlers, and slaves.[11] In LeFlore's case, Andrew Jackson's strained efforts to slander "mixed bloods" were, in short, an effort to draw sharp imaginary lines of race between people whose cultural ties were blurring racial distinctions. In LeFlore, the beliefs and practices of his Choctaw kinfolk came together with the ideas on education, political economy, and civil society that he had observed in his close contact with Anglo-American society. The Creole identity that I have ascribed to him, however, should not be confused with his political one. For if in the broadest sense LeFlore was a southern Creole, he was, in a more local sense, a Choctaw nationalist who sought to carve out a new and powerful nation for his people within the cotton kingdom of the Old South.

LeFlore's *creolité* enabled him to articulate his particular chiefly vision in ways that were consonant with both Choctaw and Anglo-American practices and beliefs. But in his day neither he nor his people were, in the end, able to withstand the increasingly racial view of the world that the citizens of the United States came to embrace in the 1820s and 1830s. In a world where the dominant political and economic powers in the South and the nation's capital sought to create a world of "whites" and "blacks," people like the Mississippi Choctaws had a hard time standing their ground. As chief of the Choctaw Nation, LeFlore tried but failed.

Sometime in the late 1790s a Canadian trader named Louis Le Fleur, who traded for the firm Panton, Leslie and Company based in Spanish Florida, married Rebecca Cravat and her sister. They were both from the western towns of what came to be called the Choctaw Nation. Typically, traders married the daughters of prominent chiefs, and it is reasonable to assume that Le Fleur gained through his marriage access to an important family. And because Choctaws reckoned kinship through the mother's line, Rebecca and Louis's children would have been well situated to assume leadership roles later in life.[12]

In 1800 Rebecca brought their first child, a baby boy named Greenwood, into the world. What might he have learned growing up in a Choctaw family? Choctaw children became men and women by learning how to do particular things. In a very basic sense young men took life. They hunted animals in the fall and winter and fought battles in the spring and summer, and they earned status by shedding blood. Women created life.[13] They raised corn, beans, cotton, and children and manufactured pottery, clothing, and other household items. Male and female roles were tied to a cosmology that reached back to the Mississippian cultures out of which the Choctaws had emerged sometime in the 1500s.[14] The cosmology found expression in a circle-and-cross motif that represented the balance they sought to maintain through the practices of their daily lives. The cross divided the circular world into discrete categories like male and female, fire and water, and sun and earth. It cropped up in all sorts of Choctaw practices. Medicine men, for example, traced the image on forest floors to conjure rain in times of drought. The winter homes that families built in their hunting camps replicated the same map of the world. The homes consisted of a circular wattle-and-daub wall topped by a conical thatched roof. Support structures inside the round dwelling partitioned the living space into four equal parts. A fire flickered in the middle of the house where the women cooked, and they used its light to illuminate different activities. When the family gathered to eat, they partook of the same bowl and sat in a circle, confirming the basic order of life.[15]

Sharing a common ethic of balance or food from the same bowl should not be taken to mean that Choctaws were egalitarian. Lines of kinship and status cut across the society in a number of ways. The women who had prepared the food had lineages to distant ancestors. The mastery of the household and its property enabled them to make many of the important decisions in life, from selecting marriage partners to endorsing political officeholders. Men belonged to the lineages but lacked the kinds of control that made women such formidable leaders. They found their sources of power in the open squares and sacred lodges that anchored public life in the towns and in the forests where women turned the deer they shot into skins that could be traded for blankets, guns, ammunition, and a host of other manufactured goods. At the top of the male hierarchy sat the chiefs, who oversaw the redistribution of various goods and services and who acted as intermediaries between the sacred and the secular. In the middle and at the bottom were other ranks of warriors and hunters whose positions were defined by kinship ties and by performance in battle, the hunt, and in the ballgame.[16]

Chiefly authority hinged on control of access to goods and sacred power. The Mississippian chiefs and priests who had inhabited the region before contact with Europeans and Africans deployed the pomp and pageantry of the sun cult to buttress their authority. They wore gorgets engraved with images of the sun, serpents, and the circle and cross. And they used large earthen mounds to connote their power and links to mother earth and father sun. Choctaws too regarded the sun as perhaps the most important power of the cosmos. Known as *Hushtahli*, "sun as divine mover," and *Ishtahullo Chito*, "great sun priest," Aba, the Choctaw sun, ordered the world through his earthly agent, sacred fire.[17] While Choctaws did not build mounds, they looked to the Nanih Waiya mound as the site where they had crawled out of the earth and emerged on her surface to begin life as the true people. As long as chiefs, Mississippian and Choctaw, maintained the delicate cosmological balance between men and women and the sun and the earth, the people prospered. But when trouble began, their leadership was imperiled.[18]

By the time Greenwood LeFlore came of age, economic trends and American treaties and political pressure had put an end to most of the hunting and warfare that young males had relied upon to gain prestige and power.[19] Any young man aspiring to a position of leadership would have to figure out how to obtain goods for redistribution and how to master sacred powers that would be strong enough to forestall the United States's invasion of the Choctaw homeland. Some Choctaw men stole horses and cattle and raided settlers' farms.[20] Others learned to read, to write, and to buy and sell slaves.

LeFlore's family believed that Greenwood would have to become acquainted with Anglo-American knowledge and power in order to survive and prosper.

In 1812, when he was twelve, he went to live with outsiders to learn new things and perhaps to acquire new responsibilities. Choctaws had sent children to live with and cultivate relationships with outsiders since at least their contact with the French in the early 1700s.[21] Rather than move in with the Taensas, Chickasaws, or the French, however, LeFlore joined the household of Major John Donly in Nashville, Tennessee.

Although LeFlore's stay in Nashville was probably a formative time in his life, we know little about what he experienced. He probably improved his ability to speak and write English, witnessed firsthand how slavery worked, and probably observed the market economy that powered the cotton boom and bust of the 1810s. Perhaps here too he heard his first sermon and learned of the racial honor that bound free men together against the slaves.[22] In addition to all of this, he also found his first wife in Rosa Donly—much to her parents' dismay.[23] When Greenwood LeFlore returned with his young wife to the Choctaw Nation in 1817, he was not yet a person of power.

The nation to which he returned, however, existed more in name than in fact. While Choctaws shared many common beliefs and practices, they did not share a common government. Before the 1820s the Choctaw Nation was a fiction of European and American imaginations. One was typically a member of the eastern or western towns, or a Coonsha or a Yannabi. What outsiders called the Choctaw Nation comprised culturally related and at times diplomatically related congeries of autonomous towns and town clusters that more often than not pursued their own local interests at the expense of what Europeans and Americans took to be a Choctaw interest.[24] As long as there was more than one European power to compete for Choctaw favors, their chiefs could "play off" one empire against another. But by the end of the eighteenth century, the French, the English, and the Spanish had pulled out of the Choctaw homeland and brought the play-off system to an end.[25]

Unable to continue to manipulate competing foreign interests after the American Revolution, Choctaw chiefs confronted the United States alone. In 1805 the federal government pried from them a large swath of land to use in extinguishing debts owed to traders. What the handful of elderly chiefs recognized on that cold day in November when they signed the Treaty of Mount Dexter was that a new generation of chiefs with a new kind of vision would have to rise if the various towns and divisions of the Choctaw people were to evolve into a nation that could withstand the expansion of the new republic.[26]

In the late 1810s LeFlore began using his skills and connections to achieve power and status in the western towns with the hopes of revitalizing the

Choctaws' economic and political fortunes. He found an eager ally in David Folsom, who hailed from the eastern towns. The two invited missionaries from the Boston-based American Board of Commissioners for Foreign Missions to build schools in their districts. In 1819 construction began on the first station, and others soon followed. Access to the mission schools and the economic benefits of having a missionary community in the midst of their own district caused great friction among the sitting chiefs and their young rivals, LeFlore and Folsom.

In 1825 and 1826 LeFlore and Folsom put together enough support to challenge the chiefs, whose debts had brought the Choctaws to the treaty table in the first place. Discontented over debts and land cessions as well as struggles over the school program, LeFlore and Folsom had initiated far-reaching political changes. In the eastern towns David Folsom ousted Chief Mushulatubbee, and in the western towns people agitated for the removal of Chief Robert Cole, who had likened the missionaries' course of instruction to slavery because the teachers drove the young boys in the fields "in the same manner that negroes were on the plantations."[27] Following the lead of the eastern council, the council of the western towns turned Cole out of office but kept the chiefly lineage intact by appointing his nephew Greenwood LeFlore to serve as chief. LeFlore pledged never to "turn his coat" on the people of the western towns.[28]

LeFlore had made his way to the top of his district by providing opportunities for his people through missionary education, but he was not solely dependent on the missions for his authority. He was, in fact, becoming a wealthy cotton planter. The purchase of slaves by LeFlore and other Choctaws offers an example of cultural consonance and creolization. By purchasing slaves, men like LeFlore, whose thirty-two slaves worked a two-hundred-and-fifty-acre plantation in the Yazoo River Valley, bought into a form of prestige and status in both southern and Choctaw societies.[29] Moreover, slaveholding made it possible for Greenwood LeFlore to amass a considerable fortune, although his wealth did not make him part of an arriviste gentry. Choctaw chiefs had always possessed more wealth than the commoners whom they governed, and if slaves and acres of cotton were different than the guns and deerskins that earlier chiefs had held, the reasons behind the acquisitive behavior were the same—to oversee the redistribution of prestigious goods. To win the support of the hierarchy of offices he commanded as well as of the people in his division, he and his allies opened their homes to all comers. "[Their] table," wrote one observer, "must be free to all who visit them, and as they wish to elevate their people, their tables must be well supplyed."[30]

The new leaders undertook to balance the practices of chiefly government with the sensibilities and systems of a contemporary nation-state. For example, the two chiefs mandated that elections would be held every four years to determine the national council's composition and that the council would meet in a house located in the geographic center of the Choctaw territory. The structure of the government, however, retained the hierarchical organization of war chiefs, council speakers, pipe lighters, and captains that had characterized government ever since contact.[31] The council house—a white-washed rectangular building made of split poplar logs—appeared to be a typical piece of Anglo-American frontier architecture, but the building was also oriented on an east-west axis so that the sun was always over the councilmen's heads.[32]

The new national government's agenda juggled the need to fashion a new civic ethnicity with a desire to retain certain indigenous beliefs. One law, for example, sought to replace kin-based revenge for the crime of murder with trials by officers of the new Choctaw state. The government also banned pole-pullings—funeral rituals that, like blood revenge, perpetuated kinship divisions at the expense of the national identity LeFlore and his allies wanted to inculcate.[33] But, like any chief, Leflore could not act out of hand; he had to maintain the support of his people if he was to remain in office. To this end he had opened his home, distributed seats in mission schools, and, as a member of the national government, wrapped himself in the mantle of a sun priest. At an 1828 national council meeting he promulgated several new laws at the Nanih Waiya mound. Here was where the first Choctaws had crawled out of the ground to live on earth. Here was where the sun had handed down the ancient law. And here was where LeFlore proclaimed the new one. By drawing on one of the most sacred objects in the Choctaw world, one that reached into every town and every home, to justify the government's innovative political and economic program, LeFlore transformed the process of creolization into a sacred movement of undeniable appeal.[34]

His sacred power, however, drew upon both Aba and Jesus Christ. While LeFlore did not personally embrace Christianity until the death of his wife, Rosa, in childbirth in October 1829, he nonetheless believed that "no other than the Almighty God, had power to produce . . . a change in the Choctaws."[35] In answer to the land-grabbing chorus of politicians in Jackson and in Washington, Choctaw commoners took heart in their chief's talk of salvation in God, and he encouraged his captains to attend church services and to speak the "Good Word."[36] In 1828, thousands of Choctaws decided to "embrace the Gospel, and walk in the straight and bright path."[37]

To find the path, in 1828 and 1829 Choctaws turned to the missionaries who since 1819 had been preaching to sparse congregations of settlers and slaves. Called *abaonompoolé*—Aba's messengers—by the Choctaws, the missionaries represented a new and vital link between Aba and the nation that held great promise for a renewal of the nation's sacred power.[38] The time had finally come, many believed, when God would outstretch "his interposing hand" and make the Choctaws strong and powerful "like white men."[39]

The camp meetings that proliferated throughout the nation followed a common pattern reflecting the confluence of Choctaw and Anglo-American practices. Though the men and boys dressed in drab homespun suits and the women were typically frocked in brightly colored calicos, they continued to gather at night, to seat themselves according to lineage around campfires, and to sing songs throughout the evening. Tearful communicants still knelt, however, at the anxious bench to make public the turmoil of their souls. Missionaries meanwhile stood at the outer edges of the gatherings and genuinely admired the multitude of voices that rose above the flickering campfires and followed the sacred smoke to Aba's home in the sky.[40]

The success of the movement LeFlore and his supporters had forged, however, was to some degree driven by outside events. Andrew Jackson's election to the presidency in 1828 signaled to Choctaws and Americans alike that the Choctaws' tenure in Mississippi would no longer be tolerated. In an attempt to hasten their departure, on February 4, 1829, Governor Gerard Brandon signed a law extending the authority of the State of Mississippi over the Choctaws' land.[41] Following the president's pronouncements in favor of the state measure, Senator Hugh Lawson White of Tennessee introduced a bill to Congress that provided funds for the removal of the Indians. Despite considerable opposition, Jackson garnered enough support in Congress to pass it, and he signed the Indian removal bill into law on May 29, 1830.[42]

In the aftermath of the passage of the two measures, LeFlore predicted that "bad white men will soon come among us, and settle on our vacant land, and cheat us out of our property."[43] William Ward, the federal agent to the Choctaws, reported to Secretary of War John Eaton that LeFlore had admitted that "if the Pres. said he would have their lands, [the Choctaws] must yeald to his power as [they] had but few people."[44] At a camp meeting held in September 1829, LeFlore made public his despair and counseled the Choctaws to accept removal because he and other leaders had agreed that armed resistance was futile.[45]

The district councils responded by reforming the national government to centralize decision making. On March 16, 1830, the chiefs of the eastern and southern towns resigned their offices, and LeFlore was "unanimously elected" chief of the entire Choctaw Nation, an office no chief had previously held.[46] In his acceptance speech LeFlore remarked that "we have long seen that to have several chiefs . . . in different parts of the nation was calculated to ruin us."[47] But given his earlier doubts about the Choctaws' chances of remaining in Mississippi, the new chief sought to secure the best possible terms for removal. The next day the national council "determined that they would not submit to Mississippi law" and decided, LeFlore wrote, to "move west, if the President would give us a good treaty."[48] LeFlore then wrote a removal treaty that was dispatched to Washington the next day. To President Jackson they pleaded, "We love our land but we cannot suffer our council fire to be extinguished by submitting to the laws of our white brothers."[49]

News of LeFlore's treaty scandalized the nation, especially because he had originally risen to power on the promise of opposing further land cessions. The old leaders whom LeFlore and Folsom had replaced used the public uproar to recoup their political fortunes. Mushulatubbee, the principal leader of the old chiefs, denounced LeFlore's actions and policies and reminded his fellow Choctaws that he "had always predicted that the Choctaws would be ruined by the introduction of Christianity."[50] The creation of a single chieftainship over the entire nation only angered him further. "The extinction of two council fires [the southern and the eastern] and the bringing of all the Choctaws under one government and one chief [the western]," Mushulatubbee charged, "were acts of usurpation not to be endured."[51] He dismissed captains who had sympathized with LeFlore and sought to extirpate all traces of the new faith from government. To this end the chief prohibited any "professor of religion" from holding political office, and he overturned the national government's bans on funeral rites, ballgames, and dances—the rituals that had given expression to the many divisions that crisscrossed the Choctaw towns.[52]

Into the confusion stepped Secretary of War John Eaton, whom Jackson had picked to negotiate a Choctaw removal treaty more to his own liking. In September 1830 nearly six thousand Choctaws convened on a small patch of land between the two forks of Dancing Rabbit Creek to discuss with Eaton their removal from Mississippi to Indian Territory. Greenwood LeFlore, resplendent in a fashionable suit and a new pair of boots, stood out as the most formidable and knowledgeable Choctaw leader, even though his support was evaporating. He oversaw the final treaty negotiations after most of the people had packed up and headed for their homes. At one o'clock on the afternoon of the twenty-seventh, he and several other chiefs signed a treaty that transferred nearly ten million acres of Choctaw land to the federal government.[53] As chief, LeFlore saw to it that each household received a reserve of land. His reserve was the largest, but, after all, as a chief he was entitled to more—to underwrite his redistributive responsibilities. In spite of the death threats against any chief who ceded land, LeFlore recollected thirteen years after the fact that he had "determined to risk [his] life in what [he] believed [was] a good cause ... [and that he] had full faith in the word of General Jackson."[54]

LeFlore's belief, however, was based upon his assumption that the federal government would uphold the treaty's crucial fourteenth article that enabled Choctaws to remain in Mississippi on their reserves of land. Had the provision not been included in the treaty, he stated, he would have refused to sign the document.[55] Agent William Ward, however, refused to enroll the Choctaw claimants' reserves. He believed that they had been put up to it by "designing men."[56] The federal agent's malfeasance in the matter completely undermined LeFlore's objectives and contributed to what LeFlore saw as the treaty's utter failure.

Shortly after the treaty council, the Western Division council declared that LeFlore was "totally unfit to rule a free people" because he had broken his pledge to never "turn his coat" on the nation. Not surprisingly, LeFlore's predecessor, Robert Cole, was the first to sign the proclamation that formally deposed his nephew.[57] In LeFlore's stead the council named as chief LeFlore's nephew George Washington Harkins. Harkins won his people's confidence by pledging "not to do what my uncle did."[58]

Over the next few years, nearly fifteen thousand of the eighteen or so thousand Choctaws moved from Mississippi to Indian Territory. LeFlore remained behind—owing to the death threats that awaited him in Indian Territory; he served briefly in the Mississippi legislature and parlayed his treaty reserves into an enormous plantation of fifteen thousand acres worked by four hundred slaves. When he died on August 21, 1865, he was buried on his estate wrapped in an American flag.[59] The end befitted the chief. Whereas centuries ago Mississippian chiefs had been interred with the things that had given them power, such as gorgets, copper ornaments, and sacred objects, LeFlore took with him to the afterlife a token of his source of power—the practices of Anglo-America and the possibilities of creolization.

Greenwood LeFlore was neither a mixed-blood nor a self-serving traitor to the Choctaw people. Nor was he a member of a new aristocracy the wealth of which was founded on the exploitation of common Choctaws. To be sure, he used slaves to grow his cotton, he sported the latest fashions, and his plantation mansion was one of the grandest the Magnolia State had ever seen, but he was first and foremost a man whose family had positioned him to draw together the Choctaw and Anglo-American worlds. He owned slaves, read and wrote, and prayed at camp meetings, but he also presided over a political hierarchy of pipe lighters and captains, provided food, shelter, and educational opportunities for his followers, and promulgated his vision of the Choctaw future at the foot of the mound that had given his people life.

Nowhere is the intersection and coalescence of cultures that occurred in LeFlore's life more clear than in the design of his mansion, Malmaison. Notwithstanding the neocolonial trappings of the lavish home, the floor plan was laid out, according to French fashion, in a square cut by hallways, forming a symmetrical cross aligned with the four cardinal points of the compass. A fireplace stood in each corner.[60] If the design was French, the style nonetheless echoed the circle-and-cross motif that had figured so prominently in the ceremonial complex of Mississippian times and that had given expression to the order and the balance that was so integral to Choctaw cosmology. Such a cultural consonance in his final home's design typified the course of Greenwood LeFlore's life. In terms of the beliefs and practices that constituted his daily life, it would be misleading to describe them as either French, or American, or Choctaw. He was a southern Creole. In terms of his politics he was a Choctaw nationalist, and he turned his personal *creolité* toward creating a Choctaw nation that would have a place in the American South.

NOTES

This chapter originally appeared as "Greenwood LeFlore: Southern Creole, Choctaw Chief," *Journal of Mississippi History* 65 (2003): 355–73.

1. Florence Rebecca Ray, *Chieftain Green LeFlore and the Choctaw Indians of the Mississippi Valley: Last Chief of the Choctaws East of the Mississippi River* (Memphis, Tenn.: C. A. Davis, 1936).

2. "Answers of Greenwood LeFlore to the interrogatories propounded on his direct examination before the board of commissioners . . . ," February 24, 1843, folder 23, p. 4, John F. H. Claiborne Papers, Southern Historical Collection, University of North Carolina, Chapel Hill,.

3. Grant Foreman, *Indian Removal: The Emigration of the Five Civilized Tribes of Indians* (Norman: University of Oklahoma Press, 1989), 22.

4. Ronald N. Satz, *American Indian Policy in the Jacksonian Era* (Lincoln: University of Nebraska Press, 1975), 67.

5. Richard White, *The Roots of Dependency: Subsistence, Environment, and Social Change among the Choctaws, Pawnees, and Navajos* (Lincoln: University of Nebraska Press, 1983), 127–28; Samuel J. Wells, "Federal Indian Policy: From Accommodation to Removal," in *The Choctaw before Removal*, ed. Carolyn Keller Reeves (Jackson: University Press of Mississippi, 1985), 206; and Clara Sue Kidwell, *Choctaws and Missionaries in Mississippi, 1818–1918* (Norman: University of Oklahoma Press, 1995), 135, 106, 141.

6. Andrew Jackson to Robert Butler, June 21, 1817, in *Correspondence of Andrew Jackson*, ed. John Spencer Bassett, 7 vols. (Washington, D.C.: Carnegie Institution of Washington, 1926–35), 2:299; and Andrew Jackson to William Lewis, August 25, 1830, in Bassett, *Correspondence of Andrew Jackson*, 4:178.

7. Another term in current use is *mestizo*, but given its origins in early Spanish notions of blood mixing, I find it equally problematic. See Claudio Saunt, *A New Order of Things: Property, Power, and the Transformation of the Creek Indians, 1733–1816* (Cambridge: Cambridge University Press, 1999).

8. Michel de Certeau, *The Practice of Everyday Life*, trans. Steven Rendall (Berkeley: University of California Press, 1984).

9. Clement Eaton, *Civilization of the Old South: Writing of Clement Eaton*, ed. Albert D. Kirwin (Lexington: University of Kentucky Press, 1968), 77–106; Virginia R. Domínguez, *White by Definition: Social Classification in Creole Louisiana* (New Brunswick, N.J.: Rutgers University Press, 1986), 13; and Sybil Klein, "Introduction," *Creole: The History and Legacy of Louisiana's Free People of Color*, ed. Sybil Klein (Baton Rouge: Louisiana State University Press, 2000), xiii–xv.

10. In historical scholarship creolization has been used mainly by students of slavery in the British Caribbean. Edward Kamau Brathwaite's *Development of Creole Society in Jamaica, 1770–1820* (Oxford: Clarendon Press, 1971) was the first and most important book in this vein. Daniel H. Usner Jr., is the first historian to explicitly link creolization to interactions between settlers, slaves, and Native Americans. Usner, "'The Facility Offered by the Country': The Creolization of Agriculture in the Lower Mississippi Valley," in *Creolization in the Americas*, ed. David Buisseret and Steven G. Reinhardt (College Station: Texas A&M University Press, 2000), 35–62.

11. See Daniel H. Usner Jr., *Indians, Settlers, and Slaves in a Frontier Exchange Economy: The Lower Mississippi Valley before 1763* (Chapel Hill: University of North Carolina Press, 1992) for an exploration of these themes in the eighteenth century.

12. Allene Smith, *Greenwood LeFlore and the Choctaw Indians of the Mississippi Valley* (Memphis, Tenn.: C. A. Davis, 1951), 19–39.

13. Gregory Evans Dowd, *A Spirited Resistance: The North American Indian Struggle for Unity, 1745–1815* (Baltimore, Md.: Johns Hopkins University Press, 1992), 4–9.

14. Patricia Galloway, *Choctaw Genesis, 1500–1700* (Lincoln: University of Nebraska Press, 1995).

15. Bernard Romans, *A Concise Natural History of East and West Florida; a Facsimile Reproduction of the 1775 Ed.* (Gainesville: University of Florida Press, 1962), 85; Gideon Lincecum, microfilm copy of "History of the Chahta Nation," 336–37, Gideon Lincecum Papers, The Center for American History, University of Texas, Austin, Texas;

Jon Muller, "The Southern Cult," in *Southeastern Ceremonial Complex: Artifacts and Analysis: The Cottonlandia Conference*, ed. Patricia Galloway (Lincoln: University of Nebraska Press, 1989), 13; Eron Opha Dunbar, ed., "Peter Chester, Third Governor of the Province of West Florida under British Dominion, 1770–1781," *Publications of the Mississippi Historical Society, Centenary Series* 5 (1925): 83–84; and George S. Gaines, "Gaines' Reminiscences," *Alabama Historical Quarterly* 26 (Fall–Winter 1964): 145.

16. James Taylor Carson, *Searching for the Bright Path: The Mississippi Choctaws from Prehistory to Removal* (Lincoln: University of Nebraska Press, 1999), 15–19.

17. Alfred Wright, "Choctaws: Religious Opinions, Traditions, Etc.," *Missionary Herald* 24 (June 1828): 179–80; Dumont de Montigny, *Memoires Historiques sur la Louisiane* . . . (Paris: C. J. B. Bauche, 1753), 1:183–84; and Lincecum, "History of the Chahta Nation," 68, 80, 311, 356.

18. Vernon James Knight Jr., "Symbolism of Mississippian Mounds," in *Powhatan's Mantle: Indians in the Colonial Southeast*, ed. Peter H. Wood, Gregory A. Waselkov, and M. Thomas Hatley (Lincoln: University of Nebraska Press, 1989), 279–91; Charles Hudson, *Southeastern Indians* (Knoxville: University of Tennessee Press, 1976), 122–31; Antonio J. Waring Jr., "The Southern Cult and Muskogean Ceremonial," in *The Waring Papers: the Collected Works of Antonio J. Waring, Jr.*, ed. Stephen Williams (Athens: University of Georgia Press, 1968), 33; Robert L. Hall, "Ghosts, Water Barriers, Corn and Sacred Enclosures in the Eastern Woodlands," *American Antiquity* 41 (July 1976): 360; and John R. Swanton, "Sun Worship in the Southeast," *American Anthropologist* 30 (April–June 1928): 206–13.

19. Carson, *Searching for the Bright Path*, 70–72.

20. James Taylor Carson, "Horses and the Economy and Culture of the Choctaw Indians, 1690–1840," *Ethnohistory* 42 (Summer 1995): 495–513.

21. Patricia Galloway, "'The Chief Who Is Your Father': Choctaw and French Views of the Diplomatic Relation," in Wood, Waselkov, and Hatley, *Powhatan's Mantle*, 271–73.

22. Bertram Wyatt Brown, *Southern Honor: Ethics and Behavior in the Old South* (Oxford: Oxford University Press, 1982); James Oakes, *The Ruling Race: A History of American Slaveholders* (New York: Vintage Books, 1983); Donald G. Mathews, *Religion in the Old South* (Chicago: University of Chicago Press, 1977); and Gavin Wright, *The Political Economy of the Cotton South: Households, Markets, and Wealth in the Nineteenth Century* (New York: W. W. Norton, 1978).

23. Allene Smith, *Greenwood LeFlore and the Choctaw Indians*, 19–39.

24. White, *Roots of Dependency*, 1–3.

25. Carson, *Searching for the Bright Path*, 26–50.

26. Treaty of Mount Dexter, November 16, 1805, reel 1, microfilm series M668, Ratified Indian Treaties, 1722-1869, Records Relating to Indian Treaties, Records of the Bureau of Indian Affairs, Record Group 75, National Archives, Washington D.C.

27. Cyrus Kingsbury to Jeremiah Everts, August 8, 1825, microfilm reel 765, *Papers of the American Board of Commissioners for Foreign Missions* (Woodbridge, Conn.: Research Publications, 1985), Indian Archives, Oklahoma Historical Society, Norman.

28. Cyrus Kingsbury to Jeremiah Everts, August 8, 1825, *Papers of the American*

Board, reel 765; Choctaw Proclamation, June 22, 1826; David Folsom to Thomas McKenney, June 27, 1826, and McKenney to James Barbour, October 21, 1827, reel 169, Choctaw Agency, microfilm series M234, Letters Received, 1824–1881, Correspondence of the Office of Indian Affairs and Related Records, Record Group 75, National Archives, Washington D.C.

29. Satz, *American Indian Policy*, 274, and Elias Cornelius, November 21, 1817, Indian Missionary Journal, part 1, Elias Cornelius Papers, Special Collections, William R. Perkins Library, Duke University, Durham N.C.; and Walter Johnson, *Soul by Soul: Life Inside the Antebellum Slave Market* (Cambridge: Harvard University Press, 1999), 216.

30. Alexander Talley to William Winans, July 5, 1830, folder 12, box 2, William Winans Papers, J. B. Cain Archives, Manuscript Collection, Millsaps College, Jackson, Mississippi.

31. "List of Choctaw Names and Ranks at a Council Held October 16, 1827," 169: M234; C. M. Thayer to William Winans, September 25, 1830, folder 12, box 2, Winans Papers; and folder 10, reel 1 and folder 25, reel 2, microfilm copy of Henry S. Halbert Papers, Mississippi Department of Archives and History, Jackson Mississippi.

32. Henry S. Halbert, "The Last Indian Council on Noxubbee River," *Publications of the Mississippi Historical Society* 4 (1901): 275–76.

33. William Ward to James Barbour, August 9, 1826, 169: M234; *Missionary Herald* 24 (December 1828): 380; ibid., 25 (May 1829): 152–53; ibid. (December 1829): 377; *Christian Advocate and Journal, and Zion's Herald* 3 (October 24, 1828): 30; and Smith, *Greenwood LeFlore*, 50–53.

34. Henry S. Halbert, "Nanih Waiya, the Sacred Mound of the Choctaws," *Publications of the Mississippi Historical Society* 2 (1899, repr. 1919): 233.

35. Alexander Talley to William Winans, October 28, 1828, folder 11, box 1, Winans Papers and quote from *Missionary Herald* 25 (April 1829): 122.

36. Alexander Talley to William Winans, August 27, 1828, folder 10, box 1, Winans Papers.

37. *Missionary Herald* 27 (May 1830): 156.

38. Adam Hodgson, *Letters from North America Written during a Tour in the United States and Canada* (London: Hurst, Robinson & Co., 1824), 1:239; emphasis is mine.

39. Thomas L. McKenney, *Memoirs, Official and Personal; with Sketches of Travels among the Northern and Southern Indians; Embracing a War Excursion, and Descriptions of Scenes along the Western Borders* (New York: Paine and Burgess, 1846), 2:120.

40. Carson, *Searching for the Bright Path*, 103–11.

41. Journal of the House of Representatives of the State of Mississippi, at Their Twelfth Session, Held in the Town of Jackson (Jackson, Miss.: Peter Isler, 1829), 214–16.

42. *Register of Debates in Congress*, 2nd Session, 21st Congress, 2nd Session, 1830–1831 (Washington, D.C.: Gales and Seaton, 1831), appendix, 9.

43. Speech by Greenwood LeFlore, April 1830, 169: M234.

44. William Ward to John Eaton, October 1, 1829, 169: M234.

45. William Ward to John Eaton, November 4, 1829, 169: M234.

46. Cyrus Byington to Jeremiah Everts, March 18, 1830, and Cyrus Kingsbury to

David Greene, April 13, 1830, *Papers of the American Board*, 756; Alexander Talley to William Winans, March 20, 1830, folder 12, box 2, Winans Papers; *Missionary Herald* 26 (August 1830): 253; and Greenwood LeFlore to Mushulatubbee, April 7, 1830, 169: M234.

47. Greenwood LeFlore to Mushulatubbee, April 7, 1830, 169: M234.

48. Ibid.

49. Greenwood LeFlore and David Folsom to Andrew Jackson, March 18, 1830, *Papers of Andrew Jackson* (Washington, D.C.: Library of Congress, 1967), reel 15, microfilm copy at William R. Perkins Library, Duke University, Durham, N.C.

50. *Missionary Herald* 26 (August 1830): 253.

51. Ibid.

52. R. D. Hall to Peter Pitchlynn, July 13, 1830, folder 16, box 1, and J. C. Hastings to Pitchlynn, June 13, 1830, folder 17, Peter Perkins Pitchlynn Papers, Western History Collection, University of Oklahoma, Norman.

53. Henry S. Halbert, "Story of the Treaty of Dancing Rabbit Creek," *Publications of the Mississippi Historical Society* 6 (1902): 374–77.

54. "Answers of Greenwood LeFlore to cross interrogatories propounded to him by Choctaw claimants," February 24, 1843, folder 23, Claiborne Papers.

55. "Answers of Greenwood LeFlore to the interrogatories propounded on his direct examination before the board of commissioners," February 24, 1843 and "Answers of Greenwood LeFlore to cross interrogatories propounded to him by Choctaw claimants," February 24, 1843, folder 23, Claiborne Papers.

56. William Ward to Samuel Hamilton, June 21, 1831, folder 8, 1831 box, Peter Perkins Pitchlynn Papers, Thomas Gilcrease Institute of American History and Art, Tulsa Oklahoma.

57. Proclamation, October 23, 1830, 169: M234.

58. Cyrus Byington to David Greene, December 1, 1830, *Papers of the American Board*, 758.

59. "Malmaison and its Memories," Greenwood LeFlore File, Greenwood-LeFlore Public Library, Greenwood Mississippi.

60. Ray, *Chieftain Greenwood LeFlore*; Wend Graf Kalnein and Michael Levy, *Art and Architecture of the Eighteenth Century in France*, trans. J. R. Foster (Baltimore, Md.: Penguin Books, 1972), 256, 320; Richard A. Etlin, *Symbolic Space: French Enlightenment Architecture and Its Legacy* (Chicago: University of Chicago Press, 1994), 136–37; and Antoine Picon, *French Architects and Engineers in the Age of Enlightenment*, trans. Martin Thom (Cambridge: Cambridge University Press, 1988), 283.

APPENDIX A

Choctaw Negotiations with the United States at Hopewell, South Carolina, 1785–1786

JOURNAL KEPT BY GENERAL JOSEPH MARTIN
DESCRIBING THE HOPEWELL TREATY NEGOTIATIONS
WITH THE SOUTHERN INDIAN NATIONS

KEY TO TEXT

- Page numbers in the text refer to the pages in the original Martin document.
- Brackets denote editorial clarification, the addition of illegible or missing text in the original, and additional text found in Benjamin Hawkin's transcription of Martin's Journal that resides in the Joseph V. Bevan Collection (Peter Force Transcripts, series 7E, vol. 11, microfilm, Library of Congress).
- Misspellings and punctuation are as contained in the original.

[p. 56] Hopewell on Keowee December 28th 1785.[1] The commissioners plenipotentiary of the United States in Congress assembled to treat with the Cherokees and all the other Indians southward of them within the lines of the United States assembled. Present Benjamin Hawkins, Andrew Pickens, J[oseph] Martin, from the state of North Carolina Mr. [William] Blount agent.[2]

The chiefs and warriors who represents the Choctaw Nation having arrived yesterday informed the commissioners that they were in such a naked distress[ed] situation they could not with any comfort to themselves meet to treat with us till they could procure some clothing to hide their nakedness—that they had been [p. 57] near three months on their way to the treaty and were [principally] retained by the villainy of Creeks who not only endeavored to dissuade them from coming but used what were supposed efficient means to prevent them by stealing all their horses—and that having taken their resolutions in their own towns agreeable to the order of their king French Chemastubee [Franchimastabé] were determined to come altho on foot to see the citizens of the United States whom they had [never] seen to be under the protection of the same sovereign with them—to unite their hands and hearts and make a firm and lasting peace.[3]

The chiefs and all their followers, a few only excepted—being destitute of Blankets, Shirts, Matchcoats, & leggings and covered only with some Bear and deer skins—and dejected and uneasy under the [severity] of their appearance.

The Commissioners were under the necessity of distributing some presents among [p. 58] them and appointed the Indians to attend and [receive] the same tomorrow and report their number and rank.

29th Dec.
Present as Yesterday

Agreeable to appointment the Indians attended and their wise four great Medal Chiefs—one gorget Captn representative of six villages—one distinguished Small Medal Chief—twelve Small Medal Chiefs and gorget captains—sixty seven warriors and twenty women.

[To the six first mentioned were given blue Regimental Coats faced with buff & yellow buttons, a hat & blue feather, a ruffle shirt, red flap leggings, and a Blanket—To the next twelve a Regimental Coat and other goods as to the first class—To the remaining officers and Warriors each a Blanket(,) Check Shirt flap & leggings(,) and to the Woman a Blanket, Petticoat, shirts & short gowns.]

On the receipt of the presents the Indians threw off what little covering they had on—dressed themselves in the presents of the Commissioners and exhibited such affection of joy and happiness as is rarely to be seen in any station of life. [p. 59] The Commissioners appointed tomorrow to meet the Indians under the Bower erected for that purpose and directed the interpreters to notify the same accordingly.

30th December
Present as Yesterday
John Pitchlynn Interpreter[4]

The Commissioners delivered the following address to the Indians.

Chiefs and Warriors who represent the Choctaw Nation

We are the Commissioners plenipotentiary from the United States in Congress Assembled who sent an invitation to you the Chief and Warriors representatives of the Choctaw Nation to meet us at this place—to give you peace and to secure you into the favour and protection of the [p. 60] United States—and to remove as far as may be all causes of future contention or quarrels that you your people—your wives and your children may be happy and feel and know the blessings of the new change of sovereignty over this land which you and with that humane and generous act of United States of America will no doubt be received by all your nation with joy and gladness and held in greatfull remembrance particularly as it flows unsolicited from their justice, Humanity, and their attention to the rights of human nature.

The Citizens of the United States and their forefathers and the people of your Nation and their forefathers were friends until the late war and altho you were under the protection of the King of Great Britain [p. 61] and in alliance with him against [us]—yet we are in the remembrance of our former friendship and in admiring your faithfull attachment of your protection.[5]

The reflection is at this juncture Pleasing to us as it affords us the Expectation of the same attachment to Congress the New Sovereign America and faith in the Engagements you may enter into with us. You will know that the troops and adherents of the king of Great Britain are all withdrawn from the Vicinity of your Nation in presence of the treaties with the United States of America—and the said king or between him and the king of Spain—and we can assure you that there is not the least probability of their ever [p. 62] Returning again.

Some of the adherents of the king of Spain may make efforts to detach you from a firm and lasting attachment to the United States of America but in so doing they do not consider your true interest consequently you should hear them—with caution—the bounds we show you on the map are really and truely from the regional treaty between our sovereign and the sovereign of Great Britain. Spain pretends to some claim in this country and they have a minister at Congress to adjust the same as will as enter into a treaty of friendship and alliance—which it is the true interest of both to do—and which will remove every cause that may disturb your domestic quiet. [p. 63]

The United States in Congress Assembled [the Continental Congress] want none of your lands or anything else which belongs to you they are now your father and friend—and as an earnest of the friendship of our declaration we propose [to] enter into articles of a treaty as may be and conformable to what we now tell you. On our own part we sincerely wish you to live as happy as we do ourselves and to promote that Happiness as far as [is] in our power regardless of any distinction of Colour—or of any difference in our Customs or manners or particular situation.

You may now retire and reflect on what you have heard and let us hear from you tomorrow or as soon as possible.

31st December
Present as Yesterday

The interpreter informed the Commissioners [p. 64] that Tobocoh [Taboca] was the ablest speaker of all the Chiefs and had always been sent by the Nation as their representative in all their important Negotiations and that now the whole of the representation was while traveling put under his immediate care—But he having lately been at Mobile and taken a Spanish medal had thereby lost the favor of his Sovereign—and most of the Leading Chiefs and he was now ordered to be disgraced for his impudence before the Commissioners of the United States by making him speak the last.

Captain John Woods laid before the Commissioners a Talk from Frenchamastuby [Franchimastabé] great medal Chief—and leading king of the Chactaw Nation a letter from Isaac Pitchlynn [p. 65] of the 16th of October containing information of a design formed at Pensacola to prevail on the Indians if practicable from coming to the Treaty—and a memorandum of a request of the King.

The Chiefs and Captains according to their appointed rank then addressed the Commissioners as follows viz[6]

YOCHENAHOMA: You see here on your table our kings talks—They are not his only but the sentiments of the Nation—He approved me as a Head Man to come and see you the beloved men who are to treat with him—Being [the] head man of the Nation he ordered me to come but not to make the Talk[s] long as he intends we [shall] [p. 66] see each other [at some] future day. You white people are strangers to our Nation and the day is come when we see you and my heart is glad. This a clear sunshiny day and I hope it will be emblematical of our future Happiness and that nothing will happen to cloud or obscure our Talks. The object of our meeting is to make a Lasting peace for all [our] warriors, women, and children—that our Nation may increase without trouble. I have said. We will now shake hands—that our friendship may never break.

YOCKEHOOPOIA: Your invitation came very unexpected to us. Capt. Wood read it to us in the Nation [p. 67] and we come to see you—the headmen of your nation and those of our Nation are of one mind and he sent me here to make peace. I am the headman of our Nation [Representative of my head men] as you are of yours and we are now here to treat with each other. My orders are to be short and explicit in what I say and that I should attend to a peace that will be lasting. I wish the headmen of our Nation [Countries] could be present to talk together. I am desirous of seeing them—This is a fine clear day and we are together to hear each other talk on the land appointed for that purpose. I am done for the present—it is proper not to be too prolix and I must think on what I shall again say.

[p. 68]MINGOHOOPOIA: I am very glad to hear the Talks of the Great headmen you represent and receive them with a sincere heart—those you represent sent you here for peace. Those I represent did the same and it is a clear day—an emblem of our future hopes. We are the headmen to [take each] other by the [hand] and make peace.

The talks sent to us from the land of the white people were very pleasing and I hope they will [be] repeated. I have done for the present but the next man will say something [Tobocah was to speak next but the first speaker directed that he should not speak till the others had done.]—he is the speaker who always [buries the hatchet] for the red people.

I TOBACAH was to speak next but the first [p. 69] Speaker insisted that he [I] should not speak till the other[s] had done—my duty has been to receive the talks from the white people for the blacks[7] and I always hold them fast.

SHINSHOMASTABE: I am a Chacktaw—and as I live in a remote corner of the Nations I am seldom seen but being before our Chiefs and you of the white people you shall hear my talks. The headman of my town being dead, I succeeded him & as desired by [the] Nation to come and meet you. We are strangers—and now having met we have joined our hands and hearts together an I am much pleased with your talks. There are others to speak who have greater abilities than I have—and as I am a young hand [head] I will not say anything more lest they should [p. 70] think me forward and not be pleased. I have done—I am not a leading man of the Nation—you will hear their talks and they may be more pleasing.

TUSCOONOHOPOIA: These around me are my Leading Men—I have heard their talks—and as they request it of me—you shall hear mine. You are the representatives of

APPENDIX A   241

your Nation and your talks were sent to our Nation and we have come to meet you and the day is come when we have met and our hands and hearts locked and we are to make a firm and lasting peace.

I am from a part of our Nation nearest to you and formerly we had a great headman but he being dead I am in his place. The talks of my predecessors [p. 71] were always true, when I was under him and a young warrior only—and I hope my talks will be true also.

POOSHEMASTABE of the Six Villages: You and our Chiefs have given in their talks and I will now give in mine. The part of the Nation where I live have never had any talks but from people on the Sea Shore [Spaniards] and when the chiefs of our nation received your talks they sent for me because I was always firmly united with them. I was told that headmen from your nation is on this ground—and the day is come when I see you and my heart is well pleased. I have done. I came of myself with a hearty good will from our Nation.

[p. 72] TOBOCAH: The day is come that I have brought many warriors here to see you and to represent my Nation. The headman in my Nation—who is not a large man—gave me all these warriors with instructions to conduct them through all nations until I shall meet you to hear you talk. The Great man above appointed this day for us to meet and talk together. I am here. It was the desire of my superior that the Chickasaws or our Eldest Brother and we should give in our talks together but they have not come and we should talk without them. You are great and we are great men [p. 73] and this day we have meet to make Peace for the Nations we respectively represent.

I am a headman in my Nation to receive and to give out talks and I have brought with me the representatives of the Whole Nation of whom I am one. It is not usual to finish our talks in one day—I have brought up the headmen—they have talked—we will now shake hands with you and take these talks back to camp. I am glad and my heart rejoices to see you take my Captains as friendly as you do. I have done and will go to camp and think of what I shall say again.

[p.74] 2nd January 1786
Present as on the day before yesterday.

The Commissioners produced a draft of a treaty which they proposed to enter into and after explaining the same with great attention the Indians expressed their perfect acquiescence therewith upon which it was agreed that two fair copies shall be made and that the Contracting Parties shall sign the same on tomorrow and that the Indians shall meet the Commissioners in order to execute the same with the ceremonies usual with them on such important Occasions

The Indians agreed that the United States in Congress Assembled shall have the exclusive right of fixing their [the three trading] posts within such parts of the lands to be allotted them to live and hunt on as the said States shall judge proper—Because the Contracting parties are not sufficiently informed to fix them properly [p. 75].

The Commissioners explained with great attention the Occurences of the late war, the extent of territory ceded to the United States of America and the humane and liberal views of Congress. Their knowledge of maps was not equal by any means to the

Cherokees and it was difficult to make them comprehend the extent of territory within the United States of America. But they had formed very exalted [ideas] of the military prowess of the American Soldiery and were ready to place implicit confidence in any promises we [the Commissioners] should make them.

When the first article of the proposed plan of the treaty was read and explained they answered that the oldest men amongst them could not remember that a Chactaw had ever shed the blood of a whiteman and that no one of their Nation had ever seen a Virginian, the term they use to express the citizens of the United States, until the present meeting. [p.76] That however great their love might be to the King of Great Britain and his adherents to whom they were under Obligation for past favors, yet they had never consented to go to war with them and boasted of being the friends of the white people whenever in their power.

The Commissioners being instructed to demand as a preliminary the restoration of negroes & agreed to qualify the instructions by the insertion: if any there be in the Chactaw Nation having some expectations that part of the property plundered from the citizens was in possession of individuals within the Nation.

3d January 1786—present as yesterday

The draught of the treat[ies] being produced in order for signing, the Indians prepared to execute the same with the ceremonies usual in such important occasions and met the Commissioners accordingly at twelve oclock. With their Eagle tale dance thus conducted, one of the Chiefs bore in his hand a white pole at twelve feet in length—three other chiefs [bore] poles with deerskins suspended as flags—two others bore alternately [p. 77] a [—] of fire with two white pipes and [one] as master of ceremonies. The six first were naked except the flaps and leggings and their bodies and faces were painted with white clay. These chiefs were followed by all the other representatives[:] warriors and women dressed in the Cloathing given them by the United States of America and singing the time for the dance. When they had approached within a few yards of the house of the Commissioners, they set up the white pole and agreeable with the established etiquett the Commissioners met them with some handkerchiefs, white pipes, tobacco and fire with some gartering or binding for the women.

The manner of coming to the house had a solemnity that would affect the Reflective mind while the decency and good order observed would impress it with a reverence for the ancient customs of a people to whom the common rights of human nature hath hither to been denied If regard is to be had to the [p. 78] constant violation of all complaints entered into with them.

The Indian Chiefs and the Commissioners were in two lines near each other and almost touching the pole, viewing each other for a few moments in silence while one of the Warriors to the tune of the dance told his war exploits and then they took each other by the hand, lit their pipes and exchanged them. After smoking the Chiefs in turn with uplifted hands returned thanks to God in a very solemn manner for having appointed this day as the Commencement of the peace and Happiness of their nation by putting them and their lands under the protection of the United States of America. The fire was then laid at the root of the pole and the Commissioners and the Agent of

North Carolina joined hands with the Chiefs and with a grave and solemn pace walked to the Bower.

After standing around the table for a short period the first chief [p. 79], the Master of Ceremonies Tobocah applied the eagle tail to the brests of the Commissioners, the agent, and some respectable Gentlemen, then covered the seat of the Commissioners with two deerskins and laid three under their feet. The Commissioners after the Chiefs were seated went and tied the handkerchiefs around their necks, and set down. Then the women approached them according to the rank of their husbands and embraced them and the agent who tied the gartering around their necks. The music was stop[ped] and the whole took their seats and after a short pause the Chactaw Commissioners in turn addres[sed] the Commissioners as follows:

YOCKENAHOMA: My address is now to the [sovereigns of your nation] who sent you here—My Eyes are Very Desirous of Seeing them—when I set out from home I heard they had sent headmen to meet headmen at this place. [p. 80] I have heard of you White People and our forefathers may have heard of you but I never saw you till now and I never heard that they ever did see you[.] Now we have met to Join our hearts and hands and talk together. This is a clear [sunshiny] day and I have set up a white pole—our token of peace—it is but a short pole but the peace will be long and lasting. I have done for the present. There are other Chiefs to speak. My talks are not long.

YOCKEHOOPOIA: I [am] thankful to the Great man above that he has brought us together this day to exchange Our Talks with each other. We are Employed by the headman of our Nations respectively to meet and give in our Talks. Our fathers and grandfathers did not ever see each other but We have met and joined our hands and hearts together. It is not for ourselves [p. 81] alone we are now making peace [but] for the people of all our respective nations and their posterity. Our Eldest Brother the Chickasaws were to have been here to treat with us but as they have not yet come we shall do it without them. I am not the principal headman of our Nation but what I do here is Valid and even the birds shall not fly over our Nation with any thing Injurious thereto. I have done for this day perhaps tomorrow something may occur.

MINGOHOOPOIA: You are headmen from Congress sent to Speak to us. I am much pleased with them. This is a Clear Sunshiny day on which we have met and it is to us as the promise of length of years. Your talks are to take us Our Women and Children under protection of and they are the most pleasing to us. I hope everything that passes among us will be remembered. On my part it shall and you may hear [p. 82] something from the whole of the chiefs tomorrow. I have done.

TOBOCAH: I am a Great man in my Nation [and] You are Great men in yours and I have brought many of my chiefs to meet you. The object of the Great men who Employed you and the Great man who sent us is accomplished as with our mouths we have locked our hands. I am a man who has been [used] to make peace. With the white clay I have washed my hands to take fast hold of yours and these feathers of the Eagle tail we always hold when we make peace. You see our Women are painted white—an emblem of peace and of their hopes of being able to raise up their Children in peace. This fire we have presented to you we brought from our Nation and we have lived on it, it is now out and we will take some of yours. I have nothing more to say but I shall have [more to say] tomorrow. It being late and cold and the chiefs naked[,] at their request the signing of the treaty is postponed until tomorrow.

[p. 83]

4th January 1786

The Interpreter informed the Commissioners that the Chiefs were desirous of postponing the signing of the treaty until tomorrow as they wish to hear some further conversation with each other. Respecting the Articles agreed upon Yesterday, Accordingly the sign[ing] was postponed.

5th January

The Commissioners assembled.

Present: Benjamin Hawkins, Andrew Pickens, and Joseph Martin. From the State of North Carolina William Blount, agent. The Commissioners of all the Choctaw Nation. John Peachlin [Pitchlynn] sworn interpreter. [p. 84] Major Samuel Taylor, Major William Hazzard, Captain John Woods, Mr. Robert Anderson, and Benjamin Lawrence, with other Respectable Gentlemen. The Commissioners of the United States of America exhibited two copies of the draught of the treaty agreed upon the second instant and which was to have been signed on the 3d. And after explaining over again the occurrences of the late war, the extent of territory ceded to the United States of America, and the human[e] and liberal views of Congress, the Articles were entered upon and every part of them fully explained as on the 2d instant so that they comprehended the whole perfectly. The Indians were then asked whether they have any objections to the whole or any part of the Articles. They answered they had not that they were satisfied with every part as they had been on the 2d instant and [p. 85] particularly so with the equitable manner of punishing the Citizens or Indians who shall be guilty of murder or robbing or other capital crime.[8]

The two copies were then signed—one for the United States of America and the other for the Chactaw Nation. The [Choctaw] Commissioners then addressed the Commissioners of the United States as follows:

YOCKENAHOMA: Now we have ended our peace talks and my heart is contented. We will after this day talk of something else. Our hearts and hands are joined together and I am desirous of returning as early as possible. Our peace talk is ended and our treaties are signed one for you and one for me as the first representative of the Nation. [I] will now [p. 86] set out as soon as possible and communicate mine as you request to my sovereign. I shall take John Pitchlynn the interpreter with me—he can tell us all our talks over again. My talks were not long when I left home and my orders were to joyn hands and hearts and return quickly. It is late now we will end our Talks and say something more tomorrow.

YOCKEHOOPOIA: Our principal talks we have had in adjusting the peace but I have a little to say. I want to know what man in the Nation is to receive your talks and publish them—The talks I have received from you I shall remember[—]I am not a man who forgets talks. Here is before you Captain John Woods, he has been with us and used us very friendly. I wish to know what objection if any [p. 87] you have against [his] Receiving and [publishing] them in our Nation. He has been very friendly to us and

APPENDIX A   245

we should have been under difficulties respecting the Way had it not been for him. We have finished our peace talks which were important. Tomorrow all the Chiefs may have something to say further. I have done, there are two more [men] to speak.

MINGOHOOPOIA: These Great Talk[s] which came from these Great men are now ended and I am desirous of returning home now. We have ended all peace talks. I will inform you that our Nation is much in Want of Match Coats, powder and lead and wish they could be supplied by your Traders as early as possible. There are many Chiefs in our Nation and if we should receive [p. 88] any Talks we should have somebody to publish them and have you any objection against Captain Woods—he is our fellow traveller.

I hope the Nation will be supported with necessaries as early as possible. We are much in want of guns & ammunition and cloathing. It was formerly a custom when I was at peace talks for the Indians to receive such guns as the white people make to carry to our nation.

This day you made a demand of prisoners and property if any there be in Our Nation, I can assure you there is not any with us but I have a demand to make on you for some. A good while ago some people from our Nation came down in your country and most of them were killed[—]two women we could never hear of. Now you have made peace with all nations, I hope you will make inquiry after them and let us know where they are. They were of the town of Bootoogoloo. [p. 89] One was young [just] in bloom the other middle aged. The young one is my niece, the other my quondam [former] wife.

The article respecting the mode of punishment of villains &c I am exceedingly pleased with and it will prevent the commission of evil. You are not the first men I have treated with on this subject. Formerly when I treated with the British we did something like it and I always punished accordingly thereto. We here are headmen and it is as impossible for us to be responsible for all the warriors as it is for you to become responsible for the disorderly people of your nation. We have bad people in our nation and there are good and bad of all nations. The peace talks are done and I am exceedingly pleased with them. I have received your talks and I love your talks and if there should be any violation of the articles we will punish immediately in the Nation. I speak for Captain Woods to be the person in our Nation to see things regulated there. I have done.

[p. 90]

TOBOCAH: Your Talks with our Chiefs and Warriors are very pleasing to us and I am now to close the whole. The English were our first friends but you have drove them across the Great Water and I have taken [you] by the hand, and now I shall hold you fast while I have breath. I have heard of the Virginia people long ago but never saw but a few of them, although I have been a Great Traveller. I have been to Charleston and there I heard they were [still] a great way off [further back]. I have now met you and am well pleased with you. I am a man of my word. Our Nation is much in want of clothing, arms, and ammunition and it is my desire that Captain John Woods should be [so situated as to be able] to see that our situation is remembered. I expressed a desire of seeing Congress some days past, what say you to it? I may have something to say tomorrow. For the present I will only request your attention to the prisoners [about who we have informed you].

[p. 91]

COMMISSIONERS: We have now finished our Treaty and [it] is such an one as will no doubt be pleasing to your whole Nation and will by them be handed down to their posterity with joy and gladness. Formerly the object of those who treated with you was mostly founded on self interest and desire for your land, the source of your misfortunes. We you know have pursued a different conduct. We protect you, your wives, and your children, and in the quiet possession of the land you live and hunt on and all this proceeds from the justice and humanity of Congress and attention to the rights of human nature.

Your prisoners will be restored to you if they are in our lands if we can know where they are. The season of the year is very unfit for your going to Congress. We told this to Yockenahoomoo yesterday and that you must wait with a little patience. When our treaty is concluded with Spain proper measures will be taken for carrying on Trade with your Nation. Congress for the present can do no more [p. 92] for you than we have done. You will now prepare to return to your Country and set out as early as possible. We shall give Yockenahoomoo a fine rifle gun made by some of our citizens, we shall give the other chiefs a musquet with some ammunition. We shall also give you proper goods to bear your expenses on the Path with such other articles as you have requested from us as necessary for your conveniency and comfort. We now take leave of you and wish you may be happy.

January 6th 1786

The Commissioners gave [the] presents as promised yesterday amounting in the whole [with those originally received] to [one thousand one hundred eighty one dollars and fifty cents]—They then directed the Interpreter of the Chactaw Tongue to the United States to hurry the departure of the Indians as early as possible. [At the same time the goods allotted to the Indians for their expenses on the path were put into the care of the interpreter and the four leading chiefs.]

The Indians appeared perfectly [satisfied] with everything except the Guns, as instead of Musquets they had been promised before they left the Nation that they should receive some Guns of the Manufacture of the United States of America and that they were rifles.[9]

Source: Draper Manuscripts, microfilm copy, ser. U, vol. 14, pp. 56–92, originals in State Historical Society of Wisconsin, Madison.

NOTES

1. Hopewell was the home of American negotiator Andrew Pickens along the Keowee (or Seneca) River in western South Carolina, now owned by Clemson University.

2. For biographies and printed papers of the American negotiators see Benjamin Hawkins, *The Collected Works of Benjamin Hawkins, 1796–1810* (Tuscaloosa: University of Alabama Press, 2003); Merritt Bloodworth Pound, *Benjamin Hawkins: Indian*

Agent (Athens: University of Georgia Press, 1951); Alice Noble Waring, *The Fighting Elder: Andrew Pickens, 1739–1817* (Columbia: University of South Carolina Press, 1962); Stephen Beauregard Weeks, "General Joseph Martin and the War of the Revolution in the West," *Annual Report of the American Historical Association* (Washington, D.C.: U.S. Government Printing Office, 1894), 401–77; and William H. Masterson, *William Blount* (New York: Greenwood Press, 1969).

3. For discussion and analysis of Franchimastabé and the entire Choctaw delegation as well as their rituals and goals in this treaty negotiation, see Greg O'Brien, "The Conqueror Meets the Unconquered: Negotiating Cultural Boundaries on the Post-Revolutionary Southern Frontier," *Journal of Southern History* 68 (February 2001): 39–72, reprinted in this volume; and Greg O'Brien, *Choctaws in a Revolutionary Age, 1750–1830* (Lincoln: University of Nebraska Press, 2002), esp. 50–69.

4. On Pitchlynn, see O'Brien, "The Conqueror Meets the Unconquered"; and the biography of his son in W. David Baird, *Peter Pitchlynn: Chief of the Choctaws* (Norman: University of Oklahoma Press, 1972).

5. As this passage by the American negotiators makes clear, Choctaws did *not* side with the United States during the American Revolution. A common misperception first promulgated by the less-than-reliable commentator Horatio Cushman in 1899 has the Choctaws assisting George Washington in the war against Britain. In fact, most Choctaws who participated in the war supported Britain, and some Choctaws supported Spain against British forces at Mobile in 1780 and at Pensacola in 1781. No Choctaw forces acted in direct support of the United States, and as the Hopewell treaty negotiation demonstrates, Choctaws had never before met citizens of the United States before 1785. For Choctaw actions in the American Revolution see Greg O'Brien, "'We are behind you': The Choctaw Occupation of Natchez in 1778," *Journal of Mississippi History* 64 (Summer 2002): 107–24; O'Brien, "The Choctaw Defense of Pensacola in the American Revolution" in this volume; and O'Brien, *Choctaws in a Revolutionary Age*. Cushman's oft-cited but erroneous assertion is found in H. B. Cushman, *History of the Choctaw, Chickasaw, and Natchez Indians*, ed. Angie Debo (Norman: University of Oklahoma Press, 1999), 238–42.

6. Although this document gives us tremendous insight into the thoughts and actions of the Choctaw diplomats, the words written down by Joseph Martin were based on his ability to copy what the translator, John Pitchlynn, told him the Choctaw speakers were saying—an imperfect process at best.

7. "Blacks" is likely a mistranscription of "flats," a common epithet for the Choctaws in the eighteenth century that referred to their traditional custom of head-flattening resulting in distinctive lengthened foreheads.

8. This optimistic assessment of Choctaw agreement with the treaty stipulations was meant for an American audience, as the Choctaws stridently disagreed with certain sections, see O'Brien, "The Conqueror Meets the Unconquered."

9. The Choctaw negotiators were upset about much more than the quality of the guns that the Americans gave them, and especially disagreed with Article Three of the treaty (see Appendix B) that called for land cessions. See O'Brien, "The Conqueror Meets the Unconquered."

APPENDIX B

The Hopewell Treaty Signed by the Choctaws and the United States

Articles of a treaty concluded at Hopewell, on the Keowee, near Seneca Old Town, between Benjamin Hawkins, Andrew Pickens and Joseph Martin, Commissioners Plenipotentiary of the United States of America, of the one part; and Yockonahoma, great Medal Chief of Soonacoha; Yockehoopoie, leading Chief of Bugtoogoloo; Mingohoopoie, leading Chief of Hasooqua; Tobocoh, great Medal Chief of Congetoo; Pooshemastubie, Gorget Captain of Senayazo; and thirteen small Medal Chiefs of the first Class, twelve Medal and Gorget Captains, Commissioners Plenipotentiary of all the Choctaw Nation, of the other part.

THE Commissioners Plenipotentiary of the United States of America give peace to all the Choctaw nation, and receive them into the favor and protection of the United States of America, on the following conditions:

ARTICLE I.
The Commissioners Plenipotentiary of all the Choctaw nation, shall restore all the prisoners, citizens of the United States, or subjects of their allies, to their entire liberty, if any there be in the Choctaw nation. They shall also restore all the negroes, and all other property taken during the late war, from the citizens. to such person, and at such time and place as the Commissioners of the United States of America shall appoint, if any there be in the Choctaw nation.

ARTICLE II.
The Commissioners Plenipotentiary of all the Choctaw nation, do hereby acknowledge the tribes and towns of the said nation, and the lands within the boundary allotted to the said Indians to live and hunt on, as mentioned in the third article, to be under the protection of the United States of America, and of no other sovereign whosoever.

ARTICLE III.
The boundary of the lands hereby allotted to the Choctaw nation to live and hunt on, within the limits of the United States of America, is and shall be the following, viz. Beginning at a point on the thirty-first degree of north latitude, where the Eastern boundary of the Natches district shall touch the same; thence east along the said thirty-first degree of north latitude, being the southern boundary of the United States of America, until it shall strike the eastern boundary of the lands on which the Indians of the said nation did live and hunt on the twenty-ninth of November, one thousand seven hundred and eighty-two, while they were under the protection of the King of Great-Britain; thence northerly along the said eastern boundary, until it shall meet the northern boundary of the said lands; thence westerly along the said northern boundary, until it shall meet the western boundary thereof; thence southerly along the same to the beginning: saving and reserving for the establishment of trading posts, three tracts or parcels of land of six miles square each, at such places as the United [States] in Congress assembled shall think proper; which posts, and the lands annexed to them, shall be to the use and under the government of the United States of America.

ARTICLE IV.
If any citizen of the United States, or other person not being an Indian, shall attempt to settle on any of the lands hereby allotted to the Indians to live and hunt on, such person shall forfeit the protection of the United States of America, and the Indians may punish him or not as they please.

ARTICLE V.
If any Indian or Indians, or persons, residing among them. or who shall take refuge in their nation, shall commit a robbery or murder or other capital crime on any citizen of the United States of America, or person under their protection, the tribe to which such offender may belong, or the nation, shall be bound to deliver him or them up to be punished according to the ordinances of the United States in Congress assembled: Provided, that the punishment shall not be greater than if the robbery or murder, or other capital crime, had been committed by a citizen on a citizen.

ARTICLE VI.
If any citizen of the United States of America, or person under their protection, shall commit a robbery or murder, or other capital crime, on any Indian, such offender or offenders shall be punished in the same manner as if the robbery or murder, or other capital crime, had been committed on a citizen of the United States of America; and the punishment shall be in presence of some of the Choctaws, if any will attend at the time and place; and that they may have an opportunity so to do, due notice, if practicable, of the time of such intended punishment, shall be sent to some one of the tribes.

ARTICLE VII.
It is understood that the punishment of the innocent, under the idea of retaliation, is unjust, and shall not be practiced on either side, except where there is a manifest

violation of this treaty; and then it shall be preceded, first by a demand of justice, and if refused, then by a declaration of hostilities.

ARTICLE VIII.
For the benefit and comfort of the Indians, and for the prevention of injuries or oppressions on the part of the citizens or Indians, the United States in Congress assembled, shall have the sole and exclusive right of regulating the trade with the Indians, and managing all their affairs in such manner as they think proper.

ARTICLE IX.
Until the pleasure of Congress be known, respecting the eighth article, all traders, citizens of the United States of America, shall have liberty to go to any of the tribes or towns of the Choctaws, to trade with them, and they shall be protected in their persons and property, and kindly treated.

ARTICLE X.
The said Indians shall give notice to the citizens of the United States of America, of any designs which they may know or suspect to be formed in any neighboring tribe, or by any person whosoever, against the peace, trade or interest of the United States of America.

ARTICLE XI.
The hatchet shall be forever buried, and the peace given by the United States of America, and friendship re-established between the said states on the one part, and all the Choctaw nation on the other part, shall be universal; and the contracting parties shall use their utmost endeavors to maintain the peace given as aforesaid, and friendship re-established.

In witness of all and every thing herein determined, between the United States of America and all the Choctaws, we, their underwritten commissioners, by virtue of our full powers, have signed this definitive treaty, and have caused our seals to be hereunto affixed.

Done at Hopewell, on the Keowee, this third day of January, in the year of our Lord one thousand seven hundred and eighty-six.

Benjamin Hawkins,
Andrew Pickens,
Jos. Martin,
Yockenahoma, his x mark,
Yorkehoopoie, his x mark,
Mingohoopole, his x mark,
Tobocoh, his x mark,
Pooshemastuby, his x mark

Pooshahooma, his x mark,
Tuseoonoohoopoie, his x mark,
Shinshemastuby, his x mark
Yoopahooma, his x mark
Stoonokoohoopoie, his x mark
Tehakuhbay, his x mark,
Pooshernastuby, his x mark,
Tuskkahoommh, his x mark,
Yoostenochla his x mark,
Tootehooma, his x mark,
Toobenohoomoch. his x mark.
Cshecoopoohcomoch, his x mark,
Stonakoohoopoie, his x mark
Tushkoheegohta, his x mark
Teshuhenoehloeh, his x mark,
Pooshonaltla, his x mark,
Okaneonnooba, his x mark,
Autoonachuba, his x mark
Pangehooloch, his x mark,
Steabee, his x mark,
Tenetchenna, his x mark,
Tushkementahock, his x mark,
Tushtallay, his x mark,
Cshnaangehabba, his x mark,
Cunnopoie, his x mark,
Witness:
Wm. Blount,
John Woods,
Saml. Taylor,
Robert Anderson,
Benj. Lawrence.
John Pitchlynn,
James Cole,
Interpreters.

Source: Charles J. Kappler, ed., *Indian Affairs: Laws and Treaties,* vol. 2 (Washington, D.C.: U.S. Government Printing Office, 1904), 11–14.

Contributors

James Taylor Carson is Associate Professor of History and Associate Dean, Faculty of Arts and Science, at Queen's University in Kingston, Ontario, Canada. He is the author of *Searching for the Bright Path: The Mississippi Choctaws from Prehistory to Removal* (Lincoln: University of Nebraska Press, 1999).

Patricia Galloway is Associate Professor in Archival Enterprise and Digital Asset Management, School of Information, at the University of Texas at Austin. She is the author of *Choctaw Genesis, 1500–1700* (Lincoln: University of Nebraska Press, 1995), *Practicing Ethnohistory: Mining Archives, Hearing Testimony, Constructing Narrative* (Lincoln: University of Nebraska Press, 2006), and editor of *The Hernando de Soto Expedition: History, Historiography, and Discovery in the Southeast* (Lincoln: University of Nebraska Press, 1997).

LeAnne Howe is a member of the Choctaw Nation of Oklahoma and an Associate Professor of English and American Indian Studies at the University of Illinois, Urbana-Champaign. She is the author of *Shell Shaker* (San Francisco: Aunt Lute Books, 2001), *Evidence of Red: Poems and Prose* (Cambridge: Salt Publishing, 2005), and *Miko Kings: An Indian Baseball Story* (San Francisco: Aunt Lute Books, 2007).

Clara Sue Kidwell is a member of the Choctaw Nation of Oklahoma and a Professor of History and Director of the American Indian Center at the University of North Carolina, Chapel Hill. She is the author of *The Choctaws: A Critical Bibliography* (Bloomington: Indiana University Press, 1980), *Choctaws and Missionaries in Mississippi, 1818–1918* (Norman: University of Oklahoma Press, 1995), and editor of *A Native American Theology* (Maryknoll, N.Y.: Orbis Books, 2001).

Greg O'Brien is Associate Professor of History at the University of Southern Mississippi, Hattiesburg. He is the author of *Choctaws in a Revolutionary Age, 1750–1830* (Lincoln: University of Nebraska Press, 2002), and coeditor of *George Washington's South* (Gainesville: University Press of Florida, 2004).

Index

Abihkas (Creek Indian group), 72, 83, 84, 85, 87, 88, 92, 94
Ackia (Chickasaw village), 79
Ada, Okla., 35
Adair, James, 50, 71, 72, 79, 84, 90, 93, 94, 95, 162
Akers, Donna, 17
Alabama, 6, 50, 54, 55, 187, 189. *See also* Mobile; St. Stephens; Tuscaloosa
Alabama Department of Archives and History, 19
Alabama Indians, 20, 74, 79, 81, 83, 88, 94, 95, 101n41. *See also* names of Alabama persons and villages
Alabama River, 32, 33, 34, 36
Alcohol (trade item), 104, 167, 189
Algonquian Indians, 203
Alibamon Mingo (Choctaw chief), 80–81, 82, 83, 86, 87, 93, 94, 97
Allotment (U.S. government policy), 27
American Board of Commissioners for Foreign Missions, 13, 19, 190, 201, 202, 204–216, 227; Prudential Committee, 202. *See also Missionary Herald*; names of missionaries; names of missionary stations
American Historical Association, 18
American Philosophical Society Library, 19
American Revolution, 8, 15, 16, 51, 114, 123–25, 127–29, 140, 143, 148–50, 152, 153, 154, 159, 164, 170, 172, 226
American Society for Ethnohistory, 7, 52
American Society for Propagating the Gospel Among the Indians and Others in North America, 201
Andover Theological Seminary, 206
Angola Prison (Louisiana), 52
Annales school, 53
Ann Arbor, Mich., 19
Apache Indians, 40

Apekimataha (Choctaw chief), 84, 91, 93, 94
Archeological Reports (published by the Mississippi Department of Archives and History), 53, 55, 59
Archeology, 51–55, 60, 67n17, 68n25
Arkansas Territory, 206, 210
Assetaoumastabé of Concha (Choctaw chief), 88
Atakabé Oulacta (Choctaw chief), 97
Atkin, Edmond, 71, 72
Atlanta, Ga., 19
Attakapas Indians, 184
Avoyelles Indians, 184
Ayanabe (Choctaw village), 112

Baird, W. David, 6
Baptist Mission Society of Kentucky, 211
Barbour (Secretary of War), 211
Bartram, William, 50
Baton Rouge, La., 123, 149
Battle Creek, Mich., 39
Battle of New Orleans (1815), 20
Battle of Oriskany (1777), 127
Battle of Pensacola (1781), 16, 123–26, 128, 129, 133, 138–43, 149
Battle of the Thames (1813), 211
Baudouin, Father Michel (Jesuit missionary to the Choctaws), 81, 86
Baumback (Hessian Captain), 138
Beauchamp, Jadart de, 85–86, 87, 88, 89
Beaver Wars (Iroquois and Hurons), 115
Bell, Amelia Rector, 190–91
Bethany mission school (among the Choctaws), 213
Bethel missionary station (among the Choctaws), 207, 214
Bethune, Farquhar, 125, 129, 130–31, 135
Bienville, Jean-Baptiste Le Moyne de, 53, 75, 78, 79, 82

255

Billy, Lucinda, 29
Black Warrior River, 12, 93
Blitz, John, 54
Blount, William, 153–54
Blue Wood (Choctaw village), 83, 86, 89
Boas, Franz, 4
Bossu, Jean-Bernard, 50
Boston, Mass., 190
Bottle Creek (archeological site), 55
Boucfouca (Choctaw village), 82, 87, 93
Bouctoucoulou Chitto (Choctaw village), 83, 84, 93
Bouctoucouloutsi (Choctaw village), 87, 95
Brain, Jeffrey, 51–52
Brainard missionary station (among the Cherokees), 202–203
Brandon, Gerard (Governor of Mississippi), 229
Brashears, Zedock
Brescia, Bill, 57; *Choctaw Tribal Government: A New Era*, 57, 68n28
Britain, 10, 11, 15, 19, 79, 103, 111, 114, 123, 124, 126, 127, 128, 129, 131, 135, 136, 140, 143, 149, 152, 154, 160, 171. *See also* London
British Southern Indian Department, 125
Broken Leg (Indian), 89
Brookes, Sam, 54
Brown, Ian, 55
Bureau of American Ethnography (Smithsonian Institution), 4
Byington, Cyrus, 18, 34, 206–207, 209, 217

Caddo Indians, 4, 20
Caffetalaya (Choctaw village), 96
Cairo, Egypt, 39
Calhoun, John C. (Secretary of War), 214
Cameron, Alexander (British Indian Superintendent), 124, 128–31, 133–38, 141–42
Campbell, John (British trader), 82, 85, 90, 92, 95
Campbell, John (Major General), 124–25, 128–29, 132–39
Canada, 103; history of indigenous First Nations people, 58
Captain Houma (Choctaw chief), 113
Captain of Boucfouca (Choctaw chief), 93
Captain of Toussana (Choctaw chief), 88
Carleton, Kenneth, 57

Carson, James Taylor, 13–14, 69n31; *Searching for the Bright Path: The Mississippi Choctaws from Prehistory to Removal*, 14
Cash, Johnny, 56–57
Catholic Church, 17
Chahta Enterprises (Mississippi Band of Choctaw Indians), 57
Chakchiuma Indians, 12, 20, 74, 84, 93, 94
Chambly (French trader), 83
Chapel Hill, N.C., 19
Charleston, S.C., 80, 90, 91, 92, 93, 94, 95, 96, 150, 169. *See also* Charles Town
Charles Town, S.C., 11. *See also* Charleston
Chávez, Thomas, 143
Cherokee Indians, 48, 60, 79, 128, 148, 152, 153, 154, 157, 166, 212, 222
Chichatalaya (Choctaw village), 87, 92, 93
Chickasaw-Choctaw Wars (1730s), 76, 78, 80, 81, 82, 84
Chickasaw Historical Society, 28
Chickasaw Indians, 4, 12, 20, 74, 76, 78, 79–80, 81, 82, 83, 84, 85, 87, 88, 90, 93, 95, 96, 97, 111, 112, 113, 124, 125, 132, 139, 142, 148, 152, 154, 163, 167, 168, 226; burial sites, 51, 54; slavers, 77. *See also* names of Chickasaw persons and villages
Chickasaw Nation (Oklahoma), 35, 67n18; Chickasaw Enterprises, 36; fair, 36; Garden Program, 36
Chickasawhay (Choctaw village), 74, 76, 81, 83, 85–86, 89, 90, 94, 95; Jesuit mission in, 76, 81
Chickasawhay River, 129
Chinnery (British trader), 90
Chitimacha Indians, 184
Choctaw Academy (Kentucky), 211–12, 214–15
Choctaw agency, 207
Choctaw-Creek War (1766–1776), 14–15, 106–115, 117n16, 120n44
Choctaw Genesis, 1500–1700 (Galloway), 12, 59
Choctaw Heritage Council (Mississippi Band of Choctaw Indians), 56–57
Choctaw historiography, 3–20, 222
Choctaw history, 56, 59, 60–61; methodology, 60; sources, 17–19, 49–55, 70–71
Choctaw Indians (*Chahtas*); adoption, 162–63; ball games, 161, 203; burial customs, 92, 189–190; cattle, 13–14, 183, 184–93; child rearing, 210, 224; civil war, 10, 16, 52, 70–98,

INDEX

99n11, 127; confederacy, 11, 12; cultural change, 8, 13, 15, 17, 188–93, 204, 210, 227; cultural continuity, 14, 15; diplomacy, 11, 15–16, 17, 113, 126–30, 139–40, 149–52, 155–73, 237–46; elites, 14–15, 107–108, 112, 114, 151, 227–28; fur trade, 9, 12, 13, 78–79, 103–107, 109, 114, 131, 136, 149–52, 163–64, 169–70, 184, 186–89, 225; gambling, 161; gender roles, 14, 16, 17, 28, 32–33, 142, 162, 184, 189, 190–93, 224–25; horses, 13; *Imoklasha* ethnicity, 10, 73, 81, 100n25; *Inholahta* ethnicity, 10, 73, 75, 81, 100n25; language, 13, 34, 57, 185, 190–93, 207; market economy, 8, 9, 104–105, 183, 188–89, 192–93, 227; oral traditions, 12, 13, 16, 26, 57, 200; population, 116n12; sociopolitical organization, 72–76, 80, 104–105, 126, 141–42, 225, 227–28; song and dance, 33, 161–62, 203; spirituality, 33–34, 43, 155–56, 161–62, 169, 203, 216, 224–25, 228, 232; stories, 26–46, 203; warfare, 77, 80, 97–98, 107, 109, 122n53, 124, 131–34, 137, 140–43. *See also* Alcohol, Corn, Literature, names of Choctaw persons and villages

Choctaw Language and Culture: Chahta Anumpa (Haag and Willis), 45

"Choctaw Missionaries in Mississippi before 1830" (Kidwell), 12–13

Choctaw Museum of the Southern Indian (Mississippi Band of Choctaw Indians), 57

Choctaw Nation of Oklahoma, 16, 27

Choctaw nationalism, 223, 232; literary nationalism, 28, 34, 45

Choctaw removal, 6, 20, 221, 229–31

Choctaw Source Book (Peterson), 18, 50

Choctaw titles; war titles, 99n13, 186; captain, 86; *fanimingo*, 73; *hopaii mingo*, 73; *mingo ouma*, 73; red shoe, 88; *soulouche oumastabé*, 73, 100n37; *taskanangouchi*, 73, 80, 86; *tichou mingo*, 73

Choctaw Trading Factory, 170, 187–88

Choctaw Tribal Government: A New Era (Brescia), 57, 68n28

Choctaws in a Revolutionary Age, 1750–1830 (O'Brien), 15

Cholko Oulacta of Ayanabe (Choctaw chief), 112

Choucououlacta (Choctaw chief), 81, 82, 84, 86, 87, 88, 92

Choucououlacta of Ebitabougoula ouchy (Choctaw chief), 110, 120n40

Christian missionaries, 12–13, 50, 78, 200–201, 203, 207–208, 229; Baptist missions, 213; Methodist missions, 213–16; Presbyterian missions, 213, 215–16; schools established by, 205–06, 208–09, 216–17. *See also* American Board of Commissioners for Foreign Missions; American Society for Propagating the Gospel Among the Indians and Others in North America; Jesuits; Missionary Society of the Methodist Episcopal Church

Christianity, 8, 34, 200–201, 207, 228, 230

Civil War (United States), 6

Colbert, James, 129

Cole, Robert (Choctaw chief), 213, 227, 231

Colorado Springs, Colo., 52

Concha (Choctaw villages, also spelled Coonsha), 76, 80, 81, 82, 83, 86, 88, 90, 91, 92, 93, 94, 95, 131, 133, 226

Conchatys (Alabama Indian group)

"Confederacy as a Solution to Chiefdom Dissolution: Historical Evidence in the Choctaw Case" (Galloway), 11

Continental Congress. *See* United States

Coosa (Creek village), 90

Coosa River, 32, 111

Coosas (Choctaw village), 112

Corn (*tanchi*), 39; hominy, 29; methods of growing, 35; origin of among the Choctaws, 27, 30–31, 35, 38–40, 44, 45; origin of in Mexico, 30; *pashofa*, 28–29. *See also* ethanol

Cornelius, Elias, 211

Cornell University, 35

Cornwell, Conn., 212

Cottonlandia Museum, 55

Couëchitto (Choctaw village), 72, 80, 83, 84, 87, 90, 93, 94

Cowetas (Creek Indian group), 84, 88

Cravat, Rebecca, 224

Creek Indians, 4, 14, 20, 79, 89, 90, 91, 92, 106–114, 124, 125, 133, 139, 140, 152, 153–54, 156, 157, 166, 168, 169–71, 178n34; Lower Creeks, 111; Red Sticks, 20, 128; slavers, 77; Upper Creeks, 72, 79, 86, 104, 107, 111–13, 153. *See also* names of Creek persons and villages

Creek removal, 20

Creoles, 222–23, 231–32

Cushman, Horatio Bardwell, 27, 28, 30, 31–34, 45, 46, 127–28, 202–203
Cushtusha (Choctaw village), 80, 83, 87, 88, 96, 97

De Verbois (French trader), 83, 84, 86, 88
Debo, Angie, 5–6; *The Rise and Fall of the Choctaw Republic*, 5
Delanglez, Jean, 50
Deloria, Vine, 52
DeRosier, Arthur, 6; *The Removal of the Choctaw Indians*, 6, 50
Desilets (French trader), 95, 96
Donly, John, 226
Donly, Rosa, 226
Du Pratz, Antoine Simon Le Page, 50
Durant family, 212

East Florida, 103, 123
East Imongoulasha (Choctaw village), 108
East Tennessee Historical Society, 18
East Yazoo (Choctaw village), 112
Eaton, John (Secretary of War), 229–30
Ebitabougoula ouchy (Choctaw village), 110
Eco, Umberto, 44, 45–46; *On Literature*, 26
Effatiskiniha (Creek chief, also called Mackay's Friend), 108
Egypt, 40. *See also* Cairo, Egypt
Eliot missionary station (among the Choctaws), 190, 193, 203, 206–207, 215; school, 204–206
Eliot, John, 203
Elsley (British trader), 90, 91
Emistecigo (Creek chief, also spelled Emistisiguo), 107, 112, 113
Espaninantela (Choctaw chief), 87
Ethanol, 39–40
Ethnohistory, 5, 6, 7, 9, 52, 53, 55, 56, 58, 59, 60, 221. *See also* American Society for Ethnohistory
Ethnohistory (journal), 11, 13
Evarts, 213–14
Ezpeleta, José de (Lieutenant Colonel), 132–34, 139–40

Faberie (French interpreter), 96
Fanimingo Tchaa of Seneacha (Choctaw chief), 87, 90, 95
Farmar, Robert, 140

Ferguson, Bob, 56
Five Civilized Tribes, 48
Florida, 123, 124. *See also* East Florida; St. Augustine; West Florida
Folsom, David, 207, 208, 212, 227, 230. *See also* Pigeon Roost
Folsom, Nathaniel, 120n39, 120n44
Folsom family, 211, 216
Foreman, Grant, 221
Fort George, 124, 133, 141, 143
Fort Moore, 90
Fort Tombecbé, 54, 78, 81, 83, 86, 87, 89, 90, 95, 96, 109, 110
Fort Toulouse, 82, 86
France, 10, 11, 19, 55, 103, 104, 127, 136, 149. *See also* Paris, France
Franchimastabé (Choctaw chief), 15, 125, 139, 141–43, 150–52, 155, 158–59, 165–67
Franklin, Benjamin, 169
Frazer, Alexander, 142
French Camps settlement, 207
French Colonial Historical Society, 53
Friend and Foe (Jaenen), 53
Frontier exchange economy, 184

Gage, Thomas (British General), 106, 113
Galloway, Patricia, 9–12, 32; *Choctaw Genesis, 1500–1700*, 12, 59; "Confederacy as a Solution to Chiefdom Dissolution: Historical Evidence in the Choctaw Case," 11; *Mississippi Provincial Archives: French Dominion*, 49, 52, 58; *Practicing Ethnohistory: Mining Archives, Hearing Testimony, Constructing Narrative*, 59; "'The Chief Who Is Your Father': Choctaw and French Views of the Diplomatic Relation," 10
Galphinton, Ga., 153–54
Gálvez, Bernardo de (Governor of Spanish Louisiana), 123, 138–40, 149
Garland, Samuel, 212
Garland family, 212
Gayoso de Lemos, Manuel (Spanish Governor of Natchez), 166–67
Gearing, Fred, 73
German Coast (Louisiana), 92, 94
Georgia, 104, 109, 114, 143, 150, 152, 153, 154, 160, 165, 188; settlers, 112–13, 171. *See also* Galphinton; Savannah

INDEX

Georgia Department of Archives and History, 19
Gibson, Arrell, 56
Gibson, Marie, 28
Glen, James (Governor of South Carolina), 90
Golden Moon Casino (Mississippi Band of Choctaw Indians), 57
Goldman, Tom, 56
Goshen, Mass., 206
Grafton, Daniel, 186
Grandpré (French commander at Fort Tombecbé), 95, 96
Gravier, Jacques (Jesuit missionary), 185
Grandpré Treaty (1749), 96–97
Great Lakes, 171
Great Tohomé (Indian), 89, 91
Greek mythology, 41
Green, Michael, 20
Gulf of Mexico, 123, 171

Haag, Marcia; *Choctaw Language and Culture: Chahta Anumpa*, 45
Haas, Mary, 190
Halbert, Henry, 50
Handbook of North American Indians (Smithsonian Institution), 69n35
Hanxladen (Hessian Colonel), 138
Harkins, George W., 212, 231
Harkins family, 212
Harvard University, 4, 52. *See also* Lower Mississippi Survey
Hawkins, Benjamin, 153, 160, 168
Henderson, Thomas, 212
Hessian mercenaries, 138. *See also* Baumback; Hanxladen; Waldeck, Philipp
Hodgson, Adam, 190
Hoklonotéshe (supernatural beings), 156
Hopankitubbe (Hopakitobi), 200
Hopewell (Andrew Picken's home), 148
Hopewell meetings (1785–86), 127–28, 148–49, 152–73, 237–47. *See also* Treaty of Hopewell
Horsman, Reginald, 154
Houma Indians, 184
Houston, John, 152
Howe, LeAnne, 16, 17, 60; *Shell Shaker*, 16, 69n35
Hudson, Charles, 11, 56; *Southeastern Indians*, 50

Hummer (automobile), 39–40
Huntington Library and Art Gallery, 19
Huron Indians, 58, 115
Hurricane Katrina, 58
Hushtahli (Great Spirit), 200
Hwoolatahoomah (Choctaw chief), 189, 209–10

Ibitoupougoula (Choctaw village), 87, 90, 92, 93
Illetaska of Immongoulacha (Choctaw chief), 87, 88
Illinois, 78
Imataha Mingo of Ibitoupougoula (Choctaw chief), 87, 92
Imataha Pouscouche (Choctaw chief, also called Little King), 84, 87, 90, 91, 92, 94, 95
Imayatabé le Borgne (Chickasaw chief, also called the Blind King), 79–80, 82, 83
Immongoulacha (Choctaw village), 84, 87, 88, 91, 92
Indian removal, 6, 8, 18
Indian slave trade, 19
Indian Territory, 6, 20, 202, 231. *See also* Oklahoma
Indians of the Southeastern United States (Swanton), 4
Indians, Settlers, and Slaves in a Frontier Exchange Economy (Usner), 8–9
Iroquois Indians, 60, 115, 127. *See also* Oneida Indians; Tuscarora Indians
Ispiahhomah (Choctaw chief), 212
Iteokchakko (Choctaw village), 110

Jackson, Andrew, 19, 212, 222–23, 229–31
Jackson, Miss., 19, 58
Jaenen, Cornelius, 53; *Friend and Foe*, 53
James, Benjamin, 142, 165
Jefferson, Thomas, 186
Jesuits, 19. *See also* Baudouin, Father Michel; Chickasawhay; Gravier, Jacques
Jewel, Moses, 207
Johnson, Richard, 211, 212
Johnson, Sir William, 18
Johnstone, George (West Florida Governor), 104, 106
Jones, Dorothy, 155
Jones, Lib Burke, 55
Jones, Robert, 212

Jordan, Terry, 188
Journal of Mississippi History, 10, 52
Juzan (Spanish trader), 139
Juzan, Charles, 188
Juzan, Pierre, 212
Juzon family, 212

Kenya, 191, 193
Keowee River, 148
Key (Captain of loyalist troops), 138
Kidwell, Clara Sue, 12, 13, 17, 18, 52, 60, 66n12, 69n35; "Choctaw Missionaries in Mississippi before 1830," 12–13; *The Choctaws: A Critical Bibliography*, 18, 50, 51
King, Charles, 212
King, Hiram, 212
King, James M., 212
King, Peter, 212
Kingsbery, Robert, 28
Kingsbury, Cyrus, 202–211, 213–14
Knox, Henry, 168, 169, 171
Kwachka, Pat, 57

Ladurie, Le Roy, 53
Lake Pontchartrain, 92
Lakota Sioux, 115
Lambert, Valerie, 17
Lankford, George, 52
La Salle, 51, 56
Le Fleur, Louis, 224
Ledbetter, Wiley, 213–14
LeFlore, Greenwood (Choctaw chief), 14, 211, 212, 214, 221–32. *See also* Malmaison mansion
LeFlore family, 207, 212, 215, 216
Lewis, Anna, 6, 17, 127–28
Lewis, Thallis, 56, 57
Library of Congress, 19
"Life of Apushimataha" (Lincecum), 6
Lincecum, Gideon, 6, 203; "Life of Apushimataha," 6
Literature; children's, 27; Choctaw literary nationalism, 28, 34, 45
Little Tallassee (Creek village, also called Paucana Talaska), 107, 113
Little Turtle (Miami Indian war chief), 171
Little Wood (Choctaw village), 83, 87
Livingood, Patrick, 54

London, England, 113, 135, 138
Louboey (French commander at Mobile), 92
Louisiana, 4, 49, 50, 52, 78, 79, 103, 223. *See also* Angola Prison; German Coast; Lake Pontchartrain; New Orleans
Louisiana colonial studies, 53
Lowe-Steen (archeological site), 54
Lower Mississippi Survey (Harvard University), 51, 67n18
Luna, Tristán de, 55
Lyle, Susan, 214

Malmaison mansion, 232
Manchac, La. (British post), 123, 149
Mann, Baxter, 54
Marakwet people of Kenya, 191
Market Revolution, 13–14, 183, 193
Martin, Joseph, 153, 157, 158–60, 167, 168, 170
Martin, Philip (Choctaw chief), 56, 57
Maryland loyalist troops, 138
Massachusetts, 201. *See also* Boston; Goshen
Mastubbee (Choctaw man), 188
Mather and Strother Company, 150
Mayhew missionary station (among the Choctaws), 207–8, 210; school, 208, 210
McComber, Stephen, 214–15
McDonald, James, 28
McGillivrary, Alexander, 153
McGillivray, John (British trader), 107
McKee, Jesse, 6
McKee, John, 202
McNaire, Charles, 90, 91, 92, 93
Merrell, James, 167, 185
Mexico, 30, 32
Michigan State University, 52
Middle Ground, 149, 172–73, 174n4
Mihesuah, Devon, 17
Mill Creek (archeological site), 54
Mill River, 185
Miller, David, 53
Mingo Houma Chito of East Imongoulasha (Choctaw chief), 108, 111
Mingo Ouma of Chickasawhay (Choctaw chief), 86
Mingo Ouma of Ibitoupougoula (Choctaw chief), 90
Mingo Ouma of Nachoubaouenya (Choctaw chief), 87, 95, 96, 97

Mingo Oumastabé of Cushtusha (Choctaw chief), 97
Mingo Pouscouche of Concha (Choctaw chief), 131–35, 143
Mingohoopoie (Choctaw chief), 158–59, 163–65
Minor, Stephen, 169
Miró, Esteban (Governor of Spanish Louisiana), 168
Missionaries. *See* Christian missionaries
Missionary Herald, 209
Missionary Society of the Methodist Episcopal Church, 213; Mississippi Conference of, 213–14
Mississippi, 6, 52, 154, 156, 184, 188, 189, 203, 205, 206, 221, 229–30; Indian education in, 50, 217; legislature, 231. *See also* Natchez; Nogales
Mississippi Archeological Association, 53
Mississippi Archeology (journal), 53, 55, 58–59
Mississippi Association of Professional Archeologists, 67n17
Mississippi Band of Choctaw Indians (MBCI), 20, 56, 57, 58, 60; Cultural Affairs Program, 57; fair, 57; hospital, 56; Pearl River Community, 58; schools, 56, 57; traditional crafts, 57. *See also* Chahta Enterprises; Choctaw Heritage Council; Choctaw Museum of the Southern Indian; Golden Moon Casino; Silver Star Casino
Mississippi Department of Archives and History (MDAH), 19, 49–50, 53, 54, 55, 56, 60. *See also Archeological Reports*
Mississippi Historical Society, 6
Mississippi Humanities Council, 54
Mississippi Provincial Archives: French Dominion (Galloway), 18, 49, 52, 58
Mississippi River, 17, 77, 78, 103, 114, 123, 125, 126, 149, 150, 155, 157, 169, 170, 171, 202, 205, 210
Mississippi State Historical Museum, 57–58; Community Advisory Committee, 58
Mississippi State University, 52
Mississippi Territory, 19
Mississippi Valley, 8, 51, 149, 171; Lower, 78, 183–86
Mississippian Chiefdoms (Indians), 11, 12, 14, 51, 53, 55, 75, 100n31, 104, 151, 225, 231–32

Mobile, Ala., 11, 71, 82, 83, 85, 86, 92, 94, 95, 96, 104, 105, 108, 109, 113, 123, 124, 129, 131–33, 135, 136, 137–39, 150, 185, 186, 210; Spanish capture of (1780), 125, 128, 129, 134, 149
Mobile Bay, 32, 137
Mobile Conference (1765), 103
Mobile Conference (1772), 112
Mobile Conference (1777), 125
Mobile Conference (1779), 125
Mobile Conference (1784), 158
Mobile River, 32, 74, 91, 95
Mobile Treaty (1784), 158
Mobile Village (also called Frenchtown), 137, 138
Mobile-Tensaw delta, 55
Mobilian trade dialect, 185
Mongoulacha Mingo (Choctaw chief), 81–82, 83, 86, 94
Mongoulacha Oupayé of Immongoulacha (Choctaw chief), 93
Monument Valley, 40
Montgomery, Ala., 19, 32
Mooney, Timothy, 54
Moore, Mary Tyler, 41
Morgan, Philip Carroll, 28
Moundville chiefdom, 12
Mt. Pleasant, Jane, 34–36
Muccolossus (Creek village), 107
Muscle Shoals, 154, 167, 169
Museum of the Cherokee Indian (North Carolina), 56
Mushulatubbee (Choctaw chief), 20, 188, 189, 203, 205, 208, 211, 212, 227, 230

Nachoubaouenya (Choctaw village), 87, 95
Nail, Joel, 210
Nail family, 212
Nambi people of Kenya, 191
Nanih Waiya (mother mound of the Choctaws), 12, 34, 53, 200, 228
Nashville, Tenn., 19, 226
Nassuba Mingo (Choctaw chief), 103–104, 115
Natchez fort, 91, 94, 96
Natchez Indians, 12, 78, 79, 81, 184; Grand Village, 51; Revolt, 76, 78, 82, 92
Natchez, Miss., 110, 123, 125, 149, 150, 151, 166, 167, 168, 186, 189
Natchez road, 207

Natchitoches, 184
National Archives (Washington, D.C.), 19
National Endowment for the Humanities, 69n35
Native American Archives Roundtable, 69n34
Native American Graves Protection and Repatriation Act, 59
Navajo Indians, 7, 40
Neihardt, John, 42
Neitzel, Stuart, 51, 52
New England, 191, 193; Presbyterian Calvinism, 201; Congregationalism, 201
New Mexico, 184
New Orleans, La., 9, 19, 92, 96, 103, 105, 108, 114, 123, 125, 140, 149, 210
New Orleans Conference (1779), 128
New York, 169
Newberry (British trader), 90
Newberry Library Center for the History of the American Indian, 53
Nogales (Vicksburg, Miss.), 167
Norman, Okla., 19
North Carolina, 153–54
Nushkobo (Choctaw village), 72, 93, 94

O'Brien, Greg, 14–15, 69n31; *Choctaws in a Revolutionary Age, 1750–1830*, 15; "The Conqueror Meets the Unconquered: Negotiating Cultural Boundaries on the Post-Revolutionary Southern Frontier," 17
Offemeko (Choctaw chief), 83
Ohio River, 153, 169
Ohio Valley, 103, 171
Ohio Valley Indian Confederacy, 20, 128
Ohoyo Chishba Osh (Unknown Woman, Corn Woman), 16, 27, 29–36, 38–44, 46
Okalusa (Choctaw village), 88, 94
Okeoulou (Choctaw village), 94, 95, 96
Oklabbee (Choctaw chief), 212
Oklahoma, 4, 6. *See also* Indian Territory; Oklahoma City
Oklahoma City, Okla., 19
Oklahoma Historical Society, 19
Olacta Houma of Iteokchakko (Choctaw chief), 110, 114
Old Northwest, 152
Old Southwest, 171, 183, 188, 193
On Literature (Eco), 26

Oneida Indians, 127
Oni (Choctaw village), 83, 86, 95, 96
Ook-tib-be-ha missionary station (among the Choctaws), 204, 206; school, 205
Opayéchitto (Choctaw chief), 84
Opelousas, 184
Osage Indians, 20
Ottoman Empire, 39
Oulitacha (Choctaw village), 87, 93
Owens, Louis, 27

Paape, Charles W., 50, 70
Paemingo of Cushtusha (Choctaw chief), 87, 88, 91, 95
Pahémingo of Immongoulacha (Choctaw chief), 92
Pahémingo of Toussana (Choctaw chief), 93, 94
Pahemingo-Amalahta (Chickasaw chief), 84
Panton, Leslie and Company, 114, 150, 153, 186–87, 224
Paris, France, 5
Parker, Jim, 54
Pascagoula Indians, 184
Pascagoula River, 74
Pastabé (Chickasaw chief), 84
Pawnee Indians, 7
Payamataha (Choctaw chief), 91
Pearl River, 12, 34, 54, 74
Peebles, Chris, 54
Penicaut, André, 50
Penn, Governor, 169
Pennsylvania loyalist troops, 138
Pensacola, Fla., 15, 105, 107, 109, 113, 124, 125, 126, 130–37, 139, 150, 186. *See also* Battle of Pensacola (1781)
Pensacola Bay, 125, 138, 139
Perdido River, 131, 140
Perdue, Theda, 59
Périer, Etienne (Governor of French Louisiana), 74
Perry family, 212
Peru, 30
Pesantubbee, Michelene, 16–17, 20, 60, 69n35
Peterson, John, 52, 56, 66n12, 68n27; *Choctaw Source Book*, 18, 50
Petit (French trader), 84, 88
Petycrou (British trader), 95–96

INDEX

Philadelphia, Pa., 19, 169
Piamingo (Chickasaw chief), 169
Pickens, Andrew, 148, 153, 160, 168
Pigeon Roost (tavern and trading post), 207
Pine Log Creek (archeological site), 54
Pitchlynn, John, 137, 156, 163, 167–68, 182n79, 188, 208
Pitchlynn, Peter, 6, 212
Pitchlynn family, 211
Plains Indians, 13
Pontiac's Revolt (1763), 106
Pooshemastubie (Choctaw chief), 159
Pope, Alexander, 212
Pouchimataha of Toussana (Choctaw chief), 87, 88–89, 95, 96, 97
Powhatan's Mantle: Indians in the Colonial Southeast, 10
Poynor, Billy, 28
Practicing Ethnohistory: Mining Archives, Hearing Testimony, Constructing Narrative (Galloway), 59
Pride, William, 213
"Protecting Trade through War: Choctaw Elites and British Occupation of the Floridas" (O'Brien), 14–15
Prucha, Francis Paul, 152
Puckshenubbee (Choctaw chief), 188, 205
Pushmataha (Choctaw chief), 6, 20, 203, 205

Quikanabé Mingo (Choctaw chief), 86

Red Captain of Shatalaya (Choctaw chief), 109, 110, 112, 114; death of, 109, 119n34
Red River, 81
Red Shoe(s) (Choctaw war leader whose actions sparked the Choctaw civil war), 16, 70, 76, 80–85, 87–90, 92, 93, 94, 100n38; death of, 90–91
Redskins, Ruffleshirts, and Rednecks (Young), 6
Replinque (French trader), 84
Roberts, Charles, 18; *The Choctaws: A Critical Bibliography*, 50, 51
Romania, 39
Romans, Bernard, 50, 184
Roullet, Régis du, 75, 185
Roussève (interpreter), 83
Royal Forresters, 137

San Marino, Calif., 19
Santa Rosa Island, 138
Satz, Ronald, 221
Savannah, Ga., 150, 151, 155, 168
Schlenker, Jon, 6
School of Information (University of Texas), 59
Searching for the Bright Path: The Mississippi Choctaws from Prehistory to Removal (Carson), 14
Sellers, Charles, 183, 193
Seneacha (Choctaw village), 87, 90, 95, 108
Seven Years War, 11, 15, 20, 103, 106, 116n3, 123, 136, 149
Seville, Spain, 5
Shatalaya (Choctaw village), 109
Shawnee Indians, 88, 111
Shell Shaker (Howe), 16, 29, 46, 69n35
Shinshomastabé (Choctaw chief), 158–59
Shulustamastabé of West Yazoo (Red Shoes, Choctaw chief), 108
Silver Star Casino (Mississippi Band of Choctaw Indians), 57
Slavery, 19, 53. *See also* Indian slave trade
Smallpox, 11, 81, 92, 93, 98, 98n11, 124
Smith, Brother, 215
Smithsonian Institution, 19. *See also* Bureau of American Ethnography; *Handbook of North American Indians*
Social history, 9
Society of American Archivists, 69n34
Sonakabetaska (Choctaw chief), 87–88
Soto, Hernando de, 11, 51, 56
Soule, Bishop, 213
Source Material for the Social and Ceremonial Life of the Choctaw Indians (Swanton), 3, 48
South Carolina, 78, 92, 94, 104, 109, 110, 148, 150, 153, 170, 188; colonial historical sources, 71, 98n7; Royal Council, 95. *See also* Charleston; Charles Town; Hopewell meetings
Southeastern Archaeological Conference, 68n25
Southeastern Ceremonial Complex, 55
Southeastern Indians (Hudson), 50
Southern Historical Collection (University of North Carolina), 19
Spain, 17, 19, 55, 114, 123, 126, 127, 128, 129–30, 133, 135, 139–40, 143, 149, 152, 154, 158, 160. *See also* Seville, Spain

St. Augustine, Fla., 150
St. Stephens, Ala., 170, 205
Steponaitis, Vincas, 54
Stuart, John (British Southern Indian Superintendent), 103, 104, 106, 110, 111, 113, 125
Stubbs, John, 67n18
Sucarnoochee Creek, 54
Suei Nantla (Choctaw man), 107
Swanton, John, 3–5, 6, 18, 48–49, 50, 73, 74, 93; *Indians of the Southeastern United States*, 4; *Source Material for the Social and Ceremonial Life of the Choctaw Indians*, 3, 48

Taboca (Choctaw chief), 15, 155–56, 158–64, 167, 168–69, 171; Hopaii Mataha, 155; Mingo Hopaii, 156
Taensas Indians, 226
Tait, Robert, 125
Taitt, David, 108
Tala (Choctaw village), 87, 96
Talapoosas (Creek Indian group), 83, 85, 88, 139–40
Tallapoosa River, 32, 111
Talley, Alexander, 214–15
Tamatlémingo (Alabama chief), 88
Taska Oumastabé (Choctaw chief), 113
Taskaoumingo of Boucfouca (Choctaw chief), 87, 88
Taskaoumingo of Concha (Choctaw chief), 90
Tatoulimataha of Little Wood (Choctaw chief), 83, 87, 88–89
Tattoully Mastabé of Coosas (Choctaw chief), 112
Tchanké (Choctaw village), 95, 96
Tchicachas Ouma of Nushkobo (Choctaw chief), 93
Tecumseh (Shawnee chief), 20, 211
Tennessee, 154, 229. *See also* Nashville
Tennessee Department of Archives and History, 19
Tennessee River, 154. *See also* Muscle Shoals
Tennessee-Tombigbee Waterway, 52, 54
Tesser, Carmen Chaves, 11
Texas, 4
"'The Chief Who Is Your Father': Choctaw and French Views of the Diplomatic Relation" (Galloway), 10

"The Conqueror Meets the Unconquered: Negotiating Cultural Boundaries on the Post-Revolutionary Southern Frontier" (O'Brien), 17
The Children of Aataentsic (Trigger), 58
The Choctaws: A Critical Bibliography (Kidwell and Roberts), 50, 51
The Mortar (Creek chief), 113
The Removal of the Choctaw Indians (DeRosier), 6, 50
The Rise and Fall of the Choctaw Republic (Debo), 5
The Roots of Dependency (White), 7, 52
Thomas Gilcrease Institute of American History and Art, 19
Thompson, Catherine, 29
Tishomingo, Okla., 36
Tomatle Mingo of Seneacha (Choctaw chief), 108
Tombecbé (Choctaw village), 88
Tombeckby. *See* Fort Tombecbé
Tombigbee River, 12, 17, 74, 78, 136, 186, 187
Tonti, Henri de, 74
Toupaoumastabé (Choctaw chief), 82, 83, 86, 88
Toussana (Choctaw village), 87, 88, 94, 95, 96, 97
Treaty of Dancing Rabbit Creek (1830), 221, 222, 230–31
Treaty of Doak's Stand (1820), 205–206, 211
Treaty of Fort Finney (1786), 152
Treaty of Fort McIntosh (1785), 152
Treaty of Fort Stanwix (1784), 152
Treaty of Hopewell (1785, between U.S. and Cherokees), 154
Treaty of Hopewell (1786, between U.S. and Chickasaws), 154
Treaty of Hopewell (1786, between U.S. and Choctaws), 15, 148–49, 162–66, 168, 172, 180n67, 186, 248–51
Treaty of Mount Dexter (1805), 186–87, 226
Treaty of Paris (1763), 11
Treaty of Paris (1783), 124, 152
Trigger, Bruce; *The Children of Aataentsic*, 58
Trouillet (French man), 135
Tubby, Roseanna, 57
Tulsa, Okla., 19
Tunica Indians, 184; burials, 52

Tunica Treasure, 51–52
Tupelo, Miss., 51, 54
Tuscaloosa, Ala., 213
Tuscarora Indians, 127
Tuscoonohopoia (Choctaw chief), 159
Tus-eam-i-ub-by (Choctaw man), 207

United States, 14, 15, 16, 19, 20, 54, 59, 114, 124, 127–28, 143, 148–49, 150, 151, 152, 153, 157, 159–60, 164–66, 170–71, 186, 187, 223, 225; Civilization Act (1819), 201; Congress, 164; Constitution, 149, 154; Constitutional Convention, 169; Continental Congress, 152–55, 158, 160, 168; Senate, 168
University of California, Berkeley, 52
University of Kentucky, 59
University of North Carolina, 54. *See also* Southern Historical Collection
University of Oklahoma, 5, 6
University of Southern Mississippi, 54
University of Texas. *See* School of Information
Usner, Daniel, 8–9, 183, 184, 188; *Indians, Settlers, and Slaves in a Frontier Exchange Economy*, 8–9

Vann (British trader), 92, 94
Vaudreuil, Pierre de Rigaud de (Governor of French Louisiana), 71, 72, 75, 82, 83–84, 90, 92, 94, 97
Vicksburg, Miss. *See* Nogales
Villebeuvre, Juan de la, 165
Virginia, 153, 154. *See also* Yorktown
"Virginians," 160
Voss, Jerome, 54

Waldeck, Philipp (Hessian Chaplain), 132, 135
War of 1812, 20, 128
War chief of Yowani (Choctaw chief), 94
Ward, William (U.S. agent to the Choctaws), 188, 212, 229, 231
Washington, D.C., 214, 222
Washington, George, 19, 26, 45, 168, 169
Weeks, Charles, 17–18, 20, 68n26
Wells, Mary Ann, 6
West Abeka (Choctaw village), 72, 84, 88, 93, 94
West Florida, 103, 111, 114, 123, 133, 140, 152
West Immongoulacha (Choctaw village), 94, 95, 96

West Yazoo (Choctaw village), 15, 94, 95, 108–109, 125, 131, 139, 151, 159, 165, 169. *See also* Yazoo
Western History Collection, University of Oklahoma, 19
White, Hugh Lawson (Tennessee Senator), 229
White, Richard, 7, 14, 52, 120n44, 172, 174n4, 183, 187, 188; *The Roots of Dependency*, 7, 52
William L. Clements Library, University of Michigan, 19, 50
Williams, Loring S., 207; and Mrs., 202–203
Williams Research Center, Historic New Orleans Collection, 19
Willing, James (American Captain), 125; raid down the Mississippi River, 127, 150
Willis, Henry; *Choctaw Language and Culture: Chahta Anumpa*, 45
Winans, William, 213–15
Winston County, Miss., 34, 200
Wolf King (Creek chief), 107–108
Woods, John, 151, 156, 164, 168–69
Woods, Patricia, 50
Worcester, Samuel, 203–205, 212
Wright, Alfred, 207

Yalobusha River, 202
Yamassee War, 78
Yanabé (Choctaw village, also spelled Yannabi), 83, 88, 94, 226
Yasi Mattaha of East Yazoo (Choctaw chief), 112
Yazoo (Choctaw village), 83, 86. *See also* East Yazoo; West Yazoo; Yazoo Iskitini
Yazoo Iskitini (Choctaw village), 89
Yazoo River, 186
Yazoo River Valley, 227
Yellow Canes (Choctaw village), 86, 95
Yockehoopoie (Choctaw chief), 158–59, 163
Yockonahoma (Choctaw chief), 157–61, 166–68, 170
York, Kennith, 56
Yorktown, Va., 152
Young, Mary Elizabeth, 6; *Redskins, Ruffleshirts, and Rednecks*, 6
Yowani (Choctaw village), 74, 94, 95

www.ingramcontent.com/pod-product-compliance
Lightning Source LLC
LaVergne TN
LVHW040734250326
834688LV00031B/288